THE EARLY
CHRISTIAN
BOOK

THE EARLY CHRISTIAN BOOK

EDITED BY

William E. Klingshirn & Linda Safran

The Catholic University of America Press

Washington, D.C.

Library of Congress Cataloging-in-Publication Data
The early Christian book / edited by William E. Klingshirn and Linda Safran.
p. cm. — (CUA studies in early Christianity)
Includes bibliographical references and index.
ISBN-13: 978-0-8132-1486-3 (cloth : alk. paper)
ISBN-13: 978-0-8132-1531-0 (pbk : alk. paper)
ISBN-10: 0-8132-1486-6 (cloth : alk. paper)   1. Christian literature, Early—History
and criticism.   2. Christian literature, Early—Publishing.   I. Klingshirn, William
E. II. Safran, Linda.   III. Title.   IV. Series.
BR67.E27 2007
002.088'2701—dc22
2006021256

CONTENTS

ILLUSTRATIONS

(following page 26)

FIG. 1. Reconstruction drawings of decorative designs on some ninth–tenth century Coptic leather book covers from Hamouli. After *The History of Bookbinding 525–1950 A.D.,* pl. X.

FIG. 2. Leather book covers removed from Morgan Library, MS M. 569. The Pierpont Morgan Library, New York. MS M. 569. Photos: The Pierpont Morgan Library.

FIG. 3. Painted wooden book covers removed from the Freer Gospels. Freer Gallery of Art, Smithsonian Institution, Washington, D.C.: Gift of Charles Lang Freer, F1906.298, F1906.297. Photos: Freer Gallery of Art.

FIG. 4. Silver book covers from the Kaper Koraon treasure. New York, Metropolitan Museum of Art, acc. nos. 50.5.1–2. Photos: Metropolitan Museum of Art.

FIG. 5. Silver book covers from the Kaper Koraon treasure. New York, Metropolitan Museum, acc. no. 47.100.36, and Paris, Musée du Louvre, AGER Bj 2279. Photos: Metropolitan Museum of Art, Musée du Louvre (reconstruction by author).

FIG. 6. Silver book covers from the Sion treasure. Dumbarton Oaks, Byzantine Collection, Washington, D.C., acc. nos. DO 63.36.8 and 65.1.3. Photos: Byzantine Collection, Dumbarton Oaks (reconstruction by author).

FIG. 7. Silver book covers from the Sion treasure. Dumbarton Oaks, Byzantine Collection, Washington, D.C., acc. nos. DO 63.36.9–10. Photos: Byzantine Collection, Dumbarton Oaks.

FIG. 8. Gold and jeweled book covers. Monza, Tesoro del Duomo. Parrocchia di S. Giovanni Battista, Duomo di Monza. Photos: Museo del Duomo di Monza.

FIG. 9. Ivory and jeweled book covers. Milan, Tesoro del Duomo. Photos: Hirmer Fotoarchiv.

FIG. 10. Ivory book covers reused on the Ejmiadzin Gospels. Erevan, Matenadaran, MS 2734. Photos: courtesy of V. Nersessian.

FIG. 11. Ivory book covers reused on the St. Lupicin Gospels. Paris, Bibliothèque nationale de France, MS lat. 9384. Photos: Bibliothèque nationale de France.

FIG. 12. Detail of Ejmiadzin Gospels cover: Christ healing a demoniac.

FIG. 13. Detail of St. Lupicin Gospels cover: Christ healing a demoniac.

FIG. 14. Photomontage reconstruction of ivory book covers from Murano. Ravenna, Museo Nazionale (Christ panel); other panels from Manchester, St. Petersburg, Berlin, and Paris (see p. 41). Photos: Victoria and Albert Museum, London; Diözesanmuseum Paderborn; The State Hermitage Museum, St. Petersburg (reconstruction by author).

FIG. 15. Central front panel of a dismantled ivory book cover. London, British Museum, acc. no. M&ME, 1904, 7-2, 1. Photo: Victoria and Albert Museum, London.

FIG. 16. P. Köln inv. 10213, flesh side. Cologne, Universität zu Köln. Photo: courtesy of Die Kölner Papyrus-Sammlung (image produced with the support of the Deutsche Forschungsgemeinschaft).

FIG. 17. P. Köln inv. 10213, hair side. Cologne, Universität zu Köln. Photo: courtesy of Die Kölner Papyrus-Sammlung (image produced with the support of the Deutsche Forschungsgemeinschaft).

PREFACE

The papers in this collection originated in a conference held at the Catholic University of America from June 6 to June 9, 2002, under the auspices of the Center for the Study of Early Christianity. The call for papers stated the organizing principle of the conference: "Christianity is assuredly a 'Religion of the Book.' It is also quintessentially a religion of books." Drawn from the multiple disciplines that make up the fields of early Christianity and late antiquity, speakers were asked to consider the production and use of books, including the Bible, between the third and seventh centuries A.D. The fact that no paper is devoted to the early Christian writings that made up the New Testament results from this chronological limitation.

The excitement and lively success of the conference suggested that the topic merited publication, and twelve speakers were asked to revise their papers for this volume. Ten short papers and eight longer ones had been delivered at the conference, and the varying length of the papers collected here to some extent reflects that feature of the original program.

We are grateful to Philip Rousseau for agreeing to write an introduction to this volume, to the authors for their conscientious revisions, and to the Press's readers, who made a number of useful suggestions and observations.

W. E. K.

L. S.

ABBREVIATIONS

ANRW	*Aufstieg und Niedergang der römischen Welt*
CCSL	*Corpus Christianorum, Series Latina*
Cod. Iust.	*Codex Iustinianus*
Cod. Theod.	*Codex Theodosianus*
CSEL	*Corpus Scriptorum Ecclesiasticorum Latinorum*
Ep(p.)	*Epistula(ae)*
GCS	Die Griechischen christlichen Schriftsteller der ersten Jahrhunderte
JECS	*Journal of Early Christian Studies*
Mansi	Sacrorum conciliorum nova et amplissima collectio, ed. J. D. Mansi
MGH, SRM	*Monumenta Germaniae Historica, Scriptores Rerum Merovingicarum*
PG	*Patrologia Graeca*
PL	*Patrologia Latina*
REAug	*Revue des études augustiniennes*
SC	*Sources chrétiennes*
VC	*Vigiliae Christianae*
ZPE	*Zeitschrift für Papyrologie und Epigraphik*

Abbreviations for authors and their texts are those of *The Oxford Classical Dictionary,* ed. Simon Hornblower and Anthony Spawforth, 3d ed. (Oxford, 1996).

THE EARLY
CHRISTIAN
BOOK

Philip Rousseau

INTRODUCTION
From Binding to Burning

Books in a bookcase present a façade. Binding, typeface, and layout carry a message of their own, inspiring reverence or pleasing the eye, presenting themselves as examples of this category or that. Yet books are also penetrable. To take one down, to open it and read, is to enter another world, to journey elsewhere, to explore an unknown territory (the point is Catherine Chin's). The second experience is modified, however, by the first. The physical book, with its edges, surfaces, and bindings, can circumscribe or define. We have to ask whether a book extends an invitation or puts up a defense, provides or protects, informs or dazzles, creates a window or a wall. Books can alter or misrepresent the territory they purport to describe. They will, at the very least, interpose a lens, creating images the writer deems acceptable. So the most welcoming of texts will still set boundaries to our imagination and understanding.

The tension between seeing and absorbing is, in the case of the early Christian book, difficult for us to recapture. Our published editions, and even the later manuscripts upon which we rely, divorce in a misleading way the content of texts from the sensation of perusing them. In a society where literacy was thinly spread, books could awaken awe or impose power, even when unopened. That was most evident, perhaps, in the case of the scriptures, texts that *others* were entitled to hold, recite from, and interpret. The same might be said of the law and of administrative decrees. The scriptures, however, were almost never *a* book. We need to bear in mind both the purpose and the effect of either combining or separating the various authors of the sacred texts. Other works, similarly, were rarely divided into the chapters that later scribes and editors have made familiar. Even the literate lacked the controlling influence of heading, spacing, and punctuation. All those features of the reading experience separate us from the early Christian world. It demands imagination to understand what it was then to see, to hear, and to look. The written word was not automatically either inviting or accessible. Consequently, its function and impact were different from the function and image of "the book" in our own day.

John Lowden's chapter, "The Word Made Visible," invites us to start with the façade and only slowly work our way inward. He provides the visible evidence of books in themselves. The treasures of Kaper Koraon and the Sion collection are striking enough, but we have to remember the wider deployment of codices bound in leather, skillfully protected with flaps, clasps, and bands, and carefully tooled or incised with geometric designs. Chrysi Kotsifou's meticulous examination of monastic book culture in Egypt illustrates the same point. She presents us with the noise and bustle, as it were, that could accompany an intellectual, even spiritual, endeavor. Here, in a wealth of humble exemplars, we see lucky survivals from a more general industry: the "portable codices" described with such wealth of evidence by Claudia Rapp. Other chapters conjure for us the same image of small, uncomplicated, unobtrusive volumes widely available to literate society.

Yet Lowden's point is that books were often far from unobtrusive. Even the simple crosses placed on the covers of smaller religious texts offered a message additional to, perhaps even more forceful than, that imparted by the texts themselves. The book as such made a statement; codicological iconography had a grammar all its own. The grandeur of gold, silver, and bejeweled covers was rare and expensive, certainly, and its detail powered a reflective interpretation more complex than that of a little psalter in the shoulder bag of a monk; but the artisan in each case was rising to the same challenge, putting a personal mark on what was often someone else's composition. Kotsifou describes similarly the potential independence of décor. She also reminds us that literacy and literary interests were not the purlieu of wealth alone.

We deduce all this not only from surviving codices but also from pictures of books (often in books). What strikes Lowden here is the way in which so many of the volumes were clearly there to be *looked at,* placed within a visual field that was itself deliberately contrived. The finest examples were constructed in such a way that the covers, back and front, created a single narrative. Such books scarcely lent themselves to reading: they were to be carried, displayed, enthroned. Suddenly, the urge to flick open covers and plunge into another world is controlled, channeled, harnessed to an agenda, even discouraged or disallowed. The boundary between reader and text (the "cover," the "binding"—such pregnant terms) acquires a veritable castellation of interpretative caveats.

Some of the other chapters—those by Daniel Boyarin, Catherine Burris, Gillian Clark, and Caroline Humfress—are focused for the most part on what can be described as single works: the Babylonian Talmud, the Syriac *Ktâbâ d-nešše* or *Book of Women,* Augustine's *City of God,* and Justinian's law code. The advantage here is the combination of detailed reflection and lateral reference.

Even to scholars with other interests, Augustine's work has to be the monster of the late antique deep, the *magnum opus et arduum.* That is why Gillian Clark insists on our reading it *as a whole.* It is, famously, a book about books: the Rome it describes (even though Augustine was familiar with the "real" city) is a library, a carefully chosen collection. The "real" city was shifting nervously from a sense of being pagan to a sense of being Christian, but the city in the book has a more reassuring stability. The *civitas dei* may have been a tent for pilgrims, but it was also safely sheltered, bound between covers, a literary tradition more than an urban complex. This explains why Augustine's prolixity, his sequential discourse, never lapses into anecdote or digression. His work has, in Jean-Claude Guy's risky phrase, a *structure logique:* the particular argument matches at every stage a single embodiment of conviction—Augustine's own, of course. Hence, to read what he says is to understand what he is. And Clark's most vivid achievement is to link the persona of this *scriptor* with Augustine the teacher. The book answers questions, whether objections or anxieties, and it draws in the process on a rich homiletic cache. The relation between Augustine's sermons and the *City of God,* at any given moment, is easy to notice and rewarding to explore, but Clark makes clear how the strongest current flows from homily to history. As with any teacher of that age, oratory preceded text. At the same time, the oratory was exegetical, whether based on Virgil or the Bible.

Caroline Humfress is also concerned to present us with a singularity: the way in which the *Digest* harmonizes the disparate. Justinian wanted to present his work as above all given by God. The Christianity of the enterprise resided most, therefore, in its defining anew (indeed, transforming) the landscape of classical law. As Humfress puts it, "[t]he *Digest* was a Christian law book despite the paradoxical fact that its fifty books contained no clearly stated Christian precepts whatsoever." To worry, therefore, whether this or that component "Christianized" the legal system is to miss the point. The singularity of the collection rested on its making present (like a book of the scriptures) the one and only God. The presence of the book within the law court, and therefore the presence there of God himself, subsumed the enduringly Roman text under divine inspiration. The heart of its message, in other words, was delivered by the book's physical presentation—Lowden's point. And the inspiration enfolded Justinian as well: he was no less related to God than were the texts he provided.

Daniel Boyarin's singularity is different again. He challenges the familiar notion that, while Christian textuality was wedded to the definition and defense of a monolithic orthodoxy, Jewish writings, even of rabbinic authority, were more tolerant of plural opinion. The latter, he agrees, may have been the case in the early rabbinic period; but contemporary Christianity, if not exactly tolerant, was equally fractured in its statements of belief. Yet there was an early difference as well as an early similarity. The rabbis were able to endow their debates with a stability that did not demean their diversity: their understanding of orthodoxy was characterized by "interpretative indeterminacy and endless dispute." Christianity found that position more difficult to adopt. So, what happened later? Here Boyarin makes his central point and identifies his singularity. Christians were indeed inclined to pack about with defensive texts a coherent dogma, integrated and timeless. Even their piecemeal *florilegia* served as proof-texts of a lasting unanimity. If in the process, however, Nicaea—one of the watersheds of coercive agreement—became the *topos* of a myth, so also the Babylonian Talmud, while continuing to reproduce tangled conversations, managed in similar fashion to mythologize the world of Yavneh. There seems to be a difference still, but it depends, for Boyarin, on "the types of books that are made." I take this to demand a sense of the dynamic within a book: the point appears to be that, within those two campaigns to capture and defend in each case one body of belief, the disposition of the logical infantry may have differed, but the strategy was the same.

Finally, Catherine Burris illustrates the impact of juxtaposition. By binding her story to the stories of Jewish heroines—Ruth, Esther, Susanna, and Judith—the *Ktâbâ* makes possible a new reading of the Christian Thecla. (The mutual influence of Judaism and Christianity becomes here a pleasing subplot.) The archetype of the footloose ascetic woman, disdainful of marriage and of civic order, is forced into textual conversation, forced to reassess, as it were, the essence of her virtue and commitment in the company of wives and widows renowned for their defense of justice, state, and people. And it is not just a question of our reading in sequence, with Thecla at the end: there is a "linear reading," certainly, but also a reading that "seeks a schema." Here a book scores over a speech, because the reader can constantly reinterpret the impact of each part on the whole. Michael Williams (in *Rethinking Gnosticism*) made a similar point in relation to the Nag Hammadi codices, where the apparently random selection of texts within each binding can be made to reveal a *structure logique* more elusive, perhaps, but no less organic than Augustine's overriding vision in the *City of God*. The process is akin to the conjunction of portraits in such "collective biographies" as the *Historia monachorum* and Palladius's *Lausiac History;* but in Burris's case we have the added excitement of different *texts* and not just different *persons*.

So, how might we combine what I called above the "lateral reference" of those four studies? They introduce us, first, to the interplay between the written and the spoken word. Nothing in the contents of a book is possible without speech and the hearing of speech. To write was to capture and preserve (even in the case of the scriptures) what had already been said and interpreted. So it is necessary to listen as we read and justifiable to identify the writer as a speaker. Indeed, the modes of speech, while not slavishly reproduced, will govern the writing. Closely connected, second, is the bond between author and text. In some sense, authors are what they write, just as readers are what they read. Some compilers remain anonymous or are unreliably identified, whereas Augustine or Justinian, for example, of whom we know so much, may appear to intrude more forcefully upon our handling of their texts; to be known or not known may accentuate or diminish the impact of an author's motives, but does not weaken their *presence,* whether recognized or not. Third, the discursive can disguise the compressed—compressed in the sense that the longest and most variegated argument can still be bound by a "schema." Here Catherine Burris appeals to Matei Calinescu; and the added implication is that "an actively interpretive reading" may create as well as discover such cohesion. Finally, texts jostle one another on readers' shelves, and are sometimes, by the writers' craft, difficult to prise apart. So much that seems accidental or convenient in the several components of a manuscript or the jumbled contents of a single binding may reflect a more devious strategy behind the processes of production.

Where, then, do such analyses carry us next? Catherine Conybeare's chapter on Prudentius might seem equally devoted to a single work (the *Hamartigenia*); but, standing on the border between focused assessments and more diffused reflections, she reminds us of the degree to which any text will pose broad questions. She expresses nicely, for example, the distinction clarified by John Lowden between "material objects, the set of tangibles that are the province of the codicologist," and "the way in which the reader constructs the book." It was a distinction that the conference that gave rise to this book did something to soften, so that one set of "constructions" was seen to be controlled or at least influenced by the other. Conybeare is attracted by such unexpected connections. She explores, for example, the relation between "literary culture" and what she calls "feigned orality," putting further spin on the distinction between text and speech. The movement from the spoken to the written word was, in a culture deeply suffused with rhetoric, "a remarkable displacement of authority." There is more here than a bookish bishop like Augustine drawing upon his homiletic repertoire. Even more striking is Conybeare's (that is, Prudentius's) evocation of Moses, the phatic *littérateur* par excellence. He served as a "bridging device," at once *historicus* and *vaticinator*. In that respect, he both summed up tradition and articulated enduring values. A word merchant of such a sort drew readers into a past while making their experience entirely present, but it took skill to effect the connection. Conybeare writes of "the difficulty of observing both the historicity of the original tales and their extension into spiritual permanence." The important word, however, is "observing." One must be able to recognize coincidence. It is not enough to recount facts and then experience transcendence, as if one will proceed to the other. The historical account and the spiritual reality are there on the page and in the voice at once and together. The surface of such a text resembles those clever exercises in perspective, where what appears distant is suddenly seen to be close. It would be hard to suppose that to close a book read in such a way would merely return readers to familiar circumstance, bring them back home from a journey. The effective book inserts the reader into its own narrative, creates, in that sense, a new present, a new circumstance for the reader to inhabit (permanently). To read, therefore, is not to escape from the present but to link one's present (indeed, one's self) to some other past, to make oneself the product of a different history. How eagerly a new Christian in an old world might seize upon such an opportunity.

Such experiences were morally and even physically demanding. Here we touch upon the *askesis* of the early Christian book, the rigor of both writing and reading. In the second case, transportation in time and transformation of self called for special energy, which enlivened Christian literature in a manner not wholly exclusive to itself but markedly a component of its particular character. The Christian writer, meanwhile, had at least to attempt and anticipate a comparable *transitus,* while displaying an urgency of motive and skill that could draw others along the same path.

Kim Haines-Eitzen and Claudia Rapp both address that shift in late Roman culture. For Haines-Eitzen, the book and the body are fields for ascetic exercise. Her use of "palimpsest" as a model of the literary process depends first on the notion that one can improve a text, like a body, by overlaying it, by inscribing it differently and in the light of a new ideal. There is then a flow of energy in return, for a book can be used to school the body—in the posture of reading, in the labor of writing and binding, and in the exhortation to change. Haines-Eitzen's chief point is that early Christians, while not unique (for some contemporaries were comparable in their handling of Homer or Virgil), were more inclined to make textual adjustments in the interests of a shared belief. That demanded not mere alteration of a word but the imputation of new meaning—a less easily detectable sleight of hand. There is something here akin to the thrust of Daniel Boyarin's chapter. We also rejoin Catherine Burris, since the illustrative dimension of Haines-Eitzen's argument depends on her rich and extended study of how Thecla, both in gender and in body, was inscribed.

Claudia Rapp builds upon the theses of contributors already mentioned by focusing on the holy: "The holy book and the holy man are the most powerful icons for our interpretation of the culture and mentality of late antiquity." A book is "a doorway for contemplation"—an echo of Catherine Chin—

but entry is sought not merely to facilitate vision but to prescribe and reform. We encounter again the conviction of Catherine Conybeare, that to read is to define (or rather redefine) the self. Conybeare is also called to mind by Rapp's sense of a need for distance, which a book can provide. The reader meets figures from somewhere else, who offer examples or explanations of what the reader finds at present either impossible or obscure. And there is what Rapp calls "a double movement," which is analogous to the "flow of energy in return" that I detected in Haines-Eitzen's descriptions: a holy text imparts that holiness to the one who writes it; and the holy man, as portrayed in the writing, imparts holiness to the text. So selective a summary does even less justice than in other instances. I pass with particular sorrow over Rapp's section "The Miraculous Hand"—returning with a vengeance to John Lowden's book as object. Another of her several themes recalls Caroline Humfress's notion of "presence." For all the distance and *étrangeté*, temporary and practical, required for successful reading, the meeting I referred to (evident above all in hagiography) overwhelms the careful construction of the "other" world: the *vaticinator*, as Catherine Conybeare presents him, supplants the *historicus*. The presence of the writer (craftily invoked in letters above all, as Rapp also notes) is here disguised or exalted in the depiction of the saint.

Mark Vessey has written persuasively about the asceticism of the writer, of Jerome especially, and about the link between writing and the fashioning of the self. His chapter here represents a different and perhaps more daring venture. It carries us beyond the apparent boundaries of the late antique text. "Apparent" is, nevertheless, the important word, for Vessey wants us to acknowledge in the fourth century the roots of our own much-vaunted attachment to literary theory. Among Christians, especially when they read the Bible, the distinction between letter and spirit, if nothing else, addressed the problem of reaching beyond the surface of the text. Even though it was an age in which writers were eager to enmesh their "public," however small, by their craft with words, a multiplicity in the levels of engagement was an essential condition for the meeting of the two. Mere decoding did not exhaust one's understanding (did not allow one to pass automatically through the "doorway for contemplation"); and creating a text carried one only part of the way toward awakening sympathy in one's readers. There was nothing "literal" about sympathy and understanding. That conviction, Vessey believes, should ring a very modern bell. The historical connection is, even so, difficult to make and startling when stumbled upon. The essay achieves its effect by avoiding the obvious. I shall not rob readers of their surprise; but it is exhilarating to discover Mallarmé rather than Heidegger or Husserl behind the pessimism, or the scruple, of the late twentieth century. And there are more technical guides in our journey from Augustine to Derrida: Curtius and Marrou. Vessey's central purpose is to help us identify what Augustine had long ago discerned: the *espace littéraire* of Maurice Blanchot, which inherited its attractiveness from Mallarmé's longing for a book beyond anyone's capacity to read or write—Augustine's celestial *patria* no less. It is a territory of the mind where text and dream become interchangeable. And for all the sensuality of much that Vessey describes, asceticism is never abandoned; there was an abstinence to these more recent writers, a whittling of their self-satisfaction, a recognition of the ideal that so often eludes an artist's grasp. Why should we distinguish sharply between that modern longing and the early Christian's wish to break through to the transcendent?

A word, finally, about burning. The fragility of the book—its combustibility is only one aspect of the matter—can always awaken the violent jealousy of the fearful or the ignorant. Christians were not alone in harboring that weakness. Daniel Sarefield's point is that the later burning of books by Christians took its cue from a long tradition of suspicious destructiveness. The particular enthusiasm that marked persecutors under Diocletian, however, reminds us of how special books were to Christians. It also reminds us of the ritualism involved: the burning was in its way ceremonial, sanctioned by public authority. It also allowed a catharsis, which made more obvious the connection between burning books and burning people. In both cases, the bodies involved were not the sole, perhaps not even the direct, object of the conflagration. The book, whether burned or preserved, was in some sense a martyr, a witness to realities beyond itself. No flame could destroy such a reference. The armory of inscription and binding, the adventure of penetrating beyond the immediately visible, created an awareness that could survive the withdrawal of those supports. Writing and reading were simply staging posts in a journey of the mind. One recalls those gifted memories that defeated, in Ray Bradbury's *Fahrenheit 451*, the myopic fanaticism of tyrannical government. Even when books are absent, we remain readers.

PART I   MAKING THE BOOK

John Lowden

THE WORD MADE VISIBLE

*The Exterior of the Early Christian Book
as Visual Argument*

Introduction

In a paper entitled "The Beginnings of Biblical Illustration," first published in 1999, I attempted to survey all the surviving biblical manuscripts that contain images made up to about the mid-seventh century.[1] There proved to

In memory of Peter Lasko (1924–2003). I am grateful to Philip Rousseau for the invitation to deliver this paper, and for organizing a most stimulating and instructive conference. Claudia Rapp's chapter in this volume in particular should be read as a kind of diptych with the present one. I also received helpful comments after repeating the lecture at a joint meeting of the Centre for Late Antique and Medieval Studies and the Centre for Hellenic Studies, King's College London. In preparing the lecture, acquiring slides and photographs, discussion before and after the event, and for advice, information, and assistance of various kinds, I am most grateful to Susan Boyd, Evangelos Chrysos, Carol Downer, Anne Duggan, Helen Evans, Carol Farr, David Ganz, Neil Grindley, Judith Herrin, Susan Holman, Tim Kirk, Kevanne Kirkwood, Marie-Pierre Lafitte, Jen Lindsay, Vrej Nersessian, Uschi Payne, Nicholas Pickwood, Julian Raby, John L. Sharpe, Barrie Singleton, and William Voelkle. The library of the Warburg Institute proved, as ever, invaluable. The annotation is primarily to recent works and those containing extensive further bibliography.

1. The paper appears in *Imaging the Early Medieval Bible,* ed. John Williams (University Park, Pa., 1999; paperback ed., 2002), 9–59. A limited account, based largely on the publications of Kurt Weitzmann, has recently been provided by Ioannis Spatharakis, "Early Christian Illustrated Gospel Books from the East," in *The Impact of Scripture in Early Christianity,* ed. J. den Boeft and M. L. van Poll-van de Lisdonk (Leiden, 1999), 102–21. In the same collection note also the articles of A. Provoost, "Le caractère et l'évolution des images bibliques dans l'art chrétien primitif," 79–101; and P. C. J. van Dael, "Biblical Cycles on Church Walls: Pro Lectione Pictura," 122–32. See also Barbara Zimmermann, "Die Codexillustration als neuer Kunstzweig: Spiegel einer geänderten Funktion des Buches in der Spätan-

be only fourteen such books, some of them mere fragments. By focusing on broadly codicological topics, such as planning and layout, rather than questions of date and place of origin, I observed and sought to emphasize the extraordinary range and unpredictability of the material. For example, the two illuminated Genesis manuscripts (the Cotton Genesis and the Vienna Genesis), despite a basic similarity, are totally different from each other in many important ways. Most of the surviving illuminated manuscripts from the period comprise gospel books, or fragments of such books, but even with these it is impossible to use one, for example, to hypothesize about the (missing) contents of another, because they show such disparity.

On the basis of my survey, I reconstructed a scenario for the use of images in early Christian books different from the theory that has long held the field. Instead of considering the survivals as more or less selective and corrupt (in the philological sense), as late copies of numerous earlier "perfect" lost archetypes—the equivalent of authorial "originals"—I proposed a less prescriptive view, in which the surviving material was varied, unpredictable, and by implication creative (albeit not in a romantic manner). According to this theory images only began to appear in biblical books at a relatively late date, say, in the fifth century; illustrated biblical books were always rare, and they were in part a response to—not the explanation for—the ubiquitous presence by the fifth and sixth centuries of Christian images throughout the public and the often overlooked private spheres.[2]

Since writing that paper I have considered the question of the "public" for images in luxury books in a variety of historical contexts,[3] observing how most

---

tike?" in *The Use of Sacred Books in the Ancient World,* ed. Leonard V. Rutgers et al. (Leuven, 1998), 263–85; Barbara Zimmermann, "Illustrierte Prachtcodices: Bücherluxus in der Spätantike," in *Epochenwandel? Kunst und Kultur zwischen Antike und Mittelalter,* ed. Norbert Zimmermann and Franz Alto Bauer (Mainz, 2001), 45–56; Barbara Zimmermann, *Die Wiener Genesis im Rahmen der antiken Buchmalerei: Ikonographie, Darstellung, Illustrationsverfahren und Aussageintention* (Wiesbaden, 2003), esp. 1–53.

2. On Christian images in the private sphere, see, for example, Thomas F. Mathews, *The Clash of Gods: A Reinterpretation of Early Christian Art,* 2d ed. (Princeton, 1999), 177–90.

3. "Byzantium Perceived through Illuminated Manuscripts: Now and Then," in *Through the Looking Glass: Byzantium Through British Eyes,* ed. Robin Cormack and Elizabeth Jeffreys (Aldershot, 2000), 85–106; "Illuminated Books and the Liturgy," in *Objects, Images, and the Word: Art in the Service of the Liturgy,* ed. Colum Hourihane (Princeton, 2003), 17–53; "'Reading' the *Bibles moralisées:* Images as Exegesis and the Exegesis of Images," in *Reading Images and Texts: Medieval Images and Texts as Forms of Communication,* ed. Marco Mostert and Mariëlle Hageman (Turnhout, 2005), 495–525; "Les rois et les reines de France en tant que 'public' des Bibles moralisées: Une approche tangentielle à la question des

illuminations played little part in shaping perceptions in their own time, unlike today, because they were generally invisible, in striking contrast to, for example, the fixed decoration of a church. My main focus in this paper is an aspect of the luxury book that was, unlike its images, undoubtedly "public" in the sense that it was exposed to public view on a regular basis—namely, the book's exterior. How were images used on the exterior of early Christian books? This is an obvious question, even banal perhaps, but, surprisingly, it is not one that has been explored before across the whole range of surviving material.[4]

I initially approached the question, it must be admitted, with a number of presuppositions. I assumed that early Christians, for whom the codex-book was such an important accoutrement, would have been interested in the possibilities that the book's exterior presented to make a visual statement of some sort to themselves and others (depending on the presumed circulation of the book). I assumed that there would be a development over time from simplicity to complexity in schemes of decoration and specifically in the use of images. And I assumed that by the sixth century Christians would be making highly sophisticated visual arguments on the exteriors of their books, as in every other area. One given was that the proportion of material that has survived is minute, but how this situation was to be controlled was less clear.

It was necessary, therefore, to assemble a body of material that could confidently be assumed to exemplify "the decorated exterior of the early Christian book." Within this large set resides the subset of decorated exteriors specifically using images, which will be of particular interest. One might expect the resulting corpus to take two forms: first, all surviving decorated early Christian book exteriors; second, all images from the period showing the exteriors of Christian books. Neither category, however, is straightforward in compilation or use, and this must be clearly acknowledged at the outset. First, there is

---

liens entre les Bibles moralisées et les vitraux de la Sainte-Chapelle," in *La Sainte-Chapelle: Royaume de France et Jérusalem céleste*, ed. Yves Christe and Peter Kurmann (forthcoming); "Under the Influence of the *Bibles moralisées*," in *Under the Influence: The Concept of Influence and the Study of Illuminated Manuscripts*, ed. John Lowden and Alixe Bovey (forthcoming).

4. Useful surveys are to be found in the early parts of Paul Needham, *Twelve Centuries of Bookbindings 400–1600* (New York, 1979), and, in particular, J. A. Szirmai, *The Archaeology of Medieval Bookbinding* (Aldershot, 1999), with further references. Still essential is Frauke Steenbock, *Der kirchliche Prachteinband im frühen Mittelalter, von den Anfängen bis zum Beginn der Gotik* (Berlin, 1965). The broad question is not considered in, for example, Harry Y. Gamble, *Books and Readers in the Early Church: A History of Early Christian Texts* (New Haven, 1995).

the problem of surviving early Christian book covers themselves: only a tiny proportion of what is already a small sample survives in situ, on the books for which they were made. This at once throws up a very serious obstacle, especially for those who attempt to understand the book by studying it in its totality (the applied codicology that I favor). Second, and even worse, the very status of a good proportion of the objects that have been referred to as early Christian book covers, precisely because they no longer perform their original function, has been challenged: are they, we must ask on a case-by-case basis, in fact book covers at all? Obviously, if they are not, and we include their evidence, our analysis could prove completely misleading.

Third, there is the matter of the representation of books in images. We have to ask on what grounds we should accept any image of a book as archaeologically accurate when it appears in a context—i.e., so-called early Christian art—in which the visual language is predominantly symbolic rather than naturalistic. With this last point in mind I have treated *images* of book covers, of which there are a large number, very cautiously, and largely for purposes of comparison with the covers themselves. To explain further: an image of a book cover in, for example, a wall painting showing Christ or an evangelist is certainly a sort of public statement. But I think such a representation needs to be treated in full awareness not just of its context but of its material and manufacture. To make a painted image of a book cover, like a painted image of clothing, or furniture, or architecture, is obviously not at all the same as to manufacture (as leather- or metal-worker, weaver, carpenter, or builder) the subject that is represented. The one exception I allow myself is the image of a book cover when it occurs *on* a book cover. Such images cannot be assumed to be strictly representational, but they must have been executed with a special awareness of their context. The presence of a degree of self-referentiality in such images opens up a possible path of inquiry.

When surveying the images in the *interiors* of biblical books, I chose to group the material by language, starting with books written in Greek. Such an approach is not possible, however, with book exteriors, for most of them, as noted above, have lost their interiors. The approach I adopt here is based instead on material considerations. I commence with a brief overview of the standard covering of the early Christian book—namely, leather—as providing the context against which the rest of the material must be studied. Because there is no evidence that in the early period leather book covers were decorated with *figurative* images (I exclude the cross), they are treated here as important principally to the main set of decorated bindings. Moving to the subset of bindings with images, I first consider the unique case of a pair of painted wooden book covers. Remaining in the subset, I then move into the luxury sphere and look at silver covers, and at the one surviving example of a cover of gold decorated with precious stones. Finally I present the ivory covers, visually the most complex by far. Throughout, I attempt to consider, in theory at least, all the evidence from the early Christian world in the period up to roughly the mid-seventh century. Despite the limitations of the evidence, I then risk some general conclusions and observations. As was the case with the reconsideration of early illuminated biblical manuscripts, I deal only in passing with the generally much debated questions of date and place of origin, focusing instead on less frequently considered topics.

Leather Book Covers

Once the codex-book was sewn, it needed a protective covering. This was true whether it was composed of a single quire of variable length or of many regular quires, and whether written on papyrus or parchment. Coverings, in addition to preventing excessive wear and tear on the outer pages of the book, could stabilize the sewing of the gatherings, help to keep the pages aligned, and, when fastened by ties or clasps, could limit buckling of the pages due to humidity. The stiffer the coverings, the greater the protection they offered, from sheets or envelopes of parchment, to leather-covered "soft boards" generally made of recycled sheets of papyrus, to stout wooden panels up to a centimeter or more in thickness equipped with clasps to hold the leaves under compression. The usual covering material for a book throughout the entire manuscript era was leather.[5]

Leather is an easy material to decorate. Especially when softened by moisture, it can be readily and permanently impressed, scored, punched, cut, and then, when dry, colored or gilded. Doubtless the many techniques by which leather artifacts of all sorts were decorated (I am thinking of such personal

5. The broadest recent survey is Szirmai, *Archaeology of Medieval Bookbinding.*

and fancy goods as shoes, saddles, harnesses, tents, and so forth) were available as potential models to those who bound manuscripts with leather covers at any date. Quite probably, leather book covers were left without any form of decoration only at the lowest levels of expense.

Cassiodorus, in a well-known chapter of his *Institutiones* (written in southern Italy around the third quarter of the sixth century), specifically mentions bindings when talking of book production. Translated literally, he says:

> We have provided workers skilled in the covering of books [*in codicibus cooperiendis*] so that a handsome external form may clothe the beauty of sacred letters. . . . For them [the bookbinders] we have represented becomingly, if I am not mistaken, numerous types of designs [*facturarum*] depicted in one book, so that the learned person can himself choose which form of covering [*tegumenti*] he should prefer.[6]

Like many things connected with Cassiodorus, his useful depictions of bindings have not survived, but I take it that he had depicted a range of designs that could be employed on the covers of sacred books and not, for example, diagrams of different sewing or structural matters, which were not relevant to his concerns. His diagrams might have looked, therefore, a little like the modern reconstruction diagrams of early decorated Coptic bindings (fig. 1).[7]

That decoration was not, however, ubiquitous on leather book covers of the earliest period is suggested by the eleven mid- to late fourth-century bindings found intact in a hoard of Coptic gnostic manuscripts at Nag Hammadi (north of Luxor) in 1945.[8] The bindings are of a quite complex wraparound envelope type, the leather covering stiffened by sheets of reused papyrus. The volume containing, among other texts, the Gospels of Thomas and Philip (Codex II) is a substantial codex of 176 pages in a single quire, 27 × 15 cm. It was the only one of the Nag Hammadi codices to have the exterior of its binding extensively decorated with incised lines and freehand spirals, volutes, and

6. *Inst.* 1.30.3, ed. R. A. B. Mynors, *Cassiodori Senatoris Institutiones* (Oxford, 1937), 77. A less literal translation is provided by Leslie Webber Jones, *An Introduction to Divine and Human Readings by Cassiodorus Senator* (New York, 1966), 134.

7. For example, the diagram in *The History of Bookbinding 525–1950 A.D.,* exh. cat., Baltimore Museum of Art (Baltimore, 1957), pl. 10; or Hugo Ibscher, "Koptische Einbände aus Ägypten," *Berliner Museen: Berichte aus den preussischen Kunstsammlungen* 49 (1928): 87, 89, 90.

8. Jean Doresse, "Les reliures des manuscrits gnostiques coptes découverts à Khénoboskion," *Revue d'Égyptologie* 13 (1961): 27–49. A general introduction is provided by James M. Robinson, *The Facsimile Edition of the Nag Hammadi Codices: Introduction* (Leiden, 1972). Szirmai, *Archaeology of Medieval Bookbinding,* 7–11, has further references.

so forth in several colors.[9] The incised designs can be resolved into crosses of both + and × type.

There are numerous other surviving Coptic bindings, beneficiaries of the preservative properties of the dry desert air of Egypt, but it is important to note that most of these are much later in date.[10] We will consider just two well-known exceptions here. The first, the Glazier codex (Morgan Library, MS G.67) is a very small fifth-century Coptic Acts (chapters 1–15.2 only; it would have been in two volumes), just 12 × 11 cm.[11] It has a leather spine strip decorated with a tooled pattern of concentric circles within horizontal lines. Because of the unusual (to modern eyes) construction of the binding, the wooden boards were left completely uncovered, and the book was held shut by wrapping it with two long leather bands, one vertical, the other horizontal. Three other fifth-century Coptic bindings with similar uncovered boards have survived, and this will be important in discussing the Freer Gospels, below.[12] Given the very limited decorative potential of such bindings, it is interesting to note that the Glazier codex closes its text with a full-page image of an ankh cross flanked by peacocks.[13] The presence of the image is remarkable, but note that there was no link between the decoration of this book's interior and its exterior, a point to which we shall return.

The second well-known example forms part of the collection of fifty or so Coptic bindings from the monastery of St. Michael, near Hamouli in the Fayyum, acquired for the Morgan Library in 1911–20 (compare the reconstruction drawings in fig. 1).[14] When excavated in 1910, the bindings were still on the books for which they were made, but all were subsequently removed.

9. Doresse, "Reliures des manuscrits gnostiques," 42–45, and pl. 6. See also *L'art copte en Égypte: 2000 ans de Christianisme; Exposition présentée à l'Institut du monde arabe, Paris, du 15 mai au 3 septembre 2000 et au Musée de l'Ephèbe au Cap d'Agde, du 30 septembre 2000 au 7 janvier 2001* (Paris, 2000), no. 18.

10. For example, the interesting bindings of the manuscripts from St. Merkourios, Edfu, dated 979–1053; see Jen Lindsay, "The Edfu Collection of Coptic Books," *New Bookbinder* 21 (2001): 31–51.

11. Needham, *Twelve Centuries of Bookbindings*, no. 1. Dimensions are of binding; the page size is less square, 12 × 9.8 cm.

12. Ibid., 9.

13. Kurt Weitzmann, ed., *Age of Spirituality: Late Antique and Early Christian Art, Third to Seventh Century*, exh. cat., Metropolitan Museum (New York, 1979), no. 444a; Harry Bober, "On the Illumination of the Glazier Codex: A Contribution to Early Coptic Art, and Its Relation to Hiberno-Saxon Interlace," in *Homage to a Bookman: Essays on Manuscripts, Books and Printing Written for Hans P. Kraus on His 60th Birthday*, ed. Hellmut Lehmann-Haupt (Berlin, 1967), 31–49. I did not include the Glazier codex in Lowden, "Beginnings of Biblical Illustration," as it has no (human) figurative decoration.

14. On the find, see Needham, *Twelve Centuries of Bookbindings*, 12–13.

The most aesthetically ambitious of the Morgan bindings was on MS M.569 (fig. 2), and measures some 38.5 × 29.5 cm.[15] It is notable that the binding is that of a gospel book (the only one among the Hamouli material), written on parchment, and covered with leather over papyrus "boards." It is generally dated to the seventh or eighth century. The decorative technique is painstaking and very elaborate: a cut red-leather openwork layer was finely sewn to a layer of parchment covered with gold leaf, over a brown leather layer. The design, similar on front and back covers, consists of a small central cross within a medallion filled with geometrical interlace, the whole within a rectangle decorated with a variety of motifs, including a small cross at the top center. The interior of the front cover has a very carefully worked inscription, "Archangel Michael," in the same cutwork technique, but a colophon in Greek indicates that the manuscript had earlier belonged to a nearby monastery dedicated to the Mother of God. The date of the M.569 binding is unclear; it might be as early as the seventh century, and might even partially predate the manuscript to which it was attached.[16] Two comparable bindings are preserved in Berlin and Vienna, and all three may be close in date.[17] As for M.569, it would appear that the highly elaborate design was employed to mark out this gospel book from others in the monastery. But in visual terms the cover did not convey specific information about, for example, the book's content or authorship.

That the Fayyum-type decoration, which goes back to simple incised patterns already found at Nag Hammadi, became ubiquitous in the late antique world is beyond dispute. Allowing for major gaps in the chronology, it can be seen that as we move out of the period considered here into the late seventh, eighth, and ninth centuries, bindings decorated in related techniques and styles have been found at the very ends of the known world—in insular Britain, for example, as in the famous case of the Gospel of John found in St. Cuthbert's coffin,[18] across the Islamic world,[19] and even among the Man-

15. Ibid., 13–16; *History of Bookbinding 525–1950*, no. 26; *Art copte en Égypte*, no. 41.

16. Needham, *Twelve Centuries of Bookbindings*, 16.

17. *P. Berol.* 14018 and *Erzherzog Rainer Pap.* inv. no. 34: see Needham, *Twelve Centuries of Bookbindings*, 15–16 and nn6–7.

18. The Stonyhurst Gospel, London, British Library, MS Loan 74; T. Julian Brown, ed., *The Stonyhurst Gospel of Saint John* (Oxford, 1969); some further references in Szirmai, *Archaeology of Medieval Bookbinding*, 95–96.

19. Szirmai, *Archaeology of Medieval Bookbinding*, 51–61, with some comments and references on early decorated covers on p. 59. See also *History of Bookbinding, 525–1950*, no. 37.

ichaeans in the Turfan region of eastern central Asia.[20] One of the fragmentary Manichaean bindings is of leather cut in interlacing geometrical patterns to reveal the gilded surface of an underlayer, and looks familiar after consideration of M.569. But are such decorative exteriors (as distinct from underlying structures) Coptic in more than a very loose generic sense?

The failure of leather covers to survive except in desert environments is hardly surprising, given that the materials of which they were made decay readily and have little or no value when recycled, and hence are unlikely to be specially preserved. Although we have not one single leather binding from the early period (up to ca. 650) that is not from Egypt, it would seem unjustifiable to locate the production of such covers in that region alone. The vast majority of all the books produced in late antiquity presumably had leather-covered bindings. The use of pattern, focused on a central motif and often symmetrical (hence potentially cruciform), was probably very common in decorating their exteriors. Even though such designs could be highly complex, and potentially open to symbolic and possibly even figurative readings, no surviving leather book cover was illustrated with human figures, although we cannot rule out the possibility that such covers might once have existed. It is against this reconstructed background of innumerable leather covers of broadly similar if individually varied type that the figured, and the far more costly luxury, bindings must be judged.

Painted Wood Book Covers

The leather-covered binding was, it is agreed, standard and hence ubiquitous in late antiquity, but the painted wood binding seems to have been very rare.[21] We have but a single surviving example (fig. 3), the covers of the early fifth-century Greek Gospels ("Codex W") in the Freer Gallery of Art in Washington, D.C. (purchased by Freer in Cairo in 1907).[22] Since they were first

20. Zsuzsanna Gulácsi, *Manichaean Art in Berlin Collections* (Turnhout, 2001), no. 70, and p. 247 (see also nos. 71–72).

21. There are examples from Antinoë (third–fourth century) of wooden panels with incised decoration without leather covers; see *Art copte en Égypte,* no. 40. For plain boards on early codices, see Szirmai, *Archaeology of Medieval Bookbinding,* 23–26. There is a twelfth-century example from Gerona of a book with figurative carved wooden covers; see Steenbock, *Kirchliche Prachteinband,* no. 85; it is not clear whether the panels might originally have been gilded or painted.

22. The panels have the accession numbers FGA 06.297 (Matthew and John), 06.298 (Mark and

published by Morey in 1913 and 1914, these panels have been little studied.[23] Their execution certainly postdates the Greek gospel manuscript they enclose, and Morey concluded that they were painted most probably in the first half of the seventh century, a date that has been accepted. Given the fragility of the painted surface, with its heavily applied encaustic-bound pigments, they are surprisingly well preserved. At some date the covers were chained, seemingly to prevent them from opening fully and hence perhaps to offer them a modicum of protection.[24]

Each beveled panel measures about 21.3 × 14.3 × 1.6 cm—quite small, about the size of a modern paperback novel. Traces of pigment on fragments of the binding structure on the edges of the boards indicate that the painting was executed with the book already bound, and this is remarkable. The standing evangelists with massive yellow haloes (imitating gold leaf—the pigment has been identified as orpiment)[25] fill the available space. On the better-preserved back cover the bearded figures are identified by inscriptions as Luke on the left and Mark on the right. The much less well preserved front cover has Matthew, presumably, on the left, and a fragment of John on the right. The order Matthew, John, Luke, Mark is the order of the Gospels in the manuscript within, and the point is important.[26] Each evangelist displays a large book with a seemingly gold and jeweled cover. The covered hands with which the figures support the books are an indication of reverence, and also perhaps a reminder of how the Freer Gospels themselves would have been carried.

Because of the fragility of the painted surfaces of the covers, their practi-

---

Luke). The text was published as *Facsimile of the Washington Manuscript of the Four Gospels in the Freer Collection,* ed. Henry A. Sanders (Ann Arbor, 1913); Charles Rufus Morey, "The Painted Covers of the Washington Manuscript of the Gospels," in his *East Christian Paintings in the Freer Collection* (New York, 1914), 63–81. See also Henry A. Sanders, "New Manuscripts of the Bible from Egypt," *American Journal of Archaeology* 12 (1908): 49–55, and pl. 3; Hugo Buchthal and Otto Kurz, *A Hand List of Illuminated Oriental Christian Manuscripts* (London, 1942), no. 309.

23. Some exceptions are Jules Leroy, *Les manuscrits coptes et coptes-arabes illustrés* (Paris, 1974), 87–89, pl. 26; Gary Vikan, "Byzantine Art as a Mirror of Its Public," *Apollo* 118 (1983): 164–67; Kurt Weitzmann, "An Early Coptic/Arabic Miniature in Leningrad," *Ars Islamica* 10 (1943): 119–34, esp. 124–25.

24. As suggested by Morey, "Painted Covers," 64.

25. See Conservation Report, April 1954, on file at the Freer Gallery of Art. I am grateful to Tim Kirk for access to this material as well as to the covers themselves.

26. This is the "so-called Western order"; Bruce Metzger, *The Text of the New Testament: Its Transmission, Corruption, and Restoration,* 3d ed. (New York, 1992), 56–57.

cality must be open to question. When it is recalled that they decorate a much older book, it seems reasonable to ask if they were perhaps made in some sense to enshrine the text, a text that perhaps had gained a relic-like status due to an association with some holy person. The later provision of chains, effectively preventing the use of the text, would seem to confirm this "enshrinement." The Greek text would have become increasingly illegible in a Coptic milieu as the bilingualism characteristic of the early centuries gradually declined. From this it follows that the images on the covers had a special function: they acted as a guide to, in effect as a substitute for, what was enclosed within. The very legible inscriptions (Matthew, John, Luke, and Mark) provided the information the viewer needed. I suggest that this was a book that, by the time the covers were painted, was intended primarily for display and for processional use, not to be routinely read from in the liturgy. It was in turn this lack of "normal" use, due to its special status, that ensured the survival of the fragile paint surface on the book's covers. When not on display, the book was probably kept wrapped in a textile for further protection.

The unique painted binding of the Freer Gospels was thus the result of exceptional historical contingencies. The boards were initially bare, because in the fifth century this was how they were left (compare the Glazier codex discussed above). Multiple holes in the top edge and fore edge of the front cover show that, like the Glazier codex, the Freer Gospels were originally secured with long leather bands. As they would have damaged the paint surface, they were presumably cut away, or had already broken off, when the boards were painted. Had the Freer Gospels been an early fourth-century manuscript, it might have had an envelope binding. Had it been a product of the sixth century, it probably would have had leather-covered boards. In either case its binding would not have been easy to paint at a later date. It was the changing technique of binding the codex in Egypt that in part explains these painted covers—this, and the desire at a later date to preserve and embellish the original binding with the venerable Greek gospel book retained within.

Silver Book Covers

The direct evidence for silver-covered bookbindings, originally partly gilded, comes from two hoards, both excavated clandestinely: one in Syria in 1908–10 and the other in southern Turkey in 1963. The first, formerly known and separately discussed as the Antioch, Hama, Riha, and Stuma treasures, is now considered to have been a single burial and is referred to, after a Byzantine settlement close to its assumed find spot, as the Kaper Koraon treasure.[27] It consists of some fifty-six silver liturgical objects from a church treasury, formed over a century or so between ca. 550 and ca. 650. The other, known as the Sion treasure after its presumed use in the church of St. Nicholas at Sion, near Myra, mentioned in some of the inscriptions, consists of more than fifty silver liturgical objects plus twenty-two pieces of silver revetment, most of strikingly massive weight and high-quality workmanship, many given by or under a Bishop Eutychianos in the mid-sixth century.[28]

The Kaper Koraon treasure had two pairs of rectangular silver plaques, now both in the Metropolitan Museum, with a fragment in the Louvre; the Sion treasure had two pairs of silver plaques, now both at Dumbarton Oaks, with a fragment in Antalya, where there are also fragments of a third pair of plaques. In every case we are dealing with silver revetments that once would have covered the wooden boards of the book's binding but that now lack any trace of their support. The designs were hammered into the sheet silver from the back and the detail then chased on the front. The silver sheets were then folded around the boards (Sion plaques) and might additionally be nailed in place on both front and back (Kaper Koraon plaques). The repoussé technique, however, results in panels in which the relief decoration is quite easily crushed or distorted.

The generally accepted function of any or all of these plaques as book covers was challenged in the 1980s,[29] but can, I suggest, be maintained on a range

27. Marlia Mundell Mango, *Silver from Early Byzantium: The Kaper Koraon and Related Treasures,* exh. cat., Walters Art Gallery (Baltimore, 1986), 3–36.

28. Susan A. Boyd, "A 'Metropolitan' Treasure from a Church in the Provinces: An Introduction to the Study of the Sion Treasure," in *Ecclesiastical Silver Plate in Sixth-Century Byzantium,* ed. Susan A. Boyd and Marlia Mundell Mango (Washington, D.C., 1992), 5–37. See also the broader account by Susan A. Boyd, "Art in the Service of the Liturgy: Byzantine Silver Plate," in *Heaven on Earth: Art and the Church in Byzantium,* ed. Linda Safran (University Park, Pa., 1998), 152–85.

29. Mango, *Silver from Early Byzantium,* 202–3, 207, 210. For example the statement on p. 203: "If, contrary to their widely accepted designation as 'bookcovers' ... these plaques [in the Metropolitan Museum] instead formed part of an iconic revetment ..." Note that Helmut Buschhausen, *Die spätrömischen Metallscrinia und frühchristlichen Reliquiare* (Vienna, 1971), cat. B 22–23, 254–56, had already questioned the function of some of the small fragments as originating from book covers rather than, for example, reliquaries.

of what might be termed circumstantial grounds: they come in pairs; their size and shape is commensurate with a function as book covers, as is their decoration; and their vertical edges, where they survive, have cuttings that could be explained as elements of the binding structure and/or clasp system of books. Their condition, with one cover sometimes considerably more worn than the other, is also characteristic. And no more satisfactory alternative function for them has yet been proposed.[30] When the silver plaques are considered in the context of the other objects gathered together in this paper, their function as book covers is confirmed beyond reasonable doubt.

Silver Book Covers: Kaper Koraon Treasure

Each leaf of the first pair of panels in the Metropolitan Museum (fig. 4) measures approximately 27.5 × 21.4 cm (max.). This implies a page format for the enclosed book twice as large as the Freer Gospels. Each plaque is decorated with a standing saint beneath an arch supported on spiral columns and flanked in its spandrels by peacocks, the whole within a vine-scroll border with a cross at the top center.[31] Originally the plaques would have been partially gilded.[32] One figure, doubtless St. Peter, turns to the left, gestures with his right hand, and with his left hand holds a large processional cross by its extended shank. The other figure, surely St. Paul, turns to the right and holds, and I would say displays, a large book in both hands. The obvious deduction is that these panels were made to cover a book of Acts and Epistles—broadly speaking, the deeds of Peter and the writings of Paul—that would be used for the epistle readings in the liturgy. The particular treatment of Peter and Paul on the covers seems to allude deliberately to the processions of a normal lit-

---

30. See also the arguments supporting their uses as book covers in Margaret E. Frazer, "Early Byzantine Silver Book Covers," in Boyd and Mango, *Ecclesiastical Silver Plate,* 71–76. Note that Catherine Metzger, in *Byzance: L'art byzantin dans les collections publiques françaises: Musée du Louvre, 3 novembre 1992–1er février 1993,* exh. cat. (Paris, 1992), 116, left open the possible use of the Louvre/Metropolitan Museum plaques as iconic revetments. The Metropolitan Museum plaques with Saints Peter and Paul were recently described as follows by the curator: "These two plaques may have framed an image of Christ, composing a tripartite icon for contemplation or veneration." See Helen C. Evans, Melanie Holcomb, and Robert Hallmann, *The Arts of Byzantium* (New York, 2001), 22. See also p. 47.

31. Nos. 50.5.1–2. See Mango, *Silver from Early Byzantium,* nos. 44–45; Weitzmann, *Age of Spirituality,* no. 554; *Early Christian and Byzantine Art: An Exhibition Held at the Baltimore Museum of Art, April 25–June 22 [1947],* ed. Dorothy Eugenia Miner (Baltimore, 1947), no. 390.

32. Frazer, "Silver Book Covers," 72n10.

urgy, or perhaps to a stational liturgy.[33] Peter carries the cross, Paul the holy book. What is more, if we look carefully at Paul's book we can see that it is not open facing us in order to reveal a text, but rather with its outside toward us, to display its covers.[34] (This would seem to be the significance of the carefully executed vertical decoration of the book's spine.) St. Paul carries and displays the silver-covered book in his hands as we assume this silver-covered book was itself carried and displayed. The self-referentiality of the image *of* the book within the image *in* the book (or on this case *on* the book) is characteristic of the possibilities of book decoration already being explored by artists in the sixth century.[35] An interesting question is which of the two was originally the front cover. The same question is raised by many of the other pairs of plaques, and some general remarks are therefore appropriate.

At issue is the interpretation of two types of physical evidence: the presence of holes and cuttings in the vertical edges of the plaques, and the strikingly greater wear and damage to one of a pair of covers. Both are problematic. Cuttings in the vertical edges of plaques (where they survive and can be examined) might be evidence of the book's binding, but they might also be evidence of the provision of clasps; i.e., we could be looking at either edge. This is the case with the Peter and Paul plaques. Frazer concludes, "On the basis of the holes, the plaques could be aligned either way."[36] In this case, however, she feels that a "tiebreak" is available: "the fact that the St. Peter plaque has suffered much more wear than that of Paul suggests that it was the lower cover."[37] This is explained by the assumption that greater wear on the back cover would have resulted from laying the book down, either for storage or on an altar. But if we stop to consider the latter point, it begins to appear less cogent. When a precious book is laid on a protective textile or cushion and then opened for

---

33. For a useful introduction and further bibliography, see John A. Cotsonis, *Byzantine Figural Processional Crosses* (Washington, D.C., 1994). See also John F. Baldovin, *The Urban Character of Christian Worship: The Origins, Development and Meaning of Stational Liturgy* (Rome, 1987), and the remarks of Thomas F. Mathews, *The Early Churches of Constantinople: Architecture and Liturgy* (University Park, Pa., 1971), 148–49.

34. Compare the description in Frazer, "Silver Book Covers," 72: "saints holding books, seemingly decorated with punched leather covers."

35. For example in the Rabbula Gospels; see Lowden, "Beginnings of Biblical Illustration," 26–30, and fig. 9.

36. Frazer, "Silver Book Covers," 75.

37. Ibid. The deduction that the back cover would have been the more worn was already made in *History of Bookbinding 525–1950*, no. 3 (and no. 4).

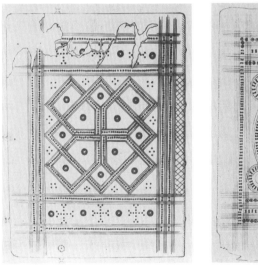

FIG. 1. Reconstruction drawings of decorative designs on some ninth–tenth century Coptic leather book covers from Hamouli.

Back

Front

FIG. 2. New York, Pierpont Morgan Library, leather book covers removed from
MS M. 569.

Back

Front

FIG. 3. Washington, D.C., Freer Gallery of Art, painted wooden book covers removed from the Freer Gospels.

Back

Front

FIG. 4.   New York, Metropolitan Museum of Art, silver book covers from the Kaper Koraon treasure.

Front

FIG. 5. New York, Metropolitan Museum of Art, and Paris, Musée du Louvre, reconstruction of silver book covers from the Kaper Koraon treasure.

Back

Front

FIG. 6.   Washington, D.C., Dumbarton Oaks, reconstruction of silver book covers from the Sion treasure.

Back

Front

FIG. 7. Washington, D.C, Dumbarton Oaks, silver book covers from the Sion treasure.

Back

Front

FIG. 8.   Monza, Tesoro del Duomo, gold and jeweled book covers.

Back

Front

FIG. 9. Milan, Tesoro del Duomo, ivory and jeweled book covers.

Front

FIG. 10.   Erevan, Matenadaran, ivory book covers reused on the Ejmiadzin Gospels.

Back

Front

FIG. 11. Paris, Bibliothèque nationale de France, MS lat. 9384, ivory book covers reused on the St. Lupicin Gospels (the front and back have been exchanged).

FIG. 12.   Detail of Ejmiadzin Gospels cover: Christ healing a demoniac.

FIG. 13.   Detail of St. Lupicin Gospels cover: Christ healing a demoniac.

Back

Front

FIG. 14. Ravenna, Museo Nazionale; Manchester, John Rylands University Library; Paris, Musée du Louvre; St. Petersburg, State Ermitage Museum; Berlin, Museum für spätantike und byzantinische Kunst, reconstruction of ivory book covers from Murano.

FIG. 15.   London, British Museum, central front panel of a dismantled ivory book cover.

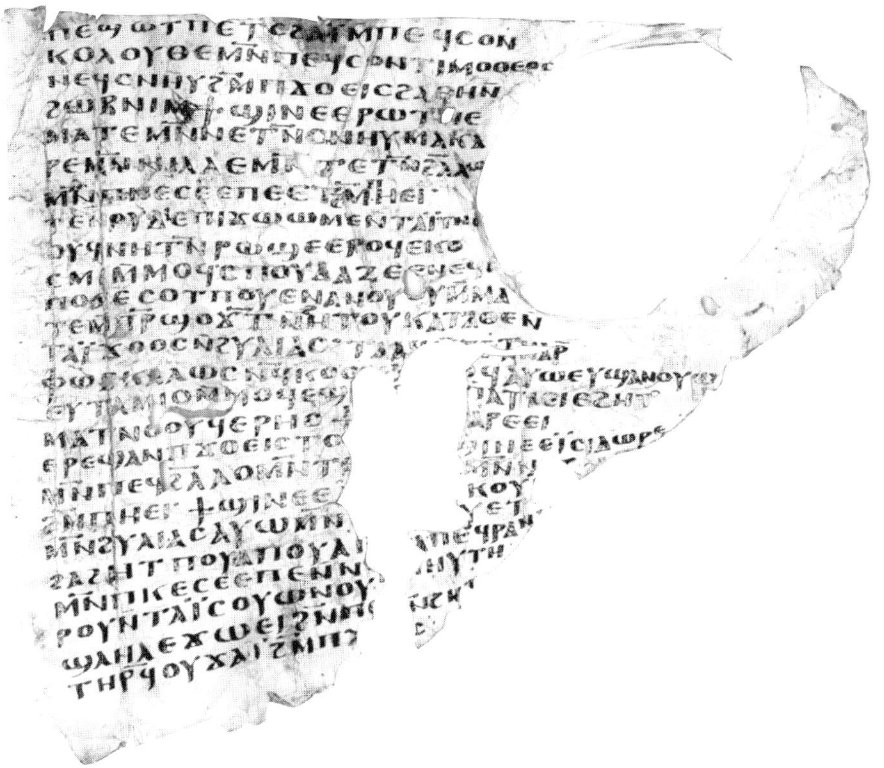

FIG. 16. P. Köln inv. 10213, flesh side.

FIG. 17.   P. Köln inv. 10213, hair side.

use, it will more probably be the *front* cover that suffers the greater wear and tear.[38] We have already seen that it is the front cover of the Freer Gospels that is the more damaged. As we proceed we shall encounter further cases in which the cover that was certainly on the front of a book is again found to be the more worn.[39] In sum, it appears to be necessary to reverse the argument from wear and, where there is no evidence to the contrary, deduce that the more worn of two precious covers is more likely to have been the front, not the back. Returning to the Metropolitan covers, I therefore conclude that Peter was on the front, and that when the book was opened flat to reveal the covers as a diptych, Paul and Peter processed with book and cross toward, rather than away from, one another.

If the first pair of covers is for a volume of Acts and Epistles, the second pair (fig. 5), slightly larger at 28.5 × 23.2 cm (max.), is surely for a gospel book. The Metropolitan Museum panel shows two standing saints, probably two of the evangelists, the one on the right with a short beard, flanking and supporting a huge cross.[40] Each evangelist also holds and displays a book. The Louvre fragment, which is all that survives of the matching cover, has a third evangelist with a long beard displaying a book and supporting a cross in the identical fashion.[41] (The Metropolitan Museum plaque, because less damaged, ought to be considered the back of the book.) There are two elements of this imagery to which I want to draw attention. The first is that the evangelists (like the St. Paul) appear to display the open exterior, i.e., the silver covers, of the books they hold; the representation of the book's spine is again very clear. This suggests once more a reference to the processional function and display of such a

38. Compare the words of Philoxenus of Mabbug (d. 523), *Letter to a Friend,* ed. G. Olinder, *Acta Universitatis Gotoburgensis* 56, no. 1 (1950): 14*–15*: "Salute the Cross and take the Gospel in your hands and put it before your eyes and your heart and go and stand on your feet before the Cross . . . and lay on a cushion every [gospel] book, in which you read . . ." Cited in Peter Brown, "Images as a Substitute for Writing," in *East and West: Modes of Communication,* ed. Evangelos Chrysos and Ian Wood (Leiden, 1999), 15–46, at 29.

39. A comparable example in repoussé gilt silver is the tenth-century Gospels of St. Eusebius in Vercelli Cathedral: see Steenbock, *Kirchliche Prachteinband,* no. 28, and figs. 42–43, clearly showing binding structure as well as much greater wear to front cover.

40. No. 47.100.36. See Mango, *Silver from Early Byzantium,* no. 46; Weitzmann, *Age of Spirituality,* no. 555; Frazer, "Silver Book Covers," 72–73, 75–76.

41. Antiquités grecques, étrusques et romaines Bj 2279 (formerly AC 98). See Mango, *Silver from Early Byzantium,* no. 47; Weitzmann, *Age of Spirituality,* no. 555; *Byzance,* no. 63; Buschhausen, *Spätrömischen Metallscrinia,* cat. B 23, 256.

book, with its covers spread open in diptych form. The second point to note
is the way in which the evangelists do not merely flank the cross, a relatively
common visual formula in the sixth century,[42] but quite unequivocally raise
and support and present the cross to the viewer. Perhaps they are processing
toward us bearing Christ himself. As the cross is an image of Christ, so is the
gospel book. As the evangelists bear Christ, so does the person who carries
this book in procession. But there is not a complete identification, for the actions of the evangelists, like their writings, are balanced and complementary.
Thus a more heavily symbolic use of images seems to have been explored on
the gospel book's cover than was the case on the accompanying volume of Acts
and Epistles.

Silver Book Covers: Sion Treasure

The Sion treasure plaques adopt related yet different approaches to the use
of images. Only one of the two pairs of covers at Dumbarton Oaks is figurative,
and we shall look at it first (fig. 6).[43] Both figured panels are very similar, albeit not identical. The better-preserved cover is 25 (originally ca. 26.5) × 23.8 cm
and weighs 317 g (perhaps originally one Roman pound).[44] Note that the proportions of the plaque indicate a book with a notably squarer page format (H:
W = 1.1:1) than can be found with any of the other silver covers. The panels are
decorated with a central standing figure of a beardless Christ, blessing with his
right hand and holding up with his left a large closed book with a cover decorated with five small bosses perhaps intended to suggest large gems. Christ is
flanked by two standing saints not holding books. Above is a scalloped niche
beneath a gable supported on spiral columns with peacocks again in the spandrels; a fragment with the fourth peacock is in Antalya.[45] Gilding is used in

---

42. A useful starting point is Erich Dinkler and Erika Dinkler von Schubert, "Kreuz," in *Lexikon
der christlichen Ikonographie,* 8 vols., ed. Engelbert Kirschbaum (Rome, 1970), vol. 2, cols. 562–90, esp.
579–81.

43. DO 63.36.8 and DO 65.1.3. Boyd, "'Metropolitan' Treasure," checklist nos. 23 a–b. Dumbarton
Oaks, *Handbook of the Byzantine Collection* (Washington, D.C., 1967), no. 69; Frazer, "Silver Book Covers," 73–76.

44. Frazer, "Silver Book Covers," 74, reconstructs the panel as 31 × 26 cm, but her initial measurements are incorrect.

45. Reproduced in Nezih Firatli, "Un trésor du VIe s. trouvé à Kumluca, en Lycie," *Studi di antichità cristiana* 27 (1969): 523–25, pl. 252, fig. 7. See also Buschhausen, *Spätrömischen Metallscrinia,* cat. B
22, 255.

an odd manner on the drapery. On the better-preserved plaque (the back, according to my interpretation) is a pointillé inscription in Greek: "For the memory and repose of Prinkipios, deacon, and Stephane and Leontia." The words "Prinkipios" and "deacon" flank the head of Christ. The more fragmentary front plaque preserves only the words "of Konon, deacon" in a similar position on either side of Christ's head. These inscriptions are quite crudely worked in comparison to the rest, and could be an afterthought. Could they also help in identifying the function of the book that the plaques decorated? The point will be considered in a moment.

The second set of plaques (fig. 7) are very much larger—ca. 37.5 × 30 cm (max.)—and more than 50 percent heavier (the better-preserved plaque weighs 495 g).[46] They are for a book with pages more than twice as big as any of the other silver covers. The excellent state of preservation of the gilding suggests they have been little handled. In the field beneath a similar conch, this time surmounted by an arch,[47] is a gilded cross decorated and treated as though it were a separate piece of metalwork attached to the cover. It is very carefully formed with a prismatic body, teardrop terminals, and beaded edges. Flanking the lower arm of the cross are two somewhat anthropomorphic stylized gilded trees, presumably palms, which appear to bend their trunks as well as their branches toward the cross.[48] The range of allusion in this composition is probably wide: at various levels we see a paradisiacal scene of the tree of life, or Christ as the tree of life; we also seem to see Christ transfigured between Moses and Elijah and Christ crucified between the Theotokos and St. John. And if, as seems very likely, these covers are from a gospel book, we probably also see Christ flanked by the evangelists (two on the front of the book, two on the back).[49]

46. DO 63.36.9–10. Boyd, "'Metropolitan' Treasure," checklist no. 22 a–b; Dumbarton Oaks, *Handbook of the Byzantine Collection,* no. 70; Ernst Kitzinger, "A Pair of Silver Book Covers in the Sion Treasure," *Gatherings in Honor of Dorothy E. Miner,* ed. Ursula E. McCracken, Lilian M. C. Randall, and Richard H. Randall, Jr. (Baltimore, 1974), 3–17.

47. Kitzinger, "Pair of Silver Book Covers," 13, interpreted the arch as a gate of paradise.

48. Cypresses, according to Kitzinger, "Pair of Silver Book Covers," 7–8.

49. The evidence of clasps/binding is puzzling since there are cuttings in the vertical edge of only one side of checklist no. 22a; i.e., either the binding or clasps have left no trace. The evidence is nonetheless interpreted as indicating that the better-preserved plaque 22a was originally on the front; Frazer, "Silver Book Covers," 74–75, and figs. S22.1–9. This supersedes the statement in Kitzinger, "Pair of Silver Book Covers," 4n8.

Returning to the figurative covers of the Sion treasure (fig. 6), we can see that although to a modern eye their visual content makes them appear more important, their much smaller size and commensurately lesser bullion value implies a lower status for them.[50] This would be consistent with their use as covers for the less important Acts and Epistles volume; the seeming repetition of the same two saints, Peter and Paul, on front and rear would thus be deliberate, no mere economy of craftsmanship. The presence of the inscriptions recording the prayers of two deacons, Konon and Prinkipios, would be fully appropriate on this book if we could be confident that it was the responsibility of the deacon to read the epistle in the sixth century. In later centuries, however, the deacon read the gospel and a lector the epistle, which suggests an entirely different explanation for our covers. St. Nicholas at Sion could well have had, indeed must have had, more than one gospel in a silver binding, just as it had numerous chalices, patens, and so forth (often in matching paired sets).[51] The duplication of silver gospel covers could have been the result of multiple donations. In this scenario the figurative covers need not have been for an epistle manuscript; the repeated saints front and rear would in this case be the four evangelists.

A fragment of Christ, flanked on the left by a long-bearded saint not holding a book, is in the museum at Antalya.[52] A further unpublished fragment provides another right arm and hand for a figure again standing to the left of Christ.[53] In other words, we have parts not just of a further cover but of a third pair of covers, although too little survives to be able to pursue the reconstruction further. The fragments might have been from yet another gospel cover, if we allow the principle of multiplication of liturgical treasures to have played an important role.

Before moving on from silver covers, three large silver plates found in a treasure of church silver at Luxor in the 1890s need to be considered briefly. They were published by Strzygowski in the catalogue of the Cairo museum, however, not as oblong plates (of the type sometimes termed a *lanx*), but spe-

---

50. Compare the Sion and Riha patens, reproduced juxtaposed and to the same scale in John Lowden, *Early Christian and Byzantine Art* (London, 1997), 80–81.

51. Boyd, "'Metropolitan' Treasure," e.g., 8.

52. Firatli, "Un trésor du VIe s. trouvé à Kumluca," 525 and pl. 253, fig. 8; Buschhausen, *Spätrömischen Metallscrinia,* cat. B 22, 255–56.

53. Visible in a photograph of the Antalya fragments kindly communicated to me by Susan Boyd. Compare the comments in Frazer, "Silver Book Covers," 74.

cifically as "book containers" *(Buchbehälterdeckel)*.[54] The three large rectangular dishes (up to 65 × 50 cm) each had a central incised and gilded cross and two had donor inscriptions. In each case the plate was supported by a rectangular foot.[55] What remains unclear from Strzygowski's discussion, not aided by a lack of photographs of the backs of the objects, is why he should have concluded that these were not merely plates with a raised foot of standard late antique type.[56] The "container" *(Kasten)* on the back was, in two of the three cases, seemingly too shallow to take a bound gospel book.[57] Could these objects (if they did once hold books) nonetheless have been early examples of so-called "book shrines"?[58] The possibility should be borne in mind. However, unless further evidence comes to light, it would seem wise to exclude the Luxor plates from a discussion of the early Christian book cover.

Gold Book Covers

Silver was a prestige material for church treasure in the sixth century, but hardly rare, even if little has survived. The nearly five hundred pounds of silver in the Sion treasure (that part that has been recovered) cannot have been unusual for an eastern Mediterranean church at the time.[59] The silver, as we

54. Josef Strzygowski, *Koptische Kunst: Catalogue général des antiquités égyptiennes du Musée du Caire. nos. 7001–7394 et 8742–9200* (Vienna, 1904), nos. 7202–4, 341–45, and pl. 39. The material was guaranteed wide circulation by its inclusion in *Dictionnaire d'archéologie Chrétienne et de liturgie* vol. 5, cols. 775–845, s.v. "Évangéliaire," esp. cols. 838–39, figs. 4218–19. Unfortunately not reproduced in Gawdat Gabra, *Cairo, the Coptic Museum and Old Churches* (Cairo, 1999), but seemingly still in the museum.

55. These were of the height × width proportions of a page of a book: no. 7202, 21.5 × 15.7 cm; no. 7203, 28.5 × 21.5 cm; no. 7204, 27.5 × 22 cm.

56. Compare, for example, David Buckton, ed., *Byzantium: Treasures of Byzantine Art and Culture from British Collections* (London, 1994), no. 15 (the Corbridge Lanx), no. 12 (Esquiline treasure); Weitzmann, *Age of Spirituality*, no. 126 (Ariadne Lanx from Augst, Römermuseum).

57. In catalogue-number order the depths of the "containers" were 2.5 cm, 4.2 cm, 2.2 cm.

58. Compare the magnificent eighth-century book shrine found in an Irish lake in 1986; Eamonn P. Kelly, "The Lough Kinale Book-Shrine," in *The Age of Migrating Ideas: Early Medieval Art in Northern Britain and Ireland,* ed. R. Michael Spearman and John Higgitt (Edinburgh, 1993), 168–74. For a superbly preserved medieval example, see Adam S. Cohen, *The Uta Codex: Art, Philosophy, and Reform in Eleventh-Century Germany* (University Park, Pa., 2000), 192–93 and col. pl. 1; see also Steenbock, *Kirchliche Prachteinband,* nos. 39, 44, 56, 59 (Uta Codex). In general on medieval books as relics, see Michelle P. Brown, *The Lindisfarne Gospels: Society, Spirituality, and the Scribe* (London, 2003), 66–72, 208–12; specifically on Coptic material, see p. 211 and fig. 80. For examples of later Coptic book shrines, see *Art copte en Égypte,* no. 45 (dated 1526) and no. 46 (dated 1255).

59. It has been estimated that when Khusro sacked the city of Edessa in 622 and removed 112,000

have seen, was partially gilded, but there can be no question that gold and jeweled book covers were, in comparison, far more costly. When in 384 Jerome
wrote to Eustochium a letter that enjoyed wide circulation, he specifically criticized books written in gold on purple parchment and "bedecked with jewels."[60] A miracle recorded by Gregory of Tours in the *Gloria Confessorum* even
hinges on the difference in value between gold and silver bindings, but here a
jewel-encrusted binding is treated positively. For a "cover for enclosing the
holy Gospels, a paten, and a chalice made from pure gold and precious gems,"
gifts of the fifth-century Emperor Leo (457–474), a devilish goldsmith sub-
stituted fakes made of silver gilt. The earth swallowed the craftsman, but the
objects were preserved at Lyon, where Gregory had seen them "many times."[61]
Nor is it surprising that in the entire period up to 650 the one and only book
mentioned in the *Liber Pontificalis,* with its extraordinary lists of gifts to or
by popes, is a "Gospels with gold covers and precious jewels, weighing fifteen
pounds," presented along with other treasures to Pope Hormisdas by the Emperor Justin around the year 520.[62] Exactly what the fifteen pounds represented in this case cannot be established, but very probably the reason why gold or
silver bindings are recorded only once is because (a) they usually did not contain much weight of precious material, and (b) such covers could not be separately weighed, as could, for example, a chalice or candleholder.

The one surviving gold and jeweled binding from the period (fig. 8), in
the cathedral treasury at Monza, is documented by an inscription carved and
inlaid with red and blue niello on narrow gold strips nailed to the two covers.[63] The placing of the strips complements the carefully considered geom-

---

pounds (more than fifty tons!) of silver from its churches, this would have represented some fifteen hundred to five thousand pounds of silver per church, a figure that no longer seems incredible. See Boyd,
"'Metropolitan' Treasure," 17. For this and other statistics, see Marlia Mundell Mango, "The Monetary
Value of Silver Revetments and Objects Belonging to Churches, A.D. 300–700," in Boyd and Mango, *Ecclesiastical Silver Plate,* 123–36.

60. Jer. *Ep.* 22.32: "Membrana colore purpureo, aurum liquescit in literis, gemmis codices vestiun-
tur," ed. Isidore Hilberg (*CSEL* 54:193).

61. Raymond van Dam, trans., *Gregory of Tours, Glory of the Confessors* (Liverpool, 1988), 68–70.

62. "Evangelia cum tabulis aureis et cum gemmis pretiosis, pens. lib. XV," *Liber pontificalis* 54.5, in
Pietro Guglielmo et al., eds., *Liber Pontificalis* (Rome, 1978), 2:137.

63. For further references, see *Splendori di Bisanzio: Testimonianze e riflessi d'arte e cultura bizan-
tina nelle chiese d'Italia,* exh. cat. (Milan, 1990), 55; Roberto Conti, *Il Tesoro: Guida alla conoscenza del
Tesoro del Duomo di Modena,* 2d ed. (Monza, 1983), 38–39, cat. 21; Roberto Conti and Carlo Bertelli,
Monza: Il duomo e i suoi tesori (Milan, 1988), 24–25; Steenbock, *Kirchliche Prachteinband,* 78–80, cat. 12.

etry of the covers perfectly, but the inscription looks like an afterthought.[64] However, the method of attachment to the ground is identical to that of the nearby cameos and gammadia. The inscription reads: "Out of the gifts of God Theodelinda, most glorious queen, offers this to St. John the Baptist, in the basilica which she founded, in Monza, near her palace."[65] There are traces of clasps on the right edge of the "Theodelinda" plaque and on the left edge of the "Monza" plaque.[66] These indicate that two clasps were attached to the fore edge of the back ("Monza") cover, and hinged forward to lock onto pins on the edge of the front ("Theodelinda") cover. The traces of the attachments for the clasps on both panels not only confirm their function as book covers but also establish that the inscription began, as we might expect, on the front cover. Unfortunately, the modern display of the covers shows them reversed. In terms of more general arguments about distinguishing fronts and backs, it can be noted that the front cover is considerably more worn and damaged, especially at the top right corner.

The Theodelinda in question was a Lombard ruler (d. 625) to whom Pope Gregory the Great sent, as gifts on the baptism of her son as a Catholic in 603, a fragment of the True Cross, and a gospel (or merely a gospel reading: *lectionem Sancti Evangelii*) kept *(inclausam)* in a *theca persica,* a container of Persian craftsmanship, long assumed to refer to these very book covers.[67] The proposed identification of the binding with Gregory's letter is problematic, however, and perhaps tells us more about how modern art history works, always keen to link objects and documents, than about late antique art patronage and gift giving. The Monza covers could well have been made not in Rome or the eastern Mediterranean but in the Milan region. To judge from

---

Note that the covers are not included in Isabella Baldini Lippolis, *L'oreficeria nell'impero di Costantinopoli tra IV e VII secolo* (Bari, 1999).

64. Conti, *Tesoro,* 38, considered it "applicato in epoca di poco posteriore." A. Lipinsky, "Der Theodelinden-Schatz im Dom zu Monza," *Das Münster* 13 (1960): 146–73, esp. 159: "auf die älteren Buchdeckel nachträglich aufgesetzt worden."

65. Conti and Bertelli, *Monza,* 24: DE DONIS DI OFFERIT / THEODELENDA REG(INA) / GLORIOSISSEMA / S(AN)C(T)O IOHANNI BAPT(ISTE) / IN BASELICA / QUAM IPSA FUND(AVIT) / IN MODICIA / PROPE PAL(ATIUM) SUUM.

66. Ibid., fig. 10.

67. Gregory the Great, *Ep.* 14.2 (*CCSL* 140A:1082–3). The reference to the gospel is in line 37. For the putative connection to the covers, see, for example, Lipinsky, "Theodelinden-Schatz," 159; Conti, *Tesoro,* 39. For the interpretation of *lectionem* as "reading," see Claudia Rapp's chapter in this volume.

the wording, Gregory's gospel might have been wrapped up in a "Persian" textile, or even enshrined in some kind of container.[68]

The Theodelinda covers are highly symmetrical, and virtually identical (in this sense reminiscent of the silver-cross covers of the Sion treasure). They are large, measuring 34 × 26 (or 26.5) cm.[69] They are both mounted on modern wood panels. Each consists of a large jeweled cross set within a cloisonné enameled frame. The rectangular fields in the arms of the cross are decorated with gamma-shaped enameled panels, and within the angles they form are recycled Roman cameos, all originally, it would seem, facing the cross. The two dark green stones representing Christ and the Virgin at the bottom are replacements made in 1773, and the cameo at the bottom right may have been moved at the same time. The four cameos per cover are probably intended to stand for the four evangelists, notwithstanding the fact that two are female heads. The nonsymbolic image content of these covers, nonetheless, is small.

In broad terms, the decorative pattern of the cover resembles that on the book held by Christ in the famous sixth-century icon at Sinai.[70] The simplicity of the design and its focus on the jeweled cross, however, are reminders that a chronological progress in the use of imagery from simplicity to complexity—one of the preliminary presuppositions of this paper—ought *not* to be assumed; this is one of the latest objects in our survey and in terms of visual content one of the least ambitious. Yet it is impressive, lavish, and beautiful. We could perhaps advance the argument that in this instance the cost of the materials outweighed any value that large-scale images could have added. In a reversal of the Ovidian tag, *opus non superabat materiam.*

Ivory Book Covers

When we move to ivory book covers we encounter a material seemingly less costly than silver, though the situation may have been different in the fifth

---

68. Strzygowski, *Koptische Kunst,* 341, drew attention to possible links between such a *theca* and the Luxor (putative) book containers discussed above.

69. Conti, *Tesoro,* 38. Note that the heights of the two panels according to Conti and Bertelli, *Monza,* 24, are 30 cm and 33.8 cm.

70. This point is often made. See the discussion in Kurt Weitzmann, *The Monastery of Saint Catherine at Mount Sinai: The Icons,* vol. 1, *From the Sixth to the Tenth Century* (Princeton, 1976), 14.

and sixth centuries, and one that was quite widely available in late antiquity.[71] We shall need to consider four sets of book covers—there are also fragments of at least five more—that are in the form of so-called "five-part diptychs."[72] These are pairs of revetments, each "wing" assembled from five separate panels of ivory in order to produce an object of a size and shape appropriate to a book cover, despite the inherent limitations of the narrow curving shape of the elephant's tusk. All of these five-part diptychs have survived in secondary use, and their relation to such imperial objects as the famous "Barberini diptych" in the Louvre has clouded their original function, so that they are sometimes treated as plaques rather than as book covers.[73] But this seems to me unwarranted: the dimensions, proportions, iconography, pairing, and later history of use and imitation of such objects are all fully consistent with a primary function as book covers. (What I have not included are any of the tall, narrow, "normal" diptychs, which, even if later reused as book covers, show no sign that this was their original intended function.)[74]

All of the five-part diptychs were originally, and most still are, mounted on wooden boards.[75] The assemblages of ivory plaques would seem to have been too unstable and fragile to function as book covers without a rigid support. Even though the vertical side panels have tenons top and bottom locked into a mortise in the top and bottom panels by two ivory dowels, thus creating a quite sturdy structure, the main panel in each case was cut with a simple rebate on all four sides, which was merely located in a shallow notch cut in the edge of the "frame."[76] As a result, the central panel cannot fall forward out of its setting, but to be secure the whole assembly would need to be held in place

71. On the cost and availability of ivory, see Anthony Cutler, "Prolegomena to the Craft of Ivory Carving in Late Antiquity and the Early Middle Ages," in *Artistes, artisans et production artistique au Moyen Age,* ed. Xavier Barral I Altet (Paris, 1987), 2:431–71.

72. See the useful general discussion in Steenbock, *Kirchliche Prachteinband,* 11–21.

73. See, for example, the treatment of the ivory "plaques," as the five-part diptychs are termed, in Weitzmann, *Age of Spirituality,* nos. 458–61, 475–76.

74. For such "single-panel" diptychs, see, e.g., Steenbock, *Kirchliche Prachteinband,* nos. 4, 6, 9. Obviously (or presumably) not originally made as book covers are her nos. 1, 2, 3, 7. No. 1 is indeed only a diptych because the ivory panel was sawn in two in secondary use. To fit such ivories, a manuscript would have to have had unusually, and hence characteristically, tall and narrow pages.

75. The Ravenna panel was recently remounted on Plexiglas. Luciana Martini and Clementina Rizzardi, *Avori bizantini e medievali nel Museo Nazionale di Ravenna* (Ravenna, 1990), 127.

76. Some preliminary remarks on construction can be found in Anthony Cutler, "Barberiniana: Notes on the Making, Content, and Provenance of Louvre, OA. 9603," in *Tesserae: Festschrift für Josef*

by a rigid backing panel of some sort; glue alone would have been inadequate to the task.

In contrast to the repoussé technique used on the silver sheets, the technique of carving in ivory permits highly detailed, even minute craftsmanship, and apart from damage and wear to the surface of the areas in highest relief, the ivories in general are in good condition. Nonetheless, the varying patterns of shrinkage and warping of the constituent panels—caused by the "grain" of the ivory curving in two planes—has created stresses that have led to opening of the joints, splitting of the mortises, and distortion of the rectangular form to a varying extent in all the examples. The resulting pattern of damage is characteristic, and where not cut away can be a useful pointer to the original provenance of now-dispersed pieces.

Ivory Book Covers: Milan Cathedral Treasury

The earliest surviving five-part ivory cover stands a little apart from the others in both material and visual content. It is now preserved in the cathedral treasury of Milan (fig. 9), where it has been since at least the first half of the twelfth century.[77] The panels are very large, measuring 37.5 × 28.1 cm. They are now separately framed and mounted on a modern wood support; the edges and backs of the panels are, unfortunately, invisible. The front cover, identifiable by the content of the images, is centered on a haloed Lamb of God composed of garnets inlaid in small cells in a silver-gilt mount, the whole set within a rich garland of fruit and grain, probably symbolizing the four seasons. At the four outer corners of the panel are simpler wreaths of bay (?) leaves enclosing, above, the winged symbol of an evangelist holding an open book: the man (Matthew) at the left, the ox (presumably Mark, following the identification proposed by Irenaeus, rather than that of Jerome)[78] at the right, with two bearded figures in the corners below—the evangelists in human form. The intervening areas are filled with eight narrative scenes, which cannot, however,

---

Engemann (Münster, 1991): 329–39 at 335–36; reprinted in his *Late Antique and Byzantine Ivory Carving* (Aldershot, 1998). His remarks are amplified here by my own observations.

77. Wolfgang Fritz Volbach, *Elfenbeinarbeiten der Spätantike und des frühen Mittelalters,* 3d ed. (Mainz, 1976), no. 119; Steenbock, *Kirchliche Prachteinband,* no. 5; Danielle Gaborit-Chopin, *Ivoires du Moyen Âge* (Fribourg, 1978), 26–27 and nos. 24–25.

78. Steenbock, *Kirchliche Prachteinband,* 69, identifies the symbol as Luke's, but she later notes that the order man-ox-lion-eagle is not biblical (70).

be read in a straightforward narrative order. Starting below Matthew's symbol at the top left we see the Annunciation to the Virgin at the spring (from the Protevangelium of James 11.2), the Magi observing the star, and the Baptism. At the right we see the Virgin introduced to the temple by the angel (Protev. 7.2), the twelve-year-old Christ teaching in the temple, and the Entry to Jerusalem. In the top panel is the Nativity, with Joseph most unusually holding a frame saw, and in the bottom panel is the Massacre of the Innocents before Herod. Insofar as the narrative images of the front cover can be said to have a program, it appears to focus on the incarnation and infancy of Christ, with a notable inclusion of nonbiblical material. The Baptism and Entry to Jerusalem images seem to stand outside the main theme.

The back cover is dominated by a jeweled silver cross on a rocky base from which flow the four rivers of paradise.[79] The four corner medallions include, as before, the evangelist symbols (lion and eagle) above holding books, and the bearded evangelists Luke (presumably) and John below. In the eight narrative panels, starting at the top we have the Adoration of the Magi, then at the left three miracles of healing: of the blind, of a paralytic, and the raising of Lazarus. At the bottom is the miracle at Cana, and then reading up the right side we have the Widow's Mite, the Last Supper, and an image of Christ, seated on the cosmos, touching the garlands extended by two flanking figures. This last scene is puzzling. In terms of a possible program on this cover we have a mixture—primarily miracles, but with infancy and perhaps postresurrection elements.

Taking the two covers together, the presence of the evangelist symbols makes it clear that we are dealing with the covers of a gospel book. Indeed, the repetition of quaternities—four symbols, four evangelists, four rivers of paradise, four seasons—is surely a form of visual commentary on the content. The technique of execution of the lamb and cross suggests north Italian manufacture, perhaps in the middle of the fifth century, and from the use of materials it appears that symbols of Christ, the lamb and the cross, were of greater importance in enhancing and communicating the significance of the object than the more naturalistic images of Christ in human form.

79. Kitzinger, "Pair of Silver Book Covers," 8, made a connection with the cross on the Sion Treasure covers at Dumbarton Oaks (see fig. 7).

Ivory Book Covers: Ejmiadzin Gospels

The three other more or less complete five-part diptychs, all made a century or so after the Milan diptych, show many similarities to one another. They differ from the Milan diptych most obviously in their lack of applied metal decoration, but this is slightly misleading, as symmetrical drill holes, for example on the crosses (top center, figs. 10, 11, 14), indicate that small metal ornaments or semiprecious stones were once applied to their surfaces.[80] The first of the group of three (fig. 10) now forms the binding of an Armenian gospel book from Ejmiadzin dated 989 (in the Matenadaran Library at Erevan). It measures 36.5 x 30.5 cm. On the front cover the central panel frames an enthroned Mother of God and Child between, it would seem, two angels. The top panel has flying angels carrying a cross in a garland. Small crowned busts appear in the corners, probably personifications of Sol and Luna. Below, on the left, we see the Annunciation, and Joseph and Mary with the water of conviction (Protev. 16). At the right are the Nativity (above), and the preceding Journey to Bethlehem (below). Across the bottom panel, moving vigorously (and somewhat surprisingly) from right to left, is the Adoration of the Magi. The third magus is pursued by a flying angel. Joseph sits at the left, and the Theotokos and Child are also attended by an angel.

At the center of the back cover is an enthroned Christ, represented young and beardless, holding a book and flanked by two bearded figures, Peter and Paul. Above, two flying angels support a cross in a garland, as on the front cover. Below, to either side, are scenes of healing: Christ curing the dropsiac (probably), and the blind man swimming in the pool at Siloam (possibly) to the left; Christ healing the palsiac and two demoniacs at the right. At the bottom is the Entry to Jerusalem, in which Christ and his followers move as forcefully to the right as the Magi move to the left on the front cover. In every scene on the back cover Christ holds a conspicuous cross staff.

In comparison with the Milan ivories, the use of images on the Ejmiadzin covers appears to have been more consistently thought out. The presence of the evangelists and their symbols has been suppressed (but we can still assume, I believe, that the covers were for a gospel book), and in place of the

---

80. Compare the Barberini diptych: *Byzance,* no. 20.

central lamb and cross we have two images of Christ in human form. The narrative structure of the panels works better. Here the Theotokos and Child are flanked by an infancy cycle, and the mature Christ and apostles by a miracle cycle. Both panels culminate, in narrative terms, in processions: the procession of the Magi bearing gifts to Christ in their covered hands on the front, and the procession of Christ himself, bearing a cross, followed by palm bearers and welcomed by the people of Jerusalem on the back. I suggest that this processional focus is not fortuitous; the makers of the Ejmiadzin covers knew they were to be displayed and viewed in processions.

A further point to emphasize is that mounting holes in the ivories leave no doubt that the Mother of God and Child/Infancy cover was on the front of the book, and the Christ enthroned/Miracle cover was on the back. Unfortunately, in Steenbock's standard work on luxury book covers, these ivories, along with all those of similar pattern, including such Carolingian derivatives as the famous Lorsch gospel covers, are reproduced and discussed with the miracle panels termed the front and the infancy panels described as the back.[81] It is also clear with the original, though less obvious in photographs, that the front (Theotokos) cover is the more worn of the two, a point to bear in mind. I shall return to the basic front/back distinction briefly in the conclusion.

81. That the Lorsch Christ panel was without a doubt originally the *back* cover of the gospel book was established by Margaret H. Longhurst and Charles Rufus Morey, "The Covers of the Lorsch Gospels," *Speculum* 3 (1928): 64–74. When the book was divided, probably not when rebound in 1479 but more likely in the mid-sixteenth century (Hermann Fillitz, "Habens tabulas eburneas: Der Elfenbeinschmuck des Lorscher Evangeliars," in *Das Lorscher Evangeliar: Eine Zimelie der Buchkunst des abendländischen Frühmittelalters,* facsimile and commentary, ed. Hermann Schefers [Darmstadt, 2000], 103–10, esp. 109–10), the cover that went with the latter half (Luke and John)—the original back cover—was remounted to form the front cover of the Luke-John volume. The book is now removed from the binding: Luke and John form MS Vat. pal. lat.50, and the ivory cover is in the Museo Pio Cristiano. Longhurst and Morey also found, by examination of the back surface, that the bottom panel of the Vatican cover recycled part of a consular diptych of Anastasius (A.D. 517). (Fillitz, 104, erroneously recorded this as the top panel.) Morey further argued that the top panel was the surviving part of a damaged five-part diptych. But he then proposed, bizarrely, that the remaining panels were a late tenth-century restoration of a Carolingian restoration of the original (72–73). Peter Lasko, *Ars Sacra 800–1200,* 2d ed. (New Haven, 1994), 21, argued that the top and bottom panels of the other cover, now in the Victoria and Albert Museum, were also reused late antique works because of their shape. While this could be true for the top panel, the figures in the bottom panel have been adapted from the start to the sloping shape (there has also been some postmedieval trimming of these edges), indicating that it must be Carolingian.

Ivory Book Covers: St. Lupicin Gospels

The second closely related five-part diptych (fig. 11) is now attached to MS lat. 9384 in the Bibliothèque nationale de France. It is a ninth-century Carolingian gospel book written in silver majuscules on purple parchment.[82] It came from the library of St. Lupicin in the Jura and measures 36.9 × 30.3 cm.[83] The present binding structure is from the reign of Charles X (1824–30), but the book and the ivories were already together in 1717, and possibly long before that. The book's pages, however, are far smaller than the ivories (roughly 32 × 25 cm), and the text is incomplete and very worn and damaged at both ends, suggesting a spell unprotected by a binding. Taken together, the evidence precludes the possibility that the book could have been made to fit the ivories; the combination is thus in some sense fortuitous, and the result is awkward (and fragile). The positions of the covers have also, I believe, been reversed vis-à-vis their original arrangement, but there are no traces on the ivories of the binding or clasps that would indicate which was the spine and which the fore edge. I shall therefore treat them with the Mother of God and Child flanked by angels as the centerpiece of what would in the sixth century have been the front cover.

Here the Christ child holds a conspicuous cross staff. At the top we see two flying angels supporting a cross in a garland, but the relief carving is shallower and cruder than Ejmiadzin and the effect is less elegant. It is notable that both angels also carry a book. At the left are the Annunciation and Visitation. At the right we see Joseph and Mary with the water of conviction, and the Journey to Bethlehem. The bottom panel has the Entry to Jerusalem, with Christ carrying a cross (this last scene was on the back cover of Ejmiadzin).

The center of the St. Lupicin back cover is occupied again by an enthroned Christ, but this time he is bearded and mature, even elderly—perhaps the Ancient of Days of Daniel's vision (Dan. 7:9). He displays a book with a cross on its cover, and is flanked as before by Peter and Paul. Above, two flying, book-carrying angels again support a cross in a garland. To the left Christ heals a

---

82. *Byzance,* no. 27; Volbach, *Elfenbeinarbeiten der Spätantike,* no. 145; Steenbock, *Kirchliche Prachteinband,* no. 10; Gaborit-Chopin, *Ivoires du Moyen Age,* 37–38 and no. 38. I am most grateful to Mme. Marie-Pierre Lafitte for permitting me to examine the manuscript.

83. The measurements are those of Danielle Gaborit-Chopin; see *Byzance,* 74. Larger measurements are given by both Steenbock and Volbach (see previous note).

blind man and the man sick with palsy. To the right he heals the woman with an issue of blood and a possessed man. It is notable that here, in comparison to the closely related image in Ejmiadzin, the bending demoniac's shackles are more visible, and the figure behind, clearly identified as a second demoniac by his naked torso and manic hair in Ejmiadzin, has become an apostle holding a book (compare figs. 12 and 13). In the panel below, Christ addresses the Samaritan woman at the well and raises Lazarus. In all the narrative images Christ, youthful and beardless, conspicuously holds a cross staff, and in three scenes one of the apostles is holding a book. These again seem to me elements appropriate to a processional function for the book whose covers we are considering.

The overall parallel between the covers of Ejmiadzin and St. Lupicin is very conspicuous (figs. 10–13). But perhaps even more striking is how neither merely repeats the other's images: the differences we see thus invite a more detailed exegetical analysis, one that will have to wait, however, for another occasion. But such differences as we see are not, I am sure, to be dismissed as merely exemplifying the results of "provincial" copying (in the St. Lupicin covers) of a "metropolitan" model (the Ejmiadzin covers).

Ivory Book Covers: Murano Diptych

The third of the three closely related five-part diptych covers is now fragmented, and one of the ten constituent panels is missing (fig. 14). In the Middle Ages the diptych was in the monastery of San Michele at Murano in the Venetian lagoon. The better-preserved back cover (as I shall term it) is now in the Museo Nazionale at Ravenna,[84] whereas the front is divided between collections in Manchester (center panel, John Rylands University Library), St. Petersburg (left panel, cut in two, Hermitage), Berlin (top panel, Museum für Spätantike und Byzantinische Kunst), and Paris (bottom panel, Louvre).[85] The Ravenna plaque measures 35.5 × 30.5 cm. In one important detail, however, the dismantled cover is better preserved than its erstwhile companion: all the con-

---

84. Martini and Rizzardi, *Avori bizantini e medievali*, 62–65, 127. See also next note.

85. Steenbock, *Kirchliche Prachteinband*, no. 8; Volbach, *Elfenbeinarbeiten der Spätantike*, nos. 126–129; Weitzmann, *Age of Spirituality*, nos. 458–61 (reconstructs Hermitage panels at right, rather than at left, on p. 511; comparison with the Ejmiadzin and St. Lupicin covers suggest the left side is correct); see also *Byzance*, no. 24 (now Louvre, OA 11149, acquired 1987 at the sale of the Marquis de Ganay collection).

stituent ivories retain extensive traces of a surface decoration comprising large gilded stars on the background and decorative motifs on the drapery. These must have been systematically cleaned off the Ravenna panel.[86] I shall examine the covers in what I presume to be the correct narrative and hierarchical order, starting with the Mother of God and Child.[87]

Beneath a fluted baldachin flanked by large crosses, an enthroned The-otokos and Child are here flanked by the Magi presenting gifts; an angel at the left provides symmetry. Below, on the same central panel but at smaller scale, is the Nativity, including the midwife Salome (see Protev. 20). In the top pan-el flying angels again support a cross within a garland. On a small scale at ei-ther end are archangels in imperial dress, each holding the orb of the cosmos and a cross standard. At the left of the central panel is the Annunciation to Anna (Protev. 4), including the unique detail of the sparrows in a laurel tree (Protev. 3). Below (now a separate panel) is the Visitation.[88] The corresponding panel at the right is lost. In the bottom panel we see the Annunciation, Mary and Joseph and the water of conviction, and the Journey to Bethlehem—here the Virgin on an ass is led by an angel holding a cross staff.

At the center of the well-preserved back cover in Ravenna, again beneath a fluted baldachin flanked by large crosses, is an enthroned youthful Christ holding a rolled scroll. He is flanked by the bearded figures of Peter and Paul, each displaying an open book held in a cloth-covered hand; probably the pag-es rather than the covers are intended to be visible, but the incised lines are too schematic for certainty. The two figures behind are probably angels.[89] (The four figures echo the four flanking figures on the front cover.) In the area im-mediately below, an angel with a cross standard rescues the three orant He-brews from the furnace (cf. Dan. 3:25). In the top panel the composition again echoes that on the front cover. The flanking panels each have two scenes at quite large scale: Christ heals a blind man (above), and a demoniac (below)

86. The conservation report records the removal of traces of old abrasive cleaning agents; see Mar-tini and Rizzardi, *Avori bizantini e medievali,* 127.

87. Note that for Steenbock, *Kirchliche Prachteinband,* 73, the Ravenna plaque was the front cover.

88. Identified by Herbert L. Kessler, "Two Carved Plaques with St. Anne," in Weitzmann, *Age of Spirituality,* 510–12, as a further Protevangelium scene preceding the Annunciation to Anna. A subse-quent scene is more probable given the usual reading of these flanking panels from the top downward. In addition, the comparison with the Visitation of the St. Lupicin cover is very close.

89. Perhaps apostles, according to Martini and Rizzardi, *Avori bizantini e medievali,* 62.

at the left, and raises Lazarus (above) and heals the man with palsy (below) at the right. In each scene Christ holds a conspicuous cross staff. At the bottom is the story of Jonah, which reads from right to left. Surprisingly, a non-biblical angel addresses the prophet as he lies in the shade of the gourd plant.[90] The simplified compositions result in a high degree of legibility. The presence on this panel of two Old Testament narratives prefiguring salvation through Christ is striking. Their widespread use in art of the fourth through sixth centuries in many media makes their absence on the other five-part diptychs notable.[91]

The Ejmiadzin, St. Lupicin, and Murano covers are widely scattered now, but their numerous similarities suggest (a) that they could originate from a single source despite differences in levels of craftsmanship, and (b) that they are probably roughly contemporary. The mid-sixth century is accepted as the most likely date for their production, but their place or places of manufacture have been much disputed. Constantinople remains a plausible default option in my view. The survival of further isolated ivory panels,[92] such as the Mother of God and Child in the British Museum (fig. 15)—closely related to the fragmentary front cover of the Murano diptych—shows that other book covers of this type were disassembled at various dates (in this case by the twelfth century, for it has a prayer in Greek inscribed on the back).[93] The reuse of the St. Lupicin covers on a Carolingian *codex purpureus* may be postmedieval, but further Carolingian evidence suggests the possibility that in the sixth century

90. The source of this detail remains to be established.

91. For a recent survey of typology, see Catherine Brown Tkacz, *The Key to the Brescia Casket: Typology and the Early Christian Imagination* (South Bend, Ind., 2002).

92. The following are fragments of five-part diptychs of an iconographic type that is close to the book covers considered here: (1) Volbach no. 131 (London, British Museum, central panel with Christ); (2) Volbach no. 132 (Paris, coll. Marquis de Vasselot, central panel with Christ); (3) Volbach no. 133 (Paris, Louvre, broken central panel with Christ [see *Byzance,* no. 23], perhaps with Volbach no. 130 (Moscow, Pushkin Museum, lateral panel [see *Byzance,* 70]); (4) the panels recently brought together by Danielle Gaborit-Chopin, "Les trois fragments d'ivoire de Berlin, Paris et Nevers," in *Byzantine East, Latin West: Art-Historical Studies in Honor of Kurt Weitzmann,* ed. Doula Mouriki et al. (Princeton, 1995), 49–63; (5) probably Volbach no. 156 (Saulieu, Mairie, two central panels recycled on the covers of the twelfth-century gospel lectionary from St. Andoche [*Byzance,* no. 26]).

93. O. M. Dalton, *Catalogue of the Ivory Carvings of the Christian Era* (London, 1909), no. 14, photograph of back on p. 12. A fine color image is available at www.thebritishmuseum.ac.uk/compass. Search under "Ivory. Adoration of the Magi." A recent survey on the ivory is provided by Antony Eastmond in *The Mother of God: Representations of the Virgin in Byzantine Art,* ed. Maria Vasilake (Milan and London, 2000), 266–67.

these ivories could well have covered *codices purpurei,* assuredly the most costly products of late antique book manufacture.[94] The comparably large dimensions of the surviving *codices purpurei* and the ivory covers are consistent with such use.

Conclusions and Proposals

To sum up, the basic structure of the binding of the early Christian book was a pair of boards, generally of wood but occasionally of some less rigid material. How such boards were decorated was in part related to the limitations and possibilities of the material used to cover them. If left uncovered, the boards could be painted, but this must always have been an unusual, because impractical, procedure. Handling of the book would have quickly eroded the pigment. Hence any binding of this sort requires an unusual explanation. If the boards were covered with leather, which was the usual practice, the leather could be and probably generally was decorated. This material lent itself to the application of geometric patterns, probably from an early date, exploiting the symbolic and symmetrical potential of the cross. Revetting of the boards with sheets of silver, when decorated in repoussé, encouraged the use of a decorative scheme comprising relatively simple large-scale forms that could then be further emphasized by selective gilding. Symmetry was again important. Figures and symbols could be used, separately or in combination, and Christ might be represented in human form or as a cross. If gold and jewels were applied to a book's binding the materials might be left little altered; the cross remained the most potent symbol. Doubtless some gold covers were decorated, like silver-gilt covers, in repoussé. It is not surprising that none survive, given the relative fragility of the result and the ease with which precious materials could be removed from the covers of books and recycled.[95] It seems that only when books were revetted with ivory plaques, which could be worked in minute detail, were really ambitious pictorial schemes attempted. The proportion of such covers that survives is relatively higher than for gold or silver revet-

---

94. Probably the best Carolingian evidence is the Lorsch Gospels; see above.

95. The earliest repoussé gold covers in Steenbock, *Kirchliche Prachteinband,* are front covers of the Codex Aureus of St. Emmeram (Munich, Clm 14000) and the Lindau Gospels (New York, Morgan Lib. M 1), nos. 20–21.

ments because the ivory plaques, while valuable, were not so easily recycled, or at least not in a form that totally obliterated their original function. The possibility that there were also other ways of presenting the early Christian book to a public—for example, in some sort of book-shrine—also needs to be borne in mind.

Crucial to all aspects of the design and use of the book is an awareness of its diptych-like form. Even so, when we look at early book covers it seems to me striking how frequently both front and back were equally, sometimes even symmetrically, decorated. (A glance into the medieval period and beyond shows that such equality of treatment was by no means universal, with high-status and high-cost decoration often reserved for the front cover—a procedure still familiar in book design today, and readily explicable in terms of storage and display.)[96] Luxury covers, it should be recalled, were merely revetments; the functional element was the underlying wooden panel, so there was no structural *need* for the gold or silver or ivory plaques to be paired. One explanation for the pairing might lie in a desire not to devalue the sacred: perhaps to decorate only the front cover could have been taken to imply that the beginning of the book was more important than the end. (At this point I am assuming that such covers were generally on gospel books.) But I do not think that that can have been a strong reason. The crucial element, I believe, was that the primary function of such covers was display. Display might have been temporary, as when the book was carried processionally during the liturgy, or it might have been long-term, as when the book was set up on an altar. At such times, such books might have been carried and/or displayed closed, or open with the sacred text visible. But I think we also have to consider a third possibility: that they were sometimes—and when given an especially costly cover may even have been intended to be—displayed open with the covers, not the text, toward the viewer. This is what some of the covers themselves show in self-referential images of the book on the book.[97]

As with all diptychs, the process of opening a book's covers for display

96. Steenbock, *Kirchliche Prachteinband*, nos. 22, 33, 38, 42, 46, 47, 49, 50, 51, 52, 54, 57, etc.

97. On the question of visibility, see Claudia Rapp's chapter in this volume. S. R. Holman kindly drew my attention to the fifth-century (?) mosaics of the Rotunda/Ag. Georgios in Thessalonike, in which books appear to stand open on altars with their covers toward the viewer. A poor reproduction is in Theocharis Pazaris, *The Rotunda of Saint George in Thessaloniki* (Thessalonike, 1985), col. pl. 4, and pls. 12, 14.

(hinging at the left) transforms the relationship between what might seem a (literally) superior front and inferior back cover to one in which the back now appears to the left, and the front to the right. This brings the left (back) cover not merely into equal prominence, but also sets up the probability of a narrative or progressive reading of the two together, from left to right. Furthermore, there exists a possible tension between these two modes of viewing, one with the book open, and the other with it closed. There can be no question that with the five-part ivory diptych covers in particular, opening them for display—primarily on an altar but also possibly in processions—would have enabled a far richer program to be communicated than could be provided by one cover alone. Yet precisely because of the division implicit in the diptych form, there could have been a danger that the imagery chosen for the two covers might have seemed to divide the human and divine natures of Christ. Perhaps, therefore, particular narrative and symbolic formulae, with their focus on the incarnation and miracles, already adumbrated in the Milan covers, were selected and arranged so as to function, diptych-like, as effective affirmations of orthodox (anti-Monophysite) doctrine.

Finally, we come to the intriguing question of the relationship between the exteriors of early Christian books and their interiors, what we might call the public and private spheres. Was there, as Kitzinger stated, a strong link between the decorative schemes of the two?[98] We can accept that the full-page cross, for example, could quite probably have been found both on the cover and occasionally inside an early Christian book, even if in the sole example that we can still investigate, the Glazier codex, this was not the case. In general, however, the treatment of book covers was much less varied, and hence is more predictable, than the treatment of images within books. Furthermore, it is important to recognize that there are no images within books in the early period that resemble in the slightest the centrally planned compositional schemes so characteristic of the five-part ivory diptychs. Is this evidence that such diptychs were in fact not made as book covers? I would dispute the point. I believe that the makers and users of luxury books had the clearest understanding of the difference between "outside" and "inside," and thought hard about what was appropriate as a cover for the Gospels. The characteristic iconography of a

98. Kitzinger, "Pair of Silver Book Covers," e.g., 2: "an inner relationship can be observed between designs on the cover and designs in the interior of codices."

five-part diptych, those themes—including the Protevangelium scenes—common to all the examples, imply that the images were intended to affirm the broad significance and meaning of the gospel texts, not to "illustrate" them by some combination of what are sometimes called the "narrative" and "iconic" modes, nor to focus on specifically liturgical events (the Last Supper, for example), nor to record or recall the major feasts of the church year.

The early Christian book cover was, I conclude, a locus for public affirmation of orthodox belief. Its decoration suggested links not with the pictorial content of the book within,[99] not even, except in the most general terms, with the text within, but rather with other public displays of imagery: the decoration of altars and ambos,[100] the items that stood on altars, other precious objects to be used processionally, particularly the cross, and the other fixed and movable decorations of the contemporary church interior.[101]

When the gospel text was written on the animal-skin sheets of a book, the word was made flesh. When the gospel was bound and its exterior decorated with images, the word was made visible. When such a book was displayed in a procession or on an altar, the viewer beheld via its exterior the *doxa* of the word, the glory, that is to say, of God incarnate.

99. Steenbock, *Kirchliche Prachteinband,* 70–71, proposed that the images on the Milan diptych were derived from a much richer lost gospel cycle ([zu rekonstruierende] Evangelienillustration), but she did not specify whether this might have been in a manuscript or not. But Kitzinger, "Pair of Silver Book Covers," 17, concluded (on the use of the cross and the gate of paradise), "it may well be that this is one of the cases where the cover designer took the lead and the miniaturist followed suit."

100. For some starting points, see Jean-Pierre Sodini, "Les ambons médiévaux à Byzance: Vestiges et problèmes," in *Thymiama stē mnēmē tēs Laskarinas Boura* (Athens, 1994), 1:303–7; Nezih Firatli, *La sculpture byzantine figurée au Musée Archéologique d'Istanbul* (Paris, 1990), nos. 178–79.

101. *Addendum.* For a reference to a pair of silver book covers, each decorated with images of saints, see the proceedings of the iconophile Council of Nicaea, 787 (Mansi 13:184), cited by Cyril Mango, *The Art of the Byzantine Empire 312–1453* (Englewood Cliffs N. J., 1972), 154. Note that these covers were not on a liturgical book, but a volume with writings of Constantine *chartophlyax.* On the other hand, the earlier reference in the same text to "two silver-bound books" from the collection of the Great Church at Constantinople (Mango, 153–54), might rather be translated as "two books decorated with images," without mention of their covers.

Chrysi Kotsifou

BOOKS AND BOOK PRODUCTION IN THE MONASTIC COMMUNITIES OF BYZANTINE EGYPT

P.Köln inv. 10213,[1] a letter on parchment of the fifth or sixth century, reads:

Flesh side (fig. 16, following p. 26):

ⲡⲉϣⲱⲧ ⲡⲉⲧⲥϩⲁⲓ̈ ⲙ̄ⲡⲉϥⲥⲟⲛ ⲕⲟⲗⲟⲩⲑⲉ ⲙ̄ⲛ ⲡⲉϥⲥⲟⲛ ⲧⲓⲙⲟⲑⲉⲟⲥ
ⲛⲉϥⲥⲛⲏⲩ ϩⲙ̄ ⲡⲭⲟⲉⲓⲥ ϩⲁⲑⲏ ⲛ̄-
ϩⲱⲃ ⲛⲓⲙ ϯⲥⲓⲛⲉ ⲉⲣⲱⲧⲛ̄ ⲉ-
ⲙⲁⲧⲉ ⲙ̄ⲛ̄ ⲛⲉⲧⲛ̄ⲥⲛⲏⲩ ⲙⲁⲕⲁ-
ⲣⲉ ⲙ̄ⲛ̄ ⲛⲓⲗⲗⲉ ⲙ̄ⲛ̄ ⲧⲉⲧⲛ̄ϩⲗⲗⲱ
ⲙ̄ⲛ̄ ⲡⲕⲉ ⲥⲉⲉⲡⲉ ⲉⲧ·ϩ·ⲛ̄·ⲡ·ⲡ·ⲏⲉⲓ :
ⲧⲉⲛⲟⲩ ⲇⲉ ⲡⲓⲭⲱⲱⲙⲉ ⲛ̄ⲧⲁⲓ̈ⲧⲛⲟ-
ⲟⲩϥ ⲛⲏⲧⲛ̄ ⲣⲱϣⲉ ⲉⲣⲟϥ ⲉⲕⲟ-

I would like to thank Professor Judith Herrin and Professor Cornelia Roemer for their help and guidance while I was working on this topic for the conference. Special thanks are also due to Dr. Arietta Papaconstantinou for her bibliographical suggestions and comments on the draft of this article. Abbreviations of papyri and ostraca in this article follow John F. Oates, Roger S. Bagnall, Sarah J. Clackson, Alexandra A. O'Brien, Joshua D. Sosin, Terry G. Wilfong, and Klaas A. Worp, *Checklist of Editions of Greek, Latin, Demotic and Coptic Papyri, Ostraca and Tablets,* http://scriptorium.lib.duke.edu/papyrus/texts/clist.html (accessed August 2005).

1. Edition of the letter by Manfred Weber, "Zur Ausschmückung koptischer Bücher," *Enchoria* 3 (1973): 53–62. There is also an English translation of the text by Herwig Maehler, "Byzantine Egypt: Urban Élites and Book Production," *Dialogos: Hellenic Studies Review* 4 (1997): 133.

ϭⲘΙ ⲘⲘⲞϤ: ⲤⲠⲞⲨⲆⲀⲌⲈ ⲈⲚⲈϤ-
ⲠⲞϬⲈ ⲤⲞⲧⲠⲞⲨ ⲈⲚⲀⲚⲞⲨⲞⲨ ⲘⲘⲀ-
ⲧⲈ ⲘⲠⲢⲰⲞⲭⲦ Ⲛ·Ϩ·ⲎⲧⲞⲨ ⲕⲀⲧⲀ ⲐⲈ Ⲛ-
ⲧⲀⲓ̈ⲭⲟⲟⲤ ⲚϨⲨⲆⲒⲀⲤ: ⲧⲀⲀϤ ⲘⲠⲈⲧⲚⲀⲢ
ⲫⲰⲂ ⲕⲀⲖⲰⲤ ⲚϤⲔⲞⲤ[Ⲙ]ι [ⲘⲘ]ⲞϤ ⲀⲨⲰ ⲈϤⲰⲀⲚⲞⲨⲰ
ⲈⲨⲧⲀⲘⲒⲞ ⲘⲘⲞϤ ⲈⲰ[ⲟϤ Ⲙ]ⲠⲀⲧⲒⲈⲒ ⲈϨⲎⲧ
ⲚⲀ ⲧⲚⲞⲞⲨϤ ⲈⲢⲎⲤ ϯ[ⲞⲨⲰⲰ Ⲅ]ⲀⲢ ⲈⲈⲒ
ⲈⲢⲈⲰⲀⲚⲠⲭⲞⲈⲒⲤ ⲧⲞ[ⲰⲦ: ϯ]ⲰⲒⲚⲈ ⲈⲒ̈ⲤⲒⲆⲰⲢⲈ
ⲘⲚ ⲠⲈϤϨⲖⲖⲞ ⲘⲚ ⲧⲈ[. . . .] ⲘⲚ Ⲛ[Ⲉ]ⲧ-
ϨⲘ ⲠⲎⲈⲒ: ϯⲰⲒⲚⲈ Ⲉ[. . . .]ⲔⲞⲨ[. .]
ⲘⲚ ϨⲨⲆⲒⲀⲤ ⲀⲨⲰ ⲘⲚ [ⲚⲈⲤⲚⲎⲎ]Ⲩ Ⲉⲧ-
ϨⲀ ϨⲎⲧ ⲠⲞⲨⲀ ⲠⲞⲨⲀ Ⲕ[Ⲁⲧ]Ⲁ ⲠⲈϤⲢⲀⲚ
ⲘⲚ ⲠⲔⲈ ⲤⲈⲈⲠⲈ ⲚⲚ[ⲈⲤ]ⲚⲎⲨ ⲧⲎ-
ⲢⲞⲨ ⲚⲧⲀⲒⲤⲞⲨⲰⲚⲞⲨ
ⲰⲖⲎⲖ ⲈⲭⲰⲈⲒ ϨⲚ ⲠⲈ[ⲧ]ⲚϨⲎⲧ
ⲧⲎⲢϤ ⲞⲨⲭⲀⲒ̈ ϨⲘ Ⲡⲭ[ⲞⲈⲒ]Ⲥ

Hair side (fig. 17, following p. 26):

ⲀⲭⲒⲤ Ⲛ[Ⲡ]ⲔⲞⲤⲘⲒⲧⲎⲤ
ⲈⲧⲢⲈϤϯ ϨⲚⲔⲞⲨⲒ̈ ·ⲚⲈⲒ-
ⲈⲠⲤⲀ ⲈⲢⲞϤ ⲈⲒⲧⲈ ⲞⲨⲠⲨⲖⲎ
ⲈⲒⲧⲈ ⲞⲨⲔⲞⲧ·[[. . ⲟ
. . ⲈⲒⲧ . . . ϨⲞⲈ
ⲖⲒ̈ Ⲛ . ⲚⲀ . . . Ⲉ Ⲏ
ⲀⲚⲞ - - - ⲚϤⲧⲈ
- - - - - ⲚⲈ
ⲈⲒⲧⲚⲞⲞⲨ ⲘⲘⲞϤ ⲚⲔⲞ-
ⲖⲞⲨⲐⲈ ⲈⲧⲘⲈ ⲚⲈϤⲚϤⲧⲈ]]

Flesh side:

Peshot writes to his brother Kolouthe and to his brother Timotheos, his brothers in the Lord. Above all, I very much greet you and your brothers Marake and Nille and your elder woman, and the rest in the house. So now, the book which I have sent you, be responsible for decorating (κοσμεῖν) it, be busy (σπουδάζειν) with its plates. Choose only those that are good. Do not cut into them as I have said to Hylias. Give it to somebody who does the job well (καλῶς), so that he decorates (κοσμεῖν) it, and if it has been completed to be received before I come to the North, send it to the South. For I wish to come, if God allows me. I greet Isidore and his elder man and Te[. . .] and those in the house. I greet E[. . .] and Hylias and the brothers who are in the North, each one by his name, and all the rest of the brothers whom I have known. Pray for me with all your heart. Be safe in the Lord.

Hair side:

Tell the illuminator (κοσμητής) to add some little ornaments to it, either a gate (πύλη) or a wheel. [Rubbed out: . . . .]²

In late antiquity, centers of book production were primarily if not exclusively in monasteries. *P.Köln* inv. 10213 attests to this practice and is the type of document on which this chapter concentrates. I hope to demonstrate that monks were involved in all stages of book production—copying, illustrating, and binding—and that these books were meant both for their personal use and for the use of their monastic community, as well as for people outside their monastery who had commissioned them. Hagiographical writings often mention books in relation to monks and ascetics. Epiphanius, bishop of Cyprus, claimed that "[t]he acquisition of Christian books is necessary for those who can use them. For the mere sight of these books renders us less inclined to sin, and incites us to believe more firmly in righteousness."³ In contrast, when "a brother said to apa Serapion, 'Give me a word,' [t]he old man said to him,

2. Since this text is integral to my study, I feel I should discuss further the points where my translation varies from the two aforementioned ones; L.6: ϩⲗⲗⲱ; the term is used to describe a woman living in an ascetic setting and thus means much more than "old woman" as in Mahler, 133. In the fifth and sixth centuries the term was used to indicate the head of a monastic community. See Walter E. Crum, *A Coptic Dictionary* (Oxford, 1939), 699a. Rebecca Krawiec also notes that "in both the men's and the women's communities, there was a position of authority known as the elder, who was an overseer of some sort," in *Shenoute and the Women of the White Monastery* (Oxford, 2002), 27, and n122 on the term 'ϩⲗⲗⲟ'. L.11: ⲡⲟϭⲉ; Crum's entries in *Coptic Dictionary*, 286a and particularly 261a, lead me to believe that this should be translated "plates" instead of "pages." In 286a, ⲡⲟϭⲉ does not feature as a single page of a book but as a part of it, while in 261a, it indicates a "thin sheet, plate," equivalent to the term ⲡⲉⲧⲁⲗⲟⲛ, another term used in papyri to suggest book illustrations or plates. Finally, L12: ⲙ̄ⲡⲣ̄ϣⲟⲭⲧ̄ ⲛ̄ϩⲏⲧⲟⲩ; Crum, *Coptic Dictionary*, 599a, notes that it means "cut, carve, hollow" and that it translates Greek verbs like γλύφειν (engrave), and that it is also used for stone carving. The verb is not widely attested, and unfortunately not together with the preposition ⲛ̄ϩⲏⲧ″. ⲛ̄ϩⲏⲧⲟⲩ, though, definitely refers to the plates, so Peshot, the sender of the letter, is most probably concerned that the brothers who will receive his book and are to select some good pages for the illustrations and then pass it on to the illuminator should not in any way mark or cut into those pages as a way of indicating to the illuminator which ones they want decorated. As we shall see in the section on binding, scribes could sometimes prepare the pages meant for writing the text by drawing lines on them; see *O.Crum* Ad. 50. Could it be that illuminators had their own way of marking the pages that they would decorate? Warm thanks to Dr. Janet Timbie for taking the time to discuss this translation with me.

3. *Apophthegmata Patrum*, Epiphanius 8 (*PG* 65:165A), in Benedicta Ward, trans., *The Sayings of the Desert Fathers: The Alphabetical Collection*, rev. ed. (Kalamazoo, Mich., 1984), 58.

'What shall I say to you? You have taken the living of widows and orphans and put in on your shelves.' For he saw them full of books."[4] Obviously, the early Christian fathers' attitudes to books were not uniform.

The written word, though, was the source of salvation and redemption. It was fundamental in the liturgy and in the education and practice of both clerics and monks. Monasteries had books thanks to the donations of pious laymen and monks[5] and copied manuscripts in order to preserve them for posterity.[6] Archaeological finds verify the importance of books. Churches and monasteries needed books for liturgical purposes, and it is safe to assume that every church had at least the Gospels and the Psalter. Furthermore, inventories of church and monastic property show that large churches and monasteries had their own libraries.[7] It is worth mentioning at this point that with the end of secular pagan education in Byzantine Egypt, schools and public librar-

---

4. *Apophthegmata Patrum,* Serapion 2 (*PG* 65:416C), ibid., 227.

5. Arnold Van Lantschoot, *Recueil des colophons des manuscrits chrétiens d'Égypte* (Louvain, 1929). For a detailed discussion of the books donated to the White Monastery from other monastic centers, see Tito Orlandi, "The Library of the Monastery of Saint Shenute at Atripe," in *Perspectives on Panopolis: An Egyptian Town from Alexander the Great to the Arab Conquest,* ed. A. Egberts et al. (Leiden, 2002), 211–19. For books donated to the Pachomian monasteries, see James M. Robinson, *The Pachomian Monastic Library at the Chester Beatty Library and the Bibliothèque Bodmer* (Claremont, 1990), 4–5. Donating books to religious institutions was also a pagan practice; see *New Docs.* 4.38 where some marvelous books (βίβλια θαυμαστά) were donated by T. Aurelius Alkibades, a Roman citizen of Nysa, to adorn the sanctuary at Rome of the association of Dionysiac artists.

6. See Claudia Rapp, "Christians and Their Manuscripts in the Greek East in the Fourth Century," in *Scritture, libri e testi nelle aree provinciali di Bizanzio,* ed. Guglielmo Cavallo et al. (Spoleto, 1991), 1:130. For the replacing of old codices with new ones in the library of the White Monastery, see Orlandi, "Library of Saint Shenute," 220.

7. For the library at the White Monastery, see Orlandi, "Library of Saint Shenute," 211–31, and Walter E. Crum, "Inscriptions from Shenoute's Monastery," *Journal of Theological Studies* 5 (1904): 564–69; for the one at the Pachomian monasteries, see Robinson, *Pachomian Monastic Library.* The rules of Saint Pachomius refer to the library. Rule 101 states that "Every day at evening, the second shall bring the books from the alcove and shut them in their case." *Pachomian Koinonia,* ed. Armand Veilleux (Kalamazoo, Mich., 1981), 2:162. In the *First Greek Life of Pachomius* (59) we are told that the books, which were kept in an alcove, were under the supervision of the house master and his second. Veilleux, *Pachomian Koinonia,* 1:338. "Alcove" translates the Greek word θυρίδιον in François Halkin, ed., *Le Corpus Athénien de Saint Pachôme* (Geneva, 1982), 32; for the one at the monastery of Arsenios at Tura, see Ludwig Koenen and Wolfgang Müller-Wiener, "Zu den Papyri aus dem Arsenioskloster bei Tura," *ZPE* 2 (1968): 41–63; for the apa Elias library catalogue, see Henry E. Winlock and Walter E. Crum, *The Monastery of Epiphanius at Thebes. Part 1* (New York, 1926), 196–208; René-Georges Coquin, "Le catalogue de la bibiothèque de couvent de Saint Élie «Du Rocher» (Ostracon IFAO 13315)," *Bulletin de l'Institut français d'archéologie orientale du Caire* 75 (1975): 207–39; and Terry J. Wilfong, *Women of Jeme: Lives in a Coptic Town in Late Antique Egypt* (Ann Arbor, 2002), 33. Orlandi, "Library of Saint Shenute," 226, has a table with the names of various other monastic libraries in Egypt, extending from the fourth to the ninth

ies diminished in number.[8] Books have also been found in hermitages, for example at Naqlun around the sixth century A.D.[9]

In this chapter I concentrate not on the theological and spiritual significance of books in monasteries[10] but rather on practical issues regarding book production and on the role and identity of scribes, as described in documentary papyri and ostraca from Egypt between the early fourth and the seventh century.[11] In the Greek and Coptic sources, books are mentioned in private letters, book lists, church inventories, and descriptions of monastic libraries.[12] Despite the fact that manuscripts of classical works have survived from late antiquity,[13] we soon realize that all the books mentioned in these lists and inventories are Christian—there is no reference to pagan or even secular works whatsoever after the fourth century[14]—and that they were produced within the confines of

---

centuries. For a general commentary on the above-mentioned libraries, see Martin Krause, "Libraries," in Aziz S. Atiya, ed., *The Coptic Encyclopedia* (New York, 1991), 5:1447–50.

8. See Maehler, "Byzantine Egypt," 134. The author goes so far as to suggest that schools and public libraries disappeared.

9. See discussion of the archaeological finds at the site, and of the role of books in hermitages, in Tomasz Derda, *Deir el-Naqlun: The Greek Papyri (P. Naqlun I)* (Warsaw, 1995), 42–49.

10. This is a whole different subject in itself, widely discussed in the past and also in this volume. Some standard works are Douglas Burton-Christie, *The Word in the Desert: Scripture and the Quest for Holiness in Early Christian Monasticism* (Oxford, 1993); Douglas Burton-Christie, "Oral Culture and Biblical Interpretation in Early Egyptian Monasticism," in *Papers Presented at the Twelfth International Conference on Patristic Studies Held in Oxford, 1995*, ed. Elizabeth A. Livingstone (Leuven, 1997), 2:144–50; Claudia Rapp, "Christians and Their Manuscripts," 127–48, esp. 136ff.; and Colin H. Roberts, *Manuscript, Society, and Belief in Early Christian Egypt* (London, 1979).

11. Two detailed studies that collect the majority of book references in papyri are Hermann Harrauer, "Bücher in Papyri," in *Flores litterarum Ioanni Marte sexagenario oblati: Wissenschaft in der Bibliothek,* ed. Helmut W. Lang (Vienna, 1995), 59–77; and Rosa Otranto, *Antiche liste di libri su papiro* (Rome, 2000), esp. 123–44. In her discussion of a twelfth-century Byzantine monastic inventory of books, Judith Waring rightly claims that "The type of data contained in the lending list can be used to qualify rather than merely quantify the range of Byzantine literacy skills." Waring, "Literacies of Lists: Reading Byzantine Monastic Inventories," in *Literacy, Education, and Manuscript Transmission in Byzantium and Beyond,* ed. Catherine Holmes and Judith Waring (Leiden, 2002), 166. This scholar, however, was working with only one document; where sources are numerous, the "type of data" can be used to both "qualify" and "quantify." For the study of the historical and theological sources of the first five centuries A.D. and the information they contain regarding the production of the early Christian book, see Harry Y. Gamble, *Books and Readers in the Early Church: A History of Early Christian Texts* (New Haven, 1995), esp. 82–143.

12. This chapter refers to numerous private letters and book lists. For examples of church inventories, see *P.Fay.* 44; *P.Prag.* I.87; *P.Leid.Inst.* 13; *P.Vindob.* 26015, discussed by Hans Gerstinger, "Ein Bücherverzeichnis aus dem VII–VIII. Jh. n. Chr. im Pap. Graec. Vindob. 26015," *Wiener Studien: Zeitschrift für klassische Philologie* 32 (1933): 185–92; and Otranto, *Antiche liste,* 129–37.

13. Maehler, "Byzantine Egypt," 125–28.

14. Ibid., 134, and Peter Van Minnen in the edition of *P.Leid.Inst.* 13, note, as the only exception to this rule, the appearance of the biography of the empress Galla Placidia in the church inventory of this

monastic or other ascetic communities. Furthermore, these manuscripts did not diverge from the appointed reading material of the monks and nuns for whom they were predominantly intended.[15] They include the four Gospels, the rest of the books of the Bible, patristic works, and hagiographical writings. The letters and lists we are dealing with are free of theological propaganda, but they still have their limitations, especially since the mention of books and their scribes is largely accidental and a by-product of other everyday activities. In addition, it must always be kept in mind that when dealing with papyri, we have only material that has survived by chance.[16] As we shall see, papyri and ostraca from the fourth to the seventh centuries A.D. offer detailed information regarding the copyists of the early Christian book, underscore the important role of monasteries as centers of book production, and attest to the involvement of monks in copying, illustrating, binding, and selling their manuscripts.

Before taking a closer look at the scribes and the various stages of their work, two general points should be made that apply to most of the material treated in this study. First, when we look at references to Christian books, and particularly the Bible, in private letters, book lists, and other inventories, we soon notice that the manuscripts mentioned are mostly selective. Allusions to a whole Old or New Testament are rare,[17] unless of course these books be-

---

papyrus. Both scholars view this work as secular. Van Minnen claims that the empress was no saint, and that it is quite unusual to find such a person's "Life" in a church library. Empress Galla Placidia, though, was indeed a saint; see Sophronios Eustratiades, *Hagiologion tēs Orthodoxou Ekklēsias* (Athens, 1995), 394, celebrated in the Orthodox Church on September 14. Thus there is no contradiction in finding this work among other theological writings in a church. As a matter of fact, the discrepancy can be found with all the pagan manuscripts that have survived from late antiquity, but they are not mentioned in our documentary sources. In his study of surviving manuscripts, Herwig Maehler counted six hundred copies, from the fourth to late seventh centuries, in both Greek and Latin and all genres. Maehler, "Byzantine Egypt," 125–28. See also Roger S. Bagnall, *Egypt in Late Antiquity* (Princeton, 1993), 104; Alain Blanchard, "Sur le milieu d'origine du papyrus Bodmer de Ménandre," *Chronique d'Égypte* 66 (1991): 211–20; and Jean-Luc Fournet, "Une éthopée de Caïn dans le Codex des Visions de la Fondation Bodmer," *ZPE* 92 (1992): 252–66, esp. 256–59.

15. Patriarch Athanasius's *Festal Letter* 39, composed in A.D. 367, addresses specifically what should be read by monks and ascetics, and warns against apocryphal writings. Admittedly, it is difficult to establish the extent to which the letter was observed or how soon that happened, but all the books that Athanasius recommends are mentioned in our documentary papyri. For an English translation of the letter, see David Brakke, *Athanasius and Asceticism* (Baltimore, 1995), 326–32. Also see C. Wilfred Griggs, *Early Egyptian Chistianity from Its Origin to 451 CE* (Leiden, 1991), 173–76; and Aziz S. Atiya, "Cathechetical School of Alexandria," in Atiya, *Coptic Encyclopedia*, 2:469–72.

16. See Frederic Kenyon, "The Library of a Greek of Oxyrhynchus," *Journal of Egyptian Archaeology* 8 (1922): 131.

17. See, for example, *P.Ashm.* inv.3; *O.CrumVC* 69; *BKU* II.313; and *O.Mon.Phoib.* 7, which reads

longed to a church and not an individual. People asked to borrow, or commissioned for copying, specific books of the Bible. Personal preferences for one gospel over another could have influenced this practice as much as did the considerable cost of acquiring a book in late antiquity. Second, I believe that the prohibitive cost of books encouraged extensive borrowing among readers.[18] Thus we find that not many people could afford to have their own books, and it was common practice to borrow from each other. *P.Köln* VIII.355 is a Coptic letter of the sixth or seventh century describing exactly this custom. Brother Sanso writes to Brother Georgios telling him that he regrets that he was unable to see him properly the last time Georgios visited him. Sanso was apparently busy baking with his father, so he asks Georgios to come back on Saturday with the book, at which point he will then give him the other. Books circulated widely in order to satisfy all the needs of the Christian audience.[19]

Scribes and Their Monasteries

Let us now turn to the scribes themselves, the copyists of Christian books. Hagiographical writings refer to copying books together with the other occupations a monk could perform in his monastic surroundings.[20] Although we cannot assume that every monastery had its own scribe, I believe it is safe

---

"Before [all things] I greet my [beloved] brother Kouloudje. [When] I left [thee] (thou saidst): 'Write the Deuteronomy.' Now, I did not write it, but [I] have written the Leviticus and the Numbers in their order. If I am able, I shall write the Deuteronomy. Give it to the master, Kouloudj, from Daueid, the most humble sinner. Farewell in the Lord" (trans. Walter C. Till).

18. For more details on the cost of books, see the section "Stages of Production: Copying, Materials, and Prices of Books."

19. *P.Mon.Epiph.* 380–97 are a collection of letters by monks borrowing and lending books to each other. Also see the story of Cosmas the lawyer: "This wondrous man greatly benefited us, not only by letting us see him and by teaching us, but also because he had more books than anyone in Alexandria and would willingly supply them to those who wished. Yet he was a man of no possessions. Throughout his house there was nothing to be seen but books, a bed, and a table. Any man could go in and ask for what would benefit him—and read it." John Wortley, trans., *John Moschos, The Spiritual Meadow,* 172 (Kalamazoo, Mich., 1992), 141. For pagan equivalents, see *P.Zenon* II.60. This is a list of books that Zenon sends his younger brother Epharmostos from his personal library in order to help him with his education; and *P.Carlsb.* III.21 and 22, two Demotic letters of the second century A.D. regarding borrowing and copying books among temple scribes. For a late Byzantine counterpart to this practice, see Waring, "Literacies of Lists," 165ff., describing a twelfth-century inventory of books lent by the monastery of St. John the Theologian to other monasteries in Asia Minor and the Aegean.

20. According to Palladius (*Lausiac History* 38.10), when Evagrius stayed at Kellia, he made a living by copying books. A. Lucot, ed., *Histoire Lausiaque* (Paris, 1912), 276.

to say that large monastic communities, for example the Epiphanius and the Pachomian monasteries, definitely did, and that they even employed groups of scribes who could copy not only for their own monastery but also for other, maybe smaller, monastic communities.[21] Laymen could also commission books from these scriptoria. In Rome during the first century B.C., rich educated people, like Cicero's friend Atticus, had their own slaves working as scribes to copy the books they required.[22] In Byzantine Egypt, on the other hand, rich persons, like the Apiones or the father of Dioscorus of Aphrodito, who were closely connected to churches and monasteries by patronage,[23] would have used these institutions for acquiring their sacred books. The lack of evidence for pagan scriptoria in Byzantine Egypt also suggests that a large number of the six hundred copies of pagan books that have survived from that period were copied by monks.[24]

Educated monks also copied books for their own personal use, as archaeological finds—for example, from the site of Naqlun—indicate.[25] The status

21. Judith Waring claims that the same role was played by the monastery of St. John and explains that "the main complex of the monastery of St. John was apparently required to provide for the textual needs of dependent communities and dependent individuals such as the anchorite Kalymnos." Waring, "Literacies of Lists," 172.

22. For Cicero, Atticus, and their scribes, see Kim Haines-Eitzen, "Girls Trained in Beautiful Writing: Female Scribes in Roman Antiquity and Early Christianity," *JECS* 6 (1998): 634, esp. n17. For more on bibliophiles in Roman times, with references to their letters of commissioning and requesting books, see Naphtali Lewis, *Life in Egypt under Roman Rule* (Atlanta, 1999), 60–61.

23. For the relations of Dioscorus and his father, Apollo, with their monastery at Pharoou, see Leslie S. B. MacCoull, "The Apa Apollos Monastery of Pharoou (Aphrodito) and Its Papyrus Archive," *Le Muséon* 106 (1993): 21–63, and "Patronage and the Social Order in Coptic Egypt," in *Egitto e storia antica dall'ellenismo all'età araba: Bilancio di un confronto: Atti del colloquio internazionale, Bologna, 31 agosto–2 settembre 1987,* ed. Lucia Criscuolo and Giovanni Geraci (Bologna, 1989), 499–500, reprinted in her *Coptic Perspectives on Late Antiquity* (Aldershot, 1993). Also see Jean-Luc Fournet, *Hellénisme dans l'Égypte du VIe siècle: La bibliothèque et l'ouevre de Dioscore d'Aphrodité* (Cairo, 1999), 669–73, for a discussion of which copies in the library of Dioscorus were written and were not written by the scholar himself.

24. Archaeological digs have found pagan books in monastic settings. For pagan manuscripts found and/or copied in monasteries, see Bagnall, *Egypt in Late Antiquity,* 104, esp. the references in n385; Kurt Treu, "Antike Literatur im byzantinischen Ägypten im Lichte der Papyri," *Byzantinoslavica* 47 (1986): 1–7, at 3–4; Robinson, *Pachomian Monastic Library,* 5, 19–21; and Raffaella Cribiore, "Greek and Coptic Education in Late Antique Egypt," in *Ägypten und Nubien in spätantiker und christlicher Zeit, Akten des 6. Internationalen Koptologenkongresses, Münster, 20–26 Juli 1996,* ed. Stephen Emmel et al. (Wiesbaden, 1999), 2:282. On a more general note, see Josep Monteserrat-Torrents, "The Social and Cultural Setting of the Coptic Gnostic Library," in *Papers Presented at the Twelfth International Conference on Patristic Studies Held in Oxford, 1995,* ed. Elizabeth A. Livingstone (Leuven, 1997), 3:464–81.

25. The anchorite in cell 25, hermitage 25, had copied chapters of the Bible for himself on scraps of papyrus. This is assumed by the editors of the texts on the basis of the informal copying of the manu-

and level of literacy of scribes was high, or at least higher than the rest of their community.[26] Considering their education and training, a look at various hands might prove helpful. In classical times texts written in a documentary hand were produced by people working in civil administration, while texts in book hands were composed by scribes working in pagan scriptoria connected to pagan libraries. Later on, in monasteries, we find that documentary hands are not different from lay handwriting, possibly indicating that these monks were originally intended for civil administration. Book hands, whether Greek or Coptic, developed in the same way, so that by the sixth century Homer could be written in the same style as the New Testament. This indicates either that both pagan and Christian books were written by monks or that monks were in close relation to possible lay scribes.[27]

Whether in the early fourth century monks' education and training came from their preparation for civil and church administration, as Claudia Rapp has argued,[28] or, like scribes of Demotic texts, from their training at temples and at home by their families, as John Tait and S. P. Vleeming have proposed,[29]

script, Derda, *Deir el-Naqlun,* 42–43 and 50. Also see Kenyon, "Library of a Greek," 13; Rapp, "Christians and Their Manuscripts," 135–36; and Robinson, *Pachomian Monastic Library,* 5, who notes when discussing the various manuscripts of the library that "the presence of relatively unskilled products alongside of relatively professional codices may indicate a plurality of places of origin, and perhaps a contrast between what was produced within the Order and what came from outside."

26. Even a casual look at the scripts of *P.Köln* inv. 10213 and the Coptic papyrus edited by Boris Turaev, *Koptskiia zamietki* [*Coptic Observations*] (St. Petersburg, 1907), 025–028 (which is also a letter among monastic scribes arranging details for copying books), reveals skilled Coptic book hands, attesting to their composers' high level of literacy. Also notice the deep knowledge and careful use of the Coptic language by the composer of *P.Köln* inv. 10213; for example, see how he distinguishes between ЕΗΑΤЕ ("very much") in lines 4–5 and ЙΗΑΤЕ ("only") in lines 11–12.

27. For the ways the book hand of Christian literary manuscripts developed, and the various ways it was influenced by pagan handwriting, see Roberts, *Manuscript, Society, and Belief,* 14–20. At the same time, though, conclusions drawn from styles of handwriting can be tricky since skilled scribes could employ different styles depending on what they were writing. See Fournet, *Hellénisme dans l'Égypte,* 245–48, for the different hands Dioscorus of Aphrodito used in his compositions.

28. Rapp, "Christians and Their Manuscripts," 134. Bagnall, *Egypt in Late Antiquity,* 249, observes that monks who came from an upper-class family before joining a monastery had also most probably received a higher education, too. Also see Annick Martin, "L'Église et la Khôra Égyptienne au IVe siècle," *REAug* 25 (1979): 14–15.

29. Sven P. Vleeming, "Some Notes on Demotic Scribal Training in the Ptolemaic Period," in *Proceedings of the 20th International Congress of Papyrologists, Copenhagen 23–29 August 1992,* ed. Adam Bülow-Jacobsen (Copenhagen, 1994), 186–87, and, in the same volume, John Tait, "Some Notes on Demotic Scribal Training in the Roman Period," 188–92. Also see John Tait, "How to Read Hieroglyphs?" in *Studies on Ancient Egypt in Honour of H. S. Smith,* ed. Anthony Leahy and John Tait (London, 1999), 317–19. On scribes in Roman times, see Lewis, *Life in Egypt,* 81–83.

eventually scribes could be trained in monasteries as part of the education an elder passed on to a novice.[30]

The Pachomian Rules clearly state that there could be no illiterate monks in the *koinonia,* and that upon entering the monastery every illiterate person had to receive enough teaching to enable him to read at least the Psalter and the New Testament.[31] Palladius, in *Lausiac History* 13.1, also tells of Apollonios, who was too old to learn a craft or to work as a scribe (ἄσκησιν γραφικὴν). This atmosphere is also mirrored in the Coptic ostracon *P.Mon.Epiph.* 140, an extensive communication in which a scribe addresses his superior, trying to appease the latter's concerns about the education of a boy. The scribe explains that he has copied in a book parts of the scripture for the boy according to the instructions of the superior, but has included nothing that could mislead the mind or spirit of his young protégé. This document illustrates two interesting points. First, it attests to the existence of scribes in monasteries, and second, it indicates how books were involved in the education of monks.[32] I believe that Judith Waring's observation about book lists also applies to this discussion:

30. I find Claudia Rapp's comment on scribal training ("there is no indication in the sources to suggest that it was provided within the monasteries," Rapp, "Christians and Their Manuscripts," 134) rather categorical. We know not only that monastic education existed but that it could also be quite advanced and demanding. Commenting on the library of the White Monastery, Tito Orlandi ("Library of Saint Shenute," 224) explains: "It is sufficiently sure that in the White Monastery, under the care of Shenute, the 'real' Coptic literature was created, and many Greek works were translated. The works of Shenute testify to a very cultivated environment, where many people read and discussed important works of spirituality, of history, and of theology. All this presupposes the possession of many books, and a cultural activity around them, possibly a school not only elementary (this must have existed in any case) but of a high level. When we try to understand how this happened, we can think of only two possibilities: either the monks dedicated to such activity relied for the organization from outside (e.g., in the large city of Shmin, Panopolis) or the cultural organization was inside the monastery. We are in favour of the second hypothesis, and we add that the existence of a school of high level at the White Monastery is to be supposed from the literary work done there." Raffaella Cribiore also notes the advanced schooling professional scribes required, in *Writing, Teachers, and Students in Graeco-Roman Egypt* (Atlanta, 1996), 28–29, and for some references to specific rhetorical and scribal exercises, 287. At the same time, there are documentary papyri, like *P.Mon.Apollo* 58 and 59, which are practice-letter formulas that may have been produced for the purpose of scribal training, possibly for secretaries working in the office of the head of the monastery. Since the evidence points on the one hand to high-level education, and on the other to scribal training in monasteries for the composition of documentary works, why exclude the possibility of scribal training in monasteries for literary texts as well?

31. *Rules of Saint Pachomius* 139 and 140, *Pachomian Koinonia* 2:166. Also see Philip Rousseau, *Pachomius: The Making of a Community in Fourth-Century Egypt* (Berkeley and Los Angeles, 1985), 70.

32. The text is rather fragmentary but the beginning of it reads: "Christ, Michael, Gabriel. Amen. I have had the letters of thy holiness, have learned thence of thy welfare and have greatly rejoiced. Now in accordance with what thy reverence wrote me regarding the boy, that I should write for him in a book

Both a writer and a reader of this text would need to have acquired a reasonable level of skill to produce and use this type of document. A writer would have been composing and constructing the content, in addition to the actual physical act of writing down this text. This is a completely different level of skill from the ability to sign one's name or indeed to copying the text of a book, which can be performed satisfactorily without the ability to understand anything of the text.[33]

Finally, I would like to consider the role of women in the matter of books and book production in the monastic communities of late antique Egypt. Obviously women composed a large part of the audience for these books. We have several letters describing the exchange of books or requests by women (we do not always know whether these were lay or monastic women) for Christian reading material.[34] But how much we can infer from the evidence about the involvement of women in the actual composition of books?[35] *P.Mon.Epiph.* 374 and *P.Köln* inv. 10213 suggest an answer. The Coptic ostracon from the Epiphanius collection includes two letters from Epiphanius to Brother Patermouthius. In the first, Epiphanius states, "regarding my book. Be so kind and agree with my mother that she may write it; take yours and bring it away in your hand and bring it up to me." The editors of this ostracon take this reference to mean an account book, but I find no evidence in the wording of the letter or the term used, ϫⲱⲱⲙⲉ, to exclude the composition of any Christian book.[36] The sec-

---

[words] from the scripture: I do not think that I have written for him [what is] outside the scripture since he hath come unto my humility, except on two days, or thereabouts, so that there be not deception. I found not [. . . .] book] at the moment, except a book [of him that is among the] saints, our holy father, A[pa . . . , arch]bishop of Alexandria, [wherein] he interpreteth the prophet [. . .], the two [. . .] having been written [. . .] that book" (trans. W. E. Crum). The editors note that instead of the word "Apa" only a name, such as Athanasius, could be supplied. Is the composer of this letter saying that he is following the guidelines of Athanasius's *Festal Letter* 39? The anguish of this poor monk is further understood if we keep in mind that Shenoute ordered forty blows to be inflicted on a nun who took it on herself to teach, while another, who practiced homosexual acts, received only fifteen. See Krawiec, "Shenoute," 42, and n100 for a translation of this text. Also see Susanna Elm, *Virgins of God: The Making of Asceticism in Late Antiquity* (Oxford, 1994), 305.

33. Waring, "Literacies of Lists," 179.

34. See, for example, *P.Oxy.* LXIII.4365, further discussed in Otranto, *Antiche liste,* 128–29. Also see *P.Lips.* 43, and Wilfong, *Women of Jeme,* 75–77.

35. Kim Haines-Eitzen's article on female scribes in Roman antiquity and early Christianity is an excellent survey of the epigraphical, historical, and hagiographical sources. Also see her *Guardians of Letters: Literacy, Power, and the Transmitters of Early Christian Literature* (Oxford, 2000), 77ff. For the early Christian era, she refers to Origen's female scribes, Melania the Younger and Caesaria the Younger, and to the possibility of a female scribe named Thecla as a copyist of the Codex Alexandrinus. The papyrological sources add to Haines-Eitzen's observations.

36. Crum, *Coptic Dictionary,* 770b–771a.

ond letter of Epiphanius to the same apa strengthens this case. He complains that he has received no reply to his messages, requests another book, and expresses his wish to meet the recipient, who is a woman. Then he adds, "send your sister's son, that he may bring . . . to the scribe Komes, that he may write it . . . and give it to Pegosh, who shall bring it." The use of the terminus technicus ⲤⲀϨ for scribe excludes the possibility of an account book.[37] This suggests that women were both copyists and recipients/commissioners of books.

Further, I believe that the greeting at the beginning of *P.Köln* inv. 10213 clearly demonstrates the participation of women in book production and, in this case, illumination. Among the brothers whom Peshot greets, there is their elder woman (ϨⲖⲖⲱ) who lives with them in the house. The word is clearly written, it is the feminine form of the noun, and there is no chance of misunderstanding it.[38] An examination of papyrological evidence from late antiquity relating to the status and role of female ascetics and nuns demonstrates that on several occasions we find women living and practicing with their male counterparts. *P.Iand.* VI.100, from the second half of the fourth century, records a certain Bessemios who had business with brothers, and greets, among others, "Aron and Maria and Tamunis together with the brothers of the monastery." In addition, *SB* VIII.9882 transmits the greetings of "amma Thaubarin and apa Dios and the brothers."[39] It must be in a setting of this sort that we can imagine the members of the illumination workshop producing their decorations.

Stages of Production

As we have seen, the ability to read and write with some degree of comprehension—and often more than that—was asked for and encouraged by

37. See ibid., 383b. For more comments on women writers among the documents from the monastery of Epiphanius, see Winlock and Crum, *Monastery of Epiphanius,* 192–93.

38. The use of the Coptic word Ⲏⲓ for the place this group of illuminators inhabits, which usually does not signify a monastery or any other ascetic setting but instead simply a house (see Crum, *Coptic Dictionary,* 66a and b), also does not pose a problem. In *New Docs.* 4.136 (also *P.Strasb.* 697) we have a sixth-century reference to a house (οἶκος, which Ⲏⲓ translates) that apparently functioned as a monastery.

39. Also see *SB* VIII.9746. These documents are also discussed in Elm, *Virgins of God,* 236–37. For more on monks and nuns living together, see Judith Herrin, "L'enseignement maternel à Byzance," in *Femmes et pouvoirs des femmes à Byzance et en Occident (VIe–XIe siècles),* ed. Stéphane Lebecq et al. (Lille, 1996), 95; and Daniel F. Stramara, "ΑΔΕΛΦΟΤΗΣ: Two Frequently Overlooked Meanings," *VC* 51 (1997): 316–20.

monastic rules for the members of their community, and several monks completed this part of their training successfully. Let us now look at some of the ways in which these literary skills were employed at the different stages of book production.[40]

Stages of Production: Copying, Materials, and Prices of Books

Scribes worked either alone or in groups of other brothers.[41] *P.Köln* inv. 10213 clearly describes a community of book illuminators working together. At the beginning of the letter, Peshot greets his brothers Kolouthe, Timotheos, Makarios, Nille, and their elder woman. *P.Köln* inv. 1473 reveals the other end of the spectrum: a scribe working alone.[42] In a Greek letter of the fifth or sixth century, Dionysios asks Father Honorios to visit him so that they can discuss the commissioning of a book. Dionysios has heard that Honorios purchased parchment, and he would like to give Honorios a book to copy for him. This letter seems to imply that Honorios is copying books on his own, that he can supply his own writing material, whether papyrus or parchment, and that the person commissioning the book most probably provided the exemplar, the book to be copied—for example, Dionysios, who gave Honorios the ἀντίγραφον.[43]

Likewise, two Coptic ostraca from the Epiphanius collection attest to scribes buying their writing material. The first letter, *P.Mon.Epiph.* 385, concerns the acquisition of papyrus rolls. Isidore writes to apa Isaac and Elias: "Be so kind, if you have good papyri, as you told us, send us them with the man

40. Judith Waring writes, "I do not wish to argue merely for the existence of literacy skills within the monastic communities; my concern is, rather, with the extent, diversity and potential uses of these skills." Waring, "Literacies of Lists," 168–69.

41. The Greek term used for a scribe of literary texts is καλιγράφος. See *P.Maspero* III.672888; *P.Touraev* (note 26 above); Rapp, "Christians and Their Manuscripts," 133; and Haines-Eitzen, "Girls Trained in Beautiful Writing," 635, 641. For a beautiful depiction of a monk-scribe on a wooden cover of the sixth to the eighth century from Bawit, see Dominique Bénazeth, "Les coutumes funéraires," in *L'art copte en Égypte: 2000 ans de Christianisme; Exposition présentée à l'Institut du monde arabe, Paris, du 15 mai au 3 septembre 2000 et au Musée de l'Ephèbe au Cap d'Agde, du 30 septembre 2000 au 7 janvier 2001* (Paris, 2000), 110–11; for the writing instruments of scribes, see, in the same volume, Anne Boud'hors, "L'Écriture, la langue et les livres," 64–65; and Marie-Hélène Rutschowscaya, *Catalogue des bois de l'Égypte copte* (Paris, 1986), 65–70.

42. *P. Köln* inv. 1473. The letter is also discussed in Maehler, "Byzantine Egypt," 130–32.

43. Finding an exemplar when one needed it often seems to have been a problem, as the letter *O.CrumVC* 69 indicates: "[G]ive us the book of Jesus of Nauê: For they are writing it for us (and) we find not a copy."

that shall bring you this sherd. But if there be two or three good rolls, send them . . . that I may write your . . ."[44] The second letter, *P.Mon.Epiph.* 380, is from Pesentius to Peter. It concerns a scribe buying the material required for binding a book. Pesenthius writes, "Be so good and go unto the dwelling of Athanasius, the son of Sabinus, the craftsman, and get good goat skins, either three or four, or whatsoever you shall find of good ones; and do bring them to me, that I may choose one from there for this book."

The terms employed in these communications to indicate writing material and the end product vary.[45] For the actual material, we have for parchment μέμβρανον in Greek and ⲛⲉϥⲣⲱⲛ in Coptic;[46] for papyrus, χάρτης, and for a papyrus roll, σχεδάριον in Greek and ⲥⲭⲓⲗⲁⲣⲏ ⲛ̄ⲭⲁⲣⲧⲏⲥ or ⲧⲉⲥⲭⲓⲗⲁⲣⲏ in Coptic. One indication we have of the cost of the material comes from a Greek papyrus letter from Oxyrhynchus, *P.Oxy.* XVII.2156 of the late fourth–early fifth century. The sender explains, "Receive through him who gives you this letter of mine the skin of the parchments in twenty-five quaternions at the price of fourteen . . . talents of silver."[47] "Book," in Greek, is βίβλιον while in Cop-

---

44. There must not have been set rules for this practice, however. In *P.MoscowCopt.* 56, a letter in which one monk commissions another to write for him the "Life of Epiphanius Bishop of Cyprus," we learn that the commissioner sends the scribe the necessary papyrus sheets.

45. The terms denoting the different writing materials used for the books, and the types of books, are common among all the papyrological references. Characteristic are *P.Fay.* 44; *O.CrumVC* 116; *P.Mon. Epiph.* 263, 380, 385, and 391; *P.Touraev; P.Leid.Inst.* 13; and *P.MoscowCopt.* 56. A notable exception is the papyrus letter, n. 76, in Eugène Revillout, "Textes coptes extraits de la correspondance de St. Pésunthius, évêque de Coptos et de plusieurs documents analogues (juristique ou économique)," *Revûe Égyptologique* 12 (1914): 28, which refers to a book written on tablets (ⲡⲗⲁⲕⲏⲗⲁⲥ). Also see the commentary of *New Docs.* 7.12 for the development of the codex, and T. C. Skeat, "The Length of the Standard Papyrus Roll and the Cost-Advantage of the Codex," *ZPE* 45 (1982): 169–74.

46. *P.Touraev* notes the preparation needed before skins were ready to write on. The sender of the letter requests of his scribe, "[L]et's prepare it. Let him have ⲁⲗⲟⲩⲗⲁⲣⲉⲓ [ἀλοηδάριον]. Let him give him the skin and let him make it softer."

47. The papyrus is also discussed in John Garrett Winter, *Life and Letters in the Papyri* (Ann Arbor, 1933), 170. Interestingly enough, in the fourth century A.D. in Oxyrhynchus, one could rent half a house for a year for the same price. Roger S. Bagnall, *Currency and Inflation in Fourth-Century Egypt* (Chico, Calif., 1985), 71. See also p. 69 for two mid-fourth-century papyri, *SB* XIV.11593, which refers to three talents for a papyrus roll, and *P.Panop.* 19 ix, which refers to six talents for a roll of papyrus. For a recent study and assessment of writing materials, see T. C. Skeat, "Was Papyrus Regarded as 'Cheap' or 'Expensive' in the Ancient World?" *Aegyptus* 75 (1995): 74–93, esp. 87–90. No matter whether the cost of the papyrus was high or not, it apparently often led monks to economize and either wash out the writing and rewrite on them (see Koenen and Müller-Wiener, "Zu den Papyri," 52) or stick together the written sides of two papyri and be left with the clean ones, which they could cut and bind as they saw fit (Robinson, *Pachomian Monastic Library,* 4).

tic it is ⲭⲱⲱⲙⲉ, as we have already seen. Further, books could be described as new (καινούργιον) in Greek documents, and ⲛⲉⲃⲉⲣⲓ in Coptic ones, or as old (παλαιόν).[48] They could also be bilingual (δίγλωσσον), and if the document is composed in Coptic, then books are described as ⲛⲉⲟⲩⲉⲛⲓⲛ.[49]

Let us now turn to the material value of the early Christian book. In both hagiographical and documentary sources, books are described as highly valuable commodities. In the *Apophthegmata Patrum* we are told that apa Gelasios owned a leather Bible containing the whole of the Old and the New Testaments, worth eighteen gold coins *(nomismata)*.[50] The *Life* of St. Epiphanius recounts that the founder of the monastery bestowed forty *nomismata* toward the purchase of Christian books.[51] Although we cannot take these prices literally, they still point to the high value of books and explain how it was possible for apa Theodore of Pherme to sell his three books and make a sizeable donation to the poor.[52] Unfortunately, papyri do not provide us with very specific information about the price of books.[53]

Keeping in mind that most of the time our documents are letters written by acquaintances, if not friends, people who were aware of the finer details of their transactions and did not feel obliged to mention everything in their letters, we also have letters that mention that the scribe will be paid for his job

---

48. *O.CrumVC* 116 juxtaposes ἀρχαῖος and καθαρός, but the meaning must remain the same.

49. Secondary literature on the various book materials can be found in Kenyon, " Library of a Greek," 132; Waring, "Literacies of Lists," 176–77; Coquin, "Catalogue," 220; and Winlock and Crum, *Monastery of Epiphanius,* 186–90.

50. *Apophthegmata Patrum,* Gelasios 1 (*PG* 65:145B–C), in Ward, *Sayings of the Desert Fathers,* 46.

51. See Ruzena Dostálová, "Der 'Bücherkatalog' Pap.Wess.Gr.Prag.I.13 im Rahmen der Nachrichten über Bücher aus frühchristlicher Zeit," *Byzantina* 13 (1985): 542. Also see Wortley, *John Moschos,* 110, where the price of the New Testament written on parchment ("extremely fine skins") is given at "three pieces of gold."

52. *Apophthegmata Patrum,* Theodoros of Pherme 1 (*PG* 65:188A), in Ward, *Sayings of the Desert Fathers,* 73.

53. This is a large topic, worth a whole article in itself, and one that I am hoping to tackle in the future. My current observations are drawn from the following papyri: *P.Touraev; O.Vind.Copt.* 292; *P.Mon. Epiph.* 286; *O.CrumST* 163, 256, 318; and *P.MoscowCopt.* 56. Also see Winlock and Crum, *Monastery of Epiphanius,* 194. For recent remarks on the subject, albeit a little earlier than the period we are concerned with, see Sigrid Mratschek, *Der Briefwechsel des Paulinus von Nola* (Göttingen, 2001), 444–53. I owe this reference to Professor Wolf Liebeschuetz. Mratschek's conclusions, detailed as they might be, should be treated with caution. There are too many different cases brought together in order to draw one conclusion, namely, the price of books, and this leads to confusion. See for example p. 446, where the cost of liturgical books is compared to the payment received by a λογογράφος. These two things are obviously incompatible, especially since this λογογράφος, as the editors of the papyrus itself (*P.Lond.* IV.1433) explain, is a notary, so we can safely assume that he was being paid differently from scribes of literary texts.

but do not say how much.[54] Or a letter might mention the price but not for which book or how many books—for example, *O.Vind.Copt.* 292, which states that a monk is sending a gold *trimesion* (one-third of a gold coin) toward the payment for a book and will send the rest in the following months.[55] Another letter, *O.CrumST* 318, requests that the value of a book be ascertained. Obviously, conclusions are difficult to draw when dealing with material of this kind. One thing that can be said with certainty, though, is that, although the scribes of these books were monks who did not work for profit, books in late antiquity still cost a considerable amount of money.

Because of their worth, both intellectual and material, books were used as guarantees, as *P.Yale* inv. 413 attests. This is a Greek document of the fourth or fifth century, which reads, "And should I refuse to return Athanasius's wares to you within a year, you shall become the undisputed legal owner of the book placed in your hands."[56] Moreover, in *P.Lips.* 43, dated to the fourth century A.D., Thaesis *aeiparthenos* is taken to court and charged with the theft of Christian books left to her in an inheritance that was contested by relatives of the deceased.[57]

Stages of Production: Punctuation

At a different stage of the production of books, separate scribes might have been employed just to punctuate a book—that is, to mark it with accents—after it was copied.[58] In the *Apophthegmata* of apa Abraham, we are told that the father was commissioned to copy a book but that, because he was deep in con-

---

54. In *P.Köln* inv. 1473, the sender of the letter explains to the scribe, "begin to write for us the book on parchment; you will not make a loss [μηδὲν βλαπτόμενος]," but does not mention how much he will be paid. Also see *P.MoscowCopt.* 56 and *P.Mon.Epiph.* 286.

55. An interesting comparison arises yet again about the exceptional worth of this book, if we consider that in Oxyrhynchus in the 430s one could rent three rooms for a year for half a solidus. Bagnall, *Currency and Inflation,* 71. *O.CrumVC* 116 is also a letter of various instructions, among which we learn that they have sent Constantine's son three solidi worth of bundles for certain books, and that Cosmas has already spent two more solidi toward the books. Also see *O.CrumST* 256.

56. George M. Parássoglou, "A Book Illuminator in Byzantine Egypt," *Byzantion* 44 (1974): 363–64. On the contrary, in *P.Touraev* the commissioner of a book is to leave a *trimesion* with the scribe as a pledge.

57. See Susanna Elm, "An Alleged Book-Theft in Fourth-Century Egypt: P.Lips. 43," *Papers of the Ninth International Conference on Patristic Studies, Oxford, 1983,* ed. Elizabeth A. Livingstone (Kalamazoo, Mich., 1989): 209–15.

58. See G. W. H. Lampe, ed., *A Patristic Greek Lexicon* (Oxford, 2000), 1260, for the various meanings of the verb στίζω, including "to mark with accents."

templation, he did a very bad job, omitting whole phrases. His omissions were spotted by the monk who had the job of punctuating it.[59] The same procedure could be described in *P.Fay.* 44, which is a list of ecclesiastical books, 105 to be exact, that have been punctuated.[60] Both cases use the same verb, στίζω.

Stages of Production: Illumination[61]

Illumination was another stage of book production, usually performed by someone other than the copyist of the manuscript.[62] Documentary sources testify to the existence of specialists in this field who received a codex after it had been written and added the decorations according to the instructions of the copyist or the person who commissioned the book. *P.Yale* inv. 1318 is a small Greek text of the fourth or fifth century witnessing such an agreement: "I the presbyter Heraclius, acknowledge that I have received from you the book for illustration (τὴν βίβλον εἰς κόσμησιν), on condition that I return it to you within a month without subterfuges."[63] *P.Köln* inv. 10213 shows that commissioners could be very particular, as we have already seen in Peshot's detailed instructions for the decoration of the book, especially his admonition to "add some little ornaments to it, either a gate (πύλη) or a wheel (ⲕⲟⲧ)."[64]

Another document that deserves our attention in this discussion of manuscript illumination is *P.Fay.* 44. This list of books that have been punctuated employs various adjectives to describe the books according to whether they are written on parchment or papyrus, are in Greek, or are old or new. Among these adjectives, the term ⲡⲉⲧⲁⲗⲟⲛ is repeatedly used. It is important to note

---

59. *Apophthegmata Patrum,* Abraham 3 (PG 65:132B–C), in Ward, *The Sayings of the Desert Fathers,* 34.

60. The list opens with the following words: ⲣ̅ ⲡⲗⲟⲅⲟⲥ ⲉⲛⲉⲭⲱⲱⲙⲉ ⲛ̅ⲧⲁⲛⲥ̅ϯⲥⲓ ⲙ̅ⲙⲁⲩ.

61. For a good article on manuscript illumination with all the recent bibliography, see John Lowden, "The Transmission of 'Visual Knowledge' in Byzantium through Illuminated Manuscripts: Approaches and Conjectures," in Holmes and Waring, *Literacy, Education, and Manuscript Transmission,* 59–80.

62. Understandably, among other excesses, Pachomius warned his followers against beautifully illuminated books. "He also used to teach the brothers not to give heed to the splendor and the beauty of this world in things like good food, clothing, a cell, or a book outwardly pleasing to the eye." *The First Greek Life of Pachomius* 63, in *Pachomian Koinonia* 1:341; also see Rousseau, *Pachomius,* 81.

63. Edited in Parássoglou, "Book Illuminator in Byzantine Egypt," 364–66.

64. Gates were a common illustration/decoration in early Christian manuscripts. See Kurt Weitzmann, *Illustrations in Roll and Codex: A Study of the Origin and the Method of Text Illustration,* reprinted with addenda (Princeton, 1970): pls. 29n89; 31nn94–96; and 33n104. All these illustrations, though, have either saints depicted or passages from the Bible written under the gate. Our scribe either did not want anything as elaborate as that or he left it to the illuminator to decide.

that the term is used only in relation to the Gospels. This is a unique reference in our papyri. The editor of the list suggests that this word is used to distinguish between codex and volume. This is a rather unsatisfactory explanation, and I would propose that the word ΠΕΤΑΛΟΝ is used here to indicate illuminated manuscripts. Under Lampe's entry for πέταλον, we learn that one of its meanings is "gold leaf used for decoration."[65] In the Greek text of Exodus 28:36, the word is used to mean a gold "plate," and it is also used similarly in the Bohairic text. Thus, what we have in this list must be references to illuminated manuscripts of the Gospels, in turn pointing to a rather wealthy institution as the owner of all these books.[66]

Stages of Production: Binding

Finally, but not to imply that this was the last stage in the process of book production, binding was crucial.[67] Books could be bound before or after the text was written.[68] Sheets of unused papyrus most commonly formed the binding.[69] Some recent archaeological finds and a Coptic ostracon from the collection in the Louvre confirm that monks made bindings from unused papyrus. In a recent issue of *Egyptian Archaeology,* the discovery of a Coptic monk's workshop in the Pharaonic tomb of Amenemope was announced.[70] A monk

65. Lampe, *Patristic Greek Lexicon,* 1078.

66. Further support for this hypothesis is given by the occurrence of the term *petalon* in the *typikon* of the monastery of the Mother of God *Petritzonitissa* in Bačkovo, A.D. 1083. In a list of articles donated to the monastery, we have the mention of "icons painted on wood with gold nimbuses" *(meta petalon).* See Robert Jordan, trans., "The *Typikon* of Gregory Pakourianos for the Monastery of the Mother of God *Petrizonitissa* in Bačkovo," in *Byzantine Monastic Foundation Documents: A Complete Translation of the Surviving Founders' Typika and Testaments,* ed. John Thomas and Angela Constantinides Hero (Washington, D.C., 2000), 2:552, esp. n42.

67. For a general introduction to bookbinding in late antique Egypt, see James M. Robinson, "The Construction of the Nag Hammadi Codices," in *Essays on the Nag Hammadi Texts: In Honour of Pahor Labib,* ed. Martin Krause (Leiden, 1975), 170–90; Myriam Rosen-Ayalon, "Bookbinding," in Atiya, *Coptic Encyclopedia,* 2:407–9; the comments by Leslie S. B. MacCoull in *Coptic Documentary Papyri from the Beinecke Library (Yale University)* (Cairo, 1986), 7–8; and Ewa Wipszycka, "The Nag Hammadi Library and the Monks: A Papyrologist's Point of View," *Journal of Juristic Papyrology* 30 (2000): 183–91.

68. See Wipszycka, "Nag Hammadi Library," 189.

69. Wipszycka (ibid.) refers to the "waste paper trade" that existed in antiquity and how this was one of the ways monks could acquire the disused papyrus needed for the bindings. Unfortunately, she does not give any bibliographical references regarding this trade, and I have not been able to find any other reference to it.

70. See Ronald Tefnin, "A Coptic Workshop in a Pharaonic Tomb," *Egyptian Archaeology* 20 (2002): 6.

named Frange occupied this workshop in the seventh or early eighth century. He worked on a loom, produced leather items and ropes, and was involved in bookbinding. Long, thin bands of papyrus, still preserving one or two characters, were found on the mud floor around the loom pit, as was a fragment of cut-up parchment—all evidence of bookbinding.[71]

This occupation by monks and other ascetics is supported by the Louvre Coptic ostracon 686, a letter that asks a monk to bring his tools to repair the bands of torn books on his next visit.[72] In addition, *O.CrumVC* 104 deals with the concerns of a monk working on book bindings. The letter is rather fragmentary but well worth citing here. It reads: "The skin will be of no use for the book. I have undone the first . . . and four quaternions. Be pleased to give a fresh . . . to me. Lo, another have I not . . . to thee for it; and (please) to give me the . . . of papyrus and that I send the pieces that I have cut off. I hope that it will be suitable this time. I have undone four and have . . . them." (trans. W. E. Crum).[73]

In conclusion, the papyrological evidence relating to book production in monastic communities of late antique Egypt includes private letters, book lists, and church and monastery inventories. These sources suggests that books were made to be used privately or for the services of the monastery itself, or were sold outside the confines of that monastery to laity or other monks who had commissioned them. Our sources demonstrate various stages of both forms of production and the existence of specialized monks at each level of production. Furthermore, it is clear that women played an important role in the different procedures.

71. See preliminary discussion of the ostraca and the rest of the findings in the workshop by Anne Boud'hors and Chantal Heurtel, "The Coptic Ostraca from the Tomb of Amenemope," *Egyptian Archaeology* 20 (2002): 7–9, with a picture of the thin bands of papyrus Frange used for bookbinding on p. 8.

72. Anke-Ilona Blöbaum, "Bemerkungen zu einem koptischen Brief: Das Ostrakon Louvre N 686," in Emmel, *Ägypten und Nubien,* 2:249–56; also in Boud'hors, "L'Écriture," 66.

73. For more references to bookbinding in documentary papyri, see *P.Mon.Epiph.* 126 and 380. Also see *O.CrumST* 163, where the cost of the book does not include the binding. Finally, *O.Crum* Ad. 50 is an interesting case. It is a Coptic letter, and the sender explains that ⲡⲭⲱⲱⲙⲉ ⲁⲓⲧⲛⲟⲟⲩ ⲛⲁⲕ ⲡⲣⲡⲛⲁ [ⲛ]ⲅⲟⲧⲟⲩ ⲛⲣⲱⲁⲗ[ⲟ̂]ⲩ ⲛⲁⲓ: "I have sent the book to you, do the kindness to pierce and mark it." ⲟⲱⲧⲟ, which means "to pierce holes" (Crum, *Coptic Dictionary,* 834a and b), in all probability refers to the holes needed for the binding of the book. ⲟⲱⲁⲟ means "to mark" but also "to draw lines" (ibid., 562a), thus referring to the lines needed sometimes by scribes in order to copy the text. Could this be an instance of a codex being bound before it was written?

PART II ❧ CONSTRUCTING TEXTS

Daniel Boyarin

TALMUD AND
"FATHERS OF THE CHURCH"
Theologies and the Making of Books

One of the most dramatic and salient differences between orthodox Christianity and rabbinic Judaism as they emerge from late antiquity is the very different kinds of books that they have made by then as their definitive statements. If, we might say, the definitive library of the church at the end of late antiquity is the collection known as the Fathers of the Church, surely the definitive library of rabbinic Judaism at that time is the Babylonian Talmud. These are not only very different books but very different sorts of books in ways that are crucial to understanding the differences between the two "religions" themselves. While the Fathers of the Church consists of a collection of tracts by named authors, the Talmud is a single text with many authors (or, rather, no author). The very idea of an author seems anathema to the Babylonian Talmud. The other salient characteristic that divides the Fathers of the Church from the Babylonian Talmud is that while the former seeks *homonoia,* that is, unanimity of opinion among the named authors of its many books, the latter seems to revel in the irresolution of disagreements among its contending speakers without an authorial voice even to tell us who is right and who is wrong. In the end, it is more than anything else the form of textuality,

Some of the material here appeared in Daniel Boyarin, *Border Lines: The Partition of Judaeo-Christianity* (Philadelphia: University of Pennsylvania Press, 2004). Reprinted by permission of the University of Pennsylvania Press. Copyright © 2004 University of Pennsylvania Press.

the types of books that are made, that marks the phenomenological differences between Christian and Jewish orthodoxies at the end of late antiquity. No
small differences, to be sure, but of a very different sort from the differences
that are usually claimed for the two "religions."

It is very tempting, of course, to see in this an essential difference between
Judaism and Christianity. This highly salient difference, however, is the product in both instances of particular histories, both discursive and literary, within the two communities. Others far more qualified than I have written of the
history that produced the Fathers of the Church.[1] Here I would like to say
something preliminary about the historical processes by which the Babylonian Talmud, as the most generative document of rabbinic Judaism, received
its characteristic and generative form.

While the earlier Palestinian Talmud shares the first characteristic of the
Talmuds, namely the lack of authorship, as indeed does all of rabbinic literature, the second characteristic is specific to the later period (and perhaps different place) of the redaction of the Babylonian Talmud. Of the two Talmuds
and their differences, Jacob Neusner has written:

> The sages of the Talmud of the Land of Israel seek certain knowledge about some few, practi-
> cal things. They therefore reject—from end to beginning—the chaos of speculation, the plu-
> rality of possibilities even as to word choice; above all, the daring and confidence to address the
> world in the name, merely, of sagacity. True, the Talmud preserves the open-ended discourse of
> sages, not reduced to cut-and-dried positions. But the [Palestinian] Talmud makes decisions.[2]

While this is a lucid characterization of the difference of the two Talmuds,
I would reframe the point in a way that places the two Talmuds more clearly in diachronic relation. Rather than present the practice of the Palestinian
Talmud as a deviation, a "rejection," I would prefer to imagine that it was the
practice of the Babylonian Talmud that was constituted through a rejection—
a rejection of the desire or hope for "certain knowledge." The making of decisions, after all, is the more obvious *telos* of an intellectual endeavor, while

1. See Patrick T. R. Gray, "'The Select Fathers': Canonizing the Patristic Past," *Papers Presented to the Tenth International Conference on Patristic Studies Held in Oxford, 1987,* ed. Elizabeth A. Livingstone (Leuven, 1989), 5:21–36; Éric Rebillard, "A New Style of Argument in Christian Polemic: Augustine and the Use of Patristic Citations," *JECS* 8 (2000): 559–78; Mark Vessey, "The Forging of Orthodoxy in Latin Christian Literature: A Case Study," *JECS* 4 (1996): 495–513.
2. Jacob Neusner, *Judaism in Society: The Evidence of the Yerushalmi; Toward the Natural History of a Religion* (Atlanta, 1991), 110–11.

the "chaos of speculation" and "plurality of possibilities," the endless defer-
ral of decision that characterizes the Babylonian Talmud, is more of a *novel-
lum.*[3] Reframing the relation between the two Talmuds in this way follows
Neusner's own documentary-history approach more plausibly, with the later
"document" responding to the earlier one. This correlates well also with the
hypothesis of David Halivni, according to which the characteristic literary
forms of the Babylonian Talmud take shape in the post-Amoraic period, that
is from 450 to 650, and "point to a shift in values that transpired in Stammai-
tic times. The Amoraim generally did not preserve the argumentation and debate but only the final conclusions. For them dialectical analysis was a means
to an end, a process through which a sage could determine the normative law
or the correct explanation of a source. The Stammaim, however, valued analysis and argumentation as ends in and of themselves."[4]

I argue that the realization of the crucial role of the late redactors, these
anonymous "Stammaim," in forming the rhetorical structures of the Talmud,
in conjunction with their increasingly appreciated role in shaping the talmudic legends[5] (especially about Yavneh), and the historical insight that the institutional Yeshiva is also a product of this period,[6] provides us with a powerful historical hypothesis, and a deeply attractive historical context, for the
formation of major structures of rabbinic Judaism in the late fifth and sixth
centuries. Institution (Yeshiva), founding and instituting text (Talmud), theological innovation (indeterminacy of meaning and halakhic argument), and
practice (endless study as worship in and of itself) all come together at this
time to produce the rabbinic Judaism familiar to us down to the present day.
The Babylonian talmudic redactors were so successful in "hiding" themselves

---

3. For an exhaustive discussion of these characteristics of the Babylonian Talmud, also dating them
to the redactional level of the text but presented in a somewhat different explanatory framework, see
David Charles Kraemer, *The Mind of the Talmud: An Intellectual History of the Bavli* (New York, 1990),
with many examples as well. Christine Hayes, *Between the Babylonian and Palestinian Talmuds* (Oxford,
1997), is also very instructive in this regard.

4. Jeffrey L. Rubenstein, "The Thematization of Dialectics in Bavli Aggada," *Journal of Jewish Studies* 53, no. 2 (2002): 1, summarizing the argument of David Halivni, *Midrash, Mishnah, and Gemara: The
Jewish Predilection for Justified Law* (Cambridge, Mass., 1986), 76–104. It should be noted that Halivni's
own dating of these phenomena is slightly different from Rubenstein's adoption and adaptation of his
theory.

5. Jeffrey L. Rubenstein, *Talmudic Stories: Narrative Art, Composition, and Culture* (Baltimore,
1999); Rubenstein, "Thematization of Dialectics."

6. David M. Goodblatt, *Rabbinic Instruction in Sasanian Babylonia* (Leiden, 1975).

that they were able to retroject those patterns and make it seem as if they were a product of a "real" Yavneh of the first century.[7]

The Palestinian Talmud seems to consider it supremely important to determine the correctness of one of the views, as did apparently the earlier strata of Babylonian (Amoraic, 200–450) rabbinism as well, whereas for the Stamma of the Babylonian Talmud it is most often the case that such an apparent proof of one view is considered a difficulty *(qushia)* requiring a resolution that in fact shows that there is no resolution, for "These and these are the words of the living God" (Babylonian Talmud Eruvin 13b). David Kraemer writes, "This contrast in overall compositional preferences may be the most important difference between the Bavli [Babylonian Talmud] and the Yerushalmi [Palestinian Talmud]."[8]

The special literary character of the Babylonian Talmud has long been recognized in the scholarly literature. The great pioneer of literary analysis of the Babylonian Talmud, Abraham Weiss, wrote evocatively, "The entire essence of the talmud which we have before us says 'becoming' and 'development,' and not final redaction."[9] For Weiss, "says" here is undoubtedly metaphorical; the Talmud, against its will, as it were, bespeaks its own unfinished character. The Talmud was in reality never redacted, but only caught at an almost arbitrary moment in its becoming. I take Weiss's metaphor a little more literally: I hypothesize that the Talmud, redacted, is redacted in order to speak its entire essence as becoming and development, to enact rhetorically the openness of its own discourse, of all discourse.

Whatever the true "history" of the canonization of the Talmud, at the end of late antiquity—at the moment of the end of ancient Judeo-Christianity—two literary canons, the patristic corpus and the Talmud, come into existence, founding the two orthodoxies of medieval Christendom, the Catholic Church and rabbinic Judaism. It was then that the final form of rabbinic textuality and implicit ecclesiology, the vaunted "pluralism" of the rabbis, was

---

7. Daniel Boyarin, "The Yavneh-Cycle of the Stammaim and the Invention of the Rabbis," in *Creation and Composition: The Contribution of the Bavli Redactors (Stammaim) to the Aggada,* ed. Jeffrey L. Rubenstein (Tübingen, 2005), 256–309.

8. Kraemer, *Mind of the Talmud,* 95.

9. Abraham Weiss, "On the Literary Development of the Amoraic Sugya in Its Formative Period" [in Hebrew], in *Mehkarim ba-Talmud [Studies in Talmud]* (Jerusalem, 1975), 245, cited in Aryeh Cohen, *Rereading Talmud: Gender, Law and the Poetics of Sugyot* (Atlanta, 1998), 9.

fully instituted. However, this pluralism is pluralism only when looked at from a very particular, rabbinic insider's, perspective. When viewed in terms of the dual canonization of the textual forms of Christianity and Judaism, it—like the patristic corpus from which is otherwise so different—is a highly efficient means for the securing of "consensual" orthodoxy. I would not want my position to be interpreted, however, as either cynical or reductive. Important theological issues were at stake: the nature of a monotheistic God and God's mediation to a physical universe, and with that the status of corporeality and all that it entails.[10]

When seen, as it traditionally is, from the point of view of the Bavli—the hegemonic work for rabbinic Judaism—the practice of the Yerushalmi can seem strange and even defective. Thus Zacharias Frankel's classic observation that "[t]he Yerushalmi will frequently raise questions or objections and never supply an answer to them. This phenomenon is extremely rare in the Bavli."[11] However, when looked at from a non-Bavliocentric point of view, this translates as precisely the willingness of the Yerushalmi to declare that one opinion is wrong and another right—Neusner's "making of decisions"—while the Bavli's practice of refusal of such closure discloses the stranger and more surprising epistemology, one that I would characterize as virtually apophatic (denying the knowability of the truth or of God) with respect to the divine mind, its text, and intentions for practice as well.

Rabbinic Judaism as Stammaitic Invention

The time of this epistemic refusal, I would suggest, is somewhere in the fifth century, when "Nicaea" was finally "taking effect,"[12] and when the Babylonian Talmud was largely redacted. (A better formulation, perhaps, would regard it as a developing emanation through the fifth and sixth centuries.) What

---

10. Although there is much in my *Carnal Israel: Reading Sex in Talmudic Culture* (Berkeley and Los Angeles, 1993), that I would now change, I stand by its central insight that orientations toward the human body and thus gender and sexuality as well as nation constituted crucial phenomenological points of difference between rabbinic Judaism and orthodox Christianity as these emerged through late antiquity.

11. As paraphrased in Kraemer, *Mind of the Talmud,* 96.

12. For a very rich account of this "taking effect," see Richard Paul Vaggione, *Eunomius of Cyzicus and the Nicene Revolution* (New York, 2000), throughout and esp. 151–57.

has often been presented as an ahistorical definitive attribute, the vaunted "pluralism" of rabbinic Judaism—perhaps its most striking feature—is the product of this specific moment in history, and not a transcendental essence of rabbinic Judaism. Keith Hopkins is perhaps the only scholar who has so far even adumbrated the point that this vaunted heteroglossia of Judaism is the product of a specific history and not a transcendental essence of rabbinic Judaism, a fortiori Judaism *simpliciter,* arguing, "Unlike Judaism after the destruction of the Temple, Christianity was dogmatic and hierarchical; dogmatic, in the sense that Christian leaders from early on claimed that their own interpretation of Christian faith was the only true interpretation of the faith, and hierarchical in that leaders claimed legitimacy for the authority of their interpretation as priests or bishops." Hopkins describes this phenomenon historically: "Admittedly, individual leaders claimed that their own individual interpretation of the law was right, and that other interpretations were wrong. But systemically, at some unknown date, Jewish rabbis seem to have come to the conclusion, however reluctantly, that they were bound to disagree, and that disagreement was endemic."[13] Rather than see this as the reluctant product of a local and particularist development within Judaism, I would prefer to see it as an instance of a wider epistemic shift taking place around the Mediterranean in the relevant centuries. At approximately the same time that rabbinic Judaism was crystallizing the characteristic discursive forms of its orthodoxy—interpretative indeterminacy and endless dispute—the orthodox church was developing the discursive forms that were to characterize it as well, their nearly proverbial "dogma and hierarchy." Without, as we shall see, ascribing any particular differentiation in social structure to the two formations on the basis of this distinction, we can nevertheless point to these shifting differences as significant moments in the epistemologies and theologies of language of the two communities. These are usually taken by scholars to be unrelated developments (insofar as they are studied as developments at all), and, moreover, to represent an enormous difference at the level of sociopolitical organization. I would like to advance the notion that, opposite as these characteristics seemingly are, they can be read as sharing a common epistemic and historical context, and that so reading them will produce interesting and perhaps useful results.

13. Keith Hopkins, "Christian Number and Its Implications," *JECS* 6 (1998): 217.

This specific moment, moreover, can be illuminated by close attention to epistemic shifts within Christian discourse that can be mapped out following some very recent scholarship on the texts of the same period. Lest it be deemed a priori unlikely that discursive histories attested for the Christian world within the empire be understood as significant context for developments within Sasanian rabbinic Judaism, it needs to be remembered that Christianity held important sway within the geocultural orbit of these rabbis. As Rubenstein has already noted, "to date the rise of the Babylonian rabbinic academy to the fifth or sixth century coheres with the broader cultural climate. Hellenistic influence increased dramatically throughout Syria and northern Mesopotamia in the fifth and sixth centuries. The Church Fathers Aphrahat (d. circa 350) and Ephrem (d. 373) wrote in Syriac and exhibit a Semitic outlook; their works are largely free of the complex Christological formulations made possible by the philosophical terminology available in Greek and Latin. In the succeeding centuries the Church Fathers within the Persian empire express themselves in a thoroughly Hellenized idiom."[14] Rubenstein, moreover, suggests that these shifts are partly to be explained by the influx of "Nestorian" scholars from the Roman Empire to the Sasanian Empire after Chalcedon. Isaiah Gafni has already identified important structural parallels between the new Christian school in Nisibis and the new rabbinic Yeshivot not so very far away.[15] In the light of these precise structural and even terminological parallels between the Christian and rabbinic foundations, it becomes much more plausible to suggest common epistemic and discursive progressions as well.[16]

The successful production of the vaunted *homonoia* of post-Nicene orthodoxy entailed or was enabled by a set of textual practices. In order for the *polynoia* of the writings of pre-Nicene theologians (those accepted into the canon of the "orthodox") to be converted into a single-voiced corpus of the fathers, discursive work had to be done, providing the canonical literary objective correlative of the legendary work that Richard Lim has described.[17] Simi-

---

14. Jeffrey L. Rubenstein, *The Culture of the Babylonian Talmud* (Baltimore, 2003), 35–36.

15. Isaiah Gafni, "Nestorian Literature as a Source for the History of the Babylonian *Yeshivot*" [in Hebrew], *Tarbiz* 51 (1981–82): 571.

16. For a more developed and longer argument to this effect, see Daniel Boyarin, "Hellenism in Rabbinic Babylonia," in *The Cambridge Companion to Rabbinic Literature*, ed. Charlotte Fonrobert and Martin Jaffee (Cambridge, forthcoming).

17. Richard Lim, *Public Disputation, Power, and Social Order in Late Antiquity* (Berkeley and Los Angeles, 1994), 187–92.

larly, the production of the actual text, the book of the Babylonian Talmud, provides a canonical literary textual fact to correspond to a legendary founding, as well as the correlate to a particular (and, I would suggest, new) theology of language in rabbinic Judaism.[18] Lim adumbrated this issue when he described the transposition of Theodosius's call for "fair and open examination of the disputed matters" to a call to submission "to the views of 'those teachers who lived previous to the dissension in the church.'"[19] As Lim points out, this shift within Theodosius's own sense of how Christian truth is found and maintained "may be regarded as part of the germinating ideological justification for the patristic florilegia that would play a large role in Christian councils."[20] Examining yet another vector in the development of Christian textual practices, Éric Rebillard has cited a Western author, Vincent of Lérins, on the justification behind the florilegia: "If no council decision has dealt with the question debated, Vincent recommends that 'one collect and examine the opinions of the ancients who, although they come from different places and times, remained however in the communion and faith of the one Catholic Church, and appeared as commendable teachers. One must understand that he too can believe without doubt what has been openly, frequently, and constantly taught, written and defended not by one or two, but by all in the same way, according to one and the same consensus.'"[21] For Augustine, as Rebillard shows, it is the agreement, the consensus, of all Catholic authorities that is the measure of orthodox truth.[22] The ecclesiastical writers speak "with one heart, one voice, one faith."[23] It is riveting that Augustine actually imagines this corpus of the writings of the fathers as both an imaginary council and as a book:

18. Boyarin, "Yavneh-Cycle of the Stammaim."

19. Lim, *Public Disputation, Power, and Social Order*, 201–2, citing Socrates, *Hist. eccl.* 5.10.

20. Lim, *Public Disputation, Power, and Social Order*, 202–3. See Marcel Richard, "Les florilèges diphysites du Ve et VIe siècle," in *Das Konzil von Chalkedon: Geschichte und Gegenwart*, ed. Alois Grillmeier and Heinrich Bacht (Würzburg, 1951), 1:721–48. See also Vaggione, *Eunomius of Cyzicus*, 368: "*Akribeia's* intolerance of ambiguity made it impossible for Eunomius or his community to take any part in the controversies of the rising generation: he was now definitively a 'heretic.' He [Eunomius] and his followers were obliged to observe the theological world of the next century from the sidelines, their proper voice audible only in (heavily doctored) *florilegia*." The point is not, of course, that controversy stopped in the Nicene church but that the modes by which it was carried out were different. See immediately below on the Pelagian controversy, and the same is true, *mutatis mutandis,* of the Nestorian controversy.

21. Rebillard, "New Style of Argument," 560.   22. Ibid., 575.

23. Augustine, *Against Julian* 1.3.5, ibid., 576.

If a synod of bishops were summoned from all over the world, I wonder whether that many men of their caliber could easily be assembled. After all, these men did not live at the same time; rather, at different periods of time and in distant places, God sends, as he pleases and as he judges helpful, a few of his faithful ministers who are excellent beyond the many others. And so, you see these men gathered from different times and regions, from the East and from the West, not to a place to which human beings are forced to travel, *but in a book which can travel to them.*[24]

This citation, I think, is sufficient to evoke the fascinating similarity of the cultural world that produced the Babylonian Talmud, also a collection of the sayings of many "excellent" rabbis over centuries and in different places made into a book that travels in space and time to the faithful. And this powerful similarity also points up the enormous difference in the mode of discourse of the two new books: one voice versus many voices, but both, I warrant, in support of the "same" kind of project, the production of a bounded, concerted orthodox "religion."

Other scholars, however, have located at least the planting of the seed of these florilegia in the textual practices of the century before Theodosius and Augustine. In a brief essay published in *Studia Patristica,* as well as in a couple of unpublished works, Patrick Gray has examined the processes through which the single-voiced institution called "Fathers of the Church" was produced in the fourth century.[25] Mark Vessey has also shown the significance of the formation of a citable patristic canon, a patristic canon of citation, in the fourth century, and its contribution to the "forging of orthodoxy."[26]

Particularly evocative, however, for the current context is Virginia Burrus's examination of the formative influence of Athanasius's literary corpus in producing the textual practices of fourth-century and later Christian orthodoxy, the modes of its discourse, its *habitus.* Positioning her mediation in relation to Lim's claim that it is with the death of the last "eye-witness," Athanasius, that the "legends about Nicaea began to emerge,"[27] Burrus writes: "Athanasius's death marked the *end* of a crucial phase in the *literary* invention of Nicaea; and, furthermore, the layered inscription of his 'historical' or 'apologet-

24. Ibid., 2.10.37, emphasis added. See also on this Mark Vessey, "*Opus Imperfectum:* Augustine and His Readers, 426–435 A.D.," *VC* 52 (1998): 271.

25. Gray, "Select Fathers."

26. Vessey, "Forging of Orthodoxy."

27. Lim, *Public Disputation, Power, and Social Order,* 186.

ic' texts—resulting in his retroactive construction of a virtual archive for the council—contributed heavily to the creation of a documentary habit that was, as Lim and others have demonstrated, crucial to the success of the late antique council in producing 'consensual' orthodoxy."[28] By substituting "end" for "beginning" and "literary" for "legendary," Burrus both supports Lim's argument and adds another dimension to it. She continues, "In Athanasius's texts—in his sensitivity to 'textuality' itself—we sense something of what Richard Lim describes as a late-antique trend toward a 'growing reliance on textual authority.'"[29]

Lim had emphasized that Nicaea, in contrast to other synods and councils, left no written record of its acts. Agreeing with him, Burrus shows through close readings of the Athanasian dossier on Nicaea that Athanasius, through the arrangement and redacting of materials, documentary and otherwise, produced ex post facto virtual *acta* for "his" council. Burrus's reading allows us to perceive that Athanasius may have made a contribution through this activity to the practice of the production of such archives and *acta* for other conciliar formations, as well as to the system of textual practices in general that constituted late ancient "patristic" orthodoxy, including especially that great late ancient Christian book of books, "The Fathers of the Church." Nicaea—the council and not only or primarily Nicene doctrine—was "invented" through the writings of Athanasius. Athanasius's literary exertions thus produced retrospectively a certain account of "Nicaea,"[30] an account that, as Burrus argues, was generative for the future history of Christian textual practices. Burrus focuses our attention on the particular form of textuality and the textual form of particular types of orthodoxy and their *habitus,* and on the correlation between those textual practices and *habitus* and the *habitus* that Lim has uncovered in his work. These literary practices (arguably centered around Athanasius, whether an Athanasius self-fashioned or fashioned by others) and their collation with the legends of Nicaea provide the richest backdrop for investigating the cognate but different relations between talmudic legends of Yavneh

28. Virginia Burrus, *"Begotten Not Made": Conceiving Manhood in Late Antiquity* (Stanford, 2000), 59, emphasis added.

29. Ibid., 56–57.

30. See also Michel René Barnes, "The Fourth Century as Trinitarian Canon," in *Christian Origins: Theology, Rhetoric, and Community,* ed. Lewis Ayres and Gareth Jones (London, 1998), 47–67.

and the textual practices that constitute the great late ancient Jewish nonbook, the Babylonian Talmud itself.

Burrus writes, "Sorting through the complicatedly intercalated writings either authored or ghostauthored or edited and published by the bishop of Alexandria [Athanasius], we observe Nicaea and its frozen Logos being produced as the cumulative effect of a series of very deliberate textual acts of self-defense, by which the armoured body of the bishop was also conceived."[31] In the even more complicatedly intercalated pseudospeech of the rabbis, as edited and published in the Babylonian Talmud,[32] a similar body, that of the rabbi, was being conceived. If, in Burrus's words, "the Alexandrian Father conceives Nicaea as the 'ecumenical' council of the Fathers who begat the immortal body of the written word," then the Talmud conceives Yavneh as the ecumenical council of fathers who transmitted the immortal (but ever-growing and shifting) body of the oral Torah. Just as Athanasius promulgated "the strikingly close identification of the divinely begotten Word with the written texts that now incarnate 'Nicaea,'"[33] so, too, did the rabbis of the Talmud closely identify their own founding text, the Mishnah, and their own commentaries on it with the divinely given oral Torah. The redactors of the Talmud are the collective rabbinic Athanasius, insofar as it is he who invented "The Fathers of the Church" as a nameable literary entity. Where the ideal of the orthodox Christian "Word" was its monovocality, its many-authored texts speaking with one voice, the ideal of the classical orthodox rabbinic oral Torah as finally formulated in the Babylonian Talmud was of one many-voiced text with no author. At a time when, as Lim shows, dialectic was being increasingly demonized by Christian orthodox writers, talmudic narrators, using the same tropes and topoi—for instance, of dialecticians as "shield-bearers"[34]—were raising forever unresolved dialectic to the highest level of religious discourse.

Just as the story of Nicaea "gives rise to the 318 conciliar 'fathers,' and also to their only begotten credal Word,"[35] the story of Yavneh gives rise to the fa-

31. Burrus, *"Begotten Not Made,"* 59.

32. It may not be entirely irrelevant to note that in the same Mesopotamian environment, the formal public debates of Manichaeans were also being recorded in writing at about the same time. Lim, *Public Disputation, Power, and Social Order,* 71.

33. Burrus, *"Begotten Not Made,"* 67.

34. See Lim, *Public Disputation, Power, and Social Order,* 119, citing Philostorgius, and cf. Babylonian Talmud Berakhot 27b.

35. Burrus, *"Begotten Not Made,"* 60.

ther rabbis[36] and their only begotten oral Torah. Yavneh was projected back into the first century, Nicaea only into the beginning of the fourth.[37] Both legendary councils claim, moreover, to have the divine truth, Yavneh its oral Torah, and Nicaea its apostolic teaching, and both authorize their claim to such truth in the same way, via a myth of apostolic succession.[38] Both are myths of foundation of an orthodoxy.[39] The Talmud itself, as the unauthored and frequently seemingly chaotic record of constant *polynoia,* is a different kind of text from both the Athanasian corpus and the monovocal "Church Fathers" that late ancient Christian orthodoxy produced. The difference in those forms of textuality is prefigured in the distinction between the exclusive orthodoxy of the end point of the Nicaea myth and the equally exclusive, divinely sanctioned heterodoxy of the end point of the Yavneh myth, embodied in the late talmudic saying "These and these are the words of the living God," which according to legend "went out" at Yavneh. For all their similarities in terms of the exercise of power, these two theologies of language were distinctly different in the kinds of books, the very notion of the book and the author, that they produced.

In an insightful and very sympathetic—if somewhat too exculpatory, I think[40]—essay on rabbinic Judaism, Rosemary Radford Ruether has described the Talmud in the following terms:

Classical Judaism, by contrast, produced a literature which looks at first sight like someone's grandmother's attic in which endless quantities of curious things which "might some day come in handy" have been passed down like so many balls of string lovingly collected over the years and piled on top of each other without apparent concern for distinctions between weighty and trivial matters. It is only with the greatest difficulty that those accustomed to systematic modes of thought, logical progression, and hierarchical ordering can adjust themselves to the discursive and unsystematic style of the rabbis and begin to discern the thread

36. Referred to frequently in the literature, indeed, as "Fathers of the World." Burton L. Visotzky, *Fathers of the World: Essays in Rabbinic and Patristic Literatures* (Tübingen, 1995).

37. If, as scholars agree, it is virtually impossible to determine what "actually" happened at the very well documented Nicaea (Vaggione, *Eunomius of Cyzicus,* 52), how much more so the virtually mythic Yavneh!

38. Daniel Boyarin, "The Diadoche of the Rabbis; or, Judah the Patriarch at Yavneh," in *Jewish Culture and Society under the Christian Roman Empire,* ed. Richard Kalmin and Seth Schwartz (Leuven, 2003), 285–318.

39. Barnes, "Fourth Century as Trinitarian Canon"; Daniel Boyarin, "A Tale of Two Synods: Nicaea, Yavneh, and the Making of Orthodox Judaism," *Exemplaria* 12 (2000): 21–62.

40. As I am sure Ruether does now, as well.

of thought that underlies what appears to be random discussion and linking of themes. But gradually one comes to see that this apparent jumble of piety and trivia is the medium of the rabbinic message which is the effort to penetrate every corner of ordinary life with God's presence. This expressed itself in an innocence of most of the Christian hierarchies of being, order, and value, and in an ability to see theological meaning in details of ordinary life. The rabbis think nothing of making their most profound comments on the nature of God in the midst of discussing the uses of cheese![41]

An example of such discussion, characterized by R. Travers Herford as "dry and tedious,"[42] will exemplify Ruether's point. This text exemplifies in both its theme and its discursive method the differentiating and distinctive workings of Babylonian rabbinic orthodoxy, via the particular nature of the one and only Babylonian rabbinic book, the Talmud:

> Rabbi Abbahu taught before Rabbi Yoḥanan: Gentiles and shepherds, one does not help them out nor throw them in, but the *minim* [Jewish heretics] and the *delatores* [informers] and apostates [to paganism],[43] they would throw them in and not help them out.
>
> He said to him, but I teach: "*all* of the losses of your brother" [Deut. 22:3] to add the apostate, and you have said: they would throw them in.
>
> Remove from here "the apostates."

The text begins with Rabbi Abbahu citing a tannaitic teaching to the effect that if idol worshippers and shepherds (considered thieves) fall into a hole, one does not rescue them, but one does not push them in either, while the second category of *minim,* delators, and apostates are to be pushed into a hole and not rescued. To this Rabbi Yoḥanan objects that he has a tradition that the verse which enjoins saving lost objects of one's brother includes even brothers who are apostates,[44] so how is it possible that Jews are enjoined to endanger the apostates' lives? The answer is that apostates are to be removed

---

41. Rosemary Radford Ruether, "Judaism and Christianity: Two Fourth-Century Religions," *Sciences Religieuses/Studies in Religion* 2 (1972): 7–8.

42. R. Travers Herford, *Christianity in Talmud and Midrash* (London, 1903; reprint New York, 1978), 176. It needs to be said, moreover, that Herford's understanding of the Talmudic passage is inaccurate in several details.

43. משומד, *mešummad,* following the manuscripts. According to the brilliant interpretation of Shlomo Pines, "Notes on the Parallelism between Syriac Terminology and Mishnaic Hebrew" [in Hebrew], in *Sefer zikaron le-Yaʾakov Fridman: Kovets meḥkarim [Yaʾakov Fridman Memorial Volume]*, ed. Shlomo Pines (Jerusalem, 1974), 209–11, to the effect that a *mešummad* is one who has become a "pagan," it follows that *minim,* Jewish-Christians, are in a much worse category than Jews who have become "pagans." This is an excellent example of how muddying the categories is the greatest threat of all.

44. By virtue of the addition of the word "all."

from the list entirely. Notice that at this point in the talmudic text—the point at which the Palestinian Talmud would have stopped[45]—we have a sharp point of disagreement. Are the apostates included in the category of the worst deviants who are to be put to death, or are they in the category of "brothers," to whom one returns a lost object? Effectively, moreover, by citing the authoritative Rabbi Yoḥanan and emending Rabbi Abbahu's tradition, the hypothetical Palestinian Talmud has decided the question in favor of the latter option: apostates are indeed "brothers."

We see here the clear difference of the layers of the talmudic text and of talmudic textual practice, for the later Talmud cannot leave this conclusion alone. The Babylonian Talmud cannot, it seems, tolerate such a situation of rational resolution of a question. The text continues:

> But he could have said to him: This is talking about an apostate who eats nonkosher meats out of appetite, and that refers to an apostate who eats nonkosher meats out of spite.
>
> He thought that one who eats nonkosher meats out of spite is a *min*.
>
> For it is said: the apostate: Rav Aḥa and Ravina disagree about him. One said, an apostate out of appetite is an apostate, and for spite is a *min,* while the other said, even for spite is still an apostate, and what is a *min?;* someone who worships an idol [i.e., a Jew who worships an idol]. [Avoda Zara 26b]

Here we are back in the world of clean and unclean meats, as Origen had put it.[46] The Talmud asks: Why did Rabbi Abbahu so readily accede to the emendation of his text in response to Rabbi Yoḥanan's objection? He had a better way out. He could have said that there are two kinds of apostates. In the case of the one who eats nonkosher meats out of appetite, we still consider him a "brother" and we rescue his lost object, and a fortiori his person, but an apostate who eats nonkosher meats demonstratively, to "spite," to make a religious point—that is the one whom we not only do not redeem but indeed endanger. To this the answer is that Rabbi Yoḥanan was of the opinion that such a one who eats nonkosher meats in order to spite the Jewish Torah is not an apostate but a *min.* The Talmud backs up this point by citing an amoraic (later

45. That is, we don't actually have a Palestinian parallel, but given the general style of the Palestinian Talmud, the pericope would have ended here. There is a chronological and geographical break, moreover, between this part of the pericope, which is early and Palestinian, and the continuation, which is later and Babylonian, so my conjecture has a further foundation.

46. *Contra Celsum* 3.11, *Origen: Contra Celsum,* trans. Henry Chadwick (Cambridge, 1953; reprint 1965), 134–35.

rabbinic, in this case Babylonian) argument as to the definition of the apostate and the *min*.

The tannaitic text projects a clear hierarchy of "evildoers." Gentiles and shepherds are obviously considered much more highly than the *minim*, the apostates, and the delators. In the course of Rabbi Yoḥanan's intervention, apostates, whatever they are, are not only raised into a higher category than the *minim* and the informers but even into a higher category than the gentiles, for the latter are neither rescued nor endangered, while the former are rescued as well. However, the most important aspect of the talmudic discussion (the *sugya*) is the new distinction it produces between the two types of apostates, a new and seemingly important category distinction not known from the earlier Palestinian text. This distinction is between apostates for appetite, the typical case being one who is desirous and sees nonkosher meat and eats it, and apostates "for spite," those who choose to disobey the laws of the Torah out of religious conviction. Now, the Talmud says, these latter are considered *minim*. In other words, *minim* are a category that is constructed ideologically, even when that ideological difference manifests itself behaviorally; it is the ideological difference that constitutes the *min*. Finally, according to one of the views of the two *amoraim*, it is an even stronger ideological difference that constitutes *minut*, namely, an improper belief in God. According to the other view, such a Christian would be considered a *min* even if she had no defects in her theological doctrine, *except for the very fact of her ideological refusal to keep the commandments, which is itself a theological statement,* and the case remains undecided.

At first glance, it would seem that the lack of resolution of such a significant question does indeed constitute an agreement to disagree, a form of epistemological pluralism. We note, however, that on either view, a person who refuses to keep the commandments for ideological reasons (e.g., Paul), whether called an apostate or a *min*, nevertheless fits into the category of those worst of deviants who are subject to righteous murder, as it were. The vaunted pluralism of the Talmud encompasses just as harsh exclusionary practices against deviants as does any earlier form of Judaism, including Christianity. Rabbi Yoḥanan, who places apostates in a very high category indeed, means, we are told, only the apostates for lust, so we take them out of the category of those to be executed, because apostates for ideology have anyway been transferred into the category of *minim*. The other position leaves the apostates, meaning the apostates for ideology, in the category of those to be executed, just not calling them *minim*. Surely to the potentially (or rather theoretically) to-be-executed ones the precise rubric under which they are being executed hardly makes a difference. Thus, while our reconstructed early—hypothetically Palestinian—*sugya* resolves the question of the status of the apostate, it does so while keeping the actual original controversy alive as a distinction that would make a difference. The Babylonian Talmud keeps a simulacrum of distinction alive, while defanging it, depriving it of any power to make a difference. It is hard to see then how Hopkins's "dogmatic and hierarchical" marks a difference of orthodox Christianity from rabbinic Judaism.

Lim describes eloquently the late fifth-century situation of orthodox textual practice:

Indeed, shedding their complexities and messiness, entire councils were reduced to icons encapsulating simple lessons. The Council of Nicaea, for example, endured as the triumph of orthodoxy and Arius's Waterloo. The number 318[47] became the canonical number of the saintly fathers who formulated the Nicene creed, the touchstone of orthodoxy, though that tally surely does not correspond exactly to the number of bishops who attended Nicaea. The power of patristic consensus exhibited in various florilegia can only be fully appreciated in light of their visual representations in Byzantine frescoes and illuminated manuscripts, in which solid phalanxes of saintly bishops in serried ranks embody the principle of *homonoia*. Against this overwhelming consensus, dissent and debate were literally swept aside.[48]

Talmudic Judaism seemingly could not be more different in its posture toward debate and disagreement than this. What must be emphasized, however, is that at one level these seeming opposites actually lead to the same point: the rejection of rational decision-making processes through dialectical investigation, the *habitus* of both earlier Christian and Jewish groups. The dual displacements of the Logos—the rabbis' by anathematizing it and the fathers' via its resurrection in the Trinity—are played out as well in the dual and parallel but different strategies for defanging logos in human discourse. If post-Nicene orthodox Christianity bound the Logos to heaven (the full transcendentalizing of the Son), the late ancient rabbis broke it (the tablets have been smashed, and the Torah is not in heaven). In both cases, there results what might be

---

47. Significantly, the number equals the number of Abraham's retainers in Genesis 14.
48. Lim, *Public Disputation, Power, and Social Order*, 227.

called a certain apophatic theology of the Divine Voice. Humans, paradoxically, have lost the power to discover truth through *ratio* and dialectic. The distinction between binding and breaking the Logos, however, seems to be a theological distinction that makes an epistemic difference. The volubility of human voices that issued from these different strategies of depriving disputation of its power to produce truth led to significant contrasts in the modes of textuality, the kinds of books that would be made, within the two religious cultures, the two orthodoxies that emerged triumphant, each in its own (unequal) sphere at the end of late antiquity.

Catherine Burris

THE SYRIAC *BOOK OF WOMEN*
Text and Metatext

A sixth-century Syriac manuscript currently in the British Library preserves a collection of texts that includes the stories of four notable women of
Jewish scripture—Ruth, Esther, Susanna, and Judith—and the story of Thecla, a disciple of Paul and almost a martyr.[1] Its title is *Ktâbâ d-neššê*, the *Book of
Women*, and while various scholars have discussed the individual texts within
this collection, no one has discussed the collection as a whole.[2]

    I am grateful to the participants in the Early Christian Book Conference for their assorted ques-
tions, comments, and suggestions on this paper. I am also grateful to Lucas Van Rompay for first bringing the sixth-century manuscript to my attention, and for later helping me turn the paper into my current
book-length project.

    1. Add. 14,652. See W. Wright, *Catalogue of Syriac Manuscripts in the British Museum, Acquired
since the Year 1838,* 3 vols. (London, 1870–72), 2:651–2 (no. 731). The British Museum manuscripts are
now in the collection of the British Library. The Peshitta Institute has accepted Wright's paleographic
dating of the manuscript, assigning it the siglum 6f1. The left number of the siglum indicates the century, the letter the category of manuscript, and the right number differentiates manuscripts within the category. The manuscript is a unified document, written in a single sixth-century hand from beginning to
end and titled in the same hand. The folios are numbered in Coptic, and the surviving quires are marked
with letters, numbers, and Arabic words. The manuscript has suffered considerable damage; it is stained
and torn, and several leaves are missing. As a result, there are gaps in four of the five texts included. The
first text, *Ktâbâ da-R‘ut* (the Book of Ruth), lacks verses 4.2b to the end. The second text, *Ktâbâ d-(’)Es-
têr* (the Book of Esther), is missing until the middle of 1:12. *Ktâbâ d-Šušan* (the Book of Susanna) appears next; it is complete. *Ktâbâ d-Ihudit* (the Book of Judith) currently lacks 15:8 to 16:2. *Tašʿitâ d-Taqlâ
talmidtâh d-Pawlos* (the History of Thecla, disciple of Paul) ends the collection; much of the latter por-
tion of the story is lost with several missing leaves, as is any original colophon that might have appeared
at the end of the *Book of Women.*

    2. This is an important manuscript in the study of Syriac literature, providing the earliest surviving

I suggest that the *Book of Women* is more than the sum of its parts, that it does considerably more than preserve early instances of certain texts. As a deliberately created, titled collection, it is an attempt to guide reading, driven by some of the same anxieties that prompted the sort of textual emendation discussed by Kim Haines-Eitzen in Chapter 9 of this volume, but accomplished by textual activity that has more in common with that outlined by Caroline Humfress in relation to Justinian's *Digest* of Roman law. If "the Christian authority of the *Digest* was not achieved by a Christianization of the substantive principles of classical Roman jurisprudence ... [but] rather created by enveloping the hallowed classical books of the Roman jurists within a new order of texts,"[3] the *Book of Women* achieves coherence not by reconciling the disparities between the texts but by enveloping existing texts within a new context. The texts acquire new meanings in their new context, altered as the contents of the *Digest* were altered "by their copying, restructuring, and complex shuffling together."[4] The *Book of Women* reveals a strategy of reading, constructing a metatextual narrative that seeks to dictate the ways in which the component texts are understood.

This collection is a construction, not merely the appropriation of or assent to an existing collection of texts for a new use. The surviving *Book of Women*

---

texts of Ruth, Esther, and Judith, and one of the earliest texts of Susanna. See the Peshitta Institute's *List of Old Testament Peshitta Manuscripts (Preliminary Issue)* (Leiden, 1961), index 2, under each book, and the institute's seven updates to the list, published in *Vetus Testamentum*. Susanna also occurs in one other sixth-century manuscript, BL Add. 14,445. It is dated 532 and contains only Daniel, with all of the apocryphal additions. As for Thecla, while there are Coptic papyrus fragments of the *Acts of Paul and Thecla,* including one large group from a sixth-century manuscript, this collection provides the earliest nearly complete text of the *Acts of Thecla* in any language and the earliest occurrence of any sort in Syriac. For references, see Wilhelm Schneemelcher, "The Acts of Paul," in *New Testament Apocrypha,* ed. Edgar Hennecke, Wilhelm Schneemelcher, and R. McL. Wilson (Philadephia, 1965), 2:326. Although attested early and well, including references by, among others, Tertullian, Methodius of Olympus, Gregory of Nyssa, and Jerome, Thecla does not have an extensive manuscript tradition in the early period. (The most recent list of early references to Thecla is Léonie Hayne, "Thecla and the Church Fathers," *VC* 48 [1994]: 209–18.) The earliest Greek manuscript of her story is from the tenth century. Even including much later manuscripts, there are only eleven surviving Syriac texts of the *Acts of Thecla,* and three of them occur in *Books of Women.* The manuscript under discussion was used by William Wright as the basis for his edition and translation of the *Acts* in his *Apocryphal Acts of the Apostles,* 2 vols. (London, 1871). Vol. 1:128–69 provides an edition of the Syriac text; vol. 2 has an English translation of same. For further details on Syriac Thecla manuscripts, see Catherine Burris and Lucas Van Rompay, "Thecla in Syriac Christianity: Preliminary Observations," *Hugoye* 5.2 (July 2002), http://syrcom.cua.edu/Hugoye/Vol5No2/HV5N2BurrisVanRompay.html.

3. Caroline Humfress, in Chapter 7 of this volume.

4. Ibid.

must be considered a Christian document; the inclusion of a text whose title refers to "Thecla, disciple of Paul" signals as much. The question, then, is whether the author simply could have appropriated an existing Jewish *Book of Women,* in which the texts of Ruth, Esther, Susanna, and Judith already traveled together, and added Thecla to that Jewish collection.

There is little to support this possibility. The Syriac translations of Ruth and Esther were made from Hebrew, while those of Judith and Susanna were made from Greek. To date, there are no indications of such a collection in Jewish commentaries; furthermore, there is great variation in the Peshitta tradition regarding the codicological context of these texts. We do not see the consistency in presence, place, and order that we would expect if this were the reuse of an existing collection. The catalogue of Old Testament Peshitta manuscripts does give the collection a siglum, but the titled collection occurs in only three places.[5] The first is in the manuscript under discussion; the second is in a tenth-century manuscript of thirty-two quires, whose entire contents are titled *Book of Women (Ktâbâ d-neššê).* This later version includes Susanna, Esther, Judith, and Thecla and comes from the same monastery where the sixth-century manuscript was acquired for the British Museum.[6] The third instance is an eighth-century manuscript containing Esther, Judith, Thecla, and Tobit; the beginning of the manuscript is lost, so it is unclear whether the title *Book of Women* was actually applied to this group, and we cannot know what else might originally have been included in it.[7] As each of these include Thecla, there is no indication of a preexisting Jewish *Book of Women.* The occurrence of both the *Book of Illustrious Women (Ktâbâ d-neššê mšabbhâtâ),* consisting of Ruth and Susanna, and the *Book on Holy Women (Ktâbâ d-ʿal neššê*

5. See Peshitta Institute, *List,* vii and 76, and Peshitta Institute, "Peshitta Institute Communications VII," *Vetus Testamentum* 18 (1968): 128–43.

6. British Library (hereafter BL) Add. 14,447. Wright, *Catalogue of Syriac Manuscripts,* 1:98, no. 156. Peshitta list siglum 10f1. A note on the first folio states that this manuscript belonged to the convent of St. Mary Deipara (Deir al-Surian); the manuscripts were purchased as a lot from Deir al-Surian in 1843 by the Rev. H. Tattam for the British Museum. The purchase is described in Wright, *Catalogue of Syriac Manuscripts,* 3:xii–xiii.

7. Ms. Deir al-Surian 27b (Peshitta list siglum 8f1). The manuscript is mentioned in "Peshitta Institute Communications VII," *Vetus Testamentum* 18 (1968): 135, in the introduction to the book of Tobit in the Leiden Peshitta edition, and in the unpublished catalogue of Murad Kamil, "Catalogue of the Syrian Manuscripts Newly Found in the Monastery of St. Mary Deipara in the Nitrian Desert," which is an unpublished English translation ca. 1960 of an earlier Arabic catalogue. The Peshitta list supplement does not mention the presence of the Thecla text, simply inserting an ellipsis in the description of the manuscript between Judith and Tobit.

qaddišâtâ), consisting of Esther and Judith, in a complete Syriac Old Testament would be suggestive if it were not in a seventeenth-century manuscript.[8]

Instances of the four books grouped together without a title offer little more. All four occur together in five relatively early Syriac biblical manuscripts, one from the seventh century and the rest from the eleventh and twelfth centuries.[9] The seventh-century manuscript—a complete Syriac Bible—does group them together, but this alone is insufficient to posit a traditional collection of, or connection between, Ruth, Esther, Susanna, and Judith that predates the sixth-century Christian example under discussion, especially given that another, eighth-century, Syriac biblical manuscript includes all four books but does not group them together.[10] Yet another manuscript from the eighth century is more suggestive; in what survives, Ruth and Susanna are grouped together. This may be a fragment of a *Book of Women;* someone clearly took it to be such, as it was combined with the eighth-century manuscript of Esther, Judith, Thecla, and Tobit mentioned above in the fourteenth or fifteenth century, inserting the ten verses of Esther missing from the latter manuscript onto the last folio of the former[11] to make a five-part *Book of Women.* Still, this is minimal support at best for the idea of a preexisting Jewish collection of Ruth, Esther, Susanna, and Judith. Four more premodern Syriac manuscripts group Ruth, Esther, and Judith together and include Susanna with the canonical Daniel and Bel and the Dragon; they are from the tenth and eleventh centuries[12] and as such do not suggest a Jewish *Book of Women* that predates the sixth-century Christian example.[13]

As there is no evidence for a preexisting *Book of Women,* I take this to be

8. BL Egerton 704, #12 and #18; Wright, *Catalogue of Syriac Manuscripts,* 1:1–3, no. 1.

9. Peshitta list sigla: 7a1, 11m1, 11m5, 12a1, 12m2. The first two are complete Bibles; the eleventh–twelfth-century manuscripts are so-called masoretic manuscripts (thus the "m" in the sigla), containing vocalized extracts from each book.

10. Peshitta list siglum 8a1 = Paris, N.L., Syr. 341. Some scholars argue for a seventh- or even sixth-century dating.

11. Peshitta list siglum 8g1 = Deir al-Surian 27. See "Peshitta Institute Communications VII," *Vetus Testamentum* 18 (1968): 135.

12. Peshitta list sigla: 10m3, 11m2, 11m4, and 11m6. These are also so-called masoretic manuscripts.

13. We cannot know whether the sixth-century version is the exemplar, but it is the earliest example and will be treated as standing earlier in the tradition of the *Book of Women* than the versions that occur in later manuscripts. Because there *are* later versions, the collection cannot be seen as a singular, aberrant classification or categorization of the component texts. We know that the tradition of the *Book of Women* continued, and the appearance of Coptic and Arabic numbering on the folios of the sixth-century manuscript indicates that it continued to be used after its removal from Syria to Egypt, which would not

a Christian collection, formed by a deliberate selection process in which each text was chosen for a specific purpose.[14] The contents of this category of manuscripts, the use of the category, and the names used for the category and its component parts provide evidence for how the included texts may have been understood in late ancient and early Byzantine Syrian Christianity.

Regarding the contents of the category, Thecla is clearly the odd woman out in this collection. After hearing Paul preach, she leaves her mother and fiancé to follow him. She enjoys two miraculous escapes from martyrdom, and baptizes herself when Paul is reluctant to do so. Finally she leaves him to begin her own career as a teacher and holy woman. The narrative exhibits a consistent disdain for family and the social order, emphasizes ascetic values, and depicts Thecla as independent and powerful. Some of this finds echoes in the other included texts, but there is one radical and seemingly fundamental difference: she is Christian, while the four women whose stories precede hers in the collection are Jewish.

That the Thecla text is both anomalous and the final text in the collection suggests several things about the editor's intentions. In choosing to group Thecla with Ruth, Esther, Susanna, and Judith, the editor of the collection implied that a Christian figure belonged in the same category as Jewish figures, and that a patently ascetic figure belonged with four nonvirginal women whose stories only occasionally included anything that might be called ascetic practice.[15] This is parallel to, but significantly different from, the textual activity discussed by Elizabeth Clark in her recent work *Reading Renunciation.* Her work deals with the ways that early Christian writers interpreted and appropriated for their own use

---

have occurred before the first half of the ninth century, and was in use after Arabic began to replace Coptic as the language of Egypt in the tenth–eleventh centuries. This evidence of continued use, combined with the existence of later *Books of Women,* indicates that the sixth-century version is an instance of an ongoing tradition. See the discussion of the Syrian presence in Egypt in Lucas Van Rompay and Andrea Schmidt, "Takritans in the Egyptian Desert: The Monastery of the Syrians in the Ninth Century," *Journal of the Canadian Society of Syriac Studies* 1 (2001): 41–60.

14. We have insufficient evidence to differentiate between intentionality on the part of this editor, and conscious or unconscious assent to, and instantiation of, widely accepted ideas of late antique Syrian Christians; there simply is not enough specific evidence for Syria in the relevant period. For the sake of convenience, I will refer to the actions and intentions of the editor.

15. Discussed more fully below, in the description of the texts.

an apparently "underasceticized" Hebrew (and earlier Christian) past. How could Israel of the flesh, with its concern for abundant reproduction, inspire those who yearned for "Jerusalem above," where marriage and family were counted as naught? If "sacred literature" could not be rejected, only interpreted, hermeneutical strategies had to be devised.[16]

Clark emphasizes the creation of new texts from old via the medium of commentaries, seeing a process of "decontextualization and relocation"; the *Book of Women* has a function analogous to the commentaries she examines. Just as a commentary on a scriptural text became itself a new, Christian text, at the least didactic and often revered as holy in itself, this collection is a thing in itself, a Christian book that appropriates Jewish figures for Christian use. While the commentators used overt exegetical manipulation to bring Hebrew scripture into their discourses, the *Book of Women* is a more subtle manipulation of scriptural texts, constructing an implicit rather than explicit commentary on its component texts. This commentary, unlike those of Clark's exegetes, not only reads Jewish texts as Christian but also reads the Christian text in light of its companion Jewish texts.

Beyond the simple presence of the Thecla text in the collection, its placement at the end suggests that Thecla is the successor of Ruth, Esther, Susanna, and Judith, perhaps even the fulfillment or the climax of the story.[17] There is at least an implied triumphalism here, and the way in which this collection was probably read (or heard)[18] would have encouraged that structural triumphalism, and the appropriation of earlier, Jewish figures into later, Christian tradition. This collection would have been used by Christians, who were probably familiar with all of the stories included in it. This would have enabled what Matei Calinescu has termed a "double reading," consisting, "naturally, of the sequential temporal movement of the reader's mind (attention, memory, hypothetical anticipation, curiosity, involvement) along the horizontal or syntagmatic axis of the work; but it also consists of the reader's attempt to 'construct' (note the building, spatial metaphor) the text under perusal, or to perceive it

---

16. Elizabeth A. Clark, *Reading Renunciation: Asceticism and Scripture in Early Christianity* (Princeton, 1999), 177.

17. It appears last in all three of the titled volumes. The eighth-century version that includes Tobit ends with that instead but may not have been a titled collection, as discussed above. The importance of titles is discussed below.

18. For the purposes of this argument it makes little difference whether the textual object was read or heard; what matters is the experience of the sequence of narratives. I shall, for the sake of convenience, refer to "readers."

as a 'construction' with certain clearly distinguishable structural properties."[19]

The second, "constructive," element of Calinescu's double reading comes into play when the reader has special knowledge of the object being read, a "deeper engagement" with the text, such as we would expect late antique Christians to have with Hebrew scripture (and probably with Thecla).[20] They would have engaged in both a linear reading that sees a beginning and an end, or climax, and an actively interpretive reading that seeks a schema for the entire textual object. This combination would favor the perception of a teleological structure in the collection, emphasizing Thecla as the climactic figure of the larger story formed by the component texts. Subsequent experiences of the text would have further encouraged the discovery of a comprehensive theme and message in the collection, drawing Thecla into a textual conversation with her companions, one in which they too have something to say about her status and identity.

This process could only have been encouraged by the titles used in the collection, which would have tended to encourage the perception of Thecla's story as somehow equivalent to those of Ruth, Esther, Susanna, and Judith, granting her almost scriptural status. First, the title *Book of Women* elides the differences between its component figures, implying that their essential femininity is their defining feature; the "Jewishness" of the first four stories is essentially lost as the reader moves through the collection, and his or her "expectations are constantly modified in light of what he or she has just read," in a continuing process of the retrospective assignment of meaning.[21] The titles used for the component texts of the collection both differentiate Thecla from her Jewish fellow-travelers and assimilate her to them. In the sixth-century *Book of Women,* her story is called "the history of Thecla, disciple of Paul"—*Taš̌itâ d-Taqlâ talmidtâh d-Pawlos*—while each of the other women has a "book" (*Ktâbâ da-Rᶜut, Ktâbâ d-(ᶜ)Estêr,* and so on). Hers is also the only text whose title mentions another, legitimating, name. By the time of the eighth-century version, she travels with Esther, Judith, and Tobit, and all four

19. Matei Calinescu, *Rereading* (New Haven, 1993), 18–19.

20. The status of Thecla in early Syriac tradition remains unexamined; she was widely known and revered elsewhere, and probably in Syria, too. This sixth-century manuscript seems unlikely to have been her first appearance in the Syriac tradition. See Burris and Van Rompay, "Thecla in Syriac Christianity," and "Some Further Notes on Thecla in Syriac Christianity," *Hugoye* 6.2 (July 2003).

21. Calinescu, *Rereading,* 45. The alternative is that Thecla is implicitly made Jewish. If so, why retain her link to Paul? What would prompt such a reading?

have "books."[22] The tenth-century volume uses one title for Susanna, another for Esther, and yet another—"history"—for Judith and Thecla. No one gets a "book" here; only the collection itself is so named.[23]

Beyond the presumptive perceived theme of the collection, the simple use of the collection as a codicological vehicle for the included texts would have affected the ways that readers understood each text. Wolfgang Iser has discussed reading as the interaction between the structure of a text and the reader, focusing on the "blanks" in the text, the perceptual places where "the different segments and patterns of the text are to be connected even though the text itself does not say so."[24] As the reader moves through the text, these blanks produce tension between "heterogenous perspective segments," and that tension is resolved by a shifting perception of the themes of the text. Perceived themes exercise influence on, and are retroactively influenced by, the themes that succeed them,

[F]or as each theme recedes into the background of its successor, the vacancy shifts, allowing for a reciprocal transformation to take place. . . . The shifting blank is responsible for a sequence of colliding images, which condition each other in the time flow of reading. The discarded image imprints itself on its successor, even though the latter is meant to resolve the deficiencies of the former. In this respect the images hang together in a sequence, and it is by this sequence that the meaning of the text comes alive in the reader's imagination.[25]

In this system the component texts of the *Book of Women* are the "heterogenous perspective segments." In the process of moving through the collection, the reader's understanding of the themes of each text would be influenced by the themes of the other texts. She or he would construct an interpretation of the texts dependent upon the components of the collection as a whole.[26]

22. Kamil, "Catalogue of Syrian Manuscripts," 27.
23. Wright, *Catalogue of Syriac Manuscripts,* 1:98.
24. Wolfgang Iser, "Interaction between Text and Reader," in *The Reader in the Text: Essays on Audience and Interpretation,* ed. Susan R. Suleiman and Inge Crosman (Princeton, 1980), 106–19. The quotation is on p. 112, where he is speaking specifically of fiction.
25. Ibid., 118–19.
26. While nothing in the published record suggests that these textual occurrences exhibit important variations from the standard Syriac version, the manuscripts have yet to be collated, and there may in fact be significant changes to the text in aid of encouraging or discouraging certain readings of it. This would not, however, affect the larger argument offered here, that the collection itself functioned to encourage or enable certain readings. The varia do not appear to be significant; many involve the presence or absence of an enclitic pronoun or of the affixed conjunction "and," or the change from the perfect indicative to the participial form of the verb. The general practice in Wright's catalogue and the Peshitta In-

By choosing texts that came complete with a variety of interpretive baggage as a result of their scriptural status, the compiler attempted to select the register of interpretation. A register "rearranges the text in such a manner that understanding may emerge" and provides "a means of access to what is interpreted, but . . . also the framework into which the subject matter is translated."[27] So, the at least partially determined register of the *Book of Women* is "superimposed on the subject matter, the liminal space is colonized by the concepts brought to bear,"[28] and the reader's understanding of the texts is thereby guided.

In particular, I suggest that it is the reader's understanding of the Thecla text that is being guided, that the *Book of Women* is a deliberate attempt to reread the Thecla text. Each of the first four texts in the *Book of Women* serves as a control for the ways in which readers were to understand the last text. Ruth, Esther, Susanna, and Judith represent Thecla, clarifying what matters and what does not in her story. She in turn influences the ways that they are understood, just as they influence one another. Space does not permit me to detail the ways in which Thecla's story could have framed Ruth, Esther, Susanna, and Judith or how these four texts interacted; briefly, reading the other texts "through" Thecla would have highlighted themes of self-sacrifice, fidelity, and chastity (as a close equivalent to virginity), and would have emphasized the possibility of effective action by women. As a group, the texts of Ruth, Esther, Susanna, and Judith contain these themes, but all are not present in each one. Just as reading "through" Thecla would highlight such themes, reading "through" each of the others would highlight some of them.

The book of Ruth emphasizes family, marriage, childbearing, and in general the proper functioning of society. Ruth, a Moabite, is a widow, faithful and obedient to her Israelite mother-in-law even though she no longer needs to be. She marries a wealthy, generous Israelite and bears a child who is part of the line of David. All of this stands in direct opposition to Thecla's rejection of her mother and fiancé, her perpetual virginity, and her repeated clashes with

---

stitute is to note any major variations in texts in the description of the manuscript, and there are no such notes for the manuscripts under discussion here. I will nonetheless undertake the collation of the manuscripts as this project progresses. Discussion of the significance of any variation will be complicated by the fact that the sixth-century manuscript preserves the earliest examples of each of its component texts.

27. Wolfgang Iser, *The Range of Interpretation* (New York, 2000), 50, 151.

28. Ibid.

civic authorities. André Lacocque has argued that Ruth's story is a reversal of a typical betrothal narrative and thus upsets gender norms,[29] but as a foreigner her breaking of social customs is to be expected, and in the end she fills her expected role admirably, marrying and producing a son to continue her dead husband's line. If Ruth filters Thecla, then the reader would focus on Thecla's fidelity to Paul and Christ in the face of danger, and relegate the extreme ascetic elements of the story to a less prominent role.

The book of Esther also emphasizes family and the proper functioning of society. The Jewish Esther joins the harem of King Ahasuerus, wins his heart, and becomes a queen. She maintains a father-daughter relationship with the uncle who raised her, and when court machinations threaten the welfare of the Jewish people, she intervenes with the king and saves the day. The once-threatened Jews are even able to achieve bloody retribution. She remains married to the king, and she and her uncle enjoy great authority in the land. The primary idea here is the salvation of the Jewish people, enacted through the skillful use of political schemes. There is no indication that the foreign king ruling over Israel is bad; he just has bad advisors. While Lacocque argues that Esther is a subversive text, framed in opposition to the "Jerusalem establishment,"[30] that opposition is nuanced at best. She does remain a queen, married to Ahasuerus, and her actions save her people, her society. Again, this emphasis on society—Jewish and more general society—would act as a filter for Thecla, downplaying the negative role society plays in her story. With this as a filter, the reader might see Queen Tryphaena, who at one point shelters Thecla, and the women who protest Thecla's apparently imminent death as representatives of the properly functioning social order, rather than as women who step outside it.

Susanna, a chaste Jewish wife, is falsely accused of adultery by two failed seducers and is saved by the inspired intervention of Daniel. The failed seducers are Jewish elders. The emphasis is on her chastity and the elders' villainy. While we would see Susanna's chastity and Thecla's virginity as closely linked, they are distinct, and the idea that chastity is just as virtuous as virginity would serve to temper the Thecla text's emphasis on asceticism. The pointed criti-

29. André Lacocque, *The Feminine Unconventional: Four Subversive Figures in Israel's Tradition* (Minneapolis, 1990), 84–117. His "four subversive figures" are, in order, Susanna, Judith, Esther, and Ruth, but he is apparently unaware of any version of the *Book of Women*.
30. Ibid., 49–83.

cism of the elders fits with the presentation of civic officials in Thecla; the important, filtering distinction is that these elders are corrupt, not fulfilling their proper social function or role. So the authority figures who cause Thecla problems might be read as aberrant and therefore bad, rather than as socially powerful and therefore bad.

Finally, the book of Judith presents the reader with a wealthy, beautiful Jewish widow who seduces and kills the commander of the army that threatens her people when the elders of her town are helpless. She does not remarry, remains very wealthy, and enjoys great honor in the land both before and after her death. As in Esther, the important thing is the survival of her people, and she operates not only within society but at its upper echelons. This would reinforce the filtering of Thecla's interactions with the existing social order. Also, while there is a much clearer gender reversal here than in any of the previous three texts—Judith is the action hero of the piece—she acts by emphasizing and utilizing her sexuality rather than denying it. Being a woman has a positive function here. As in Esther, this might encourage us to see Queen Tryphaena and the protesting women as more important to the Thecla text than an unfiltered reading might suggest.

Thus by the time readers reached Thecla, the last character in the *Book of Women,* they already would have encountered ideas about virtuous women that were in some ways opposed to those of the Thecla text. These ideas would suggest certain understandings of the story of Thecla, understandings that downplayed or tamed certain potentially troubling aspects of the text.

We know that there were those who did find parts of the story troubling. Our earliest witness to the story of Thecla is Tertullian, in his baptismal treatise.[31] He is unhappy with women who use the story as a license to teach and to baptize. There are few other indications of specific, overt objections to Thecla's story; in fact, some Christian writers had positive things to say about her. Methodius of Olympus, Isidore of Pelusium, and Severus of Antioch all lauded her chastity.[32] Sometimes, though, admiration can mask concern. Severus, for instance, while praising her, explains in detail and at length why most women cannot and should not follow her virginal and notably independent example.[33]

31. Tertullian, *De baptismo,* 17.5 (*CCSL* 1:291–92).

32. Methodius, *Symposium* 8 (*SC* 95:200ff.); Isidore, *Letter* 1.87 (*PG* 78:244A); and Severus, *Homily* 97 (*Patrologia Orientalis* 25.1:121–38).

33. I have explored the rhetorical and exegetical devices he deploys to this end in a paper titled

Basil of Seleucia, or a contemporary imitator, wrote a *Life* of Thecla in the third quarter of the fifth century,[34] in which he changed two notable features of the story. First, he simply eliminated the scene in which Paul denies knowing Thecla and leaves her alone to face her attacker in Antioch. The second change is more involved, and more insidious. In the *Life*, we are given explanations for Thecla's actions, explanations based on accepted social norms. Thecla knows that in going to visit Paul in prison she is acting inappropriately, and so she is consumed with fear and trembling; she does not answer her accusers in the arena because it would be inappropriate for her to speak in public. Throughout, she is a good, moral girl rather than a heroine who steps outside the boundaries of her life in order to pursue a life of Christian chastity.[35]

In addition to these instances of apparent discomfort with certain potential uses of Thecla's story, a number of modern scholars have argued for other late antique receptions or understandings of Thecla's story that might have caused concern to the developing institutional church. Dennis MacDonald argued in 1983 that Thecla's story was so strongly against the empire, the city, and even the household that the author of the pastoral epistles made a deliberate attempt to counteract its radical rejection of social norms.[36] Soon thereafter, Virginia Burrus made a strong case for understanding the apocryphal acts, including the *Acts of Thecla*, as championing the creation of "a new community, in which traditional sex roles and authority roles were abolished."[37] Johannes Vorster has argued more specifically that the dominant paradigm of personhood or self in antiquity was andro- and sociocentric, and that the *Acts of Thecla* undermined those standards, suggesting the possibility of an alternative construction of personhood.[38] Most recently, Melissa Aubin, expanding on the work of Kate Cooper on the ancient romances, has suggested that the

"Imagining Thecla: Rhetorical Strategies in Severus of Antioch's 97th Cathedral Homily," in *Papers Presented at the Fourteenth International Conference on Patristic Studies Held in Oxford, 2003*, forthcoming.

34. Gilbert Dagron, *Vie et miracles de sainte Thècle: Texte grec, traduction et commentaire* (Brussels, 1978). See now on this *Life*, Scott F. Johnson, *The Life and Miracles of Thekla* (Washington, D.C., 2006).

35. Discussed in Monika Pesthy, "Thecla in the Fathers of the Church," in *The Apocryphal Acts of Paul and Thecla*, ed. Jan N. Bremmer (Kampen, 1996), 175.

36. Dennis Ronald MacDonald, *The Legend and the Apostle: The Battle for Paul in Story and Canon* (Philadelphia, 1983).

37. Virginia Burrus, *Chastity as Autonomy: Women in the Stories of the Apocryphal Acts* (Lewiston, Maine, 1987); quotation on 118.

38. Johannes N. Vorster, "Construction of Culture through the Construction of Person: The *Acts of Thecla* as an Example," in *The Rhetorical Analysis of Scripture: Essays from the 1995 London Conference*, ed. Stanley E. Porter and Thomas H. Olbricht (Sheffield, 1997), 445–75.

primary function of the Thecla story was to upset accepted gender norms.[39] What seems to be an inescapable emphasis on breaking, or at least bending, social and especially gender expectations must have been increasingly troubling as the church became ever more closely linked to the empire and ever more institutional in nature.

Syriac writers used a variety of strategies to tame this potentially troubling story. The sixth-century *Book of Women* is only one of their attempts to frame the Thecla text in a particular way, encouraging particular readings. The tenth-century *Book of Women* mentioned above may well derive from this one, but the eighth-century manuscript containing Esther, Judith, Thecla, and Tobit is either a separate framing device or an important modification of the sixth-century collection. Tobit's narrative centers on family, presenting a romantic adventure, complete with angelic intervention, that ends in marriage, procreation, and the continuation of the family line. This is strongly opposed to the ideas of virginity and cutting of family ties that play so large a role in Thecla. In Tobit the biological family is the focus of the story. While Ruth and Esther agree with the Thecla text in championing adoptive or alternative parent-child relationships, Tobit is concerned with one large extended family group. With this story in mind, the reader might tend not to see Thecla's separation from her mother and fiancé as an important positive event in her spiritual progress.

Thecla does appear in other, more predictable contexts in Syriac; we are not surprised to find her in collections of admirable Christian women. Those contexts are important as well, but I have chosen to focus on an apparently anomalous grouping in the hope of communicating a broader and more complicated picture. The *Book of Women* is one instance of an ongoing struggle to dictate acceptable understandings of Thecla's story. This struggle is only apparent when we broaden the scope of our investigations from the text itself to the contexts in which it occurs. We are all familiar with textual studies and understand the importance of discussing the changes that occur within a text in the process of transmission. By also discussing the changing manuscript contexts in which a given text occurs, we can better understand the ways that it was understood and used.

39. Melissa Aubin, "Reversing Romance? The *Acts of Thecla* and the Ancient Novel," in *Ancient Fiction and Early Christian Narrative,* ed. Ronald F. Hock, J. Bradley Chance, and Judith Perkins (Atlanta, 1998), 257–72. Aubin relies on Kate Cooper, *The Virgin and the Bride: Idealized Womanhood in Late Antiquity* (Cambridge, Mass., 1996).

PART III ⚜ PASSAGES AND PLACES

Catherine M. Chin

THROUGH THE LOOKING
GLASS DARKLY

Jerome Inside the Book

As the other papers in this volume show, the early Christian book served, in its various forms, as a means of drawing boundaries and defining Christian identities.[1] By comparison with the heightened contrast that the book could produce at the borders between imagined communities, however, what existed on either side of these boundaries—heresy, paganism, Christianity, Judaism—may begin to seem a little vague. If, for example, books could mark heresies on the early Christian ideological map simply as "Here there be dragons," how carefully, in turn, was the terrain within Christian territory explored? In this chapter I would like to consider one way in which late ancient Christians imagined the contents of books literally to constitute that terrain, and to provide them with an opportunity to enter, and chart, a Christian utopia through the act of reading. Jerome's correspondence with Paulinus of Nola offers an example of one outstanding Christian reader who understood books as imaginative "spaces" containing landscapes that the reader could enter and explore by reading. Thus Christian reading practices, at least in these letters, created a

---

1. An earlier version of this paper was read at the Duke University Department of Classical Studies/Center for Late Ancient Studies colloquium, "Paideia and Power in the Fourth Century," April 1, 2002. I would like to thank the colloquium participants for their comments and suggestions, which have much improved the work. I would also like to thank Andrew S. Jacobs, whose comments on both earlier and later versions of the paper have been most helpful.

conceptual territory for Christianity by conflating the idea of travel with the idea of reading.

Jerome's three letters from Bethlehem to the aristocrat-turned-ascetic Paulinus[2] have been studied primarily with respect to two separate themes: first, fourth-century attitudes toward pilgrimage,[3] and second, Jerome's introduction of an "art of scripture," intended to supersede non-Christian arts of all kinds.[4] The confluence of these themes in the letters is not accidental; rather, Jerome uses the language of travel in order to create an imagined Christian landscape, visible, however, only through the mediations of fragmented literary texts. That is, Jerome imagines the word-by-word or phrase-by-phrase commentary as the standard form of authoritative biblical reading, following common grammatical practice, and it is this kind of commentary that, he argues, allows the reader to enter Christian textual space most successfully. The letters valorize the reading practices involved in ancient commentary writing, making literate acts the defining gestures of Christian identity, and making the textual commentary the only "place" in which the imagined Christian landscape appears. The commentary, which inserts words and meanings between the words and phrases of the original text, signals the possibility that the original text contains space in which the reader or commentator can move. The act of reading, in this sense, entails conceptual if not physical space.

2. For an overview of Jerome's relations with Paulinus, see Stefan Rebenich, *Hieronymus und sein Kreis* (Stuttgart, 1992), 220–39; a briefer statement of the place of these letters in Jerome's life is in J. N. D. Kelly, *Jerome: His Life, Writings, and Controversies* (London, 1975), 192–94; Pierre Nautin, "Études de chronologie hiéronymienne (393–397): III. Les premières relations entre Jérome et Paulin de Nole," *REAug* 19 (1973): 213–39, is standard for the dating of the letters; cf. Dennis Trout, "The Dates of the Ordination of Paulinus of Bordeaux and of His Departure for Nola," *REAug* 37 (1991): 237–60; and Dennis Trout, *Paulinus of Nola: Life, Letters, and Poems* (Berkeley and Los Angeles, 1999), 90–101. On Paulinus as Jerome's correspondent, see also Catherine Conybeare, *Paulinus Noster: Self and Symbols in the Letters of Paulinus of Nola* (Oxford, 2000), 128–30. For the text of Jerome's letters, I have relied on the edition of Jérôme Labourt, *Saint Jérôme: Lettres,* 8 vols. (Paris, 1949–63).

3. For discussion, see especially Hillel I. Newman, "Between Jerusalem and Bethlehem: Jerome and the Holy Places of Palestine," in *Sanctity of Time and Space in Tradition and Modernity,* ed. A. Houtman, M.J.H.M. Poorthuis, and J. Schwartz (Leiden, 1998), 215–27; cf. Blake Leyerle, "Landscape as Cartography in Early Christian Pilgrimage Narratives," *Journal of the American Academy of Religion* 64 (1996): 130–32, which concentrates primarily on Jerome, *Epp.* 46 and 108; Leyerle does note, however, that in *Ep.* 58 to Paulinus, "[t]he real city to visit is, apparently, the city of the book" (132). E. D. Hunt, *Holy Land Pilgrimage in the Later Roman Empire, A.D. 312–460* (Oxford, 1982), 192–94, uses the exchange to describe the theological politics of pilgrimage during the Origenist controversy, which I shall discuss further below.

4. Especially Mark Vessey, "Conference and Confession: Literary Pragmatics in Augustine's *Apologia contra Hieronymum*," *JECS* 1 (1993): 179–85, on Jerome's "professionalizing" of Christian reading; cf.

Learning as Traveling

Language of physical space, however, is the means by which Jerome marks out conceptual space. Jerome first establishes Christian reading as a spatial practice through metaphors of travel. Letter 53 begins by comparing Paulinus's course of scriptural study to journeys undertaken by famous learned figures of Christian and pagan antiquity: Plato traveled to Sicily, Apollonius to India, and Pythagoras to Egypt;[5] Paul traveled to Jerusalem to be taught by the apostles.[6] Paulinus, then, is in good company if his study takes him away from home. The letter entreats Paulinus to "cut, rather than untying, the rope of your ship, dallying at sea."[7] While this may be, on one level, an invitation to Paulinus to travel to Palestine,[8] it is also a conflation of literal travel with the task of learning. To a certain extent, this language merely reflects an educational fact of the later Roman Empire: persons belonging to the classes for whom extensive education was an option were often expected to travel for the sake of that education. Jerome, of course, had himself traveled to Rome to study with Donatus, and given the difficulty of maintaining a teaching corps in any small town, it was common for students and teachers to cluster in larger urban centers, rendering travel necessary for anyone based outside them.[9] On the other hand, the fact that Jerome associates travel with such figures as Plato, Pythagoras, and Paul indicates that he is doing more than acknowledging travel as a sometime necessity. Instead, travel is given a highly distinguished intellectual pedigree. Paulinus is advised to "live in the midst of" his studies; and this figurative "place" of study is called the "small earthly dwelling of the heavenly kingdom."[10] Even at the outset of Jerome's correspondence with Paulinus, the attraction of travel is literary learning rather than pilgrimage.

Mark Vessey, "Ideas of Christian Writing in Late Roman Gaul" (D.Phil. diss., Oxford University, 1988), 49–56.

    5. 53.1.   6. 53.2.

    7. 53.11: et haerentis in salo naviculae funem magis praecide quam solve.

    8. This is the standard reading of *Ep.* 53, with *Ep.* 58 as Jerome's "change of mind" in the midst of the Origenist controversy. Nautin, " Études de chronologie hiéronymienne," 224–39; cf. Rebenich, *Hieronymus und sein Kreis,* 228–35. I would not argue that *Ep.* 53 does not contain an invitation, but would like to read that invitation as applying primarily to joint scriptural study, possibly but not necessarily undertaken with both parties at Bethlehem. Certainly the language of *Ep.* 53 is very different from that of *Ep.* 46, which is a clear exhortation to travel in Palestine.

    9. Cf. Robert Kaster, *Guardians of Language: The Grammarian and Society in Late Antiquity* (Berkeley and Los Angeles, 1988), 106ff.

    10. 53.10: inter haec vivere ... nonne tibi videtur iam hic in terris regni caelestis habitaculum?

The material to be learned is in turn construed as the space into which the learner moves. In 53.5, Jerome uses the story of the Ethiopian eunuch to indicate multiple levels of spatial practice: the eunuch's reading of Isaiah in his chariot suggests the simultaneity of learning and travel, but Jerome claims that the eunuch's true goal is "Jesus, who was hidden, concealed in the text."[11] The ultimate end of traveling study, in this anecdote, is the space enclosed in the book. Such spatial metaphors recur throughout Letters 53 and 58. Paul, for example, is called a "repository" of the scriptures,[12] becoming himself a space to be entered through study; Jerome also offers to "lead [Paulinus], not through Aonian mountains and the heights of Helicon . . . but through Zion and Tabor and Sinai, and the high places of scripture."[13] This configuration of learning fundamentally suggests the spatialization of knowledge; thus scripture is not merely the written word but is "Zion and Tabor and Sinai." That this description occurs in Letter 58, which is generally taken as a letter discouraging Paulinus from literally traveling to Palestine, further suggests that Jerome intends these places to be read primarily as metonyms, not for the entirety of literal Palestine but for the entirety of scripture, imagined as a holy space.

Simultaneously real and symbolic scriptural places are used in the letters to create a very different "Palestine" from the one in which Jerome himself was living at the time of the correspondence, and it is this ideal Palestine to which Jerome invites Paulinus through the act of reading.[14] Letter 53.8 lists place after place in its review of biblical books: Egypt, Judah, Israel, Assyria, Ephraim, Canaan, Edom, and Nineveh are placed side by side in Jerome's account. The juxtaposition of sites from vastly different narrative time periods without distinction of location or history collapses the entire geography of the Bible into a single collective place, in which notable places and events coexist without reference to chronology or literal possibility.[15] Even in the ostensibly "pro-

11. 53.5: *Iesum qui clausus latebat in littera.*

12. 53.3: *armarium.*

13. 58.8: *non per Aonios montes et Heliconis vertices . . . sed per Sion et Itabyrium et Sina et excelsa ducere scripturarum.*

14. On Jerome's use of biblical knowledge to "Christianize" Palestine, see Andrew S. Jacobs, "The Imperial Construction of the Jew in the Early Christian Holy Land" (Ph.D. diss., Duke University, 2001), esp. 82–100, on Jerome and the *Judaeus biblicus.*

15. Cf. Michel de Certeau, *The Writing of History,* trans. Tom Conley (New York, 1988; originally published as *L'écriture de l'histoire* [Paris, 1975]), 312, on Freud's *Moses and Monotheism:* "Through metaphor, a rhetorical means, and through ambivalence, a theoretical instrument, many things are in play in the same spot, transforming each spatial element into a volume where they intersect, and introducing the

pilgrimage" Letter 53, Jerome in Bethlehem is not offering to show to Paulinus any literal Egypt, Canaan, or Nineveh; rather, like "Zion and Tabor and
Sinai" in Letter 58, these names function metonymically to suggest an entirety
of scriptural space. This imagined country—simultaneously Egypt, Israel, and
Judah—becomes the homogenizing site of that which Jerome claims is enclosed in such scriptural *topoi,* namely, Christianity itself, since "[Christ], hidden in a mystery . . . was predestined and prefigured in the law and the prophets."[16] In other words, the list of places to which Jerome advocates traveling
does not refer exclusively to different literal places. It refers to the single object
Christ, who is accessible through spatialized text. All of Jerome's places are
markers of an essential sameness, since all of them figure an iconic Christianity. Or, perhaps more accurately, they signify an iconic "Christianicity," since
it is the elusive quality of "being Christian" that is evoked, rather than any specific set of Christian teachings or practices.[17] Thus Jerome's conflation of reading and travel serves fundamentally to suggest the goal of an ideal Christian
space enclosed in texts.

In order for Jerome to project this figural country adequately, however,
he must clearly distinguish it from the literal Holy Land, while at the same
time maintaining its connection to scriptural locations.[18] Christianicity is ab-
stracted from fourth-century Palestine most markedly in Letter 58, in which,
famously, Jerome claims that "what is praiseworthy is not to have been in Jerusalem, but to have lived rightly in Jerusalem."[19] Similarly, Jerome contrasts
the Jerusalem that was the setting for Christ's Passion with the fourth-century
city, "in which there is a court, soldiers, prostitutes, mimes, and idlers."[20] It is

---

movement of a quid pro quo (what comes in place of what?) everywhere." Michel Foucault, "Of Other
Spaces," trans. Jay Miskowiec, in *Diacritics* 16, no. 1 (1986): 25, argues that "[t]he heterotopia is capable of
juxtaposing in a single real place several spaces, several sites that are in themselves incompatible."

16. 53.4: qui, in mysterio absconditus . . . praedestinatus autem et praefiguratus in lege et prophetis.

17. The term "Christianicity" is here to be understood as analogous with Roland Barthes's use of the
term "Italianicity," "the condensed essence of everything that could be Italian," in "The Rhetoric of the Image," in his *Image, Music, Text,* trans. Stephen Heath (New York, 1977), 48. Christianicity, then, is the condensed essence of everything that could be seen as within the purview of the Christian, in this case, from
Egypt to Nineveh.

18. Cf. Gillian Clark's discussion of Augustine's clear separation of literal fifth-century Rome from
literary Rome, in Chapter 6 of this volume. Jerome is certainly not alone in his projection of idealized
landscapes for apologetic purposes.

19. 58.2: Non Hierosolymis fuisse, sed Hierosolymis bene vixisse laudandum est.

20. 58.4.

in the former that Paulinus should live, "praying alone on the Mount [of Olives] with Christ"[21] rather than seeking out the literal city. The idea that Paulinus should have as his goal the insertion of himself into scriptural narrative, and thereby into both scriptural places and the company of Christ ("hidden in the text"), sustains the spatialization of study and text while at the same time clearly indicating that such scriptural spaces are not accessible through physical travel. Letter 58 in this sense does not contradict Letter 53 but brings the idealization of scriptural space in Letter 53 to its logical conclusion. The Holy Land is best reached through reading, and the ideal space produced by reading is not the literal land of Palestine but the space of Christianicity.

Although they are not coterminous, the ideal Holy Land and literal Palestine can nevertheless be usefully linked. If Jerome is not merely caught here in an either/or dilemma on the usefulness of pilgrimage, the slippage between the literal terrain of Palestine and the conceptual space opened for Christianity in reading strongly suggests that Christianity is not pure fantasy. Reference to real sites anchors Christianity in the physically real, even if the importance of the physically real is then disavowed. By tying the metaphorical space of scriptural study to actual places, Jerome can "naturalize"[22] the idea that Christianity does, indeed, occupy space—that is, that the ideal Christian "place" is a real entity. Even in his disparaging view of fourth-century Palestine, Jerome nonetheless attempts to ground Christian reading in actual space, the better then to idealize it in fantastic space.

The concomitant Christianizing of space and spatializing of Christianity is played out in Letter 58 through Jerome's rhetoric of "wilderness."[23] Jerome advises Paulinus to live "in a small field . . . in solitude" and to "leave behind cities and their crowds."[24] The empty spaces here envisaged are themselves conflated with biblical wildernesses: Jerome appeals to the examples of Elijah and Elisha as precedents, and to the "sons of the prophets, who lived in wilderness and solitude."[25] This solitary existence will allow Paulinus to "pray alone

---

21. 58.4.   22. Barthes, "Rhetoric of the Image," 44.

23. On Jerome's use of "the desert" as a symbolic site in other work, see Patricia Cox Miller, "Jerome's Centaur: A Hyper-Icon of the Desert," *JECS* 4 (1996): 209–33; for the symbolism of the desert in other ascetic literature, see especially James Goehring, "The Encroaching Desert: Literary Production and Ascetic Space in Early Christian Egypt," *JECS* 1 (1993): 218–96.

24. 58.4: si urbibus et frequentia urbium derelicta in agello habites, et Christum quaeras in solitudine.

25. 58.5: filii prophetarum, qui habitabant in agris et solitudine.

on the mount with Jesus."[26] The trope of "wilderness" allows Jerome both to emphasize the unity of imagined Christian space with the space described in biblical texts, and at the same time to distance this space from the literal environs of Palestine, and particularly from the urban center of fourth-century Jerusalem.

The ultimate effect of the language of travel and geography in Letters 53 and 58, then, is to create a kind of Christian utopia—a hypothetical space of "pure" Christianity imperfectly mirrored in the actually existing sites of fourth-century Palestine. Christianity is configured as a conceptual place in which all scriptural sites meet,[27] its ontological reality implied through the reality of the literal places that Jerome uses to create it. This conceptual place, clearly not accessible to literal pilgrimage, becomes the "essential cipher of all possible" Christianities, the cipher "of the purest idea of" Christianity.[28] In a sense, Letters 53 and 58 are *both* attempts by Jerome to persuade Paulinus to travel to the Holy Land, but it is not the literal Holy Land to which Jerome invites him; rather, it is the imagined country of Christianity, or the utopia of Christianicity.

Ars as Spatial Strategy

Getting to Christianicity, however, requires a passage. In Jerome's letters the biblical text provides both the occasion and the means for imagining Christianity as a utopian space. The words of the book function as what Foucault has called a heterotopia,[29] that is, a really existing place or object that can project and contain an imagined space—and for which Foucault's primary example is the mirror, which projects into itself a space that inverts the mundane world.[30] Jerome's theory of textual exposition in these letters uses scrip-

---

26. 58.4: ores solus in monte cum Iesu.

27. Cf. Louis Marin, "The Frontiers of Utopia," in *Utopias and the Millenium,* ed. Krishan Kumar and Stephen Bann (London, 1993), 12: "[Utopia] offers the synthetic unity of the same and the other, of past and future, of this world and the beyond—and the frontier would be in this case the place where conflicting forces are reconciled." On utopian writing in antiquity more generally, see Doyne Dawson, *Cities of the Gods: Communist Utopias in Greek Thought* (New York, 1992), who argues (284–87) that the tropes of classical utopian theory are taken up by patristic authors in writing about monastic life. I am grateful to Jeremy M. Schott for this reference.

28. Barthes, "Rhetoric of the Image," 48.   29. Foucault, "Of Other Spaces," 24.

30. Ibid.: "The mirror is, after all, a utopia, since it is a placeless place. . . . But it is also a heteroto-

tural passages, in turn, as "mirrors" in which to posit ideal Christian space. As we have seen, Jerome uses the idea of real Palestine to ground Christianity in space, but also to superimpose on that space an ideal Holy Land accessible only through reading. The mechanism that Jerome introduces to establish this idealization and inversion is the textual commentary. Letters 53 and 58 are certainly about travel, but in both cases travel is transformed through Jerome's notion of scriptural "art," to which I now turn.

The standard etymology of *ars* in late ancient grammatical literature derived the word from Greek *aretē* and related it conceptually to *technē* and *scientia*,[31] that is, a learned skill possessed by a trained practitioner. Jerome uses this idea of an art to tie the opening of scriptural space to learned practice, arguing that Christian space is not open to just any reader but requires a specific kind of schooling. The art of scriptural exposition is introduced in Letter 53.7 with reference to Horace's *Ars poetica* and Horace's quip that even the unlearned write poetry. Despite his gesture toward poetry, Jerome's art of scripture, as theorized in these letters, is more closely related to the techniques of the *ars grammatica*.[32] Grammatical commentary in late antiquity generally took the form of a word-by-word, phrase-by-phrase, or line-by-line analysis of a text's philological, historical, scientific, religious, or philosophical content as understood by the commentator—not altogether unlike commentary today.[33] In practice, this meant the insertion of commentarial words between the words of the original text, so that, quite literally, space was created within the text in the process of commenting. Although neither Letter 53 nor Letter 58 is a commentary of this formal sort, Jerome nonetheless performs this spatializ-

---

pia in so far as the mirror does exist in reality, where it exerts a sort of counteraction on the position that I occupy."

31. See discussion in Martin Irvine, *The Making of Textual Culture: "Grammatica" and Literary Theory 350–1100* (Cambridge, 1994), 63–68.

32. Significant work has been done on the dependence of patristic exegesis on ancient grammatical writing. See especially Bernhard Neuschäfer, *Origenes als Philologe,* 2 vols. (Basel, 1987); Christoph Schäublin, *Untersuchungen zu Methode und Herkunft der antiochenischen Exegese* (Cologne, 1974); Frances Young, *Biblical Exegesis and the Formation of Christian Culture* (Cambridge, 1997). Adam Kamesar, *Jerome, Greek Scholarship, and the Hebrew Bible* (Oxford, 1993), emphasizes Jerome's dependence on Origen, Antiochene exegetes, and rabbinic method. Y.-M. Duval, "Les premiers rapports de Paulin de Nole avec Jérôme," *Studi Tardoantichi* 7 (1989): 177–216, considers the different valences of "poetry" and "exegesis" in Letter 53; cf. Vessey, "Ideas of Christian Writing," 51–54.

33. For a detailed analysis of one such commentary, and its social and ideological location, see Kaster, *Guardians of Language,* chapter 5, on Servius's commentary on the *Aeneid.*

ing task in miniature in these letters, inserting his comments between various biblical *nomina*. Where standard commentarial practice in antiquity isolated the line, line segment, or individual part of speech and surrounded it with linguistic, historical, or cultural meaning, Jerome in Letters 53 and 58 isolates the names of biblical books and figures and uses the resulting gaps between them as openings into generalized Christian meaning. Exodus is full of "mysterious and divine teachings";[34] Zephaniah "knows the secrets of the Lord";[35] and David "sounds out Christ in his lyre."[36] The names of biblical books and characters are here occasions for Jerome to project depths of meaning invisible at the text's surface. Jerome's scriptural art, like ancient grammatical work, uses the component parts of a text to open passages into extratextual meaning.

Despite its usefulness as a reading technique, however, the art of scripture presents Jerome with a serious problem: simply that the paths into the projected utopia may be mapped very differently by different readers. Hence Jerome's scathing remarks on scriptural commentators who use the same technique but with different results: "I pass over those like me, who come to the holy scriptures after learning worldly letters ... who juxtapose otherwise incongruous passages in order to make up their own meanings, as if this were some great thing, and not the faultiest teaching method of all, to distort the meaning and to force the reluctant scriptures to their bidding."[37] This is, says Jerome, a perversion of the art of scripture.[38] Jerome is not in this case simply being inconsistent: in order to ensure both the accessibility of the Christian utopia and its credibility as a "real" place with definite boundaries, the art of scripture must chart specific interpretive paths rather than claim that all ways lie open.[39] In other words, in order for Jerome to configure Christianity as a place at which one can arrive, he must also configure it as a place at which one can *not* arrive. Here again the concept of the *ars* serves Jerome's rhetorical needs. By configuring real Christianity as available primarily through technical training in the

---

34. 53.8: mysticis divinisque praeceptis. 35. Ibid.: arcanorum Domini cognitor.

36. Ibid.: Christum lyra personat.

37. 53.7: Taceo de meis similibus, qui si forte ad scripturas sanctas post seculares litteras venerint . . . , sed ad sensum suum incongrua aptant testimonia, quasi grande sit et non vitiosissimum dicendi genus depravare sententias, et ad voluntatem suam scripturam trahere repugnantem.

38. 53.7.

39. Foucault, "Of Other Spaces," 26: "In general, the heterotopic site is not freely accessible like a public place." Cf. Kaster, *Guardians of Language,* 17–31, on the exclusionary uses of grammatical training.

ars scripturarum, Jerome can introduce levels of scriptural competence that qualify (or disqualify) readers for interpretive entry. His criticism of interpreters who teach the scriptures before having learned them[40] indicates that for Jerome simple reading of the Bible is not enough; this reading must conform to certain technical standards if it is to be properly Christian.

Moreover, the art of scripture is also clearly spatialized, not merely as the physical product of written commentary but along the lines laid out in Jerome's configuration of reading as travel. Hence Jerome argues at 53.6, "it is not possible to enter into the holy scriptures without a guide to show you the path."[41] Jerome asserts his own cartographic skills for the mapping of Christian space, offering himself as Paulinus's companion on his scriptural journey.[42] The metaphor of path and guide occurs again in 58.8 and 9: "If only it were possible for me to lead such a genius, not through the Aonian mountains and the heights of Helicon, as the poets say, but through Zion and Tabor and Sinai, and the high places of scripture."[43] Paulinus must "listen to what path [he] ought to follow in the holy scriptures."[44] Jerome is effectively plotting Paulinus's route, configuring Christian space as territory difficult to chart and himself as the explorer able to chart it. Jerome's competitors, by contrast, are castigated primarily for leaving this utopian space underexplored. In Jerome's sarcastic account of wrong reading practices, "Genesis is perfectly obvious. . . . Exodus is clear. . . . Leviticus is easy."[45] Where Jerome's "art" consists in opening these texts to the scriptural traveler, and in showing readers the appropriate "paths" into the Bible, other (less knowledgeable) interpreters, he claims, leave the scriptures closed to advanced interpretation. The art of scripture is fundamentally a matter of knowledgeable travel inside the Christian utopia.

The emphasis on "opening" and "entering" may also explain Jerome's condemnation in Letter 53 of Christian *centones,* and in particular, apparently, the Cento of Proba.[46] Jerome here claims that the cento as a poetic form distorts

---

40. 53.7.

41. 53.6: in scripturis sanctis sine praevio et monstrante semitam non posse ingredi.

42. 53.10–11.

43. O si mihi liceret istius modi ingenium non per Aonios montes et Heliconis vertices, ut poetae canunt, sed per Sion et Itabyrium et Sina et excelsa ducere scripturarum . . . .

44. 58.9: ausculta paulisper quo in scripturis sanctis calle gradiaris.

45. 53.8: Videlicet manifestissima est Genesis . . . Patet Exodus . . . In promptu est Leviticus liber.

46. For discussion of the literature on Proba in relation to Jerome, see Carl P. E. Springer, "Jerome and the *Cento* of Proba," in *Papers Presented at the Eleventh International Conference on Patristic Studies*

the original meaning of texts. At first sight, the centonist practice of breaking down texts for use in new texts may seem like Jerome's own reading practice. Further, the biblical cento, as imagined by Proba, is clearly an interpretive text, in the sense that it recasts biblical narrative in Virgilian terms and Virgilian language in biblical terms, using Virgil and the Bible in tandem to come to new understandings of the meanings and possibilities of both. What the centonist does not do, however, is leave the text open for overt interpretive entry by a technician who is marked in the text as such: the joining together of passages from Homer or Virgil effectively closes off this kind of interpretive space in favor of creating an apparently new and unbroken text.

Proba, in fact, appears to reject the ideal of the commentator's self-insertion in favor of a more strictly "poetic" self-presentation in the opening lines of the cento: nullus enim labor est verbis extendere famam / atque hominum studiis parvam disquirere laudem: / Castalio sed fonte madens imitata beatos / quae sitiens hausi sanctae libamina lucis / hinc canere incipiam.[47] Jerome, for whom the visible status of the commentator is a vital part of interpretation, dismisses this poetic practice as "childish" and "a game";[48] like the schoolroom practice of composing speeches on epic themes,[49] writing *centones* is, for Jerome, not representative of an interpretive art. As noted above, Jerome's insistence on scriptural reading as an art involves the insertion of extratextual commentarial words into a text understood to be an original object whose meaning is to be extrapolated precisely through the addition of such words. Centonist practice relies, however, not on the insertion of new commentarial words but on the rearrangement of what are understood to be original words.[50] To the ex-

---

Held in Oxford, 1991, ed. Elizabeth A. Livingstone (Louvain, 1993): 5:96–105; Karla Pollmann, "Sex and Salvation in the Vergilian Cento of the Fourth Century," in *Romane Memento: Vergil in the Fourth Century,* ed. Roger Rees (London, 2004), 79–96; on Proba and the *Cento* more generally, Elizabeth A. Clark and Diane F. Hatch, *The Golden Bough, the Oaken Cross: The Virgilian Cento of Faltonia Betitia Proba* (Chico, Calif., 1981), remains fundamental, but see also the work of Danuta Shanzer, "The Anonymous Carmen contra paganos and the Date and Identity of the Centonist Proba," *REAug* 32 (1986): 232–48, and "The Date and Identity of the Centonist Proba," *Recherches Augustiniennes* 27 (1994): 75–96.

47. Lines 18–22; Clark and Hatch, *Golden Bough, Oaken Cross,* 16–17, translate this as: "It is not my task, indeed, to publicize / My fame on the strength of words, thereby / To seek some small acclaim from human favor. / But wet from the Castilian font have I, / In imitation of the blessed, and thirsting, / Drunk the offerings of the holy day. / And here I shall begin my song."

48. 53.7: puerilia . . . ludo.

49. As Quintilian recommends and describes in *Institutio oratoria* 1–2.

50. For a full study of centonist practice, see Scott McGill, *Virgil Recomposed: The Mythological and Secular Centos in Antiquity* (New York, 2005).

tent that the *ars* presupposes a separate, unoriginal set of words supplied by a "technician" rather than an author, the cento fails to be an art. The later history of Proba's Cento as a schoolroom text reflects not the rightness of Jerome's dismissal but the fact that the fragments of Virgil put together in the cento are themselves ripe for refragmentation and opening into pedagogical interpretive space.[51] Jerome, for whom the insertion of words into the interstices of fragments is the essential "artistic" act, will not allow the re-formation of fragments into "whole" texts to usurp his own commentarial art.

In contrast, Jerome's own quotations of classical authors leave texts in fragmentary form, opening rather than closing gaps in the text. When Jerome quotes a fragment of Horace to introduce the concept of a scriptural "art,"[52] the line becomes an opportunity to reinterpret Horace's "art" as a specifically Christian practice. The reinterpretation takes place in the lines surrounding the fragment—that is, in the gaps created around the fragment of Horace's text. Horace provides the fragment, but the art occurs in Jerome's insertion of his own words around the fragment. This use of the interpretive art allows even non-Christian texts to provide openings into idealized Christian space; here Jerome's words create that space in the fragmentation of a classical text. The projection of Christian space into such gaps is precisely the method Jerome prescribes for the art of scripture. The art is not coterminous with the reading of scripture per se but is defined primarily by the opening of texts onto imagined Christian space. Jerome can insist upon the fragments themselves as "non-Christian"—"nor . . . can we call Virgil a Christian without Christ"[53]— but can still use them to mark Christian space. His conversion of the *ars grammatica* into an *ars scripturarum* thus allows him to claim that the Christian "art" now completes the task of classical reading: as a technique of reading and composing, the art of scripture perfects the "Latin" linguistic arts; or, as Jerome puts it, "if you had this foundation . . . nothing would be more beautiful, nothing more learned, nothing more Latin than your works."[54] Jerome's

51. Cf. Clark and Hatch, *Golden Bough, Oaken Cross,* 98–100.

52. 53.7.

53. 53.7: ac non sic etiam Maronem sine Christo possimus dicere Christianum (despite the fact that many of Jerome's contemporaries, and certainly later Latin tradition, did grant Virgil special "Christian" status).

54. 58.9: Si haberes hoc fundamentum . . . , nihil pulchrius, nihil doctius, nihilque latinius tuis haberemus voluminibus.

confidence in the art of scripture brings even "Latinity" into the art's compass. Christian space can ultimately take over the spaces of the classical, while still preserving classical texts' original status as "non-Christian."

Closing the Frontier

Perhaps inevitably, Jerome's Christian utopia comes into sharp contrast with his experiences of day-to-day life in Palestine.[55] The open space of Christianicity created in Letters 53 and 58 is altogether closed in Letter 85, the last extant record of communication between Jerome and Paulinus.[56] Whereas in Letter 53, Jerome's enthusiastic mapping of Christian space caused him to "exceed the bounds of a [single] letter,"[57] in Letter 85 Jerome excuses himself from writing, and from finishing his commentary on Daniel, by citing the burdens of nonscriptural work: the translating of Origen's *On First Principles*,[58] and the writing of more pressing letters.[59] In contrast to the perfect Latinity Jerome promises Paulinus as a result of scriptural travel, Jerome here claims that his own Latin style is at the mercy of the shipping schedule between Palestine and Rome: "When it is time for ships to sail west, so many letters are asked of me that if I wanted to reply to them all individually I would never be able to do it. Hence it happens that I dictate whatever comes to my mouth, leaving aside the arrangement of the words and the care of a writer."[60] It is, of course, a commonplace in ancient letter writing that the writer had to compose in haste,[61] but it is precisely the blunt banality of the excuse that contrasts so strikingly with Jerome's earlier picture of a perfect style that would result from an imagined journey east. Letter 85's description of the circumstances of writing is anything but utopian.

55. On the problem of utopias and their implied dystopias, see Anthony Stephens, "The Sun State and Its Shadow: On the Condition of Utopian Writing," in *Utopias: Papers from the Annual Symposium of the Australian Academy of the Humanities,* ed. Eugene Kamenka (Melbourne, 1987), 1–19.

56. Cf. Trout, *Paulinus of Nola,* 223, who describes the letter as "formal and curt."

57. 53.9: excessisse modum epistulae; on this as a trope in ancient letter writing, see Conybeare, *Paulinus Noster,* 23–24.

58. 85.3.

59. 85.1.

60. 85.1: uno ad Occidentem tempore navigandi, tantae a me simul epistulae flagitantur, ut si cuncta ad singulos velim rescribere, occurrere nequeam. Unde accidit ut omissa compositione verborum et scribentium sollicitudine dictem, quicquid in buccam venerit.

61. Conybeare, *Paulinus Noster,* 22–24.

The abrupt closing of scriptural space[62] highlights two of the difficulties with Jerome's configuration of study as travel: first, the fundamental "otherness" implied between the traveler and the landscape[63] in which he[64] travels, and second, the resultant ambiguity as to the identity or affiliation of the traveler.[65] It is clear from Jerome's absence from the Christian utopia in Letter 85 that he is not, as it were, a permanent resident there. He has had to postpone writing his Daniel commentary,[66] and his cursory answers to Paulinus's scriptural questions appeal more to other biblical "guides" than to Jerome's own expertise.[67] The harried and overburdened Jerome of Letter 85 is decidedly not "living amongst" the scriptural texts that form the "dwelling of the heavenly kingdom on earth," as he had described them to Paulinus five years earlier. He moves instead more fitfully in and out of his ideal realm, and this movement is reflected in his reading and writing practices.

More dangerously, Jerome worries in Letter 85 that he seems to move out of Christianicity through his connections with Origenism. While it is not within the scope of this chapter to discuss Jerome's relationship to Origen in detail,[68] it is nonetheless noteworthy that Jerome here justifies his acceptance of Origen only on the basis of the art of scripture.[69] On the one hand, Jerome

62. Marin, "Frontiers of Utopia," describes utopian spaces as "constantly, unceasingly displaced, about to be inscribed at the very moment when [they are] about to be erased amidst all the real islands that travellers register."

63. Cf. Tzvetan Todorov, "The Journey and Its Narratives," trans. Alyson Waters, in *Transports: Travel, Pleasure, and Imaginative Geography, 1600–1830*, ed. Chloe Chard and Helen Langdon (New Haven, 1996), 293: "The first important feature of the travel narrative as it is unconsciously imagined by today's reader seems to be to be a certain tension (or a certain balance) between the observing subject and the observed object." Or Foucault, "Of Other Spaces," 24, on the heterotopic mirror: "it exerts a sort of counteraction on the position that I occupy. From the standpoint of the mirror I discover my absence from the place where I am since I see myself over there."

64. Jerome's traveler is imagined primarily as male; the injunction to study is to Paulinus rather than to Therasia; and Jerome seems to be averse to "learned women" as such in *Ep.* 53.7, though obviously this does not hold in all of Jerome's configurations of women and erudition. Cf. Elizabeth A. Clark, *Jerome, Chrysostom, and Friends* (Lewiston, Maine, 1979), 35–106, on the conditions of friendship between men and women for Jerome.

65. Cf. Foucault, "Of Other Spaces," 24–25, on the uses of heterotopias to mark transitions or deviances in identities.

66. 85.3, 6. On Jerome's connection from Bethlehem to Pammachius and Rome, see Rebenich, *Hieronymus und sein Kreis*, 193–207; on Jerome's use of this connection during the Origenist controversy, see Elizabeth A. Clark, *The Origenist Controversy: The Cultural Construction of an Early Christian Debate* (Princeton, 1992), 11–42.

67. 85.3: Origen; 85.5: Tertullian.

68. For this discussion, see Clark, *Origenist Controversy*, 121–51.

69. Origen is, of course, Jerome's model of scriptural practice—a modeling that at times caused

is willing, even in the midst of the controversy over Origen's orthodoxy, to refer Paulinus to Origen's exegesis of Romans 9:16; on the other, he glosses Origen's unorthodoxies not as wrong scriptural practice but as wrong "doctrine."[70] Origen the "scripture artist" is, according to Jerome, within the bounds of Christianicity, but Origen the theologian is not.[71] Jerome, himself accused of Origenism, claims to be "safe" in using Origen's scriptural practices but must strenuously distance himself from Origenist "dogma": "Do not think that I disapprove of everything that Origen has written, like some rustic fool would do . . . I only reject his bad doctrine."[72] Here the alterity of the commentator from the textual spaces he opens is again evident: both Jerome and Origen move into and out of Christian space depending on how closely they follow the art of scripture. The art places the reader within the bounds of Christianicity, while other reading practices are less certain. "Being Christian," then, is a decidedly tenuous matter, depending as it does on the use of a literary process that continuously suggests the potential gap between the practitioner and the practice. Jerome's Christian utopia is a nice place to visit, but it is ultimately impossible to live there.

Jerome's last surviving words to Paulinus are thanks for the small hood Paulinus has sent as a gift,[73] "small in cloth but great in love [*textura breve, caritate latissimum*], good for warming an old man's head."[74] It is tempting to read in these lines a further apology for the brevity of Letter 85, itself small in its "text" and perhaps great in its love, but I would also like to refer these words to the reading practices that are the theme of the correspondence as a whole. Jerome has argued throughout that "smallness" in a text can signify much larger meaning, and indeed that it is the obligation of the well-trained reader to look for this signification. By using the language of travel, Jerome creates an image of scriptural exegesis as the exploration of a utopian Christian space contained

---

Jerome acute discomfort. Cf. especially Mark Vessey, "Jerome's Origen: The Making of a Christian Literary *Persona*," in *Papers Presented at the Eleventh International Conference on Patristic Studies Held in Oxford, 1991*, ed. Elizabeth A. Livingstone (Louvain, 1993), 5:135–45.

70. 85.4: prava dogmata.

71. Cf. also *Ep.* 84.8, which praises Origen's scriptural learning, and 84.3, which several times condemns Origen's "dogma": e.g., uenenata sunt illius dogmata, aliena a scripturis sanctis.

72. 85.4: ne me putes in modum rustici balatronis cuncta Origenis reprobare quae scripsit . . . , sed tantum prava dogmata repudiare.

73. *Ep.* 53.1 also acknowledges gifts; on Paulinus' epistolary gifts, see Conybeare, *Paulinus Noster*, 26–31.

74. 85.6: palliolum textura breve caritate latissimum, senili capiti confovendo.

within the bounds of individual textual heterotopias—real sites that serve as springboards into an imagined world of pure Christian meaning.

The image, however, simultaneously implies the closeness of the scripture artist to the meaning of the text and the great distance between the commentator's and the text's "native countries." Jerome can venture into Christian space through his commentarial art, but he cannot, at least in the mundane reality of fourth-century Palestine, stay there. The art of scripture creates Christianicity, but cannot bestow it on its practitioners in the world in which they find themselves existing. The difficulty with locating the quality of "Christianness" within the space of the book is thus that, from time to time, the book will simply be closed, a circumstance that raises the question of how long the Christian reader in this world can continue to be a Christian when he ceases to be a reader. Ultimately, for all its invocation of larger meaning and of utopian, pure Christianity, in a certain sense the main practical benefit of Jerome's art of scripture, like that of Jerome's new hat, may simply be to keep the commentator's head warm.

Gillian Clark

CITY OF BOOKS

Augustine and the World as Text

The earliest and most famous portrait of Augustine, a mid-sixth-century fresco in the Lateran, may have been painted for a Christian library.[1] He sits in what looks like a butterfly chair, a stylized version of the *cathedra* used by professors and bishops. His left hand holds a scroll, as in the traditional representation of the educated man, the *mousikos aner*. His right hand rests on an open codex, another sign of learning, that lies open on a bookstand turned to face the viewer, and he too looks out at the viewer.[2] Through the centuries, illustrations and portraits have shown Augustine sitting in his book-littered study, dressed like the clerical scholars of the time and equipped with the latest in reading desks and adjustable lighting. The tradition continues. Augustine was the first saint to have a home page on the Internet. He continues to inspire innumerable books and papers and electronic resources, and secular scholars still find it very easy to identify with him.[3] They see a professor of rhetoric

1. On the use of this portrait in interpreting Augustine, see Mark Vessey, "The Demise of the Christian Writer and the Remaking of 'Late Antiquity': From H.-I. Marrou's Saint Augustine (1938) to Peter Brown's Holy Man (1983)," *JECS* 6, no. 3 (1998): 401. It was the cover illustration for the first edition of Peter Brown, *Augustine of Hippo: A Biography* (London, 1967, rev. ed. 2000).

2. Henri-Irénée Marrou, Μουσικòς άνήρ: *Étude sur les scènes de la vie intellectuelle sur les monuments funéraires romains* (Grenoble, 1937); Paul Zanker, *The Mask of Socrates: The Image of the Intellectual in Antiquity,* trans. Alan Shapiro (Berkeley and Los Angeles, 1995), 290–97, for representations of Christ, apostles, and bishops holding books. For fuller discussion of the portrait, see Karla Pollmann, *St. Augustine the Algerian* (Göttingen, 2003), 18–21.

3. On continuing interpretations of Augustine, see James J. O'Donnell, "The Next Life of

who cannot find time for research in the midst of teaching and administration (*Conf.* 6.11.18), a priest who responds to forced ordination by pleading for study leave (*Ep.* 21), a bishop who recycles his sermons in his treatises and vice versa and who takes fifteen years to produce the big book because there is always another more urgent deadline (*Ep.* 23A*.4).[4]

The big book is, of course, *City of God.* It has a strong claim to be *the* early Christian book (as distinct from the collection of books that made up the Bible), for its content, its scale, and its influence. Augustine chose to present the confrontation of Roman and Christian religion in the form of a massive book, "this huge book," he called it as he signed off (*De civ. D.* 22.30). *City of God* ranges over the moral and philosophical heritage of Greco-Roman culture, the history of the world and of God's people within it, the purpose and limitations of human society, and the distinctive teachings of Christian theology. It is the biggest book Augustine ever wrote, and in extant patristic writing there is no obvious competitor. Of all of Augustine's works, this was the most often and most carefully copied: only in the mid-twentieth century did his *Confessions* begin to overtake it in the publishing history.[5] Even the mention of *City of God* usually prompts a respectful response. The earliest known commentary on the text dates from the fourteenth century, when an Oxford Dominican, Nicolas Trevet, decided that his students needed help with the classical references. It continues, most recently in the form of a collaborative English-language commentary designed both as books and as an electronic version that can be updated and adapted for new kinds of readers.[6]

But how many people, in the fifth or the thirteenth or the early twenty-first century, have actually read *City of God,* or even some of it, as opposed to thinking that some day they really should? A letter from Augustine to Firmus (*Ep.* 2*) shows that suspicion started early. Augustine is pleased that Firmus read books 1–10 with such attention, but does not know whether he has yet read books 11–22. Firmus is surely not alone. The textual city that is *City*

Augustine," in *The Limits of Ancient Christianity: Essays on Late Antique Thought and Culture in Honor of R. A. Markus,* ed. William E. Klingshirn and Mark Vessey (Ann Arbor, 1999), 215–31.

4. For the dating, see Gerard O'Daly, *Augustine's City of God: A Reader's Guide* (Oxford, 1999), 34–35.

5. Bernardus Dombart and Alfonsus Kalb, eds., *Sancti Aurelii Augustini De civitate Dei, CCSL* 47 (Turnhout, 1955), 1:v*.

6. For Trevet, see Beryl Smalley, *English Friars and Antiquity in the Early Fourteenth Century* (Oxford, 1960). For the commentary in progress, see www.augustinecityofgod.net.

of God is, like all great cities, too much to take in. It is very big, and like Babylon as described by Herodotus (1.191), or early imperial Rome as described by Dionysius of Halicarnassus (4.13–15), it has no obvious limits. There is an overall plan, quite frequently signposted, but visitors may sometimes suspect that the plan was made after the development happened.[7] There are through routes and detours, new housing and ancient monuments, demolition and adaptation. Some parts have three stars in the tourist guides, others are generally avoided. There are also some strange byways, the result of questions Augustine had encountered in pastoral work or in debates with Manichaeans (*De civ. D.* 15.26) and of his assumption (also very recognizable to present-day scholars and teachers) that others share his delight in exegesis. Augustine had himself taught in the educational system that trained him in the classics of Latin culture, and he often asks the kind of questions, and supplies the kind of information, that his contemporary Servius thought useful for the study of Virgil.[8] Why were the beams of Noah's ark square in cross-section, and how did God ensure that there were only two fleas, male and female (*De civ. D.* 15.26–27)? After the flood, how did animals get back to islands, if they were not the kind of animals that humans look after? Was it by angelic airlift for those that could not swim (*De civ. D.* 16.7)? Many Latin translations of scripture use the word *campestria* for the fig-leaf aprons made by Adam and Eve: it means an athlete's loincloth, because athletics happen on the campus (*De civ. D.* 14.17).

Some readers find it all too much. Augustine characterized *City of God*, in the preface, with the Ciceronian tag *magnum opus et arduum* (Cicero, *Orator* 33), a phrase once translated by Robert Markus as "this great and exhausting work." Others find Augustine just too bookish, too preoccupied by reading books and by writing books about books. He wrote so much that, before machine-readable texts, it was almost impossible to survey his usage of a particular word or image; though it is not quite true that anyone who claimed to have read all his books must have been lying.[9] The proposal for the Early Christian Book Conference noted that Augustine's *Confessions* is the most famous

---

7. O'Daly, *Augustine's City of God*, 72–73.

8. Don Fowler, "The Virgil Commentary of Servius," in *The Cambridge Companion to Virgil*, ed. Charles A. Martindale (Cambridge, 1997), 73–78; Sabine MacCormack, *The Shadows of Poetry: Vergil in the Mind of Augustine* (Berkeley and Los Angeles, 1998); for Augustine as teacher of Virgil, Gillian Clark, "City of God(s): Augustine's Virgil," *Proceedings of the Virgil Society* 25 (2004): 83–94.

9. For the inscription that says this, written below Augustine's portrait in the library of Isidore of Seville, and its predecessors, see Vessey, "Demise of the Christian Writer," 378n4.

example of early Christian reading. Brian Stock's study of Augustine focused critical attention on Augustine the reader, the person who discovers himself and God through the activity of reading.[10] James O'Donnell warns that the Augustine with whom it is so easy to identify is Augustine the writer, Augustine as we meet him in his books.[11] It was Augustine who ensured, by surveying all his works in *Retractations,* that we are able to meet him in at least some of the 1,030 works listed and classified by Possidius in the *Indiculum.*[12] When he had the idea of collecting everything he now disliked in his books, he said that it would show *quam non sim acceptor personae meae,* perhaps "how far from satisfied I am with who I am." Possidius said that he was working on the *Retractations* in his last days, correcting anything that was *aliter quam sese habet ecclesiastica regula,* "divergent from the Church's rule." Possidius may have been mistaken about Augustine's reasons, but both men knew that Augustine would be known by his books.[13]

Augustine was particularly aware of *City of God* as a book, a physical object used by readers. He wrote it after years of preaching experience, and he wanted to ensure that his readers could follow a long sequence of argument. He provided signposts, summaries, and cross-references; he made a summary *(breviculus)* of the whole.[14] In book 19 he reassures readers that he has not forgotten a promise made in book 2, which was written a decade earlier (*De civ. D.* 2.21 and 19.21). Even more interesting is a sentence in book 19 (19.5) that uses the length of *City of God* as evidence for the long development of the City of God: "here we are with the nineteenth book on the City of God in our hands." The Latin phrase *versamus in manibus* can mean "I am working on book 19"; it could also remind readers that they are in action as readers, turning over the pages of book 19 and aware of how much has gone before.[15] We

---

10. Brian Stock, *Augustine the Reader* (Cambridge, Mass., 1996).

11. O'Donnell, "Next Life of Augustine."

12. *Retract.* 2.41, *in opusculorum meorum indiculo.* Goulven Madec, "Possidius de Calama et les listes des oeuvres d'Augustin," in *Titres et articulations du texte dans les oeuvres antiques,* ed. Jean-Claude Fredouille (Paris, 1997), 427–45, considers the *indiculum* of Augustine in relation to that of Possidius.

13. Aug. *Ep.* 143.2. For the date, see John Burnaby, "The 'Retractations' of St Augustine: Self-criticism or Apologia?" in *Augustinus Magister* (Paris, 1954), 1:85–92. Possidius, *Vita* 28; for the purpose of the *Vita,* see further Louis I. Hamilton, "Possidius' Augustine and Post-Augustinian Africa," *JECS* 12 (2004): 85–105.

14. On the *breviculus* and other divisions of the text, see O'Daly, *Augustine's City of God,* 277–28.

15. He may intend an allusion to Horace, *Ars P.* 269: vos exemplaria Graeca / nocturna versate manu, versate diurna.

know that they are turning pages, not unrolling a scroll, because of another letter from Augustine to Firmus (*Ep.* 1A) that demonstrates his awareness of the book as an object. He advises Firmus on how to bind the twenty-two *quaterniones* in two codices of ten and twelve books, or in five of two fives and three fours. These divisions are not merely practical: they are the basic divisions of the text. The first ten books refute the claims of Roman popular and philosophical religion, with five books for each. The later twelve books discuss the origin, development, and goal of the two cities, with four books for each.[16] Book 18, on the history of biblical Israel, is seriously overlong (but Firmus was very attentive to the reading, *Ep.* 2*.3).

So what's wrong with bookishness, preoccupation with books, awareness that you are reading or writing a book, recognition that a book is both text and a particular kind of physical object? Awareness of how you respond to what you read, and of how readers of your work might handle your book, has caused an outpouring of critical theory in the past thirty years. It is a cliché to speak of the "towering figure of Augustine" and the "massive *City of God*," but why should it matter if the tower and the textual city are built up of books? A first answer to this question starts from Augustine's engagement with another city, namely, Rome. Hostile critics or puzzled students can claim that much of *City of God* is shadowboxing. It is a clever man using his rhetorical training to set up and then demolish a construct of Rome, to confront a history that is centuries out of date and problems that no longer matter. Worse, Augustine thereby evades immediate problems in a time of crisis, in a book addressed to refugees who had seen the ravaging of a city they thought eternal. In early October 2001 my final-year students were struck by the difference between Augustine's response to the Gothic sack of Rome in A.D. 410 and the anguish they saw in every newscast. Was Rome, for Augustine, only a city of books, a construct made from the literature he had read at school? Did he just not care?

Of course he cared, as he insisted in one of the few sermons that address the sack of Rome.

---

16. See the chart in James J. O'Donnell, *Augustine* (Boston, 1985), 45. *Ep.* 1A was first published in 1939 and is printed in *CCSL* 47: iii–iv. See below for divisions into fives and fours in the work of Iamblichus.

Just don't let him talk about Rome, they've said about me: please let him keep quiet about Rome! As if I gloated, rather than praying to God and encouraging you as best I can .... Didn't we have many fellow-Christians there? Don't we still? Isn't that where a large part of the city of Jerusalem lives abroad?[17]

"The city of Jerusalem living abroad," *peregrinans,* is a scriptural image that did not need explaining to Augustine's congregation. Just as Israel lived in exile in Babylon, God's people, displaced from their homeland in heaven, live as migrants and refugees on earth, resident aliens in the Roman Empire.[18] Rome, of all cities, is full of these displaced Christians, both laity and committed religious, and full of the shrines that commemorate the great Christian dead.

Peter's body lies at Rome, they say, Paul's body lies at Rome, Lawrence's body lies at Rome, the bodies of other holy martyrs lie at Rome: but Rome is wretched, Rome is devastated: Rome is afflicted, ground down, in flames; there is so much slaughter, by starvation and epidemic and weapons.[19]

Pagans and Christians alike wanted to know why the God of the Christians had not protected the city. The answer was to be found in *the* Christian book, the scriptures.

One of Augustine's sermons now has the title *De excidio urbis,* "On the Destruction of the City."[20] This title gives a misleading impression and is most unlikely to be Augustine's own. He did not have time, at the end of his life, to revisit the texts of his letters and sermons as well as his books. His sermons were often recorded in shorthand and circulated without his knowledge, and their titles vary in manuscript collections.[21] In this case Augustine's sermon was partly, but not wholly, concerned with the Gothic sack of Rome, and he said explicitly that the city was not destroyed: he used the word *vastatio,* "rav-

17. *Serm.* 105.9 (*PL* 38.621); the complete sermon (*PL* 38.618–25) is translated by Edmund Hill in *The Works of Saint Augustine for the Twenty-First Century,* ed. John E. Rotelle, part 3, vol. 4: *Sermons on the New Testament, 94A–147A* (Brooklyn, N.Y., 1992), 88–96.

18. For Augustine's use of *peregrinatio* to mean "being away from home," not "pilgrimage," see M. A. Claussen, "*Peregrinatio* and *peregrini* in Augustine's *City of God,*" *Traditio* 46 (1991): 33–75; Gillian Clark, "Pilgrims and Foreigners: Augustine on Travelling Home," in *Travel, Communication, and Geography in Late Antiquity: Sacred and Profane,* ed. Linda Ellis and Frank Kidner (Aldershot, 2004), 149–58.

19. *Bibl.Casin.* 1.133, in *Miscellanea Agostiniana,* ed. Germain Morin, vol. 1 (Rome, 1930), 404–5.

20. See the excellent annotated translation by Margaret Atkins in *Augustine: Political Writings,* ed. E. M. Atkins and R. Dodaro (Cambridge, 2001).

21. François Dolbeau, "Les titres des sermons d'Augustin," in Fredouille, *Titres et articulations,* 447–68.

aging," not *excidium*, "destruction." He was quite right, and this is important in relation to his response. There is archaeological confirmation of burning in some areas, and there was no doubt much individual suffering, but there was no widespread destruction and the Goths were bought off after three days; they may never have intended an invasion.[22] *De excidio* starts, as Augustine's sermons usually do, from the scripture readings that the congregation had just heard: we cannot be certain how the readings for the day were chosen, but they are not the most obvious choice for a sermon on the sack of Rome.

Augustine's preaching was shaped by books, by two collections of texts (known to him as the Old and New Testaments) from very different periods and contexts. He used them as if they were as closely integrated as the poems of Virgil, drawing on one passage of scripture to interpret a word or phrase in another.[23] The first reading was from the book of Daniel, and Augustine spends at least five minutes of preaching time on the theme of Daniel, a good man and a prophet, confessing his sins. Only then does he say, "You have also heard the reading from the book of Genesis. If I am not mistaken, it made us all very attentive when Abraham asks the Lord whether if he finds fifty just individuals in the city he will spare the city for their sake, or if he will destroy the city with them in it." Augustine continues to expound Abraham's negotiation with the Lord. How about forty-five just individuals? Forty? Then (maybe ten minutes into his sermon) he acknowledges why the congregation went quiet at that point in the reading. Surely there were fifty just individuals in Rome?

Augustine sees no problem here. Either God did find enough just people in Rome and spared the city; or, if he did not spare the city, it is because he did not find enough just people. But surely it is obvious that God did not spare the city? No. Rome has not been wiped off the face of the earth like Sodom and Gomorrah; many people survived, or escaped and will return, or took refuge in holy places. True, people were taken captive, but that happened to Daniel; people were killed, but that happened to prophets and apostles and to Jesus; people were tortured, but think of the sufferings of Job. True, dreadful things have happened. "The most awful things have been reported to us:

22. Neil Christie, "Lost Glories? Rome at the End of Empire," in *Ancient Rome: The Archaeology of the Eternal City,* ed. Jon Coulston and Hazel Dodge (Oxford, 2000), 306–31.

23. On this exegetical technique, see Joseph Lienhard, "The Christian Reception of the Pentateuch: Patristic Commentaries on the Books of Moses," *JECS* 10 (2002): 373–88.

slaughter, arson, looting, murder, human torture have taken place. It is true: we have heard many reports, we have grieved about it all, we have often been in tears, it is hard for us to be comforted" (*De exc.* 3). But his audience should compare the sufferings of Job and contrast the pains of hell. The purpose of physical suffering is to test the faithful and to heal their sins, and no one is sinless. The city is its citizens, not its walls (*De exc.* 6.6): Rome is the Romans (*Serm.* 81.9). Many escaped, and the faithful who died are safe with God.

Only a handful of Augustine's extant sermons deal with the Gothic sack of Rome.[24] For him, 410–11 was the year of maximum effort to deal with the Donatist problem, not the year of the sack of Rome. In each of these sermons Rome is similarly approached through scripture and read through scripture, and the central concern is the right understanding of human suffering. Augustine dealt with the sack of Rome as he did with other human tribulation. "Tribulation" derives from *tribula,* the wooden sled, studded with sharp stones, that separated grain from chaff (*De exc.* 9); in other sermons Augustine used the image of the olive press whose *pressura* results in exhausted olive lees but also in pure gold oil (*Serm.* 19.6; 296.9–10).[25] For Augustine, the invasion of Rome is not a disaster after which the world will never be the same. It is one more instance of tribulation, to be kept in perspective by the sufferings of Job and the destruction of Sodom and Gomorrah, and to be understood both as punishment and as remedy for human sin. Cities, built environments and centers of power, last while God allows it; a vision showed the destruction of Constantinople, the Christian city (*De exc.* 7). What matters is not the fall of lofty towers and massive circuit walls, constructions of wood and stone, *lapides et ligna,* "so built that they would collapse" (*Serm.* 81.39)—it is the experience and response of individual human beings. Rome is the Romans, the people who were actually living there in 410. But what has happened to that city of the present when Augustine began, in 412, writing *City of God?*

Late antique Rome is scarcely present in Augustine's text. Rome the eternal city, *caput mundi,* "the city" that needed no further adjective or description, really is, for Augustine, a city of books. It is a heritage constructed and

<hr />

24. François Paschoud, *Roma Aeterna* (Paris, 1968), 239–45; Theodore de Bruyn, "Ambivalence within a Totalizing Discourse: Augustine's Sermons on the Sack of Rome," *JECS* 1 (1993): 405–21; Jean-Claude Fredouille, ed., *Augustin d'Hippone: Sermons sur la chute de Rome* (Turnhout, 2004).

25. On these images, see Suzanne Poque, *Le langage symbolique dans la prédication d'Augustin d'Hippone: Images héroïques* (Paris, 1984), 1:157–70.

preserved by literature. The Rome he deconstructs is made of books and of his commentary on those books. It is adorned with classical literary *spolia* just as the arch of Constantine is adorned with samples of classical art,[26] and it collapses like the wood and stone that made up the lofty towers and the massive walls of Rome. Augustine devastates this textual Rome with more precision than the Goths used in laying waste the ancient city; but he gave himself an easier task. Instead of debating with live Roman adherents of the traditional religion, he challenges Virgil's account of the gods Aeneas brought to Rome, harangues Virgil's near-contemporary Varro about his interpretations of archaic Roman cult, and mocks Roman foundation myths. In the early fifth century, why would anyone care that Rome, twelve hundred years before, was founded in fratricidal conflict by a handful of asylum seekers (*De civ. D.* 3.6, 4.5)? Augustine's letters show that he had been explicitly asked to provide a rhetorically impressive response to anti-Christian arguments (*Ep.* 138). But his response seems to be rhetoric in the bad sense, someone firing off forensic ammunition to distract attention from the real questions. It is as if Augustine is trying to return to his school days, when there were prizes on offer for representing in prose the emotions of Virgil's Juno. As he so rightly asked in *Confessions,* what is the point? *Ut quid mihi illud?* It is all smoke and wind (*Conf.* 1.17.27).

There is a first line of defense in the purpose of *City of God.* It is often described as "Augustine's response to the sack of Rome," but this is not exact. The programmatic opening sentence says that it was written to defend the city of God against those who prefer their own gods to its founder. Augustine's letters from the years 410–12 show how strongly this preference was expressed by distinguished Romans who had fled Rome and made the short sea crossing to Carthage, and in *Retractations* (2.69) he specifies that the Gothic sack made the pagans blaspheme the true God more bitterly than usual. It was the old argument: no rain, blame the Christians; in Christian times, Rome has fallen (*De civ. D.* 2.3). So there was a case for demonstrating that Roman history was a sequence of disasters, starting from the moment when Aeneas imported to Rome the gods who had failed to protect Troy (*De civ. D.* 1.2). That demonstration had to use the textual record. "I had to show, from the books in which their own authors committed to memory the history of times past,

26. Jaś Elsner, *Imperial Rome and Christian Triumph* (Oxford, 1998), 187–89.

that it was far otherwise than they think" (*De civ. D.* 4.1). There was also a case for deconstructing Rome the glorious and enduring city as it was constructed by the late antique classical curriculum.[27] Virgil describes the fall of Troy and its abandonment by the gods; Virgil proclaims Rome's divinely given mission "to spare the humbled and fight down the proud," *parcere subiectis et debellare superbos* (*Aen.* 6.853). The preface of *City* immediately confronts Virgil with the proclamation of the true God, declared in his scripture: God gives grace to the humble and resists the proud (Prov. 3:34). This is one of the citations from scripture that means most to Augustine; it echoes through his own history in *Confessions,* and here it applies to Roman history.[28]

Augustine was out to show that he shared the classical education and the cultural referents of his opponents. He too could write the Latin of five centuries ago that was the hallmark of the educated man. *City of God* is his most consciously and consistently Ciceronian work, both in content and in style. Latin-speaking schoolboys worked through Terence and Sallust and Virgil as well as Cicero, and there they all are, reinforced by Livy for the legends of the early republic and Varro for its religion.[29] So perhaps this is what "Rome" was for Augustine and his opponents, or for the worried Christians who also needed reassurance. Rome is a city of books because books are the collective memory, the "societal archive."[30] For the refugees who fled to Carthage, Rome was Cicero and Virgil, just as, for many refugees from Nazism who are still living in Britain, Germany was Goethe and Schiller, Beethoven and Brahms. Augustine argued in *De magistro* that we know the past only in and as the mind.[31] How else, then, could he engage with Roman history and religion and philosophy, except in the books that presented them most authoritatively? In the Roman imperial period Varro became the authoritative text on Roman religion precisely because there was nowhere else to look, no liturgy or sacred scripture. In a fifth-century library described by Sidonius Apollinaris, where

27. Robert Kaster, *Guardians of Language: The Grammarian and Society in Late Antiquity* (Berkeley and Los Angeles, 1988); *De civ. D.* 1.2, for the place of Virgil in education.

28. "Almost every page of the holy books proclaims 'God resists the proud and gives grace to the humble'" (*De doctrina Christiana* 3.23.33); see further James J. O'Donnell, *Augustine: Confessions* (Oxford, 1992), 2:11–12.

29. Augustine's citations are collected by Harald Hagendahl, *The Latin Fathers and the Classics: A Study on the Apologists, Jerome, and Other Christian Writers* (Gothenburg, 1958).

30. Stock, *Augustine the Reader,* 13.

31. John Rist, *Augustine: Ancient Thought Baptized* (Cambridge, 1994), 74.

pagan classics were balanced by Christian authors, Varro was paired with Augustine (Sid. Apoll. *Ep.* 2.9.4).

But there is an answer to the rhetorical question "how else?" in Augustine's own experience of the city of Rome. That was part of the furniture of his mind: he had been there, he had lived and taught and written in the city, he had expected to settle there as a teacher. Rome was exceptionally rich in buildings and monuments that were also a "societal archive" of history and religion. Augustine quoted in *City of God* Cicero's praise of Varro for making this archive accessible:

We were like foreigners in our own city [*in nostra urbe peregrinantes*], visitors who had lost their way, and your books showed us the way home, so that we could finally recognize who and where we were. You explained to us the age of our country, distinctions of times, the rules of rituals and priesthoods, how things are done in public and in private life, where regions and places are, and the names and kinds, the functions and causes, of everything human and divine. (Cic. *Acad.* 1.3.9, cited in *De civ. D.* 6.2)

Nevertheless, in Augustine's books, the absence of Rome is striking. He moved to Rome, according to the *Confessions,* because he wanted students of rhetoric who were less disruptive than the Carthage "wrecking crew" (*Conf.* 3.3.6). His friends thought the move would mean an increase in money and status, but (like all good academics) he did not mind about that, he just wanted good students (*Conf.* 5.8.14). His enemies later claimed that he was one jump ahead of arrest as a Manichaean (*Contra litteras Petiliani* 3.35.30), and Manichaeism dominates the few chapters of *Confessions* (5.8.14–12.22) that deal with Rome. The absence of Rome is the more noticeable in that Augustine's departure from Carthage for Rome is, inevitably, framed by Virgil. He does not make the allusion explicit: there is no need, because the implied readers of *Confessions* soaked up Virgil in their early youth (*poeta . . . teneris ebibitus animis, De civ. D.* 1.3) just as Augustine did. They could be expected to hear Virgil when the story's hero, at the harbor of Carthage, lies to a woman who loves him and sails off in secret to Rome, on a journey directed by God (*Conf.* 5.8.14).[32] But there is no Virgilian tour of the city such as Evander gave to Aeneas (*Aen.* 8.307–69).

Rome, when it makes a brief appearance in *Confessions,* is a place of fever

32. Clark, "City of God(s)."

and intellectual delirium. That is to say, in less dramatic language, Augustine arrives and immediately falls ill (*Conf.* 5.8.15–9.16), perhaps with the notorious Roman malaria. He continues his journey on the high road to hell, laden with the baggage of his sins. He is nursed in the house of a Manichaean hearer and associates with the Manichaean elect. Manichaean errors, counterpointed by Monica's grief, dominate his account of his time in Rome. A commentary published in 1931 has a disapproving footnote on his arrival (5.9.16): "A strange abruptness on the part of a provincial, from whom we could expect, even in a spiritual biography, a record of the impressions made on him by the capital of the Empire."[33] But Augustine records instead how he studied Academic philosophy and attended some anti-Manichaean lectures. When he finally starts to teach rhetoric (5.12.22), he learns that Rome has its hazards too. Students are polite, but they do not pay their fees. So, when (5.13.23) a request comes from Milan for the urban prefect to find a civic professor of rhetoric, Augustine uses his Manichaean contacts to get a tryout and is appointed; and so he comes to Milan, to Ambrose the bishop. This rapid narrative reflects his own: in *Confessions,* his time in Rome is literally transitional.

Augustine was in Rome in 383–84. That year saw the death of Praetextatus, consul-elect and an open supporter of the traditional religion, which had just lost much of its funding. It also saw the death of Damasus, bishop of Rome for almost twenty years, who had maximized the claims of Rome as the city of Peter and Paul and innumerable other martyrs. Damasus insisted on Rome's status in the universal and especially the Western church, and enhanced the visible Christian presence in urban Rome by martyr shrines and churches and elegant inscriptions. In 383–84 Jerome, encouraged by Damasus, was starting on what became a much more important task, the revised translation of the Latin Bible. Symmachus became urban prefect and tried to have the traditional altar of victory restored to the senate house. It was an exciting moment in the relationship of Christianity and traditional religious practice.[34] Macrobius, writing at about the time of Augustine's death, chose it as the dramatic setting for his *Saturnalia,* the great textual commemoration of Roman

33. James M. Campbell and Martin R. P. McGuire, eds., *The Confessions of St Augustine, Books I–IX (Selections)* (Englewood Cliffs, N.J., 1931; reprint Chicago, 1984), 136.

34. Praetextatus and Symmachus: Neil McLynn, *Ambrose of Milan* (Berkeley and Los Angeles, 1994), 165–66; Damasus: Dennis Trout, *Paulinus of Nola: Life, Letters and Poems* (Berkeley and Los Angeles, 1999), 42–45; and Jerome: J. N. D. Kelly, *Jerome: His Life, Writings and Controversies* (London, 1975), 86.

religion and culture as attested in classical learning and (above all) in Virgil.[35] Did Augustine also recognize the significance of the time? On the evidence of *Confessions,* he was absorbed by debate on Manichaeism.

There is nothing in Augustine's books to suggest that he toured the ancient monuments of Rome, the new basilicas, or the newly restored shrines, or that he saw Roman tradition displayed in political assembly and defiant religious ceremonial. Late fourth-century Rome, in one of Peter Brown's wonderful phrases, was a "pagan Vatican, a punctiliously protected city of great temples."[36] An anonymous "poem against pagans" claims that the people of Rome saw a prefect of the city lead a procession of senators at the games in honor of the Magna Mater. This may well have been Praetextatus in 384.[37] If so, the episode would have been a perfect target for Augustine's antipagan polemic in *City of God.* The mother of the gods with her votaries, the self-castrated *Galli* whom Varro did not plausibly explain (*De civ. D.* 7.25), is *Berecynthia mater,* the goddess with the turreted crown and progeny of gods whom Virgil used as the image of Rome and its empire (*Aen.* 6.781–87). Augustine describes how he himself, as a young man, saw the obscene ceremonial for the mother of the gods, eagerly attended by Roman senators who would not want their own mothers to see it (*De civ. D.* 2.4). Here is one of the few connections made in *City of God* between Roman religion according to Varro and Roman religion as lived late antique experience. But it was Carthage, not Rome, that supplied Augustine's experience in youth. The disgraceful ceremonies were offered to "the virgin Caelestis and Berecynthia mother of all" (2.4): the cult of Caelestis reached Rome, but Caelestis the virgin was Tanit, the guardian deity of Carthage.[38] Augustine nowhere suggests that he had seen the temples and ceremonies of the gods of Rome, or the civic monuments of the Roman glory that was supposedly owed to their protection.

Augustine made a second transitional visit to Rome, in 387, but *Confessions* does not even mention it: once again Monica and grief, this time grief for Monica's death, displace Rome from his narrative. Only his *Retractations* (1.6–

35. For December 17–19, 384, as the dramatic date of the *Saturnalia* (written ca. 431), see Alan Cameron, "The Date of Macrobius' *Saturnalia,*" *Journal of Roman Studies* 56 (1966): 25–38, at 28–29.

36. Brown, *Augustine of Hippo,* 287.

37. *Carmen adversus paganos* 103–9, ed. Theodor Mommsen, "Carmen codicis Parisini 8084," *Hermes* 4 (1870): 350–63; McLynn, *Ambrose of Milan,* 165–66.

38. G. H. Halsberghe, "Le culte de Dea Caelestis," *ANRW* 2, no. 17.4 (1984): 2203–23, esp. 2220–21.

8) show that he went from Ostia to Rome and was there long enough to write some short treatises.[39] His only mention of personal experience in Rome is a comment in one of these, *De moribus Catholicae ecclesiae,* on the organization of monastic communities: he had seen one in Milan and several in Rome (*vidi ego,* 1.33.70). That was what mattered about Rome. There are no other recollections of the city where he lived and taught and wrote for at least some months of his life: no traveler's tales, no casual mentions of "when I was in Rome," no useful contacts. One explanation is that Augustine was a provincial, with an African accent (*De ordine* 2.16.45), whose socially undistinguished career gave him no access to Italian grandees, pagan or Christian, in Rome or in Carthage.[40] But one does not need important contacts to be impressed by the heritage of a great city; and it seems that Augustine was not. There is no visible emotional impact, no acknowledged response either to the "pagan Vatican" or to the city of Peter and Paul. In the first chapters of *City of God* Augustine moves swiftly from the sack of Rome to the fall of Troy, but this is not for the poignant sense that *urbs antiqua ruit, multos dominata per annos:* "the ancient city falls that long time ruled the world."[41] It is a forensic attack on the gods of Rome, imported from a city they had failed to protect.

Rome, then, remained for Augustine a city of books, a literary construct that deluded people into preferring its gods to the founder of the most glorious city of God (*De civ. D.,* preface). Literature, like theater, displays false gods. Augustine differs from Plato (*Resp.* 379d–83c) in that he does not think theater misrepresents the gods: he thinks it represents exactly what the demonic gods of Rome want, an obscene and corrupting display (*De civ. D.* 1.31–32). These gods were credited with the triumph of Roman history and culture; Roman history and culture and religion were displayed in the "societal archive," the books of Roman authors; so Augustine attacks the books, both by direct confrontation and by displacing them from the center of attention. When *City of God* is considered as a physical object, it is immediately clear

---

39. *De quantitate animae, De moribus Manichaeorum, De moribus Catholicae ecclesiae,* and the beginning of *De libero arbitrio.*

40. McLynn, *Ambrose of Milan,* 169; argument developed in Neil B. McLynn, "Augustine's Roman Empire," in *History, Apocalypse, and the Secular Imagination: New Essays on Augustine's City of God,* ed. Mark Vessey, Karla Pollmann, and Allan D. Fitzgerald (Bowling Green, Ohio, 1999), 29–44.

41. Contrast Jerome (*Ep.* 127.12–13), who juxtaposed Virgil (*Aen.* 2.315–6 and 369) with Isaiah (15:1) and the Psalms (78:1–3). See further P. Laurence, "Rome et Jérôme: Des amours contrariés," *Revue Bénédictine* 107 (1997): 227–49.

that Augustine decenters Rome. In the two-codex division that he suggested to Firmus, the second codex includes books 11 to 22.[42] Augustine's second preface, at the beginning of book 11, declares that he has now replied to the enemies of God's city and is moving on to discuss the rise, the development, and the destined ends of the two cities. Even in the first half, Rome dominates only the first volume of the five-volume division and is disappearing from view by book 8, as Augustine embarks on the serious philosophy and theology that is best illustrated by Platonism. In the second half of the text Rome is firmly put in perspective in the history of the world so far, read through scripture, carefully synchronized with Assyria and Sicyon and Athens and biblical Israel. Classical literature plays a minimal role in comparison with the Bible; a rapid scan of footnote references makes this point very clearly. As Augustine had already said of scripture, "I have known no other books that can so bring down the proud" (*Conf.* 13.15.17).

In this passage of *Confessions,* one of his many exegeses of the creation narrative in Genesis, Augustine uses biblical images of books to explore the relationship between divine scripture and human writing. Philip Burton translates as follows:

And who but you, our God, made us the "firmament" of authority that is above us in the divine Scriptures? *Heaven will be rolled up like a scroll* (Is. 34.4), and even now is *stretched out like the skin of a tent* (Ps. 104.2) above us. Your divine Scriptures are all the more highly exalted in their authority inasmuch as the mortals through whom you dispensed them to us have died the mortal death. And you know, O Lord, you know how you clothed mankind in skins when as a result of sin they became mortal. Hence you have stretched out like a skin the firmament of your Scriptures, those words of yours that chime out in harmony, which by the ministry of mortals you have set over us.

Henry Chadwick's translation handles the Bible quotations differently.

For "the heaven will fold up like a book" (Isa. 34:4), and now "like a skin it is stretched out" above us (Ps. 103:2).[43]

Skin can be made into parchment: is heaven a parchment scroll to be rolled up, or a parchment codex to be closed? Either way, it is skin that makes

---

42. *Corpus Christianorum* achieved, in 2003, a single-volume paperback, the "Scholars Version."

43. Philip Burton, trans., *Augustine: The Confessions* (London, 2001); Henry Chadwick, trans., *Saint Augustine: Confessions* (Oxford, 1992). Burton's numbering of the psalms is that of the Hebrew text, which is followed in most English translations, Chadwick's that of the text as Augustine knew it, in which psalms 9 and 10 formed one psalm.

a text. In Philip Burton's translation it is also skin that makes a tent. This is certainly one meaning of *pellis,* "skin": soldiers in camp were *sub pellibus,* as they used to be "under canvas" (e.g., Cic. *Acad.* 2.2.4). But it seems not to be Augustine's own exegesis of *pellis.* His interpretation of Psalm 103:2 is a classic example of his exegetical technique, both in its focus on words and phrases that he explains through other passages of scripture and in its adaptation to different audiences.[44] One of his sermons on this psalm (*Enarrationes in Psalmos* 103 s.1.8) offers, in simpler expository style, the same explanation as *Confessions:* "skin" signifies mortality, because when Adam and Eve were expelled from paradise, they were clothed in skin tunics to signify their mortality. The heaven that is like skin is holy scripture, which is "stretched out like skin" because the words of the mortal dead are spread out. That is, the fame of prophets and apostles was more widespread after their death. *De Genesi ad litteram* (2.9.21–22) explicitly refers to the exegesis given in *Confessions,* but it also deals with people who think "stretched out like skin" means that heaven is not spherical, and therefore contradicts other references to the vault of heaven. Skin can be curved, Augustine replies: think of leather balls, or leather bottles.[45]

So mortal readers, unlike the angels, are below the firmament of heaven. They look up to read God's word in scripture, just as, in philosophic tradition, humans (unlike other animals) stand upright and look up to find the divine power proclaimed by the order of the universe and the "visible gods," the sun and moon and stars. The scriptures are uniquely authoritative because they are God-given; but, like the skin clothing of fallen mortals, these skins written by fallen mortals are ambivalent. They are necessary protection for humans, but it is the separation of humans from God that makes them necessary as damage limitation. The protective firmament, the written text that declares in the heaven the glory of God, also marks our separation from the angels who read God's face.

But it might be permissible to extend the image in a way that would appeal to Augustine. The "skin tent" of the scriptures is one coherent covering

44. I owe the references to O'Donnell, *Augustine: Confessions,* 3:371–72. This commentary is a brilliant demonstration of Augustine's technique applied to Augustine.

45. In an earlier paper I connected the images of a skin tunic and the skin of the firmament with a skin container *(uter)* that prevents water from dissipating. It is an Augustinian exegesis, in that it is the kind of connection Augustine might well have made, but I no longer think that he made it in *Confessions* 13. See further Gillian Clark, "Adam's Womb and the Salty Sea," *Proceedings of the Cambridge Philological Society* 42 (1996): 89–105.

for the encampment of strangers and sojourners, the *civitas peregrina* of God's people for whom scripture is the collective memory, the history, and the authoritative text. *City of God,* by contrast, is a built environment, a textual city constructed of books: the books of the earthly city coexist with the scriptures as the citizens of the earthly city coexist with the citizens of God's city. In *City of God* (15.1) Augustine contrasts the righteous Abel, a *peregrinus,* with Cain, who built the first city.

So, according to Augustine, the world in which we live is shaped by a text. A text helps to heal the separation of fallen humans from God, and human history is to be interpreted by that text. Rome, city and empire, culture and religion, is a city of books. Its history, ancient and recent, is subject to interpretation by "our" book, the Christian book, the one authoritative book that God has entrusted to mortal writers and readers. Augustine's heavenly city is like a late antique Roman city in that it has a *curia* of angels (*De civ. D.* 10.7) who transmit the pronouncements of the Ruler. But the words of God must still be written and interpreted by mortals who are resident aliens, *peregrini,* in the earthly city of their time, and who share the local customs and culture. Augustine's own big book is a city of books, built up from "their" classics of Roman culture and from "our" scripture, from his own work of exegesis and reflection on human society and from earlier Christian apologetic and reflection on Rome.[46]

A final question, then: is all this bookishness distinctively Augustinian, or distinctively Christian? The papers in this collection strongly suggest that it is not: rather, bookishness is a late antique characteristic. Christian holy books were adorned and handled with reverence, and when Mani launched a new religious movement, he produced books, beautifully crafted objects that were repositories of wisdom to be handled only by the elect.[47] Augustine fought against Manichaean books in *Contra Adimantum* and *Contra Faustum.*[48] The

46. For earlier apologetic, see Simon Price, "Latin Christian Apologetics: Minucius Felix, Tertullian, and Cyprian," in *Apologetics in the Roman Empire,* ed. Mark Edwards, Martin Goodman, and Simon Price (Oxford, 1999), 105–29; Mark Edwards, "The Flowering of Latin Apologetic: Lactantius and Arnobius," ibid., 197–221; Oliver Nicholson, "*Civitas quae adhuc sustentat omnia:* Lactantius and the City of Rome," in Klingshirn and Vessey, *Limits of Ancient Christianity,* 7–25. Augustine's specific debt to Lactantius is discussed by Peter Garnsey, "Lactantius and Augustine," in *Representations of Empire: Rome and the Mediterranean World,* ed. Alan K. Bowman et al. (Oxford, 2002), 153–79.

47. Iain Gardner and Samuel N. C. Lieu, *Manichaean Texts from the Roman Empire* (Cambridge, 2003).

48. For *Contra Adimantum,* see N. Baker-Brian, "*. . . quaedam disputationes Adimanti:* Reading

books of the Talmud collect the oral tradition and debate of many generations, including rules on the reverent handling of the scriptures.[49] The books
of Roman law, reverently received by Roman officials, attempt to codify and
clarify the decisions of many centuries.[50] All these books are works of reference, authoritative texts for consultation, though all (especially the Talmud)
provide more than one answer. All offer comparisons with Christian use of
books. But the closest comparison is the philosophical tradition that Augustine regarded as the highest achievement of Greco-Roman religious thinking
(*De civ. D.* 8.5–12), namely, Platonism.

Platonist tradition included warnings against books. In the *Phaedrus*
(275ab) Plato told the myth of the Egyptian god Thoth, who invented writing, but was told by king Ammon that writing is a device for recollection as
opposed to memory, and that students will acquire information without instruction. Augustine noted (*De civ. D.* 8.4) that it is not easy to discover Plato's own opinions from his books. But Platonist philosophy became increasingly concerned with canon and commentary, in particular with interpreting
texts that were thought to conceal wisdom, and in general with the attempt to
ensure that people read the right texts, in the right sequence, with the right interpretation.[51] Commentary was as much a way of doing philosophy as Christian exegesis was a way of doing theology. Later Platonism, it has been argued,
absorbed a specifically Christian intolerance of heresy.[52] It could equally be argued that Christians shared a general concern for correct reading and correct
formulation of belief.

The study of philosophic commentary has transformed understanding of
late antique philosophy.[53] The principles of commentary and canon were well

---

the Manichaean Biblical Discordance in Augustine's *contra Adimantum*," *Augustinian Studies* 34, no. 2
(2003): 175–96.

49. See Boyarin's chapter in this volume.

50. See Humfress's chapter in this volume.

51. On esoteric wisdom, see Gillian Clark, "Translate into Greek: Porphyry of Tyre and the New
Barbarians," in *Constructing Identities in Late Antiquity,* ed. Richard Miles (London, 1999), 112–32. For
Platonist commentaries, see Robert Lamberton, "The Neoplatonists and Their Books," in *Homer, the Bi-
ble, and Beyond: Literary and Religious Canons in the Ancient World,* ed. Margalit Finkelberg and Guy
Stroumsa (Leiden, 2003), 195–211.

52. Polymnia Athanassiadi, "The Creation of Orthodoxy in Neoplatonism," in *Philosophy and Power in the Graeco-Roman World,* ed. Gillian Clark and Tessa Rajak (Oxford, 2002), 271–91.

53. Peter Adamson, Han Baltussen, and M. W. F. Stone, eds., *Philosophy, Science, and Exegesis in
Greek, Arabic, and Latin Commentaries* (London, 2004).

established by the late first century B.C.[54] In the mid-second century A.D. the great doctor Galen, who thought of himself as a Platonist philosopher, listed the books that represented him to the world, with notes on their context. He said he wanted to counter bad copies and mistaken interpretations (*Libr. Propr.* 8–11), but he probably envisaged future commentaries, like his own commentaries on Hippocrates.[55] Someone also listed the extensive works of Varro, for Jerome was able to compare the output of Varro and of Origen, another prolific author and commentator. Even halfway through the list of Varro's works, he said, his readers were growing weary (*Ep.* 33.2).[56]

Porphyry and Iamblichus, Platonist philosophers of the later third century, both engaged in ordering and commenting on texts. Porphyry brought the Chaldaean Oracles into the philosophical tradition by writing a commentary on them.[57] His teacher Plotinus is the great exception to the bookishness of philosophers, but Porphyry worked to ensure that there were adequate texts of Plotinus and that people read them in what he, Porphyry, thought was the right sequence, with headings and (in some cases) discussion (*Plot.* 24–26). His *Life of Plotinus and the Order of His Writings,* written as an introduction to his edition of Plotinus's *Enneads,* is dated by an internal reference to the year 301, just before the effort of Diocletian and his colleagues to eliminate Christian scriptures in the "Great Persecution."[58] Were the *Enneads* envisaged as rival scriptures, presentations of the great tradition for the use of students? There is no indication that Porphyry considered (as Augustine did for *City of*

54. David Sedley, "Philosophical Allegiance in the Greco-Roman World," in *Philosophia Togata: Essays on Philosophy and Roman Society,* ed. Miriam Griffin and Jonathan Barnes (Oxford, 1989), 97–119.

55. Galen, *Libr. Propr. (My Own Books)* and *Ord. Lib. (The Order of My Books),* are included in P. N. Singer, trans., *Galen: Selected Works* (Oxford, 1997).

56. Harry Y. Gamble, *Books and Readers in the Early Church: A History of Early Christian Texts* (New Haven, 1995), 121, suggests that Jerome's list of Origen's works came from the catalogue of the library at Caesarea. See further Ronald E. Heine, *The Commentaries of Origen and Jerome on St Paul's Epistle to the Ephesians* (Oxford, 2002), 23–35, for philosophical and literary commentary, and Eric Plumer, *Augustine's Commentary on Galatians* (Oxford, 2003), 5–59, for commentary on scripture.

57. Andrew Smith, "Porphyrian Studies since 1913," *ANRW* 2, no. 39.2 (1987): 763n286; 749–54 for Porphyry as a commentator on Plato.

58. For dating, see Gillian Clark, trans., *Porphyry: On Abstinence from Killing Animals* (London, 2000), 5; Elizabeth DePalma Digeser, *The Making of a Christian Empire: Lactantius and Rome* (Ithaca, N.Y., 2000), 91–114, argues that Porphyry was the unnamed philosopher who, according to Lactantius, attacked Christianity; see her bibliography for opposing views. On the headings and discussions, now lost, see Mark Edwards, trans., *Neoplatonic Saints: The Lives of Plotinus and Proclus by Their Students* (Liverpool, 2000), 53.

God) how they would work as a book, on scrolls or in codices. He grouped them in sixes and nines (both are significant numbers in Pythagorean tradition), but the groupings are often forced, and vary greatly in length. In other respects Porphyry is a classic case of bookishness. His treatise *On Abstinence from Killing Animals* is on subjects of the most profound importance: it is about how to live as a human being in relation to God and to the human and nonhuman beings with whom we share the world. But it is mostly made up of other people's books, recycled almost without acknowledgment.[59] Iamblichus organized Pythagorean texts into an encyclopedia, also with a numerically significant structure, possibly intended as two codices of four and five books with a table of contents. He also devised an improved Platonic curriculum with appropriate commentaries, and disputed with Porphyry and others the proper understanding of Plato's text and its implications for religious practice.[60]

This small selection of examples shows how philosophers had become bookish: they did philosophy from books, taught it from books, and used books as guides to living. Caroline Humfress has pointed to the connection of legal and philosophical *praecepta*. Theodosius II and Justinian wanted their officials to have authoritative handbooks of law; philosophers in several traditions carried authoritative little books of calm. Augustine borrowed from Gellius the story of the Stoic, pale and trembling in a shipwreck, who was mocked by a fellow passenger for failing to live by his principles (*De civ. D.* 9.4). He responded to a serious enquirer by pulling out a book and explaining the difference between "first movements," the physical reactions that are not within our control, and assent to the judgments that accompany those movements. But Platonic caution about books also survived in philosophical tradition. It was not restricted to those who shied away from a Stoic with an *Introduction to Philosophy* (Porphyry, *Abst.* 3.22.2).[61] Epictetus (1.4.29) praised the books of Chrysippus, but issued a warning in the same lecture:

59. Clark, *Porphyry*, 19–20.

60. Dominic J. O'Meara, *Pythagoras Revived: Mathematics and Philosophy in Late Antiquity* (Oxford, 1989), esp. 31 on the organization of the encyclopedia.

61. Loveday Alexander, "The Living Voice: Scepticism towards the Written Word in Early Christian and in Graeco-Roman Texts," in *The Bible in Three Dimensions: Essays in Celebration of Forty Years of Biblical Studies in the University of Sheffield*, ed. David J. A. Clines, Stephen E. Fowl, and Stanley E. Porter (Sheffield, 1990), 221–47.

"Take the treatise *On Choice* and see how I have read it!" you say. . . . If you are acting in harmony with nature, show me that, and I will tell you that you are making progress. If you are not acting in harmony, off you go: don't just expound books, write some. And what good will that do you? Don't you know that the entire book is worth five *denarii?* (1.4.14–16)

So it seems that bookishness was general in the early centuries A.D. As Augustine's own work so clearly acknowledges, Christians did not live in some separate city, isolated from the language and culture and customs of their time (*De civ. D.* 19.17). Late antique Christianity looks exceptionally bookish because it had (so to speak) the technology: devoted scribes and monastic *scriptoria* to multiply copies, precious covers and ritual to enhance the status of books.[62] But there remains one distinctive factor in early Christian preoccupation with the book, and Augustine is the ideal illustration. Christians had a book, and it was someone's job to explain that book to anyone who would come and listen. The Christian book was used analogously with the books of the law or the philosophers. A standard public building, a basilica, could be used as a Christian church with the bishop seated on his *cathedra,* as a law court with the judge seated on the tribunal, as a lecture room with a philosopher in his professorial chair. The bishop, the judge, and the philosopher all had an authoritative text. Christ himself was represented as a judge and as a philosopher.[63] But untrained people could not understand the law: they had to hire an expensive lawyer with a degree from Berytus, and even then he might be wrong.[64] Late antique philosophical books are also notoriously difficult: they require an advanced education and either private means or a strong ascetic commitment, so that the learner can devote the necessary hours to study. But, as Augustine said (*Ep.* 138.10), a Christian church was like a classroom for all ages, both genders, and all levels of education.[65] If literacy levels were low, it did not matter, because the book would be read aloud and explained.

62. Gamble, *Books and Readers in the Early Church,* especially 120–23, 158–59; R. N. Swanson, ed., *The Church and the Book: Papers Read at the 2000 Summer Meeting and the 2001 Winter Meeting of the Ecclesiastical History Society* (Woodbridge, 2003).

63. Examples in Thomas F. Mathews, *The Clash of Gods: A Reinterpretation of Early Christian Art,* 2d ed. (Princeton, 1999), 98–114.

64. On the difficulty of interpreting late antique law, see Jill Harries, *Law and Empire in Late Antiquity* (Cambridge, 1999), esp. 8–19.

65. See further Gillian Clark, "Pastoral Care: Town and Country in Late-Antique Preaching," in *Urban Centers and Rural Contexts in Late Antiquity,* ed. T. Burns and J. Eadie (East Lansing, Mich., 2001), 265–84.

Not everyone was lucky enough to have it explained by the former professor of rhetoric at Milan, but someone would at least try, and if there was no one available, some conscientious bishop would try to provide clergy. The Christian book was not secret. It could be understood without a prior commitment, such as the Manichaeans required, to a strange and demanding lifestyle. It did not have to be difficult, and if it was, someone would help. In the book of another conference co-organized by Philip Rousseau, I wrote about a vocabulary of commitment shared by Christians and non-Christians, a common willingness to make spiritual progress by the study of challenging texts and by an appropriate lifestyle.[66] Bookishness, like asceticism, is a late antique tendency; to understand the distinctive character of Christian bookishness, we need to move from Augustine as reader and writer to Augustine as preacher.

66. Gillian Clark, "Philosophic *Lives* and the Philosophic Life," in *Greek Biography and Panegyric in Late Antiquity,* ed. Tomas Hägg and Philip Rousseau (Berkeley and Los Angeles, 2000), 48; see also Clark, *Porphyry,* 15–19.

PART IV ❦ CEREMONY AND THE LAW

Caroline Humfress

JUDGING BY THE BOOK

*Christian Codices and Late Antique
Legal Culture*

The Emperor Justinian and New Christian Books

By 533, the Christian God, according to the emperor Justinian, had authored a new Christian book, a book of law, known today as the *Digest* or *Pandects*. The divine authorship of this new Christian book is stated explicitly in Justinian's imperial constitution *Tanta*. This constitution effectively promulgated the authority of the *Digest* text, the second of Justinian's new authoritative law books that made up his tripartite "body of the civil law" (what we today term the *Corpus Iuris Civilis*). The opening sentence of the constitution reads, "So great is the providence of the Divine Humanity toward us that it ever deigns to sustain us with acts of eternal generosity."[1] The particularly expansive acts of eternal generosity that Justinian goes on to specify include the end of the Parthian wars, the extinction of the Vandal nation, and the reconquest of the whole of Libya for the Roman Empire. Christ then apparently turned his providential attention toward reducing more than five hundred years' worth of internally inconsistent imperial constitutions and nearly fourteen hundred years' worth of confused Roman jurisprudence into a single

---

1. Justinian, *Constitutio Tanta* pr. (addressed to the senate and all peoples, dated 533), ed. Theodor Mommsen, in Paul Krueger et al., eds., *Corpus Iuris Civilis*, 3 vols. (Berlin, 1877–95), vol. 1: *Digesta,* xviii: "Tanta circa nos divinae humanitatis est providentia, ut semper aeternis liberalitatibus nos sustentare dignetur."

concordant "body" of civil law. With respect to the creation of a single harmonious text of juristic opinions (the *Digest* itself), the author of the constitution *Tanta* goes on to observe that:

for the heavenly providence this was certainly appropriate, but for human weakness in no way possible. We, therefore, in our accustomed manner have resorted to the aid of the Immortal One and, invoking the Supreme Deity, have desired that God should become the author and patron of the whole work.[2]

In the rhetoric of the compilers of Justinian's *Corpus Iuris Civilis,* the volume that now contained the supposedly harmonious sum of ("pagan") classical juristic science between its covers was literally a Christian book. The triune Christian God, working through the agency of the emperor Justinian, was both its author and patron.

There is the same insistence on divine providence, inspiration, and patronage in the Justinianic legislation that refers in detail to the mechanics of compiling the *Digest.* The constitution *Deo auctore,* in which Justinian ordered the volume's composition, paints a vivid and highly rhetorical picture of an emperor imploring divine assistance from the Christian God:

In our haste to extricate ourselves from minor and more trivial affairs and attain to a completely full revision of the law, and to collect and amend the whole set of Roman ordinances and present the diverse books of so many authors in a single volume (a thing which no one has dared to expect or to desire), the task appeared to us most difficult, indeed impossible. Nevertheless, with hands stretched up to heaven, and imploring eternal aid, we stored up this task too in our mind, relying upon God, who in the magnitude of his goodness is able to sanction and to consummate achievements that are utterly beyond hope.[3]

2. Ibid.: "namque hoc caelestis quidem providentiae peculiare fuit, humanae vero inbecillitati nullo modo possibile. nos itaque more solito ad immortalitatis respeximus praesidium, et summo numine invocato deum auctorem et totius operis praesulem fieri optavimus." For further discussion of the Justinianic compilation and Roman law under Justinian, see Caroline Humfress, "Law and Legal Practice in the Age of Justinian," in *Cambridge Companion to the Age of Justinian,* ed. Michael Maas (Cambridge, 2005), 161–184.

3. Justinian, *Constitutio Deo auctore* 2 (addressed to Tribonian, dated 530), ed. Mommsen, xiii: "Hocque opere consummato et in uno volumine nostro nomine praefulgente coadunato, cum ex paucis et tenuioribus relevati ad summam et plenissimam iuris emendationem pervenire properaremus et omnem Romanam sanctionem et colligere et emendare et tot auctorum dispersa volumina uno codice indita ostendere, quod nemo neque sperare neque optare ausus est, res quidem nobis difficillima, immo magis impossibilis videbatur. Sed manibus ad caelum erectis et aeterno auxilio invocato eam quoque curam nostris reposuimus animis, deo freti, qui et res penitus desperatas donare et consummare suae virtutis magnitudine potest."

The consummation of this daring project involved the collection, emendation, and reduction of nearly two thousand separate books *(libri)* and more than three million lines of text written by classical Roman jurists into the fifty books of the *Digest*. By attributing the completion of this monumental volume to the "inspiration of heaven and the favor of the Supreme Trinity" (*Constitutio Tanta* 1), and indeed by confirming the *Digest*'s authority in an imperial prologue issued "In the Name of Our Lord God Jesus Christ," Justinian effected the rhetorical Christianization of all the non-Christian classical juristic books contained within it. The *Digest* was a Christian law book, despite the paradoxical fact that its fifty books contained no clearly stated Christian precepts whatsoever. In other words, the Christian authority of the *Digest* was not achieved by a Christianization of the substantive principles of classical Roman jurisprudence; it was rather created by enveloping the hallowed classical books of the Roman jurists within a new order of texts.

It was precisely this new order of texts, the completion of a complex and difficult project of sorting, excerpting, and ordering, that was (according to Justinian) guided to completion by the supreme Christian Trinity. The emperor also ordered that the divine status of the *Digest* ought to govern the material form of the book in which the final text was to be copied: "Since this material will have been composed by the supreme indulgence of the Deity, it is necessary to set it out in a most handsome work, consecrating as it were a fitting and most holy temple of justice."[4] However we read this metaphorical reference to the actual physical form of the book as a "holy temple of justice," the example of Justinian's *Digest* serves as a salutary reminder of how the meaning of texts can be subtly altered by their copying, restructuring, and complex shuffling together into a new, monumental physical form.

During the course of the fifth and sixth centuries there is, of course, concrete evidence for precisely the same process of textual "monumentalizing" with reference to Judeo-Christian scriptures. Sacred Judeo-Christian books were themselves collected and ordered into new pandect forms, pandects that monumentalized the transformation of the Hebrew Bible into the Christian Old Testament by literally binding it together with books of the New Testament (for example the *Codex Vaticanus,* the *Codex Sinaiticus,* and the *Codex*

4. Ibid., 5:xiii. See also *Constitutio Tanta* 20, where the *Digest* is described as a "temple of Roman justice" *(iustitiae Romanae templum).*

Alexandrinus). The hermeneutical arts that paved the way for a harmonious Christian exegesis of the "Old Testament" and the "New" were also in the process of being developed. In this respect the Christian deity's capacity for monumentalizing a collection of disparate, often conflicting, but potentially harmonious writings into a single codex was well attested before Justinian singled out that power explicitly for his own early sixth-century authoritative project.

It has in fact been argued by some modern Roman legal scholars that the specific use of the codex form for the copying of early Christian texts acted as an inspiration to the later codification of Roman law. Henryk Kupiszewski has suggested that a general preference for codex-books in early Christian circles may have influenced the evolution of a peculiarly "legal" use of codices in late Roman judicial contexts: "Around the middle of the third century, the Christians were followed by the jurists and by legal practice. Within this milieu the 'codex-book' became, slowly but irresistibly, a physical collection of legal rules and more precisely of imperial constitutions."[5] Other scholars, however, have argued more strongly for a causal relationship between the Christian production of pandect Bibles, such as the *Codex Vaticanus,* and the emperor Theodosius II's project of producing a single pandect volume of Roman law (eventually promulgated in 438 as the *Codex Theodosianus*). Yet it should be noted in this context that the compilers of the *Theodosian Code* themselves stated clearly that their codex was arranged "in the likeness of *(ad similitudinem)* the Gregorian and Hermogenian [codes]."[6] The pattern for the *Theodosian Code* was thus specified as two Diocletianic "collections" of imperial rescripts.[7] If the compilation of the *Theodosian Code* was inspired by Christian codices or *pandectae,* its compilers were not concerned with noting that Christian lineage.

The only direct comparison between the form of an early Christian book and the form of a late Roman legal codex comes from within a Christian ambit: in the mid-fifth century the ecclesiastical writer Sedulius drew a (curious) analogy between the third-century theologian Origen's three editions

---

5. Henryk Kupiszewski, "Dal codice-libro al codice-raccolta di precetti giuridici," *Journal of Juristic Papyrology* 20 (1990): 84. "Intorno alla metà del III sec. i cristiani furono seguiti dai giuristi e della prassi giudiziaria. In quest'ambito il codice-libro diventava, lentamente ma inarrestabilmente, una raccolta materiale di norme giuridiche e più precisamente di constituzioni imperiali."

6. *Codex Theodosianus* 1.1.5 (429) = *Gesta Senatus* 4 (438), ed. Theodor Mommsen, in Theodor Mommsen and Paul M. Meyer, eds., *Theodosiani Libri XVI cum Constitutionibus Sirmondianis,* 2d ed. (Berlin, 1954), 1:28.

7. On the so-called Gregorian and Hermogenian "codes," see Simon Corcoran, *The Empire of the Tetrarchs: Imperial Pronouncements and Government AD 284–324* (Oxford, 1996), 25–42.

of his *Hexapla* (a text that placed different Greek versions of the Hebrew Bible in parallel with a Greek transliteration of the Hebrew text) and Hermogenian's three editions of his *opera* (i.e., the *Hermogenian* legal "code," discussed above). Sedulius, engaged in his own work of poetic (re)composition, makes the comparison between the "Christian" and the "Roman" legal text by way of a self-apology for his literary activity:

> Some will say that a translation is untrustworthy and flawed, because (of course) things are unambiguous in a speech that cannot be so regarded in a poem. If they make this objection, they expose themselves as having no understanding. Whether they are deemed to have pursued a secular education or to have been instructed in the divine books, they ought to review the examples set by the ancients, before they embark on the unjustified abuse of those acting in a similar way. Let others learn that Hermogenian, that most learned lawgiver, composed three editions of his work. Let them learn that Origen, expert in the divine law, put together almost all that he wrote in, precisely, three editions. Neither of them has suffered the abuse of a sharp tongue. Rather, the greater praise is extended to them because, thanks to the work of their fertile intellects, those coming after them have been equipped with a more firmly grounded confidence of comprehending the truth. It is, clearly, one thing to alter finished compositions, and another to give them fresh life.[8]

Sedulius's analogy between the editions of Origen and Hermogenian thus seems to point toward a symbiotic culture of book production and revision, rather than any particular causal relationship between "Christian" and "Roman" legal texts.

With respect to this general culture of book production, Franz Wieacker has argued convincingly that the development of the codex book form in both Christian and Roman legal contexts should be considered, rather, as the expression of a definite late antique cultural style. This style is characterized by a new relationship to the written transmitted word (upheld by Sedulius himself in the passage quoted above). As Wieacker notes, the codex book could be closed and its front and back covers lavishly ornamented; it was thus symbolic of a new culture of written language and a new conception of the authority and value of the text.[9]

The emperor Justinian's sixth-century "codification" project, however, took the transformation of late Roman legal culture a step further. Justinian's

---

8. Coelius Sedulius, *Epistola ad Macedonium* (*CSEL* 10:172) = *Dedicatio operis Paschalis* (*PL* 19:547B–C). My translation.

9. Franz Wieacker, *Textstufen klassischer Juristen* (Göttingen, 1960), 95. On the exterior ornamentation of early Christian books as a form of visual argument, see John Lowden's chapter in this volume.

insistence on the Christian God's involvement in the production of the *Corpus Iuris Civilis* was certainly influenced by Justinian's own conception of his imperial theocracy. This is, after all, the same emperor who could state that "any difference between priesthood and empire is small," and could count himself as an expert theological exegete in his own right.[10] Justinian and his compilers, moreover, were insistent on the fact that the Christian God inspired the very workings of their legal hermeneutics. The concept of the "spirit" and the "letter" of Roman law had been discussed by Roman jurists and forensic rhetoricians as early as the late republican period. According to Justinian's legal rhetoric, however, the "spirit" that was seen to animate written law was no longer a vague sense of equity or justice, but rather the Christian Holy Spirit itself. The project of reducing the imperial constitutions in Justinian's *Codex* (the first book of the Justinianic *Corpus Iuris*) to one harmonious whole involved amending "anything that was found to be dubious and uncertain and (reducing) it to a proper form." This very particular task of legal exegesis, the constitution *Tanta* states, was undertaken "in reliance on the Heavenly divinity." Turning its attention to the *Digest*, the constitution *Tanta* again insists that the specific task of reducing and clarifying the 3 million lines written by the ancient jurists was only accomplished "by the inspiration of the Holy Spirit." If we take Justinian's theocratic rhetoric seriously for a moment, then what gives Tribonian and the various imperial commissioners the authority to alter the hallowed texts of the jurists and previous emperors (of "divine memory" in their own right) is the authority of the Holy Spirit itself, channeled through Justinian to his imperial commissioners.

It is tempting to note here that the divine aid allegedly supplied by the Holy Spirit to the Justinianic legal commissioners seems curiously analogous to the miraculous divine aid attributed in later Christian legends to the seventy-two (or in some accounts seventy) Hebrew translators of the biblical Septuagint text.[11] The legend was refashioned by Augustine in the late fourth century,

---

10. Justinian, *Nov.* 7.2.1, ed. Rudolf Schoell and Wilhelm Kroll, in Krueger et al., *Corpus Iuris Civilis,* 3:53. On Justinian's particular contributions to the development of (political) theology, see Claire Sotinel, "Emperors and Popes in the Sixth Century: The Western View," in Maas, *Cambridge Companion to the Age of Justinian,* 267–90, and for broader discussion of the whole concept of "cesaro-papism," see chapter 9 of Gilbert Dagron, *Emperor and Priest: The Imperial Office in Byzantium,* trans. Jean Birrell (Cambridge, 2003).

11. A narrative first told, rather more prosaically, in the pseudepigraphic *Letter of Aristeas.*

in the aftermath of his dispute with Jerome over the translation of the Old Testament books of the Vulgate from the Hebrew rather than the Greek. According to Augustine, the translators owed no human bondage to the original Hebrew words being translated, as the divine power of the Holy Spirit filled and ruled the mind that was translating:

For the same Spirit that was in the prophets when they spoke was present also in the seventy men when they translated them; and the Spirit could have said something else also, with Divine authority, as if the Prophet had said both things, because it was the same Spirit who said both. The Spirit could also have said the same thing in a different way, so that even though the words were not the same, the same meaning would still shine forth upon those who rightly understood them. He could also have omitted something, or added something, so that it might be shown in this way also that the work of translation was accomplished not by the mere human labor of one slavishly interpreting the words, but by the power of God filling and directing the mind of the translator.... For just as the one Spirit of peace was present in the prophets when they spoke the truth with no disagreement, so also was the same one Spirit present in the seventy translators when, without consulting one another, they still translated the whole as if with one voice.[12]

For Augustine, the Holy Spirit animated both the Hebrew prophets and the seventy Hellenistic translators; the devout human translators who produced the Greek Septuagint were thus liberated by the Holy Spirit and owed no slavish bondage to the original Hebrew text. The new text of the Septuagint was accordingly sacred and divinely sanctioned, immune from the censorious work of mundane philologists (a thinly veiled Augustinian jibe at Jerome's own translation of sacred scripture into Latin, directly from the Hebrew).[13] The rhetoric of Justinian's legal commissioners, at least, was certainly inspired by this peculiarly Christian relationship between Holy Spirit and sacred texts.[14]

Returning to Justinian's appeal to the Holy Spirit in his own imperial legislation, it is clear that his legal officials were expected to be familiar with the

---

12. Augustine, *De civitate Dei* 18.43, in R. W. Dyson, trans., *The City of God against the Pagans* (Cambridge, 1998).

13. On Augustine, Jerome, and the Christianicity of books, see the chapters in this volume by Gillian Clark and Catherine M. Chin, respectively.

14. The legal expert who drafted Justinian's *Novel* 146 (553) even included a reference to (one version) of the Septuagint's miraculous drafting within section 1 of the *Novel* itself: "We make this proviso that those who use Greek shall use the text of the Septuagint, which is the most accurate translation, and the one most highly approved, since it happened that the translators, divided into two groups, and working in different places, all produced exactly the same text" (Krueger et al., *Corpus Iuris Civilis*, 3:715).

concept that the physical presence of particular Christian codices actually invoked the spiritual presence of God.[15] Much more than the sum of the words contained within them, certain Christian books literally invoked God as a virtual participant in legal trials under Justinian's jurisdiction. This concept was applied to clever effect in a constitution, dated 530, concerning contumacious proceedings (trials where one of the litigants was absent). In the case of contumacious proceedings, Justinian explicitly provides that when a copy of scripture is present in the courtroom, the absence of the litigant is to be understood as remedied by the presence of God: "When either the plaintiff or the defendant is in default, the examination of the case should proceed without any impediment, for as soon as the Holy Scriptures *(scripturae terribiles)* are brought forward, the absence of the litigant is supplied by the presence of God."[16] Justinian thus neatly extricates himself from a potentially tricky conflict of Roman law and Christian canon law: traditional Roman procedural regulations allowed contumacious proceedings, whereas ecclesiastical practice enshrined in the unanimous agreement of the church councils insisted that defendants should not forfeit their cases unheard. Justinian manages to uphold both Roman and canon law by substituting God for the absent defendant, God's presence being guaranteed by the sacred scriptures themselves.

In a constitution issued in the same year (*Cod. Iust.* 3.1.14) Justinian ordered that every judge who decides cases according to Roman law (including all types of arbitration) must not start his proceedings until a copy of the *scripturae sacrosanctae* has been placed before the judge in the tribunal hall, where it was to remain until after the sentence had been delivered:

All judges learned in the Roman law shall not undertake to hear a case, unless the Holy Scriptures *(scripturae sacrosanctae)* have previously been placed before the judicial seat, and remain there, not only during the beginning, but also throughout the entire examination, until the very end, and the promulgation of the final decision.[17]

15. Claudia Rapp's chapter in this volume discusses broader contexts concerning the tangible holiness of the written word in early Christian contexts.

16. *Codex Iustinianus* (hereafter *Cod. Iust.*) 3.1.13.4 (530), in Krueger et al., *Corpus Iuris Civilis,* 2:121: "Cum autem eremodicium ventilatur sive pro actore sive pro reo, examinatio sine ullo obstaculo celebretur. Cum enim terribiles in medio proponuntur scripturae, litigatoris absentia dei praesentia repletur."

17. *Cod. Iust.* 3.1.14.1 (530), 2:122. The entire text of section 1 reads: "Cum igitur et viam non inusitatam invenimus ambulandam et anteriores leges nostrae, quae de iuramentis positae sunt, non minimam suae utilitatis experientiam litigantibus praebuerunt et ideo ab omnibus merito collaudantur, ad hanc in

The text goes on to specify that through the physical presence of the *scripturae sacrosanctae* the judges, and by implication the courtroom itself, will be "consecrated by the presence of God" and the litigation aided "by a higher power." Justinian also avails himself of this opportunity to terrify his legal officials by reminding them that they might judge now, but they will be judged in turn. Late Roman judges were thus to proceed "by the book" of *scripturae sacrosanctae,* yet they would in turn be judged by that book. This eschatological threat of future judgment is equally leveled against the litigants, their advocates, and their witnesses in Byzantine papyrological reports of courtroom proceedings.[18] The centrality of texts, of books, to the act of judging was, of course, a fundamental tenet of Judeo-Christian religion. The (often visionary) pictures of divine judgment found in the Hebrew Bible and pseudepigrapha, as well as in the New Testament and Christian apocrypha, each imply to varying effects that human souls will be judged "by the book(s)."[19] Leaving the threats of divine retribution aside, however, the question arises of what we are to understand by the phrase *scripturae sacrosanctae* in Justinian's own legislation. What "book," exactly, was to be placed before every judge who heard cases "according to the Roman law" in the age of Justinian?

To a modern reader the term *scripturae sacrosanctae* might plausibly suggest the placing of a pandect Bible, containing the holy scriptures of both the Old and New Testaments, in every courtroom. However, it is clear from two later Justinianic constitutions, each dealing with the same provision in slightly different contexts, that *scripturae sacrosanctae* refers here to the Gospels in

---

perpetuum valituram legem pervenimus, per quam sancimus omnes iudices sive maiores sive minores, sive qui in administrationibus positi sunt vel in hac regia civitate vel in orbe terrarum, qui nostris gubernaculis regitur, sive eos, quibus nos audientiam committimus vel qui a maioribus iudicibus dantur vel qui ex iurisdictione sua iudicandi habent facultatem vel qui ex recepto (id est compromisso, quod iudicium imitatur) causas dirimendas suscipiunt vel qui arbitrium peragunt vel ex auctoritate sententiarum et partium consensu electi, et generaliter omnes omnino iudices romani iuris disceptatores non aliter litium primordium accipere, nisi prius ante iudicialem sedem sacrosanctae deponantur scripturae: et hoc permaneat non solum in principio litis, sed etiam in omnibus cognitionibus usque ad ipsum terminum et definitivae sententiae recitationem." Discussed briefly by Biondo Biondi, *Il diritto Romano Cristiano* (Milan, 1954), 3:377.

18. *Cod. Iust.* 3.1.14.2. Compare the report of legal proceedings given in the papyrus *P.Cair.Masp.* I, 67089 = III, 67294, at line 13: "They shall see what it means, facing the terrible Judgment Seat of a mightier one [God]."

19. For example, Deut. 28:58–62 and 31.23–26; Ps. 69:27–28; Dan. 7:9–10; Rev. 20:11–12; and Enoch 47:3–4. For a patristic exegesis of the Last Judgment proceeding "by the book," see Origen, *Commentary on Matthew* 14.9, ed. E. Klostermann and E. Benz, *Origenes Werke* 10.1, GCS 40 (Berlin, 1935–37), 295–98.

particular and not to pandect Bibles. The first relevant constitution, issued in 531, actually appeals directly to *Cod. Iust.* 3.1.14. The constitution of 531 begins: "As We have already decided that judges shall not dispose of cases unless in the presence of the Holy Gospels *(sacrosanctis evangeliis)* . . . We consider it necessary to promulgate the present law."[20] The phrase *scripturae sacrosanctae* in the text of 530 is now clarified by the phrase *sacrosanctis evangeliis.* Moreover, a constitution issued in 537 allows the senate body at Constantinople the right of hearing cases, on appeal, "in the presence of the Holy Gospels." Hence a copy of the Gospels was to be placed before the senators, as before imperial magistrates and other legal arbitrators.[21]

In fact the Justinianic constitutions relating to procedural oath swearing regularly specify that those oaths are to be made while touching gospel books *(sacrosanctis evangeliis tactis). Cod. Iust.* 3.1.14.4 (530) simply states that before a trial can take place "the advocates employed on both sides shall be sworn with their hands upon the Holy Gospels." A further constitution, however, clearly implies that the advocates are to swear their legal oaths on the copy of the Gospels that has already been placed before the judge in the tribunal.[22] This stress on the gospel books in legal contexts is also recorded by Procopius in his *Secret History.* According to Procopius, Justinian himself was made to abjure his faults to his Constantinopolitan subjects during the Nika riots of 532 by an oath sworn while touching a gospel codex in the public arena of the

---

20. *Cod. Iust.* 2.58 (59).2.pr (531), 2:118: "Cum et iudices non aliter causas dirimere concessimus nisi sacrosanctis evangeliis propositis et patronos causarum in omni orbe terrarum, qui romano imperio suppositus est, prius iurare et ita perferre causas disposuimus: necessarium duximus et praesentem legem ponere."

21. Justinian, *Nov.* 62 (537). For other specific references to gospel books in legal contexts see Justinian's *Nov.* 35 (535), *Nov.* 112 (541), and *Nov.* 137 (565).

22. *Cod. Iust.* 2.58 (59).2.pr (531). Other Justinianic constitutions referring to oath swearing on sacred scripture are *Cod. Iust.* 2.58 (59).1.1 (529), *Cod. Iust.* 4.1.12.5–6 (529), and *Cod. Iust.* 5.70.7.5–6 (530). Nicholas Everett, *Literacy in Lombard Italy c. 568–774* (Cambridge, 2003), 171, notes the use of gospel texts in legal oath swearing within Lombard Italy, from at least 643 onward: "Rothari made the act of swearing oaths upon the Gospels an integral element of Lombard law, and valued it more highly than oaths sworn upon arms. Later legislation appears to have dropped oaths sworn upon arms as an option. . . . Biblical quotations, oaths sworn upon the Gospels, and even letters from the Pope advising on family law, all testify to the permeating influence of a literate Christian culture within the [Lombard] code." For records of contemporary dispute settlements written down in the interlinear margins of gospel texts in early medieval Ireland, see Richard Sharpe, "Dispute Settlement in Medieval Ireland: A Preliminary Inquiry," in *The Settlement of Disputes in Early Medieval Europe,* ed. Wendy Davies and Paul Fouracre (Cambridge, 1992), 170, 173, and 174.

Hippodrome. It was thus copies of the Gospels, rather than pandect copies of the Bible or "sacred scripture" in general, which were given a preeminent status in early sixth-century legal contexts. What, then, are we to conclude concerning this emphasis on codices of the gospel books in particular?

Justinian's stress on the gospel books mirrors the church's own formalization of its conciliar and liturgical practices. The fourth ecumenical council at Chalcedon (451) was conducted with a copy of the Christian Gospels at the center of the assembly, as apparently was the first ecumenical council at Nicaea (325). With respect to the liturgy of the Christian divine service, in early fifth-century Egypt a letter of Isidore of Pelusium describes how, when the true shepherd appears at the opening of the Holy Gospels, the presiding bishop rises up and lays aside his bishop's stole *(omophorion),* thus signifying that the Lord himself, the author of the pastoral function, his God and his master, is present *(Ep.* 136).[23] We have already noted the emperor Justinian's own application of this belief that when the Gospels are present, so too is the Lord. On the other hand, codices of "four-in-one" Gospels had already acquired a symbolic status in relations between church and empire during the reign of Constantine (although the fact that the emperor Julian's copy of St. Luke's Gospel did not contain the narrative of the agony at Gethsemane serves as a reminder that variant forms of the gospel text were in use).[24] Constantine himself had asked Eusebius of Caesarea to furnish him with fifty copies of the Gospels in Greek, for use in his new city of Constantinople.[25] The emperor Constans' request that Athanasius send him copies of the *theiōn graphōn* should perhaps equally be seen as a demand for gospel books rather than pandect Bibles.[26] In fact, within the broader question of surviving manuscript copies, John Lowden has noted the relatively high survival rate of gospel books, in relation to other scriptural books, from the late antique period.[27]

23. On this passage, see also Claudia Rapp's chapter in this volume.

24. Noted by Henry Chadwick, *The Church in Ancient Society: From Galilee to Gregory the Great* (Oxford, 2001), 307–8.

25. Eusebius, *Vita Constantini* 4.36. On these "fifty copies" as gospel books, see Geoffrey A. Robbins, "'Fifty Copies of the Sacred Writings' (*VC* 4.36): Entire Bibles or Gospel Books?" in *Papers Presented to the Tenth International Conference on Patristic Studies Held in Oxford, 1987,* ed. Elizabeth A. Livingstone (Louvain, 1989), 1:91–98.

26. Athanasius, *Defence before Constantius* 4.2 (*SC* 56:92), noted in Timothy D. Barnes, *Athanasius and Constantius: Theology and Politics in the Constantinian Empire* (Cambridge, Mass., 1993), 39.

27. See John Lowden's chapter in this volume.

In the context of relations between imperial bureaucrats and Christian bishops, the church historian Socrates narrates a curious though nonetheless illuminating incident involving a physical copy of a book of the Gospels (*Ecclesiastical History* 7.13). Socrates' narrative tells of the bloody and violent struggles between Jews and Christians in early fifth-century Alexandria, highlighting the increasingly strained relations between Cyril, the bishop, and the imperial prefect Orestes. The prefect Orestes, as Socrates portrays him, was a Jewish sympathizer: in the wake of Cyril's own Christian congregation driving the Jews out of the city of Alexandria and "permitting the multitude to plunder their goods," Orestes had the nerve to be outraged at the Christians' behavior. Cyril of Alexandria attempted to placate the prefect with letters and personal Christian embassies, but when words failed the bishop resorted to symbolic action: "And when Orestes refused to listen to friendly advances, Cyril extended toward him the book of Gospels, believing that respect for religion would induce him to lay aside his resentment. Even this, however, had no pacific effect on the prefect, but he persisted in implacable hostility against the bishop."[28] Cyril's presentation of the gospel to Orestes is symbolic in the sense that the gospel books were the books of Jesus Christ par excellence. This, of course, is not to deny the fact that Cyril would also have viewed the books of the Old Testament as Christian texts. But when the issue was one of differentiating between Jewish and Christian identity (as it was in this case), the Gospels were the books to be relied upon. In this sense Socrates' narrative points toward a much more widespread cultural phenomenon: that of ascribing identity through the deliberate choice of possessing a collection (or even a canon) of particular books.

The idea that identity could be constructed by the mere possession of particular books was not of course new: in the late second century A.D. the sophist Lucian had used exactly that premise in order to lampoon ignorant "book collectors" who thought that the mere possession of handsome volumes guaranteed them a place within the social elite.[29] Within the context of early Christian self-definition through book possession, one might think immediately of Marcion in the mid-second century, Mani in the third century, and indeed the

28. Trans. A. C. Zenos, *Nicene and Post-Nicene Fathers,* 2d ser. (New York, 1890), 2:159–60, slightly adapted.

29. Lucian of Samosata, *Diatribe against the Ignorant Book Collector* (ca. 170), trans. A. M. Harmon, *Lucian,* vol. 3 (Cambridge, Mass., 1921), 175–211.

angst of certain late Roman ecclesiastics over whether knowledge and/or possession of classical Greco-Roman texts was compatible with being a Christian
at all. The case of Cyril and Orestes, however, highlights the fact that identity
differences between Jews and Christians could be made materially concrete by
laying out a book of the Gospels. Can the emperor Justinian's insistence on the
particular use of the Gospels in legal contexts be understood in a similar way?

Justinianic legislators were certainly well aware of the relationship between identity politics and the possession of books. Justinian's *Novel* 146
seeks to regulate the use of sacred scripture in Jewish synagogues. The preface opens with the words "Necessity dictates that when the Hebrews listen to
their sacred texts they should not confine themselves to the meaning of the
letter, but should also devote their attention to those sacred prophecies which
are hidden from them, and which announce the mighty Lord and Savior Jesus Christ." In other words, the drafters of this constitution are primarily concerned with converting Jews into Christians. Section 1 of *Novel* 146 specifies
that Jewish congregations must not use sacred scriptures written in Hebrew,
but must use translations either in Greek (from the Septuagint text or the literal version of Aquila) or from other translations into Latin, "or any other
tongue." The specific (legislative) reasoning here is that those who make use
of the Hebrew texts alone will henceforth be unable to corrupt or falsify them
without the knowledge of non-Hebrew speakers (both within Jewish communities and outside them). The text then continues, "But the Mishnah, or as
they call it the second tradition, we prohibit entirely." According to the drafter
of this imperial constitution, the Mishnah is not part of the sacred books, nor
was it handed down by divine inspiration: it is profane and mundane, "having nothing of the divine in it." The use of the Mishnah is thus forbidden in
synagogue, and the sacred "Hebrew" books which remain licit (the equivalent of the Christian "Old Testament") are no longer to be read in Hebrew.
Hence Justinian concludes in section 3 of the *Novel* that every Jew will have
the chance to read, interpret, and understand sacred scripture for themselves
without having to rely upon Hebrew teachers:

For it is acknowledged that he who is nourished upon the sacred scriptures and has little need
of direction, is much readier to discern the truth, and to choose the better path, than he who
understands nothing of them but clings to the name of his faith alone, and is held by it as by a
sacred anchor, and believes that what can be called error in its purest form is divine teaching.

Thus Justinian attacks the power structure and self-identity of Jewish communities through defining and regulating the community of books they are to use.[30]

The reference in Justinian's *Novel* 146 to the treatment of Hebrew scriptures as "prophecy" has, of course, a long, complex, and contentious history within all kinds of Judeo-Christian contexts. By the late fourth century exegetical techniques for treating the Hebrew scriptures as a prophetic revelation of later Christian events were well developed.[31] Thus a "Christian" identity could be claimed for "Judaic" books of holy scripture. "Judaic" books of holy scripture were treated (by Christian communities) as "Christian" books. However, one particular source of contention that persisted throughout late antiquity was how an aspiring model Christian *ought* to read (and especially ought to act upon) the thousands of literal, specific, and binding Mosaic laws in the books of Genesis, Exodus, Leviticus, Numbers, and Deuteronomy.[32] An important identity issue for (at least some) late antique Christians was whether they could, or indeed should, conceive of a concrete *lex Christiana*, a Christian law based on the New Testament, that could stand over and against the Judaic *lex Dei*.[33] This poses a further question concerning whether late antique Christians and/or non-Christians conceived of the Gospels as the source of a specific written-down, binding Christian *lex*. Were the gospel texts, in effect, treated as books of Christian law? This line of inquiry introduces much broader questions concerning the extent to which sacred scripture was considered an authoritative legal text that could be cited in cases at law, and how the books of sacred scripture were handled in various (ecclesiastical and "secular") forensic contexts up to the age of Justinian himself.

---

30. For the broader context concerning Jewish communities within the Justinianic empire, see Nicholas de Lange, "Jews in the Age of Justinian," in Maas, *Cambridge Companion to the Age of Justinian,* 401–26.

31. An early fifth-century example of a hermeneutic strategy for reconciling the "Old" and "New" Testaments is discussed in Catherine Conybeare's chapter in this volume.

32. The relevance of the (probably late fourth-century?) *Mosaicarum et Romanarum legum Collatio* to this question depends on whether Christian or Jewish authorship is ascribed to the text. For discussion, see Giorgio Barone Adesi, *L'età della "Lex Dei"* (Naples, 1992), and Giovanni Pugliese, "A Suggestion on the Collatio," *Israel Law Review* 29 (1995): 161–75.

33. See, for example, Publicola's letter to Augustine and the latter's response (Augustine *Letters* 46 and 47).

The Christian Gospels: Judging by the Book(s)?

The "law" of Christ is, in Pauline terms at least, a spiritual law. As Lactantius wrote in the early fourth century, the *lex Christi* is a *lex animata,* a "living law."[34] The precepts of Christ contained in the gospel narratives—and indeed the precepts of the evangelists and apostles—were treated by early Christian communities as concrete pieces of advice that gestured toward a spiritual law. In this sense the gospel books outline a *lex Christiana* or *nomos tou Christou,* a Christian "way of life" (reading *lex/nomos* in their normative Greco-Roman sense). By the second century A.D. Epicureans and Stoics carried handbooks of *praecepta* and *leges* in their pockets, just as Christians might have carried gospel books in theirs. In the *City of God* (9.4), Augustine tells a story, originally from Aulus Gellius, concerning a Stoic philosopher who carried a handy book of Epictetus on his person (probably the *kyriai doxai,* a set of Epicurean maxims in book form). Having blanched during a storm at sea, Aulus Gellius asked the "stoic" what the reason for his fear had been: "And the philosopher, willing to teach a man so zealous in his pursuit of knowledge, at once drew forth from his satchel a book of the Stoic Epictetus, in which were written doctrines in keeping with the utterances of Zeno and Chrysippus, who were, as we know, the founders of the Stoic school." According to Augustine, Aulus Gellius was apparently impressed enough to acquire a copy of the *leges Epicuri* for himself.[35] Epicurean precepts or *leges* were described by Diogenes of Oenoanda in the mid-second century as "remedies which bring salvation"; thus Diogenes decided to have them chiseled into the walls of a courtyard in Oenoanda, Lycia, to the general edification of the surrounding populace: "For we have had this writing inscribed in public not [for ourselves] but for you citizens, so that we might render it available to all of you in an easily acceptable form without oral instruction."[36] Diogenes was providing precepts (advice) for liv-

34. Lactantius, *Divine Institutes* IV.17.

35. The striking phrase *leges Epicuri* is Ciceronian, *Tusculan Disputations* 5.108. On the circulation of Epicurean texts, see J. G. Keenan, "A Papyrus Letter about Epicurean Philosophy Books," *J. Paul Getty Museum Journal* 5 (1977): 91–94. On Epictetus's celebrated *Enchiridion,* see Gerard Boter, *The Encheiridion of Epictetus and Its Three Christian Adaptations: Transmission and Critical Editions* (Leiden, 1999), and A. A. Long, *Epictetus: A Stoic and Socratic Guide to Life* (Oxford, 2002).

36. Fragment 29, quoted in Martin Ferguson Smith, *Diogenes of Oinoanda: The Epicurean Inscription* (Naples, 1993), 380, with the Greek text at 194. On the inscription itself, see also Martin Ferguson Smith, "Excavations at Oinoanda 1997: The New Epicurean Texts," *Anatolian Studies* 48 (1998): 125–70.

ing well, through the inscribing of his monumental "limestone handbook."[37] These tantalizing glimpses of a shared bookish culture, across philosophical and religious sects, remind us that early Christian communities would have approached the Gospels as texts containing *praecepta:* advice on how to live according to a law that was only "metaphorically" written down, in the fleshy tablets of the heart, rather than in a "lawbook" grasped by the hand.

In mid-third-century north Africa, Cyprian of Carthage invoked what he termed the "law of the Gospel" in his attempts to gain authoritative control over Christian martyrs and confessors in the wake of the Decian persecutions.[38] This specific concept of an authoritative gospel law, spelled out and elaborated upon in its precise details as it was laid down in written texts, became increasingly elaborated well into the Middle Ages. In summary, we might conclude that while the *lex Christiana* retained its status as a spiritual living law for practicing Christians, its contents were increasingly textualized. This process of "textualization" was effected by the canons of church councils and papal letters (the beginnings of what would eventually be termed "canon law"), the ecclesiastical procedures of individual Christian communities (later referred to as ecclesiastical *ius* or custom),[39] and of course the exegesis, sermons, and catechetical instructions of such theologians as Clement of Alexandria and Cyprian. The Christian *lex* became increasingly identified as a law that could be textualized and, moreover, written down. Was the *lex Christiana,* then, increasingly conceived of as a distinct type of written law to be spelled out authoritatively?

The concept of the gospel texts in particular as containing *praecepta,* advice on how to live according to a spiritual law, certainly continued, but in the context of the late fourth-century church I would suggest that we can isolate a trend toward understanding the gospel books themselves as a textualized *lex Christiana.* This trend can be illustrated by comparing various theological exegeses of a scriptural lemma from Psalm 110:2: "The Lord will send forth the rod of your strength out of Sion, and rule you in the midst of your enemies." Augustine declares the meaning of this text to be "so clear that to deny it would imply not merely unbelief and error, but downright idiocy." And what is the

---

37. The phrase is from Pamela Gordon, *Epicurus in Lycia: The Second-Century World of Diogenes of Oenoanda* (Ann Arbor, 1996), 2. Compare H. Gregory Snyder's discussion on "the rhetoric of stone" in his *Teachers and Texts in the Ancient World: Philosophers, Jews, and Christians* (London, 2000), 61–63.

38. Cyprian, *Letters* 10.1 and 29.1.   39. See especially Tertullian, *De Corona* 4.

clear meaning of this text, according to Augustine? That "out of Sion has been sent the *lex Christiana, which we call the Gospel,* and acknowledge as the rod of his strength" (*De civitate dei* 17.17). A similar exegesis of this lemma is given by Basil of Caesarea and John Chrysostom. Augustine's own, rather ominous, tying together of the gospel, the *lex Christiana,* and a "rod of strength" also gestures toward an increasingly polemical use of the term *lex Christiana:* heretics, like Jews and pagans, are now said to transgress its commandments.[40]

The conversion of Constantine in the early fourth century provoked serious questions concerning the status of a *lex Christiana* vis-à-vis Roman law. How was the concept of a *lex Christiana* to be handled by the imperial chancellery, and indeed in forensic contexts, in the post-Constantinian era? Was the *lex Christiana* incorporated or absorbed into Roman law under the Christian emperors? In other words, was Roman law itself "Christianized"? One concrete way of approaching this question is to look for evidence of Christian scripture within imperial legislation from Constantine onward, in the sense of either direct quotations or even oblique references. However, it is a striking fact that there are only two references to what the imperial chancellery obliquely calls "precepts of the apostles" in the entire surviving corpus of the Theodosian Code and late Roman jurisprudential writings before the Justinianic era. The first occurs at *Cod. Theod.* 16.6.2. pr. (dated 377) and condemns those who trample the "precepts of the apostle" underfoot by repeating holy baptism. The second is *Cod. Theod.* 16.2.27. pr. (390), where again the "precepts of the apostles" are mentioned with reference to Christian deaconesses. There is thus little evidence that the emperors "Christianized" their legal enactments by quoting from Christian scripture, that is, by literally bringing the words of the Christian book into the new Theodosian Code.

The term *lex Christiana,* however, does occur in the Theodosian Code. In 318 Constantine issued a rescript concerning the translation of (civil?) cases to the judgment of the Christian bishop and described that translation as a "transferral of the case to the *lex Christiana*" (*Cod. Theod.* 1.27.1). Constantine thus seems to imply, at least, a transferral of the case to a different "law," as well as a transferral of jurisdiction. Later imperial constitutions, however, do not specify what this "Christian law" might consist of exactly, and it would be a

---

40. Augustine, *Letter* 88 (406), from the clergy of Hippo to the Donatist bishop Januarius; compare Jerome, *Letter* 69.2.

mistake to assume that bishops did not use Roman legal principles when they judged concerning "sheep and farms." Once again the phrase *Christiana lex* is used by the imperial chancellery more as a way of marking a difference between Christians and the rest of late Roman society.[41]

One further possible hypothesis is that fourth- and fifth-century imperial officials understood the phrase *lex Christiana* in a deliberately vague context, frequently producing a hendiadys in which the terms "most holy religion" and *lex Christiana* simply appear as two in one. Terms such as *lex divina, antistes, sacerdotes, sacrosancta lex* and even *sacrosanctae scripturae* had a field of application before the era of imperial Christianity. The drafters of imperial constitutions in the fourth and fifth centuries must often have found it necessary to distinguish the new Christian context of such terms from their previous fields of practical application. This hypothesis is useful, as it reminds us that semantic terms themselves, as much as books, could be reordered and reshuffled from one field of application to another. The "distinguishing" application of the term *lex Christiana* would have become increasingly redundant as the old fields of application faded into a historical context and as the church began increasingly to elaborate a distinct system of (canon) law for itself; from at least the mid-sixth century onward, books of "canon law" became the archetypal textualized *lex Christiana*.[42]

In Justinianic courtrooms, however, it was enough to have copies of the gospel texts on display during legal processes and to rely upon them in procedural contexts, such as the swearing of oaths. Justinian thus harnessed the power and identity of the quintessential Christian books, without the need to actually open those texts in order to consult their words during every legal process. What was important to Justinian was that the Christian God should be literally called into the courtroom, should be spiritually "present," and the gospel books functioned as the avenue of invocation. The placing of gospel books within Justinianic courtrooms thus ensured that the place of judgment and the legal participants were animated by the Holy Spirit, but the cases themselves were still judged according to the letter of "Roman" law.

41. See *Const. Sirm.* 6 (425), in Mommsen and Meyer, *Theodosiani Libri XVI,* 911–12, which states that those belonging to the *lex Christiana* shall not be slaves to Jews and pagans.

42. For discussion relating to the sixth century, see the introduction to Nicolaas van der Wal and Bernard H. Stolte, eds., *Collectio Tripartita: Justinian on Religious and Ecclesiastical Affairs* (Groningen, 1994).

Daniel Sarefield

THE SYMBOLICS OF BOOK BURNING
The Establishment of a Christian Ritual of Persecution

As we reflect on the varied uses of the early Christian book, it is appropriate to consider one unintended use that has important implications for the social milieu of these texts.[1] I refer to the ritual destruction of a book by fire—a book burning. To willfully destroy a text by placing it in a fire is to perform an ancient and persistent action that is in its essence a ritual of purification. Yet a book burning is more than a ceremonial act; it is a spectacle that transmits forceful social and religious messages to victims, witnesses, and participants alike. As ritual and spectacle it served as an "idiom of authority" for those who deployed it.[2] The following discussion traces the development of book burning from its roots in the Roman Republic through the fifth century A.D. Although this analysis covers a long period, it is unified by its interest in certain consistencies in the rite's practical features, its meanings, and the *mentalités* behind the authorities' recourse to it. These changed little over the centuries, whether authorities were incinerating the books of unsanctioned ritual experts and diviners, magicians, Manichaeans, or Christians. But with the transi-

---

1. I would like to thank the organizers of the Early Christian Book Conference for the opportunity to present an earlier version of this paper, and the participants in the conference, whose insightful comments and questions greatly improved it. I must also thank my advisor, Professor Timothy E. Gregory, and Professors Anthony Kaldellis and David Pettegrew of Ohio State University, who read and discussed it with me. All errors are entirely my own.

2. On "idioms of authority," see Raymond Van Dam, *Leadership and Community in Late Antique Gaul* (Berkeley and Los Angeles, 1985), 20–25.

tion to a Christian Roman empire, former victims became book burners. The gradual appropriation of this ancient rite by Christians presents an opportunity to examine how early Christians reformulated one particular element of their Greco-Roman inheritance.[3]

Burning Books in the Roman World

Throughout antiquity communities employed rites of purification to establish and maintain relations with the gods. Some ceremonies were performed at regular intervals; others were occasional, undertaken in periods of crisis brought on by famine, plague, war, or other catastrophes. In hard times, such rites demonstrated that the authorities were "doing something" to confront the problems threatening society.[4] According to popular belief, such crises often indicated that the gods were angry, and that the harmony between human and divine had been soured by some breach in relations, such as by the introduction of new and improper religious beliefs and practices; hence the need for purification. Often these rites used fire, which served the dual purposes of destruction and purification.[5]

The Roman government long used this method to destroy religious texts whose ideas and ritual techniques were at odds with established religion and thus perceived as a threat to society. Since many incidents are known only through brief references, a few examples will illustrate this phenomenon in its Roman context. As early as 213 B.C., the Roman government took steps to confiscate religious texts it deemed dangerous. This early instance took place in

3. Scholarly interest in the adaptation of Greco-Roman ceremonies and spectacles by Christians has expanded in recent years. See, for example, ibid., 115–40, in which Van Dam discusses how the Christian community at Tours, "which was familiar with the traditional military and imperial idioms of authority that had successfully ensured the stability of central Gaul during the fourth century, now used those same idioms to define the leadership of their new bishop," Martin of Tours. For other examples, see Geoffrey Nathan, "The Rogation Ceremonies of Late Antique Gaul: Creation, Transmission, and the Role of the Bishop," *Classica et Mediaevalia* 49 (1998): 275–303; and Javier Arce, "Imperial Funerals of the Later Roman Empire: Change and Continuity," in *Rituals of Power: From Late Antiquity to the Middle Ages,* ed. Frans Theuws and Janet L. Nelson (Leiden, 2000), 115–29.

4. John E. Atkinson, "Turning Crises into Drama: The Management of Epidemics in Classical Antiquity," *Acta Classica* 44 (2001): 37.

5. Wolfgang Speyer, *Büchervernichtung und Zensur des Geistes bei Heiden, Juden und Christen* (Stuttgart, 1981), 31: "Das Feuer hat so eine zweifache Aufgabe: es befreit die Gemeinschaft von der ansteckenden Befleckung des fluchbringenden Buchs und reinigt sie."

the midst of Hannibal's invasion of Italy during the Second Punic War, when the rural population was forced into the city, causing severe social and economic disruption. Many, led by "petty priests and prophets," turned to foreign practices, and when the government attempted to disband their gatherings it met with resistance. In response, the senate ordered all those in possession of books of prophecy, prayers, or instructions for the performance of rituals to hand them over to the urban praetor.[6] What happened to the books after they were confiscated is left out of the account. Another incident, the earliest actual Roman book burning recorded in our sources and well known to both pagan and Christian writers, occurred in 181 B.C., at the close of a decade most famous for the violent suppression of the Bacchanalia. In that year, books attributed to Numa Pompilius, Rome's semilegendary second king who was credited by the Romans with founding some of their most ancient rites and festivals, were discovered in stone chests buried in fields below the Janiculum Hill.[7] The senate took a strong stand on these potentially dangerous sacred texts. Upon investigation, some were preserved while others were burned by the praetor in the *comitium,* "in sight of the people."[8] Sacrificial attendants prepared the bonfire. The customs of established religion informed the decision to retain or destroy each book. Those written in Latin and concerned with pontifical law escaped the flames, while those in opposition to established religion were burned. By such public destruction, the unmistakable message was conveyed to witnesses that the Roman state wholly rejected the beliefs contained and represented in these books. Moreover, by their public destruction, the power and authority of Rome and its religious beliefs and practices were confirmed.

During the principate, emperors assumed the role of earlier magistrates in carrying out such purges. In 12 B.C., Augustus's first act as *pontifex maximus* was to burn publicly more than two thousand magical and divinatory writings

6. As Livy explains concerning the events of 213 B.C., a complaint was made to the senate that many Roman women had abandoned traditional rites and were publicly offering unconventional prayers and sacrifices under the direction of "petty priests and prophets" *(sacrificuli ac vates).* The praetor urbanus, M. Aemilianus Lepidus, backed by a *senatus consultum,* ordered that all persons in possession of books of prophecy, prayers, and ritual instructions hand them over to the praetor by April 1 of that year and that no one should offer sacrifice in a public place according to strange or foreign rites. See Livy 25.1.6–12.

7. This event is recorded in several versions. See Valerius Maximus 1.1.12; Lactantius, *Divinae institutiones* 1.22.5–8; Livy 40.29; Pliny, *Naturalis historia* 13.84–87; Augustine, *De civitate Dei* 7.34.

8. Val. Max. 1.1.12.

determined to have "anonymous or unsuitable authorship."[9] Suetonius places this action in the context of other religious reforms enacted by Augustus as Rome's chief priest.[10] Just as had been the case for the magistrates of the republic, the protection and maintenance of the *pax deorum* were among Augustus's primary concerns as Rome's preeminent civic and religious leader.

So far as sources indicate, most emperors prior to the fourth century A.D. did not, like Augustus, authorize the burning of texts on religious grounds. More commonly, persons guilty of performing or participating in unsanctioned rites and practices received corporal punishment. The persecution of the Christians is the best-known example.[11] Astrologers were also expelled from the city or from Italy as an occasional, temporary measure, while those convicted of black magic were burned alive, a form of execution routinely used for those whose actions were regarded as a threat to society.[12] However, the possession by the accused of books of magic may have been decisive in determining guilt.[13] These texts were burned in public.[14] This pattern is also evident in the burning of Manichaean books, which began in the reign of Diocletian.[15]

9. Suetonius, *Divus Augustus* 31.1: *nullis vel parum idoneis auctoribus.* See also Dio Cassius 54.27.2–3.

10. See Suet. *Aug.* 30–32.

11. At Lyons in 177, the Christians were first banned from public places and then assaulted and beaten in the streets. After arrests, interrogations, and torture, many of the Christians from the vicinity were executed in prison or the arena; their bodies were exposed to public ridicule for six days before finally being burned and the ashes scattered into the Rhone River. Eusebius, *Hist. eccl.* 5.1.59–60. See W. H. C. Frend, *Martyrdom and Persecution in the Early Church: A Study of a Conflict from the Maccabees to Donatus* (Oxford, 1965), 1–30; and David S. Potter, "Martyrdom as Spectacle," in *Theater and Society in the Classical World,* ed. Ruth Scodel (Ann Arbor, 1993), 53–88.

12. Summarized in the late third-century compilation attributed to Iulius Paulus: "Magicae artis conscios summo supplicio adfici placuit, id est bestiis obici aut cruci suffigi. Ipsi autem magi vivi exuruntur," *Sententiae* 5.23.17 (*Fontes Iuris Romani Anteiustiniani* 2:409). See Frederick H. Cramer, "The Expulsion of Astrologers from Ancient Rome," *Classica et Mediaevalia* 12 (1951): 21–28, and Frederick H. Cramer, *Astrology in Roman Law and Politics* (Philadelphia, 1954), 276–81; Clyde Pharr, "The Interdiction of Magic in Roman Law," *Transactions and Proceeding of the American Philological Association* 63 (1932): 278. For a detailed discussion of the constraints placed on magicians prior to Constantine, see also Matthew W. Dickie, *Magic and Magicians in the Greco-Roman World* (New York, 2001), 142–250.

13. Cramer, *Astrology in Roman Law,* 269–95.

14. Ps.-Paul., *Sent.* 5.23.18: "Libros magicae artis apud se neminem habere licet; et penes quoscumque reperti sint, bonis ademptis ambustis his publice in insulam deportantur, humiliores capite puniuntur. Non tantum huius artis professio, sed etiam scientia prohibita est" (*Fontes Iuris Romani Anteiustiniani* 2:410).

15. Most scholars, from Theodor Mommsen to Peter Brown, have favored a date around 302 for the beginning of the persecution of the Manichaeans under Diocletian. See Samuel N. C. Lieu, *Manichaeism in the Later Roman Empire and Medieval China* (Manchester, 1985), 92–95. On the possible date of 297, see Lorne D. Bruce, "Diocletian, the Proconsul Iulianus, and the Manichaeans," in *Studies in Latin Lit-*

The emperor's concern was that the sect threatened the harmony between Romans and the gods by turning people away from traditional observances. The rescript of the emperor to the proconsul Iulianus illustrates this clearly: Manichaeism was a new and seemingly foreign religion that, "like the poison of a malignant serpent," disturbed the harmony of Roman society and threatened the stability and prosperity of its communities. In consequence, books of the Manichaeans, along with leaders of the sect, were ordered to be burned publicly.[16] Throughout the period, then, authorities of the Roman state burned books they considered dangerous on religious grounds.

During the empire, a wider circle of authorities also began to use the ritual spectacle of book burning, among them leaders of religious communities who were similarly engaged in local conflicts over proper religious beliefs and practices. Lucian of Samosata's *Alexander* is a key piece of evidence for this development. In the Paphlagonian town of Abonouteichos in the late second century, Alexander, founder of a thriving oracular shrine centered on the so-called New Asklepios, the serpent Glykon, came into conflict with the local Epicurean community and the Christians, who both opposed the oracle and regarded its founder and god as a hoax.[17] As Lucian reports, Alexander's followers resorted to street violence as the conflict escalated. When the Epicureans disrupted the ceremonies of Glykon and mocked the cult publicly, Alexander responded by burning an Epicurean book in the agora of the city, "as if he were burning the man himself."[18] The incineration was performed ceremonially, using fig wood, a combustible material with specific religious connotations.[19] As Alexander put the book into the flames he enjoined others to do

---

erature and Roman History, ed. Carl Deroux (Brussels, 1983), 3:336–47. Bruce argues from indirect evidence that the emperor was in Egypt that year carrying out important tax reforms.

16. *Lex Dei sive Mosaicarum et Romanarum legum collatio* 15.3.4, 6–8, *Fontes Iuris Romani Anteiustiniani* 2:580–81.

17. This book-burning incident is discussed in greater detail in "Bookburning in Religious Conflict in Roman Asia Minor: The Case of the Epicureans," chap. 3 of my dissertation, "'Burning Knowledge': Studies of Bookburning in Ancient Rome" (Ph.D. diss., Ohio State University, 2004).

18. Lucian, *Alexander* 47: εὑρὼν γὰρ τὰς Ἐπικούρου κυρίας δόξας, τὸ κάλλιστον, ὡς οἶσθα, τῶν βιβλίων καὶ κεφαλαιώδη περιέχον τῆς τἀνδρὸς σοφίας τὰ δόγματα, κομίσας εἰς τὴν ἀγορὰν μέσην ἔκαυσεν ἐπὶ ξύλων συκίνων ὡς δῆθεν αὐτὸν καταφλέγων, καὶ τὴν σποδὸν εἰς τὴν θάλασσαν ἐξέβαλεν, ἔτι καὶ χρησμὸν ἐπιφθεγξάμενος· "Πυρπολέειν κέλομαι δόξας ἀλαοῖο γέροντος."

19. As Macrobius, writing ca. A.D. 400, states, fig trees were under special protection from chthonic deities and could signify good or ill omen depending on the circumstances. The black fig, in particu-

likewise, saying, "I command this: Burn the teachings of this blind old man!"[20] Afterward, the ashes were scattered on the sea.

Other priests may well have heeded his injunction and burned Epicurean texts elsewhere, as is suggested by the testimonial of a miraculous healing from the early third century recorded by Aelian.[21] An ailing Epicurean named Euphronios was brought to a temple of Asklepios after other, more rational cures had failed. The priest advised the sufferer to burn his Epicurean texts and make a plaster from the ashes. The philosopher did so and was cured. With Alexander and his successors, book burning became an act of religious destruction that was not exclusive to the magistrates and interests of the Roman government, but was used by religious authorities for their own purposes, namely, to further the interests of their own community in its competition with other groups. This change foreshadows developments in book burning in relation to Christianity.

Burning Christian Books

Before the early fourth century, Christian books do not appear to have been specifically targeted for destruction by the Romans, neither in the numerous local persecutions nor in the empirewide assaults initiated by Decius and Valerian in the third century. Lucian's account is suggestive in this regard: Alexander's cult was "at war" with both the Epicureans and the Christians, but Christian books were left out of the spectacle and only the book of Epicurus was burned.[22] By contrast, the fury of the early fourth-century persecutors was

---

lar, was a wood that was to be used to destroy materials that were considered polluted or an abomination (*Saturnalia* 3.20.2).

20. Lucian, *Alex.* 47.

21. Aelian, fr. 89. See Emma J. Edelstein and Ludwig Edelstein, *Asclepius: A Collection and Interpretation of the Testimonies* (Baltimore, 1945; reprint, New York, 1975), 200–201.

22. Another work of Lucian's, *De morte Peregrini,* makes clear that Lucian understood how important sacred texts were for the Christians. Peregrinus was a Cynic philosopher best remembered for how he ended his life—by throwing himself into a great bonfire at the conclusion of the Olympic Games of 165. As Lucian recounts, when Peregrinus was a younger man, he was for a time a Christian. During his Christian phase, he became a leader of his local community and was said by Lucian to be responsible for interpreting some of their texts and for writing others. Although Lucian's intention is to lampoon Peregrinus, his discussion makes clear that he understood holy books were important for Christians. See *De mort. Peregr.* 11–12. On his self-immolation, which Lucian describes as a spectacle with religious connotations, see *De mort. Peregr.* 35–36.

directed specifically at Christian texts, indicating that an important change had occurred in their understanding of this religion, in particular regarding the role books played in its practice and dissemination.

Sacred texts had come to be used by Christians in a variety of ways. Books were among the most essential elements of Christian religious life. Indeed, the Christian mission was, from its beginnings, "substantially invested in texts."[23] Although by no means were all Christians literate, the scriptures, as texts to be read or to be heard or as symbols, were prominent in nearly every Christian activity: they were displayed in processions and read aloud to the congregation during worship services, interpreted in preaching and in instruction of catechumens, and deployed in apologies and for settling internal theological disputes. Many Christian communities had their own libraries, and production centers oversaw the manufacture and distribution of sacred texts.

The Roman state's recognition of the roles played by books in the transmission and practice of Christianity must have developed slowly over time. Most of this process is irrecoverable, but glimpses are visible in the *Acta* and *Passiones* of martyrs and other sources.[24] Some Christians brought their holy scriptures to hearings before government officials. A Numidian Christian named Speratus, for example, brought a *capsa* to his arraignment before the proconsul of Africa in the late second century.[25] When asked what it contained, he responded, "books and epistles of Paul, a just man."[26] It is likely that he intended to make use of them in his defense, although it is certain that this did not occur, for he was promptly led away.[27] What happened to these texts after Speratus and his companions were executed is not recorded.[28] The Christian apologists

23. Harry Y. Gamble, *Books and Readers in the Early Church: A History of Early Christian Texts* (New Haven, 1995), 99, 104. The aural reception and visual character of these texts are also major aspects of their role among early Christians. On which, see Averil Cameron, *Christianity and the Rhetoric of Empire: The Development of a Christian Discourse* (Berkeley and Los Angeles, 1991), and Frances Young, *Biblical Exegesis and the Formation of Christian Culture* (Cambridge, 1997).

24. Although the historicity of many *acta, passiones,* and hagiographies has been called into question, their value as social documents for the period in which they were written is considerable. See Sebastian P. Brock and Susan Ashbrook Harvey, trans., *Holy Women of the Syrian Orient* (Berkeley and Los Angeles, 1987), 2–3.

25. See Herbert Musurillo, trans., "The Acts of the Scillitan Martyrs," in *The Acts of the Christian Martyrs* (Oxford, 1972), 86–89.

26. *Passio Sanctorum Scillitanorum* 12, ibid., 88.

27. More than a century later, during the Great Persecution, another Christian, Euplus, was granted the opportunity to read from the book he brought before the *corrector Siciliae;* see below.

28. The symbolic value of the scriptures was tremendous for Christians in the second and third

of the second and third centuries addressed their works to the emperors and, more generally, to a non-Christian audience. Their works refer frequently to Christian sacred books to make their defense.[29] No matter what their opinion of Christianity, readers would be left with little doubt that books were a source of tremendous authority and inspiration for many Christians.

During the second and third centuries the Christian movement became an institution, identifiable by growing congregations served by a hierarchy of priestly officials, buildings for conducting services, and other property, such as books. Government opponents of Christianity recognized that they would have to eradicate its leaders and destroy its property if they were to check the spread of this dangerous cult.[30]

In the late third century, Diocletian, in his devotion to ancient Roman practices, struck out at the Christians. Like other emperors of provincial origin whose path to the throne was military service, Diocletian adopted the conservative *mos maiorum* and deemed traditional expressions of piety to the Roman gods beneficial to himself and the state.[31] The emperor took Jupiter as his divine patron and styled himself as the god's son, Jovius. In accordance with his sacred obligation to preserve the empire from threats to the *pax deo-*

centuries. This also can be inferred from an episode of the mid-third century reported by Eusebius. During the reign of the emperor Gallienus (253–68), a Christian in the Roman army named Marinus was ordered to sacrifice to the emperor in order to gain a promotion. The local bishop spirited him off to a nearby church, where he could consider his situation. There the bishop offered him the same choice, pointing first to the sword at his side and then to the Gospels on the altar. His fateful decision made, Marinus returned to the emperor and declared that he was indeed a Christian, for which he was later beheaded. Euseb. *Hist. eccl.* 7.15.1–5. See also Geoffrey A. Robbins, "'Fifty Copies of the Sacred Writings' (*VC* 4.36): Entire Bibles or Gospel Books?" in *Papers Presented to the Tenth International Conference on Patristic Studies Held in Oxford, 1987*, ed. Elizabeth A. Livingstone (Louvain, 1989), 1:91–98.

29. See Robert M. Grant, *Greek Apologists of the Second Century* (Philadelphia, 1988).

30. The period leading up to the outbreak of the general persecution witnessed the development by Rome's pagan intelligentsia of "the most formidable assault on Christianity in its brief history." Michael Bland Simmons, *Arnobius of Sicca: Religious Conflict and Competition in the Age of Diocletian* (Oxford, 1995), 22. Porphyry, arguably the greatest anti-Christian writer of the ancient world, published several works attacking Christianity, refuting its holy books, and calling on Christians to return to honoring the gods according to "ancestral tradition." See, for example, Porphyry, *Ad Marcellam* 18. Sossianus Hierocles, consular governor at the beginning of the Great Persecution, wrote the *Lover of Truth*, which also sought to prove the falsehood of the Christian scriptures. See Anthony Meredith, "Porphyry and Julian against the Christians," *ANRW* 2, no. 23.2 (1980): 1120–21. See also Timothy D. Barnes, "Sossianus Hierocles and the Antecedents of the Great Persecution," *Harvard Studies in Classical Philology* 80 (1976): 239–52.

31. For Diocletian's religious beliefs, see Stephen Williams, *Diocletian and the Roman Recovery* (London, 1985).

rum, he strengthened its borders by constructing religious shrines along the frontiers and by proscribing beliefs and practices, such as sorcery and Manichaeism, that jeopardized the harmony between Rome and the gods.[32] Although he avoided the problems posed by Christianity for nearly twenty years of his reign, accusations by a priest finally compelled the emperor to take action. The purported catalyst was that the Christians had interfered with a sacrifice and prevented omens from being taken.[33] By undermining rites crucial to the well-being of the state, the Christians jeopardized continued good relations with the gods.

On a "fit and auspicious day," February 23, 303—the day of the ancient Roman festival of the Terminalia—Diocletian began his assault on the church.[34] His selection of this particular festival underscores his conservatism, for according to tradition the Terminalia had been established by Numa.[35] The rite was connected with the stones that marked the boundaries between fields, offering sacrifices to the spirits presiding over them. To disturb such stones was forbidden, and an individual who tampered with one was considered accursed by the community.[36] On the same day, a public sacrifice and celebration commemorated the symbolic perimeter of Roman territory, separating the realm of peace and order from that of chaos and warfare.[37] In the republican era, Terminus, the god of boundaries, had become associated with Jupiter, Diocletian's patron de-

32. In the summer of 298, when the emperor traveled up the Nile River to make a lasting settlement with the desert nomads of Numidia, the Blemmyes and Nobatae, the boundary of Roman dominion moved downriver to the island of Philae. The Romans stationed a garrison there and, equally important, erected religious shrines that marked the boundaries of the Roman world. Diocletian's reign witnessed a massive program of fortification along the frontiers to promote security and internal stability. This project had religious overtones. At Palmyra, only recently retaken by the emperor Aurelian, Diocletian constructed a temple complex known as the Principia between 293 and 305. Its high point was dominated by the "Temple of the Standards," which boldly advertised the tetrarchs in a Latin inscription as "the repairers of the world and propagators of the human race." See the discussion by Fergus Millar, *The Roman Near East 31 B.C.–A.D. 337* (Cambridge, Mass., 1993), 174–207, esp. 176–90.

33. Lactantius, *De mortibus persecutorum* 10.1–5.

34. Ibid., 5.1.12: "Inquiritur peragendae rei dies aptus et felix ac potissimum Terminalia deliguntur, quae sunt a.d. septimum kalendas martias, ut quasi terminus imponeretur huic religioni."

35. H. H. Scullard, *Festivals and Ceremonies of the Roman Republic* (Ithaca, N.Y., 1981), 79–80.

36. Ibid., 80.

37. See Ray Laurence, "Ritual, Landscape, and the Destruction of Place in the Roman Imagination," in *Approaches to the Study of Ritual: Italy and the Ancient Mediterranean,* ed. John B. Wilkins (London, 1996), 111–21; and Ray Laurence, "Emperors, Nature, and the City: Rome's Ritual Landscape," *Accordia Research Papers* 4 (1994): 79–88. See also Clifford Ando, "The Palladium and the Pentateuch: Towards a Sacred Topography of the Later Roman Empire," *Phoenix* 55 (2001): 369–85.

ity.[38] The emperor deliberately chose this day, connected with the maintenance of community boundaries, to initiate his campaign against a cult that he considered a threat to the survival of the Roman community.[39] Having breached the sacred boundaries of the community by their refusal to honor the gods, the Christians were to be punished in the appropriate traditional manner.

In the morning twilight, the doors of the church in Diocletian's capital, Nicomedia, were forced open and the building ransacked. Scriptures and other books discovered inside were brought into the public square and burned.[40] By the end of the day the church had been dismantled, and the same fate befell other buildings that housed Christian books. The first edict of the Great Persecution was made public on the following day, and with its promulgation throughout the empire local authorities set about the process of searching for, seizing, and publicly destroying Christian books. Eusebius reports that he saw with his own eyes holy scriptures committed to the flames in the marketplace.[41] Some bishops surrendered their books willingly, others under compulsion.[42] Some evaded the order by turning over other books, including heretical texts, instead.[43] Others believed that anything less than defiant resistance was a betrayal of their religion, and suffered the consequences. Felix, the bishop of Thibiuca in Africa, refused to hand over the scriptures of his congregation and was decapitated.[44]

38. On the "imperial theology" of the tetrarchy, see J.H.W.G. Liebeschuetz, *Continuity and Change in Roman Religion* (Oxford, 1979), 237–41. See also the comments of J. Rufus Fears, "The Cult of Jupiter and Roman Imperial Ideology," *ANRW* 2, no. 17.1 (1981): 118–21.

39. Scullard argues that the purpose of the rite was to foster feelings of neighborliness and restrain territorialism, but this is inconsistent with its original purpose, which was to emphasize the importance of these boundaries for the well-being of the community and to maintain the proper relationship with their guardian spirits. See Scullard, *Festivals and Ceremonies,* 80.

40. Euseb. *Hist. eccl.* 8.2.4. See also Eusebius, *De martyribus Palaestinae, praef.* 1, and Lactant. *De mort. pers.* 13.

41. Euseb. *Hist. eccl.* 8.2.1.

42. As Augustine describes, during the persecution in North Africa a man by the name of Victor of Rustica was compelled by the magistrate Valentinianus to throw a copy of the Gospels into the fire with his own hands. As Victor pleaded before the tribunal organized after the persecution to investigate the surrendering of the scriptures, the copy he destroyed was unreadable. See Augustine, *Contra Cresconium* 3.27.30 (*CSEL* 52.435–37).

43. Bishop Mersurius of Carthage claimed that he allowed heretical works to be discovered and destroyed by Roman officials while successfully hiding copies of the true Christian scriptures. See Augustine, *Breviculus collationis cum Donatistis* 3.13.25 (*CSEL* 53.73–75). Bonanus of Calama claimed that he handed over medical treatises, and Marinus of Aquae Tibilitana also claimed that he had handed over other papers. See August. *Contra Cresc.* 3.27.30 (*CSEL* 52.435–37).

44. *Acta S. Felicis Episcopi* (*PL* 8:680–83).

Other edicts followed, widening the scope of the state's attack on the Christians, but the centrality of the scriptures is evident even in incidents where they were not burned. In 304, for example, the future saint Euplus walked into the council chambers at Catania where the *corrector Siciliae,* Calvisianus, was in the midst of a hearing. Euplus presented himself to the authorities as a Christian. His proof: personal possession of the Christian Gospels, which he carried before himself as he shouted aloud, "I am a Christian and I want to die for the name of Christ."[45] The governor asked him, "Why did you retain these writings which the emperors have forbidden, and why did you not give them up?" He replied, "Because I am a Christian and it [is] forbidden to give them up.... Whoever gives them up loses eternal life."[46] When he would not relent under torture, Euplus was sentenced to die by the sword. Led off to execution, his copy of the Gospels was hung about his neck. A herald proclaimed, "Behold Euplus, the Christian, an enemy of our emperors and our gods!"[47]

Burning Books in the Christian Roman Empire

The reign of Constantine witnessed the beginning of the toleration of Christianity and set it on course to become Rome's state religion, but the transformation of the book-burning rite was a gradual process. In the fourth century, Christian writers began to call on the emperors to defend their faith against beliefs that were a threat to Rome and the Christian religion.[48] Christian emperors used the forces at their disposal to combat these threats more frequently and more violently than had their predecessors.[49] This increase in violence, at least in regard to the persecution of such heresies as Manichaeism, can be seen as a fusion of the strident Roman patriotism of emperors like Diocletian and the doctrinal intolerance of Christianity.[50] Old foes continued to be assaulted: Valentinian and Valens, for example, placed a ban on astrology in

---

45. *Acta Eupli* 1.1, Musurillo, *Acts of the Christian Martyrs,* 315.

46. Ibid., 2.1–2, 317.

47. Ibid., 3.2–3, 319.

48. See, for example, Firmicus Maternus, whose *De errore profanarum religionum* urged the emperors to persecute pagan practices and beliefs.

49. See Ramsay MacMullen, "Judicial Savagery in the Later Roman Empire," *Chiron* 16 (1986): 43–62.

50. See Peter Brown, "The Diffusion of Manichaeism in the Roman Empire," *Journal of Roman Studies* 59 (1969): 97–98.

373, and transgressors convicted of practicing, learning, or teaching it suffered capital punishment.[51] Sorcery continued to be prohibited, but with the growing influence of Christian beliefs on society it came to be understood not as an illegitimate form of interaction with the gods but as communion with demonic forces acting in opposition to God.[52]

In their role as defenders of the Christian faith, emperors also burned texts whose ideas they regarded as heretical and therefore a threat to the unity of Christian society. Following the accession of the emperor Theodosius I in 379, non-Nicene forms of Christianity were proscribed. The "noxious" writings of such radical theologians as Eunomius, and those of the heretical Montanists, were ordered burned.[53] Most emperors of the late fourth and early fifth centuries also continued to forbid the practices of sorcerers and astrologers.[54] Their books and the teaching of these arts were prohibited. In this period the beliefs of heretical sects, and eventually even traditional Roman religion itself, came to be understood in the same light.[55] To this end, fifth-century emperors ordered the public burning of such unorthodox books as the writings of Nestorius and such anti-Christian tracts as those of the Platonist Porphyry.[56]

Representatives of the church also began to adopt these methods for set-

51. *Cod. Theod.* 9.16.8.

52. See Valerie I. J. Flint, "The Demonisation of Magic and Sorcery in Late Antiquity: Christian Redefinitions of Pagan Religions," in *Witchcraft and Magic in Europe,* vol. 2, *Ancient Greece and Rome,* ed. Bengt Ankarloo and Stuart Clark (Philadelphia, 1999), 315–16.

53. *Cod. Theod.* 16.5.34: "The clerics of the Eunomian and Montanist superstitions shall be expelled from the association and intercourse of all municipalities and cities. . . . We command that the books containing the doctrine and matter of all their crimes shall be immediately sought out and produced, with the greatest astuteness and with the exercise of due authority, and they shall be consumed with fire immediately under the supervision of the judges. If perchance any person should be convicted of having hidden any of these books under any pretext or fraud whatever and of having failed to deliver them, he shall know that he himself shall suffer capital punishment, as a retainer of noxious books and writings and as guilty of the crime of magic." Clyde Pharr, trans., *The Theodosian Code and Novels and the Sirmondian Constitutions* (Princeton, 1952), 455–56.

54. Dickie, *Magic and Magicians,* 251–321.

55. As H. A. Drake explains, following the brief but eventful reign of Constantine's nephew, Julian, the emperors moved toward a more coercive posture. Within the church, the threat posed by heresy was instrumental in unifying Christians in the belief that coercion was necessary. See H. A. Drake, "Lambs into Lions: Explaining Early Christian Intolerance," *Past and Present* 153 (Nov. 1996), esp. 22–36. See also A. H. Armstrong, "The Way and The Ways: Religious Tolerance and Intolerance in the Fourth Century A.D.," *VC* 38 (1984): 1–17; and Anthony Meredith, "Orthodoxy, Heresy, and Philosophy in the Latter Half of the Fourth Century," *Heythrop Journal* 16, no. 1 (1975): 5–21.

56. On the destruction of Nestorian books, see *Codex Iustinianus* 1.1.3 (448). See also Mansi 5:418, where, regarding Porphyry's books, Theodosius II and Valentinian had stated, "We order to be committed

tling theological and other internal conflicts. In the mid-fourth century, for example, Bishop Paulinus of Dacia was accused of practicing magic and expelled from the church. Another bishop, Macedonius, personally burned his offending writings.[57] In the fifth century the role of the bishop expanded. In 409, for example, when the emperors Honorius and Theodosius II again attacked astrology, they ordered all practitioners of the art to hand over their books to be burned in the presence of a bishop.[58] The location of public incinerations began to shift as well, from traditional Roman civic spaces to more explicitly Christian religious venues. Hence at Berytos in the 490s, the immolation of magical texts was carried out by the bishop in front of the Church of the Theotokos.[59] Similar burnings of Manichaean texts were performed before other churches in Rome.

Roman emperors continued to authorize the rite, and books continued to be burned publicly on their authority and in witness to their power, but in the Christian world, violent acts like book burning came to be understood as spiritually beneficial for anyone who performed them.[60] In Gaza, for example, Bishop Porphyry conducted a campaign to eradicate pagan practices in the late fourth and early fifth centuries.[61] During the culmination of that campaign in 402, the city's most celebrated temple, the Marneion, was burned down by a mob of Christians. In the wake of its destruction, eager participants spilled into the streets and began to conduct door-to-door searches of near-

---

to the fire everything that Porphyry, impelled by his own madness, or anyone else has composed against the Christian religion, no matter in whose possession the books are found. For all the writings that move God to wrath and harm the soul we do not want to come even into men's hearing."

57. See Hilarion, *Quindecim Fragmenta ex Opere Historico,* fr. 3.27 (*PL* 10:663).

58. *Cod. Theod.* 9.16.12: "We decree that the astrologers shall be banished not only from the city of Rome but also from all the municipalities, unless, after the books of their false doctrine have been consumed in flames under the eyes of the bishop, they are prepared to transfer their faith to the Catholic religion and never return to their former false doctrine. But if they should not do this and, contrary to the salutary constitution of Our Clemency, should be apprehended in the municipalities or should introduce there the secrets of their false doctrine and profession, they shall receive the punishment of deportation," Pharr, *Theodosian Code,* 238–39.

59. Zacharias, *Vita Severi* 18, ed. M.-A. Kugener, *Zacharie le Scholastique: Vie de Sévère d'Antioch, Patrologia Orientalis* 2, no. 1 (1907), 68–71.

60. See, for example, Michael Gaddis, "'There Is No Crime for Those Who Have Christ': Religious Violence in the Christian Roman Empire" (Ph.D. diss., Princeton University, 1999), 143–93; and David Frankfurter, "'Things Unbefitting Christians': Violence and Christianization in Fifth-Century Panopolis," *JECS* 8 (2000): 273–95.

61. See Mark the Deacon, *Vita Porphyrii* 70–84, in Henri Grégoire and M.-A. Kugener, eds., *Marc le diacre: Vie de Porphyre, évêque de Gaza* (Paris, 1930), 56–66.

by non-Christian homes. Many books and idols were uncovered, and these were burned in bonfires or cast into public latrines. Such incidents were frequently accompanied by sudden conversions to Christianity. The seizure and destruction of forbidden texts had become an act considered pleasing to God, no matter who performed it.

A precedent for this kind of piety had been established by Paul during his stay in Ephesus. As described in the Acts of the Apostles, Paul accomplished miracles there that demonstrated that the power of his god was greater than that of pagan gods.[62] Members of the local populace, including some in possession of books of magic, were spontaneously converted: "Many also of those who were now believers came, confessing and divulging their practices. And a number of those who practiced magic arts brought their books together and burned them in sight of all."[63] By burning these books, no less indispensable for performing and preserving magical practices than the books of the Christians for their religion, these individuals demonstrated their sincere rejection of past beliefs. Personal destruction of one's private forbidden texts came to signify genuine conversion. The story of the third-century magician Cyprian of Antioch, although probably a hagiographical invention, is evidence of the power of book burning as a symbolic act.[64] Cyprian, whom Prudentius describes as "pre-eminent among the young men of Antioch for his skill in perverse arts," became a convert following his failure to corrupt a Christian virgin through sorcery.[65] Conceding defeat, he is reported to have publicly confessed his occult practices and burned his books. Book burning would continue to be a sign of sincere conversion throughout late antiquity. As the Bithynian monk Hypatius responded to another magician-convert some two hundred years later, "If you want to become a Christian, bring me your book!"[66]

In the Roman world, book burning was an ancient civic ritual of purification and a spectacle that transmitted powerful religious and ideological messages. Roman magistrates burned books in times of crisis to restore good

62. Acts 19.

63. Acts 19:18–19.

64. Gregory Nazianzen, *Oratio 24, In laudem S. Cypriani* (*PG* 35:1169–93); Prudentius, *Peristephanon* 13.21–4; Eudocia, *De martyrio sancti Cypriani* 1.240, ed Arthur Ludwich (Leipzig, 1897), summarized in Photius, *Bibliotheca,* codex 184 (*PG* 103:537–41).

65. Prudent. *Perist.* 13.21: unus erat iuvenum doctissimus artibus sinistris.

66. Kallinikos, *Vita Hypatii* 43.8 (*SC* 177:259).

relations with the gods when society seemed threatened by the pollution of improper rites and beliefs. Beginning in the second century A.D., book burning came to be used by other religious authorities engaged in intercommunal conflicts over the same issues. This development continued as bishops, other Christian authorities, and even laypersons came to appropriate book burning in the fourth century and thereafter.

This is not to suggest that all Christians were comfortable with the appropriation of this pagan rite and spectacle, which, indeed, had consumed their own holy books. Augustine, commenting on the destruction of the "Books of Numa," insisted that the senate had rightly destroyed these texts since they were not fit to become known by the people, members of the senate, or even the priests.[67] By destroying them they prevented the state from being thrown into chaos. Not all Christians agreed, however. Lactantius, remarking earlier on the same event, criticized the burning of books as a method for resolving religious problems:

That was done foolishly, indeed, for to what advantage were the books burned when this very action, namely, that they were burned because they were derogatory to religion, was memorialized? There was no one in the Senate at that time who was not very foolish, however; because the books could be destroyed, yet the affair itself could not be erased from memory. So while they wished to prove to posterity with what great piety they defended religion, they lessened the authority of that very religion by their testimony.[68]

Such is the ambiguous legacy of a very unambiguous ritual.

67. August. *De civ. D.* 7.34.
68. Lactant. *Div. inst.* 1.22.5–8, in Mary Francis McDonald, trans., *The Divine Institutes, Books I–VII* (Washington, D.C., 1964), 89.

PART V   TEXTS AND THE BODY

Kim Haines-Eitzen

ENGENDERING PALIMPSESTS
Reading the Textual Tradition of the
Acts of Paul and Thecla

In January 1892 twin sisters Agnes Lewis and Margaret Gibson, scholars of Semitic languages from Cambridge, made their first of many trips to St. Catherine's monastery in Sinai.[1] The primary aim of their visit was to study the manuscripts in the library and to photograph the Syriac codex of the Apology of Aristides discovered earlier by James Rendel Harris. But their most significant discovery on this trip came not from rummaging through the monastic library; rather, it occurred at the dining table. I quote here at length from the story, as told by Lewis and Gibson's biographer, A. Whigham Price (italics are mine):

Hospitality in an *all-male community,* though cordial, is apt to be of a somewhat *rough-and-ready kind.* At St Catherine's, meals tended to be served on the firm principle that one eats to live, and no more. Butterdishes, for instance, were scorned: when, at breakfast, butter was required, it was simply planked down on an old sheet of discarded manuscript, and put thus on the table. After all, vellum is a tough material, and will resist grease for at least the period of one meal; and its use reduces the washing-up. Such, at any rate, was the monks' normal custom, and they saw no reason to vary it for their *feminine visitors.* They had been so long out of the world that they had forgotten that *women attach considerable importance to such trifles.* So the butter for the twins' meals appeared on the same ersatz tableware. Our *heroines* were somewhat disconcerted but, as *well-bred women,* naturally made no comment.

1. The story of this trip is told by A. Whigham Price, *The Ladies of Castlebrae: A Story of Nineteenth-Century Travel and Research* (Gloucester, 1985), 107ff.; for later trips see also Agnes Smith Lewis, *In the Shadow of Sinai: A Story of Travel and Research from 1895 to 1897* (Cambridge, 1898).

Agnes, indeed, saw in such unusual arrangements an excellent opportunity to combine study with eating, to blend intellectual refreshment with the somewhat clumsy methods prescribed by the Lord for refuelling the human frame. Hence it soon became her custom to scrutinise the 'butterdish' with an unobtrusive scholarly eye, to see whether it offered anything of interest. As a rule it did not; but one morning the grubby sheet proved to be a fragment of a palimpsest, and at the edge of the 'dish', disappearing under the lump of butter, was a line or two of the underwriting—clearly visible—which she at once recognised as a verse of the Gospels. This happened to be in Syriac, Agnes' newly-acquired language (and therefore one in which she happened to be especially interested at that moment). Tactful and casually-worded enquiries, after the meal, led her to a certain basket in the glory-hole where they had been working. There, she found a complete Syriac palimpsest of three hundred and fifty-eight pages, the leaves of which were mostly glued together by dirt and damp—so firmly, indeed, that the least force used to separate them resulted in instant crumbling. . . .

The problem was how to investigate it, so frail was the condition of the codex: even the most delicate and careful manipulation with the fingers resulted in immediate damage to the vellum. Suddenly Agnes had an inspiration. Of course!—*her tiny tea-kettle,* that indispensable item of luggage for any British traveller. The very thing! Maggie was dispatched to the tent for it; the little spirit lamp was lit, and the kettle put on to boil. As soon as it began to steam, they held the leaves in the vapour; and to their satisfaction, the pages separated easily. The British passion for tea had once more paid dividends.

When the pages were dry enough to examine, Agnes scrutinised them carefully under her lens. After a few minutes, she straightened her back and reported excitedly that while the upper (or more recent) writing seemed to contain an account—*very well-thumbed in places!*—of the lives of *certain rather frisky women saints,* the underlying and more ancient script was evidently a copy of the four Gospels of a very early date indeed.[2]

The immediate interest of the palimpsest, of course, lay in the underwriting—the four Gospels dated to the fifth or even late fourth century. Some eight years later Agnes Lewis transcribed and published the upper writing, the eighth-century copy of the lives of so-called "frisky women saints." Lewis herself noted the asymmetry of value: "Although these 'Select Narratives' cannot pretend to much value when compared with the ancient Gospel-text which underlies them, and which has been preserved for their sakes alone during eleven centuries, and though it would be a difficult task to sift the few grains of historical truth which they contain from their bushels of imaginative chaff, they are not without some literary beauty."[3]

2. Price, *Ladies of Castlebrae,* 125–26.
3. Agnes Smith Lewis, ed., *Select Narratives of Holy Women from the Syro-Antiochene or Sinai Palimpsest* (London, 1900), vi.

Why begin with this lengthy narrative? First, it is an example of a highly gendered and multilayered narrative regarding a late nineteenth-century event—the unearthing of the Syriac palimpsest.[4] Price's telling of the event casts the characters as "rough-and-ready" men—the monks of St. Catherine's who, Price winks, appear to have thoroughly enjoyed reading the lives of the "frisky women saints"—and the monks' "feminine visitors," "well-bred women" who attached "considerable importance" to the "trifles" of dishware. Likewise, the narrative produced by both Price and Lewis herself in 1900 highlighted the asymmetry of the two layers of the palimpsest itself: the Gospels produced by the male evangelists far outweighed in importance the "imaginative chaff" of the lives of those "frisky women."[5]

Yet to some extent the palimpsest bears witness to a different hierarchy: old gospel texts reused for the lives of exemplary women saints—a palimpsest engendered in multiple senses. The "lives" of Thecla, Eugenia, Mary/Marinus, Euphrosyne, Pelagia, Onesima, Drusis, Barbara, Mary (slave of Tertullius), Irene, Euphemia, Sophia, Cyprian, and Justa are written over the Gospels of Matthew, Mark, Luke, and John. Thecla is written above—on top of—Mark; Eugenia on top of Mark, Luke, and Matthew; Euphrosyne on top of Matthew and Luke; Pelagia on top of Mark, and so forth. The colophon itself offers the scribe's rationale: "I, the mean one, and the sinner, John the Stylite, of the monastery of Beth-Mari-Qanun in the town of Ma'arath Kaukab of Antioch, by the mercy of God, I have written this book for the profit of myself, of my brethren, and of those who are neighbors to it."[6] Palimpsests, of course, are not uncommon: similar to our Sinaitic palimpsest is the better-known Codex Ephraemi Rescriptus, on whose early fifth-century text of the Bible the Greek translation of the sermons of Ephrem were copied in the twelfth century.[7]

4. On this Sinaitic Syriac palimpsest, see Bruce M. Metzger, *The Early Versions of the New Testament: Their Origin, Transmission, and Limitations* (Oxford, 1977), 37–38; Robert L. Bensly et al., *The Four Gospels in Syriac Transcribed from the Sinaitic Palimpsest* (Cambridge, 1894); and Agnes Smith Lewis, *Some Pages of the Four Gospels Re-transcribed from the Sinaitic Palimpsest* (London, 1896); see also Agnes Smith Lewis's standard edition of the manuscript: *The Old Syriac Gospels, or, Evangelion da-Mepharreshê* (London, 1910).

5. I am reminded here of Wettstein's eighteenth-century acceptance of the attribution of the fifth-century Codex Alexandrinus to the hand of Thecla on the basis of its many mistakes (see my *Guardians of Letters: Literacy, Power, and the Transmitters of Early Christian Literature* [New York and Oxford, 2000], 51).

6. Lewis, *Select Narratives*, 206.

7. See Bruce M. Metzger, *The Text of the New Testament: Its Transmission, Corruption, and Restoration*, 3d ed. (New York and Oxford, 1992), 12, 48–49.

More typically, however, palimpsests were used to "retire" classical literature and prepare a new copy of a Christian text; thus we find Augustine's *Commentary on the Psalms* copied over a fourth-century copy of Cicero's *De republica* (Vat. lat. 5757). The term, of course, usually refers to manuscripts in which one text was "rubbed out" or "erased" (-ψηστος from ψάω), so that the material, usually parchment but sometimes papyrus, could be reused (πάλιν). In the Sinaitic palimpsest we have a vivid example of a palimpsest (en)gendered—created and gendered in its first creation, gendered in its late nineteenth-century context, and gendered in a late twentieth-century reading of the account of its find.

But the phrase "engendering palimpsests" might be taken less in a material sense and used profitably in a text-critical context. I want to turn now to the light that textual criticism can shed on contested interpretations of texts and the ways these interpretations affect the very words of the texts. More precisely, I want to look at the ways in which text transmission intersected with notions about the human body, the divine body, competing understandings of the roles of women, and conflicts over the rise of early Christian asceticism.

Books and Bodies in Early Christianity

The transmission of early Christian literature from the second through fourth centuries was remarkably interwoven with the rise and development of early Christian asceticism. The relationship between early Christian books and early Christian bodies can, in fact, be configured in several ways and located at various sites of early Christian religiosity. Books and bodies shared certain qualitative similarities: just as bodies were considered malleable, porous, corruptible, and susceptible to invasion, pollution, and disease, as well as to shaping and formation, so too were books and the texts they contained susceptible to modification, misinterpretation, and misuse, as well as correction and reformation; indeed, these things could not be prevented.[8] Like bod-

---

8. The ancient and modern literature on ancient constructions of the human body—and the gendered body in particular—is enormous. The following secondary treatments have been most helpful in my work: Michel Foucault, *The History of Sexuality,* vols. 1 and 2, trans. Robert Hurley (New York, 1980); Dale B. Martin, *The Corinthian Body* (New Haven, 1995); Aline Rousselle, *Porneia: On Desire and the Body in Antiquity,* trans. Felicia Pheasant (Oxford, 1988); David H. J. Larmour, Paul Allen Miller, and Charles Platter, eds., *Rethinking Sexuality: Foucault and Classical Antiquity* (Princeton, 1998); David M.

ies, books were anything but fixed. Hence the need for marginal notes that read, "Fool and knave, can't you leave the old reading alone and not alter it!"[9] Clement of Alexandria, Irenaeus of Lyon, Rufinus of Aquileia—these church fathers and others attest to an awareness that texts were subject to scribal tampering, and they include curse formulas to protect their books: "I adjure you, who will copy out this book, by our Lord Jesus Christ, by his glorious advent when he comes to judge the living and the dead, that you shall compare what you transcribe and correct it with this copy that you are transcribing, with all care, and you shall likewise transcribe this oath and put it in the copy."[10] Books and bodies were vulnerable, and that pains were taken to protect both of them attests to their power.

We might also locate a more direct link between books and ascetic bodies, for within some channels of early Christian ascetic movements books took on acute and particular importance. Take, for example, the story of a certain balsam grower early in the fourth century named Ammon of Nitria. Palladius reports that Ammon, unable to withstand family pressures, finally agreed to marry at the age of twenty-two. On his wedding night, he called his bride to his side and said, "Come, my lady, and I will explain this matter to you finally. The marriage that we have just entered is not necessary. We will do well if from now on each of us sleeps alone so that we may please God by keeping our virginity sacred." And then he took a small book from his cloak and read to her "from the apostle and the saviour himself as it were, for she lacked knowledge of scriptures. And adding to most of what he read ideas from his own mind, and he explained the word about virginity and purity, so that she was convinced by the grace of God."[11]

Halperin, John J. Winkler, Froma I. Zeitlin, eds., *Before Sexuality: The Construction of Erotic Experience in the Ancient Greek World* (Princeton, 1990); Judith P. Hallett and Marilyn B. Skinner, eds., *Roman Sexualities* (Princeton, 1997); and Peter Brown, *The Body and Society: Men, Women, and Sexual Renunciation in Early Christianity* (New York, 1988). On ancient concerns about the "misuse" and "corruption" of books, see Haines-Eitzen, *Guardians of Letters,* 105–11.

9. The thirteenth-century marginal note found in the fourth-century biblical Codex Vaticanus. See Bruce M. Metzger, *Manuscripts of the Greek Bible: An Introduction to Greek Palaeography* (New York and Oxford, 1981), 74–75.

10. Irenaeus, *On the Ogdoad,* as quoted by Eusebius, *Hist. eccl.* 5.20. Translations of ancient texts are mine unless otherwise indicated.

11. Palladius, *Historia Lausiaca* 8; my translation is based on the Greek text found in vol. 2 of Cuthbert Butler, *The Lausiac History of Palladius* (Cambridge, 1904). English translation in Robert T. Meyer, *Palladius: The Lausiac History* (New York, 1965).

What did they do? They proceeded to live together but sleep "in separate beds"; they lived this way until they "had reached a state of insensibility to
lust," and then Ammon, at his wife's encouragement—for she wanted him to
display his virtue—departed into the mountains of Nitria to take up the life
of a hermit. This story, paradigmatic of many narratives about the emergence
of monasticism in Egypt, offers a causal link between books and bodies. It is
the book, and the texts therein, that effects a bodily response of protected and
preserved virginity and lifelong celibacy.

The relationship between books and bodies in early Christianity can also
be located in the very genesis of Christian literature, for human bodies were,
of course, the producers and (re)producers of early Christian books. That
copying was a task for the body, and a continual reminder of embodiment, is
clear from marginal notes and colophons found in ancient and medieval manuscripts: "He who does not know how to write supposes it to be no labor; but
though only three fingers write, the whole body labors"; "Writing bows one's
back, thrusts the ribs into one's stomach and fosters a general debility of the
body"; "As travellers rejoice to see their home country, so also is the end of a
book to those who toil in writing"; "The end of the book; thanks be to God."[12]
So write the scribes who labored at copying books.[13] And yet, while we know
that it was human bodies that copied written texts throughout antiquity, we
still know little about the persons responsible—their location, their work environment, their socioeconomic standing, their gender. Our literary evidence
provides little by way of comment, though one can infer from the combination of epigraphic evidence and literary comments about women as scribes—
in the context of Eusebius's comments about Origen's female calligraphers, in
the vitae of Melania the Younger and Caesaria the Younger much later, and in
the Coptic *Lausiac History*'s mention of Litia/Lydia of Thessalonike, who was
"a scribe writing books"[14]—that women were involved in the copying of early
Christian literature.

12. Metzger, *Text of the New Testament*, 17–18.

13. On writing as ascetic devotion, see especially Derek Krueger, "Writing as Devotion: Hagio-
graphical Composition and the Cult of the Saints in Theodoret of Cyrrhus and Cyril of Scythopolis,"
Church History 66 (1997): 707–19; Derek Krueger, "Hagiography as an Ascetic Practice in the Early
Christian East," *Journal of Religion* 79 (1999): 216–32.

14. Butler, *Lausiac History*, 1:150; Eusebius, *H.E.* 6.23; *Life of Melania* 26 (*SC* 90:178–80); *Life of
Caesarius* 1.58 (*MGM, SRM* 3:481).

The earliest Christian papyri contain clues as to their copyists. The use of handwriting that falls somewhere between documentary and literary hands, the use of such stylistic features as the *nomina sacra,* the appearance of harmonistic tendencies—such features suggest that during the second and third centuries, early Christian scribes worked privately and individually to reproduce early Christian texts.[15] While some of these scribes may have been professionals, many of them—in contrast to the scribes who copied Greco-Roman literature more generally—seem to have been nonprofessionals who had a vested interest in the texts they were copying. Herein lies the significance of exploring the identities of early Christian scribes. They were not mindless copyists, the ancient equivalent of photocopy machines. Rather, they often took the "care" to change, to manipulate, and (to their minds) to correct the text they were copying to make it say what they thought it meant.[16] It is no coincidence that in the earliest Christian texts we find the most fluidity and variety of readings. This brings us to yet another link between texts and bodies: some of the variant readings in early Christian texts appear to intersect with issues of gender—especially the roles of women in the early church—and the rise of asceticism.

Take, for example, the textual tradition of the book of Acts. A number of scholars have noted the variant readings that appear especially in the fifth-century Codex Bezae.[17] In Acts 17:4, the description of Paul's converts includes "many of the devout Greeks and not a few prominent women"; the fifth-

---

15. Haines-Eitzen, *Guardians of Letters,* esp. 77–104.

16. The best treatment of the intersection of theological/Christological debates and text transmission is that of Bart D. Ehrman, *The Orthodox Corruption of Scripture: The Effect of Early Christological Controversies on the Text of the New Testament* (New York and Oxford, 1993).

17. Ben Witherington, "The Anti-Feminist Tendencies of the 'Western' Text in Acts," *Journal of Biblical Literature* 103 (1984): 82–84; Bart D. Ehrman, "The Text as Window: New Testament Manuscripts and the Social History of Early Christianity," in *The Text of the New Testament in Contemporary Research: Essays on the Status Quaestionis,* ed. Bart D. Ehrman and Michael W. Holmes (Grand Rapids, Mich., 1995), esp. 368; Bart D. Ehrman, "The Text of the Gospels at the End of the Second Century," in *Codex Bezae: Studies from the Lunel Colloquium June 1994,* ed. D. C. Parker and C.-B. Amphoux (Leiden, 1996), esp. 116; Elizabeth Schüssler-Fiorenza, *In Memory of Her: A Feminist Theological Reconstruction of Christian Origins* (New York, 1983), esp. 51–52; Curt Niccum and Jeffrey Childers, "'Anti-Feminist' Tendency in the 'Western' Text of Acts?" in *Essays on Women in Earliest Christianity,* ed. Carroll D. Osburn (Joplin, Miss., 1993), 1:469–92; and Eldon J. Epp, *The Theological Tendency of Codex Bezae Cantabrigiensis in Acts* (Cambridge, 1966). This issue was addressed most recently by Dominika Kurek, "Some Textual Problems with Prisca and Aquila," a paper delivered to the Society of Biblical Literature, Toronto, Nov. 25, 2002.

century Codex Bezae, however, changes the case ending for "women" from genitive to nominative, thereby stating that many devout Greeks were converted, along with "wives of the prominent men"! Just a few verses later, Codex Bezae changes the word order so that the text places emphasis on the men of prominence rather than the women. In Acts 18:26, Codex Bezae minimizes the prominence of Priscilla by placing her name after the mention of Aquila, her husband. Even better known is the case of 1 Corinthians 14:34–35 ("Let women in the churches be silent. For it is not permitted for them to speak, but let them be subordinate, just as the law says. If they wish to learn anything, let them ask their husbands at home. For it is shameful for a woman to speak in church"). Without rehearsing the arguments for and against the attribution of this passage to Paul, it should be noted that there is an emerging scholarly consensus that these verses were interpolated into Paul's letter by a writer who shared much ideologically with the author of 1 Timothy.[18] There are other examples of textual variants that seem to have emerged within the context of early Christian debates about the roles of women in churches, debates that were particularly virulent precisely when they intersected with theological issues and condemnation of various "heresies."[19]

Theological debates more generally provided ample occasion for the correction or corruption (depending on the side one took) of early Christian texts.[20] Did Christ have a real body, for example? What does it mean to say the Word became flesh? Does God have a body? Is there a resurrection of the flesh? Such were the questions that inspired intense combat among patristic writers, desert monks, and a host of other adherents to early forms of Christianity.[21] Each of these contests found its way into the textual arena: combat over "bodies"

18. In addition to works cited in n16, see also Gordon D. Fee, *The First Epistle to the Corinthians* (Grand Rapids, Mich., 1987), 669–708; Curt Niccum, "The Voice of the Manuscripts on the Silence of Women: The External Evidence for 1 Cor. 14:34–35," *New Testament Studies* 43 (1997): 242–55; Philip B. Payne, "Fuldensis, Sigla for Variants in Vaticanus, and 1 Cor. 14:34–35," *New Testament Studies* 41 (1995): 240–62; Philip B. Payne, "Ms. 88 as Evidence for a Text without 1 Cor. 14:34–35," *New Testament Studies* 44 (1998): 152–58; Antoinette Wire, *The Corinthian Women Prophets: A Reconstruction through Paul's Polemic* (Minneapolis, 1990), esp. 149–52.

19. Other examples can be found in 1 Cor. 16:19; Rom. 16: 3, 7; and Col. 4:15.

20. See, most comprehensively, Ehrman, *Orthodox Corruption of Scripture*.

21. For one particularly excellent treatment, see Elizabeth A. Clark, *The Origenist Controversy: The Cultural Construction of an Early Christian Debate* (Princeton, 1992). Other secondary literature that treats this subject is enormous; see, most helpfully, Elizabeth A. Clark, *Reading Renunciation: Asceticism and Scripture in Early Christianity* (Princeton, 1999); Brown, *Body and Society;* Virginia Burrus,

entailed combat over the interpretation of scripture and required a textual response. Take, for example, the Passion narrative in the Gospel of Luke. Throughout the narrative of trial and execution scenes, Jesus appears completely calm, in control, and without pain—in stark contrast to Mark's Gospel. Indeed there were Christians in the second century who may have favored Luke because it depicted a less emotional Christ. Some scribes who copied Luke's Gospel, however, appear to have taken pains to inscribe Christ's bodiliness into their texts by adding the following passage: "Then an angel from heaven appeared to him and gave him strength. In his anguish he prayed more earnestly, and his sweat became like great drops of blood falling on the ground" (Luke 22:43–44). The addition of bloody sweat is but one example of how texts, written by embodied scribes, in turn inscribe the body, here the body of Christ.[22] Particularly significant is that while debates over the corporeality of Christ and God ensued, contests over the ascetic body—and especially the bodies of virgins—were waged, and in a similar fashion made their way into the textual arena.

Let us look now at some examples taken from the Acts of Paul and Thecla. Here I am interested less in establishing the "original" text of the apocryphal Acts and more in how the competing readings within the Greek tradition and in subsequent versions can enhance our understanding of contests over asceticism, the proper relations between men and women, and women's roles in earliest Christianity.

The Acts of Paul and Thecla: Engendering Multiple Readings

The apocryphal Acts are by now familiar: a collection of second- and third-century Christian texts, written by anonymous different authors, that contain stories about the missionary travels of Jesus' apostles. Thus we have the Acts of Peter, Paul, John, Andrew, and Thomas.[23] While it is impossible

---

The Making of a Heretic: Gender, Authority, and the Priscillianist Controversy (Berkeley and Los Angeles, 1995); Virginia Burrus, *"Begotten Not Made": Conceiving Manhood in Late Antiquity* (Stanford, 2000).

22. On this passage, see Ehrman, *Orthodox Corruption of Scripture,* esp. 187–94; Bart D. Ehrman and Mark A. Plunkett, "The Angel and the Agony: The Textual Problem of Luke 22:43–44," *Catholic Biblical Quarterly* 45 (1983): 401–16.

23. English translations of these works are best found in vol. 2 of Edgar Hennecke, Wilhelm Schneemelcher, and R. McL. Wilson, eds., *New Testament Apocrypha* (Philadelphia, 1965), and J. K.

to determine with any degree of certainty where and when these texts were written, occasionally we are able to make some educated guesses. The Acts of Thomas, for example, probably written originally in Syriac, records stories of Jesus' twin brother Judas Thomas's travels to eastern Syria, and appears to have affinities with certain eastern Syrian and Persian theological movements, including Manichaeism.[24] In contrast, the Acts of Paul and Thecla appears to have a provenance in Asia Minor. The attestation for the Greek Acts of Paul and Thecla is, by my count, found in three papyrus fragments from the fourth century and forty-three ninth- to sixteenth-century manuscripts; it is also found translated into Coptic, Syriac, Latin, Armenian, Ethiopic, Slavic, and Arabic.[25] Especially important versions, in Coptic, are the sixth-century papyrus in Heidelberg, which contains the most extensive fragments of the entire Acts of Paul; in Syriac, a sixth-century manuscript and the eighth-century Sinaitic palimpsest with which I began; and at least four independent Latin versions.[26] Unfortunately, our textual evidence is not always sufficient to locate precisely when a variant reading entered in, although in some cases where scribes produce readings that are nowhere else attested, we might be inclined to view this singular reading as deriving from the scribe him- or herself.

Central to nearly all of the Christian Acts is the rather conspicuous prominence of female characters, a feature that has led to long-held but problematic arguments regarding the female authorship of or audience for these texts.[27] The

---

Elliott, *The Apocryphal New Testament: A Collection of Apocryphal Christian Literature in an English Translation* (Oxford, 1993). For the Acts of Paul and Thecla, upon which I focus, the standard critical edition continues to be that of Richard A. Lipsius and Maximilian Bonnet, *Acta Apostolorum Apocrypha,* vol. 1 (Leipzig, 1891). A new critical edition is needed, particularly one that would incorporate all of the manuscripts identified in M. Geerard, *Clavis Apocryphorum Novi Testamenti* (Turnhout, 1992).

24. See especially Elliott, *Apocryphal New Testament,* 439–42; Wilhelm Bousset, "Manichäisches in der Thomasakten," *Zeitschrift für die neutestamentliche Wissenschaft und die Kunde der älteren Kirche* 18 (1917–18): 1–39; A. F. J. Klijn, *The Acts of Thomas: Introduction, Text, Commentary* (Leiden, 1962).

25. The best listing of the manuscript and versional evidence is in Geerard, *Clavis Apocryphorum.*

26. For the Coptic, see Carl Schmidt, ed., *Acta Pauli aus der Heidelberger koptischen Papyrushandschrift Nr. 1* (Leipzig, 1904; reprint, Hildesheim, 1965); for the Syriac, William Wright, *Apocryphal Acts of the Apostles,* vol. 1 (London, 1871; reprint Hildesheim, 1990); for the Latin, see especially Oskar von Gebhardt, *Passio S. Theclae Virginis: Die lateinischen Übersetzungen der Acta Pauli et Theclae* (Leipzig, 1902). In what follows, I depend on Lipsius for the Greek, Schmidt for the Coptic, Wright for the Syriac, and von Gebhardt for the Latin.

27. There is extensive bibliography on this issue, which is related to similar arguments about the ancient novel more generally. For the earlier idea that the Apocryphal Acts should be attributed either to female composition or creation or connected to a female audience/readership, see Virginia Burrus, *Chastity as Autonomy: Women in the Stories of the Apocryphal Acts* (Lewiston, Maine, 1987); Dennis Ronald

narrative framework of the Acts of Paul and Thecla unravels as follows: Paul is speaking in some kind of public or private forum; Thecla hears him speak (and the women in the apocryphal Acts are variously married women, betrothed virgins, or widows); she proceeds to "fall head over heels" for him and his message; she converts, turns her back on her husband or severs ties with her betrothed, causing an uproar in her village; she and the apostle are brought to trial and variously condemned to death or torture but manage miraculously to escape death; she commits herself to celibacy, is baptized, and embarks on a life of traveling with the apostle and preaching. What is striking about these stories is the paradoxical use of erotic language to describe the relationship between the female converts and the apostles, paradoxical not only because the stories present celibacy as the highest ideal of spiritual reverence and devotion, and in some cases as the path to salvation, but also because celibacy is the only route through which women can transcend their bodily existence. At certain junctures in the story, particularly where the erotic element comes to the fore, some scribes profess discomfort with the erotic language and with the notion that women are able to transcend their bodies, and by manipulating the book—that is, by changing their texts in subtle ways—they both remove the erotic language and reinscribe and recircumscribe women's bodies.

The first instance is found in Paul's opening sermon in Onesiphorus's house. Paul has just arrived in Iconium, and when Onesiphorus learns this, he goes out to meet Paul and invites him into his home. Paul's speech has parallels with Matthew's and Luke's beatitudes, but they take on both Pauline and ascetic overtones.

Blessed are the pure in heart [οἱ καθαροὶ τῇ καρδίᾳ], for they shall see God.

Blessed are they who have kept their flesh pure [οἱ ἁγνὴν τὴν σάρκα τηρήσαντες], for they shall become a temple of God.

Blessed are the self-controlled [οἱ ἐγκρατεῖς], for to them will God speak.

Blessed are they who have renounced this world [οἱ ἀποταξάμενοι τῷ κοσμῷ τούτῳ], for they shall be well pleasing unto God.

MacDonald, *The Legend and the Apostle: The Battle for Paul in Story and Canon* (Philadelphia, 1983); and Stevan L. Davies, *The Revolt of the Widows: The Social World of the Apocryphal Acts* (Carbondale, Ill., 1980). Recently this notion has been revived in Stephen J. Davis, *The Cult of St. Thecla: A Tradition of Women's Piety in Late Antiquity* (Oxford, 2001). The critique of this view is most compelling in Kate Cooper, *The Virgin and the Bride: Idealized Womanhood in Late Antiquity* (Cambridge, Mass., 1996).

Blessed are they who have wives as if they had them not [οἱ ἔχοντες γυναίκας ὡς μὴ ἔχοντες], for they shall be heirs to God. (APTh 5)

Purity, renunciation, and self-control: these are the qualities worthy of blessing throughout the apocryphal Acts. ἐγκρατεία, which in earlier Greek classical literature as well as Jewish Greek writing meant temperance or self-control, throughout the apocryphal Acts designates sexual abstinence or celibacy. The Latin translations further extend this meaning of ἐγκρατεία by using the term *abstinentes*.[28]

Paul's speech continues with themes that are less specifically ascetic: "Blessed are they who fear God, for they shall become angels of God. Blessed are they who tremble at the words of God, for they shall be comforted. Blessed are they who have received the wisdom of Jesus Christ, for they shall be called sons of the Most High," and so forth. The climax of Paul's speech, however, is concerned with bodies: "Blessed are the bodies of the virgins [τὰ σώματα τῶν παρθένων], for they shall be well pleasing to God, and shall not lose the reward of their purity" [ἁγνείας] (6). This last blessing is particularly striking: in light of the renunciation, transcendence, or transformation of the body in early Christian asceticism, the affirmation of the bodies (σώματα) of the virgins is rather peculiar; moreover, it is found in our best witnesses to the Greek text as well as in the sixth-century Coptic papyrus in Heidelberg. While it may be that this blessing is linked to Pauline notions of bodies as temples of the Holy Spirit (and this is supported by earlier statements in "Paul's" speech in Onesiphorus's house), it is precisely here that we find evidence of a textual contest over the virginal body: some scribes have re-formed the text by adding two words. In several eleventh- and twelfth-century Greek manuscripts the text reads, "Blessed are the bodies and spirits/souls/breath [τὰ πνεύματα] of the virgins" rather than "Blessed are the bodies of the virgins." Likewise, the Syriac has "blessed are the bodies and the souls [*ruah*] of the virgins"; the Armenian has "souls and bodies of the virgins."[29] The addition of these words tempers the blessing of the body. Even more striking is a reading found in one

---

28. Similarly, as Elizabeth Clark has pointed out, Jerome's Latin translations of the Pastorals "pressed verses in an ascetic direction" by, for example, rendering the Greek σωφροσύνη (sound-mindedness and/or self-control) "as *castitas* or as *incorruptio*" (Clark, *Reading Renunciation,* 166).

29. For the Armenian, I am depending upon the translation of Frederick C. Conybeare, ed., *The Apology and Acts of Apollonius and Other Monuments of Early Christianity* (London, 1894).

fifteenth-century Latin manuscript in which "the bodies" are eliminated altogether and replaced with *beati spiritus virginum*. However we choose to translate spiritus—breath, soul, spirit—it is the incorporeal part of the body. Such
variant readings betray a textual contest over the bodies of virgins.[30]

Thecla is transfixed by Paul's speech. She stays at her window, listening
"night and day," watching the women and virgins going in to Paul. Her betrothed, Thamyris, comes looking for her, and her mother bemoans Thecla's state: "She sticks to the window like a spider, is moved by his words, and
gripped by a new desire and a fearful passion; for the maiden hangs upon the
things he says and is taken captive" (9). Once again, "a new desire and a fearful
passion" (ἐπιθυμίᾳ καινῇ καὶ πάθει δεινῷ) is odd or, at the very least, paradoxical language in a text so overtly promoting celibacy. Evidently it was also
problematic for some scribes and translators. Some Greek manuscripts replace
καινή (new) with δεινή (strange), clarifying that Thecla's desire for Paul is of
a different kind from her desire for her betrothed. In one Latin manuscript
(identified by von Gebhardt as "m") "and a fearful passion" has been replaced
with *atque nouae doctrinae*—a phrase that certainly carries little of the overtly
erotic overtones of "a new desire and a fearful passion." In Conybeare's translation of the Armenian, the erotic element is excised altogether: "she strains
her eyes to gaze upon a strange man, and hearkens to his words as if they were
pleasing, though they are illusive and vain and disgusting."

Another contest over words takes place when Thecla visits Paul in prison—the erotic climax, if you will, of the entire story. Some time has passed
since Paul's initial speech in Onesiphorus's house; by now Thecla, thoroughly
"gripped by a new desire," has severed ties with her fiancé. In his anger, Thamyris brings Paul before the authorities, claiming that "he has destroyed the city of
the Iconians, and my betrothed, so that she will not have me" (15). After a brief
exchange, the governor has Paul bound and "led off to prison until he should
find leisure to give him a hearing" (18). As we can expect, Thecla searches for
Paul. After bribing the doorkeeper (apparently she was locked in her room),
Thecla goes to the prison. There she bribes the jailer, and then, we read, she

---

30. Such variants may also be attempts to harmonize this text with the gospel texts, particularly
Pauline, Matthean, and Lukan passages; I am grateful to Georgia Frank for reminding me of this scribal
tendency and the likelihood that scribes copying the apocryphal acts were influenced by their knowledge
of canonical passages.

"went in to Paul and sat at his feet and heard [him proclaim] the mighty acts of God. And Paul feared nothing, but comported himself with full confidence in God; and her faith was increased, as she kissed his fetters" (18). Before long, Thamyris and others come looking for Thecla and find her in the prison, "so to speak [or "in a certain way"], bound with him in affection" (19). It is impossible to miss the erotic language here: τρόπον τινὰ συνδεδεμένην τῇ στρογῇ.

The erotic image was not lost on the scribes who copied the passage. One of the scribes who added τὰ πνεύματα (the spirits) in the passage considered above has here chosen to eliminate the whole phrase "in a certain way bound with him in affection." Simple haplography—that is, the possibility that the scribe simply skipped a line accidentally in the process of copying—cannot explain the omission. Rather, I would suggest that this omission is quite deliberate; it removes the erotic element, with its potential dangers. No longer can readers (or hearers) "misread" or "misconstrue" the passage as suggesting an erotic embrace between Paul and Thecla; the purity of the passage, and the relationship, is preserved.

The evidence is even more striking in this instance, though not altogether uniform. For the phrase "so to speak, bound with him in affection," the Latin readings found in various manuscripts are as follows: "as though joined to his feet" (quasi colligatam ad pedes eius); "sitting by Paul's feet" (Pauli pedibus assidentem); "listening to God's teaching from Paul" (doctrinam dei a Paulo audientem); "sitting at the feet of Paul, joined in the desire of Christ" (eam sedentem ad pedes Pauli, colligatam desiderio Christi). Talk about cleaning up the story! But one Latin scribe goes in the opposite direction, daringly describing Thecla as "having been bound with him in some kind of affection" (quodam affectu eidem copulatam).

The Syriac and Armenian versions appear to approach the problem from a different direction. Perhaps in response to the Greek narrative's problematic notion that Thecla was found alone with Paul in prison—and in a compromising position—the Syriac and Armenian translations make it clear that others were in the prison, thus preserving some sense of propriety. The Syriac, for example, reads, "And they went, as the doorkeeper told them, and found her sitting at Paul's feet, she and many persons, and they were listening to the great things of the Most High."[31] The Armenian reads, "So they went and found

---

31. Wright, *Apocryphal Acts,* 126.

her as the doorkeeper told them; they came and found her sitting at the feet of Paul, and saw several other people as well who were listening to the great things of Christ."[32]

Another example occurs at a crucial juncture. Woven throughout the Acts of Paul and Thecla is the notion of transgressing gender boundaries. This motif or image is by now quite familiar from our early Christian materials: the Passion of Perpetua, for example, in which Perpetua is "stripped naked and becomes a man"; Jesus' closing statement in the Gospel of Thomas, "I will make Mary male"; the Sayings of the Desert Mothers that play with this notion; the quasi-transvestite narratives of Eugenia, Mary/Marinus, Pelagia, and others; Augustine's mother, who is manly in her faith; and so forth.[33] In the Acts of Paul and Thecla, Thecla's desire to bend genders pushes the limits of ancient gender constructions: at different junctures she proposes to cut her hair short, wear a man's tunic, and follow Paul wherever he goes. The first declaration of her desire follows her visit to Paul in prison. By this time, Thecla's refusal to marry Thamyris has caused an uproar in town. When she is found in prison with Paul, the governor (apparently in an effort to keep some measure of peace) brings Paul and Thecla to trial. He asks her, "Why do you not marry Thamyris according to the law of the Iconians?" She remains silent, whereupon her mother cries out, "Burn the lawless one! Burn her that is no bride in the midst of the theater, that all the women who have been taught by this man may be afraid" (20). The governor then sentences Paul to be flogged and sent out of the city, and Thecla he condemns to be burned.

Thecla, however, survives the fire; indeed, "the fire did not touch her" (22). She is therefore released, and once again she seeks out Paul. She finds him with Onesiphorus and his wife and children, praying and fasting in a tomb. Her arrival is the cause for joy: "within the tomb there was much love,

---

32. Conybeare, *Apology and Acts of Apollonius,* 70–71.

33. Again, there is extensive bibliography on "transvestite saints" as well as motifs of the manly woman. See especially Elizabeth Castelli, "'I Will Make Mary Male': Pieties of the Body and Gender Transformation of Christian Women in Late Antiquity," in *BodyGuards: The Cultural Politics of Gender Ambiguity,* ed. Julia Epstein and Kristina Straub (New York, 1991), 29–49; Evelyne Patlagean, "L'histoire de la femme déguisée en moine et l'évolution de la sainteté féminine à Byzance," *Studi Medievali,* ser. 3, 17 (1976): 597–623; John Anson, "The Female Transvestite in Early Monasticism: Origin and Development of a Motif," *Viator: Medieval and Renaissance Studies* 5 (1974): 1–32; and Susan Ashbrook Harvey, "Women in Early Byzantine Hagiography: Reversing the Story," in *That Gentle Strength: Historical Perspectives on Women in Christianity,* ed. Lynda L Coon, Katherine J. Haldane, and Elisabeth W. Sommer (Richmond, 1990), 36–59.

Paul rejoicing, and Onesiphorus and all of them" (25). Then Thecla makes her proposition: "I will cut my hair short and follow you wherever you go"; but Paul denies her, saying, "The season is unfavorable, and you are comely. May no other temptation take hold of you, worse than the first, and you not endure it but play the coward." Thecla replies, "Only give me the seal in Christ, and temptation will not touch me." And Paul says, "Thecla, have patience and you will receive the water" (25). Note the adjective "comely"—εὔμορφος—well formed. The gender ambiguity of this word is significant: εὔμορφος is an adjective of two endings, masculine and neuter, where the masculine doubles for the feminine. Such gender ambiguity serves to reemphasize exactly what Thecla is requesting—that she become like a man. Such subtlety was not lost on the scribes. The same scribes who amended the passages quoted above have taken it upon themselves here to reemphasize Thecla's womanhood: they insert the word γυνή—γυνή εὔμορφος (a comely woman). If there was any doubt about Thecla's ability to transcend or transgress gender boundaries, these scribes eliminate it. On a small scale, we find here a process similar to that identified by Stephen Davis in his recent article on intertextuality in the stories of "transvestite saints," in which he argues that these "legends themselves never quite allow their readers to forget that the transvestite saint is still a woman by nature."[34]

I offer one final case of engendered textual variants, appearing this time in the scene of Thecla's persecution in the arena. "When she had finished her prayer, she turned and saw a great pit full of water, and said: 'Now it is time for me to wash.' And she threw herself in, saying: 'In the name of Jesus Christ I baptize myself on the last day!'" (34). We have some independent help in understanding how this particular passage might have been interpreted, for Tertullian admonishes those who take "Thecla's example as a license for women's teaching and baptizing," arguing that this text was written not by Paul but by a presbyter in Asia who was removed from office when his authorship was discovered (*De Baptismo* 17). What is interesting here is that the problem of Thecla baptizing herself can be solved textually quite easily. Some Latin manuscripts simply excise the whole passage: "And she threw herself in, saying: 'In the name of Jesus Christ I baptize myself on the last day!'" Others use not a re-

34. Stephen J. Davis, "Crossed Texts, Crossed Sex: Intertextuality and Gender in Early Christian Legends of Holy Women Disguised as Men," *JECS* 10 (2002): 29.

flexive construction but rather a simple passive, so that Thecla declares not "I baptize myself" but "I am baptized" *(ego baptizor)*. The Syriac and Armenian also use a simple passive construction.

In these passages I would argue that we see scribes emphasizing the incorporeal aspect of virgins, excising erotically suggestive passages, and reaffirming Thecla's inability to transcend her female body. Blessing the bodies of virgins was as problematic as depicting them bound in affection with an apostle and/ or able to become like a man. In each case, the effort to circumscribe and control the virginal body is paramount. Carlin Barton has illuminated "the paradox of the eye" in Roman antiquity.[35] I would suggest a similar paradox here: it is precisely because the body is both powerful and vulnerable that we find it so hotly contested in early Christian books. Books, likewise, were a powerful resource and arena for debates about the human body among early Christians, and perhaps because of their power they were vulnerable to corruption and manipulation. Not only could they be erased and reinscribed—reused as palimpsests—but their words could be altered in the process of copying and translation.

35. Carlin A. Barton, *The Sorrows of the Ancient Romans: The Gladiator and the Monster* (Princeton, 1993), esp. 91–95: "The eye realized the polarization that magnetized Roman culture during this period: the operation, concurrently, of the extremes of power and powerlessness" (93); "it was the paradox of heightened power and heightened vulnerability that made the eye especially fascinating: it injured and was injured simultaneously" (94).

Claudia Rapp

HOLY TEXTS, HOLY MEN, AND HOLY SCRIBES

Aspects of Scriptural Holiness in Late Antiquity

Exposure to individual verses of scripture often triggered life-changing events.[1] A famous case is St. Anthony, who understood Matthew 19:21—"If you wish to be perfect, go sell everything you possess and give it to the poor and come, follow me and you will have a treasure in heaven"—when he heard it read in church as being directly addressed to him, "as if the passage were read on his account," and under its impact relieved himself of all his possessions and worldly obligations.[2]

It is significant that our first work of hagiographic biography begins in this manner, with an oblique reference to the common practice of *sortes biblicae* or *apertio libri,* i.e., the direct application of individual verses or sentences of scripture, encountered by opening a book at random, to the current predicament of the searching individual.[3] This use of the written text was a common divinatory

1. This work was presented at the Early Christian Book Conference at the Catholic University of America, and later the same year at the Late Antique Seminar in Princeton. I am grateful to the participants in both venues for their valuable feedback. Among them, Mark Vessey and Derek Krueger deserve special mention for their insightful comments. I am also grateful to Peter Brown, Mildred Budny, Michael Haslam, Thomas Head, Kevanne Kirkwood, Chrysi Kotsifou, Maged Mikhail, Lawrence Nees, and Els Rose for pointing me to further literature that I would otherwise have missed. Valuable research assistance was provided by Alex Effgen, Andrew Fogleman, and Sarah Madole.

2. *Life of Antony* 2.3–4 (*SC* 400:132–34); Robert C. Gregg, trans., *Athanasius: The Life of Antony and the Letter to Marcellinus* (New York, 1980), 31.

3. The practice of the *sortes biblicae* should not be confused with the *sortes sanctorum,* which

practice in the Middle Ages, but its origins reach far back into classical antiquity, when Virgil's *Aeneid* was a popular proof text.[4] By the time of St. Anthony, guidebooks for the oracular use of scripture were being produced in Egypt.[5] It is equally significant that the *Life of Anthony* itself later played a similar role in Augustine's narration of the process of his own conversion. Here the story is refracted through the narration by a third person, Augustine's friend Ponticianus, who reminisces about his two friends, high-ranking officials both, and their instantaneous conversion to the ascetic life after they literally stumbled across a copy of the *Vita Antonii* outside Trier, in the modest dwelling of some Christians, possibly hermits.[6] In this instance, it is the hagiographic text that provides specific guidance to a searching and questioning soul.

The examples of Anthony and Augustine illustrate what might be called a "chain of *imitatio*," scriptural and personal, that is an essential part of hagiographic discourse. The active force of the word in and of itself, especially in its written form, and its nexus with the holy life of monks and saints is the theme of this chapter. In the background is the question of whether hagiography can operate as "scripture once removed," embodied in the saints. For lack of a better term in English, one might perhaps speak of the "materiality" of the holy text, whether scriptural or hagiographic. Joseph-Claude Poulin refers to similar phenomena in the fifth- to tenth-century Latin West with the expression *utilisations marginales de l'écrit*.[7] Germans use the term *Schriftlichkeit* for the various facets of the power of the written word that resides precisely in the fact that it is written.

William E. Klingshirn has shown to be a text widely known (and condemned) in late antiquity; see his "Defining the *Sortes Sanctorum:* Gibbon, DuCange, and Early Christian Lot Divination," *JECS* 10 (2002): 77–130.

4. Theodore of Pherme, the successor of Pachomius, engaged in this practice: *Bohairic Vita of Pachomius* 94, in Armand Veilleux, trans., *Pachomian Koinonia,* vol. 1 (Kalamazoo, Mich., 1980), 127. For examples from early medieval Francia, see Valerie I. J. Flint, *The Rise of Magic in Early Medieval Europe* (Princeton, 1991), 273–81.

5. David Frankfurter, *Religion in Roman Egypt: Assimilation and Resistance* (Princeton, 1998), 195.

6. Augustine, *Confessions* 8.6.15 (*CCSL* 27:122–23).

7. Joseph-Claude Poulin, "Entre magie et religion: Recherches sur les utilisations marginales de l'écrit dans la culture populaire du haut Moyen Age," in *La culture populaire au moyen âge: Études présentées au Quatrième colloque de l'Institut d'études mediévales de l'Université de Montréal, 2–3 avril 1977,* ed. Pierre Boglioni (Montréal, 1979), 123–43. A similar study, focusing on small-sized manuscripts and on manuscripts that are autographs of holy men in the Latin West from the fourth to the ninth century, was undertaken by Jean Vezin, "Les livres utilisés comme amulettes et comme reliques," in *Das Buch als magisches und als Repräsentationsobjekt,* ed. Peter Ganz (Wiesbaden, 1992), 101–16.

The following is an investigation of the supernatural connotations that are tied to the materiality of the text, arising from the holiness of the text or the holiness of the scribe, or from a combination of both. This study is based on the rich monastic and hagiographic literature of the patristic age up to the seventh century, with occasional forays into later periods.[8] As my interest lies in the beliefs and perceptions of late antique Christians, I will follow their lead in using the term "holiness" in the vaguest sense to describe phenomena that are perceived to be beyond the human realm of understanding and explicable only as the result of divine intervention.

Holy Scripture as Divine Presence

The Christian religion has a deep affinity with scripture, writing, and *Schriftlichkeit*. God made his Word manifest in the world through Christ, the incarnate Logos. The Gospels and other New Testament writings contain this "good news" in written form, easily accessible to readers and listeners, and readily available for ownership in the form of manuscripts. These physical depositories of the Word of God shared in the holiness of the message they contained. The possible associations of the particular appearance of the Christian book in codex form and of special kinds of scripts (such as Guglielmo Cavallo's *maiuscola biblica*) with the holiness of the Christian text have been the subject of intense study, including John Lowden's chapter in this volume.

To what degree the divine presence fused into the gospel book was understood to be real, or symbolic, or anything in between, is often difficult to gauge. Our sources seem to indicate a whole spectrum of possible interpretations. The gospel book could act as a stand-in for the real or intended presence of Christ, a theme elaborated in this volume by Caroline Humfress with regard to its application in law. Justinian formally required the presence of the holy scriptures throughout the duration of judicial trials in a law of 530.[9] In the same year, he also affirmed that the presence of God, signaled through the

8. For the intersection between saints and the miraculous use of written texts up to the fifteenth century, see Edina Bozóky, "Saints, Legends, and Charms," in *Telling Tales: Medieval Narratives and the Folk Tradition,* ed. Francesca Canadé Sauterman, Diana Chonchado, and Giuseppe C. Di Scipio (New York, 1998), 173–88, esp. 176–78.

9. *Codex Iustinianus* 3.1.14.1 (530), in P. Krueger et al., eds., *Corpus Iuris Civilis,* 3 vols. (Berlin, 1877–95), 2:122 (hereafter *Cod. Iust.*). See further Caroline Humfress's chapter in this volume, at n. 17.

presence of the "awesome scriptures," can substitute for the absence of one of the litigants in a court case.[10] The use of Gospels or complete Bibles for the swearing of oaths also belongs in this context and was normal judicial procedure by the time of Justinian.[11] To touch the holy scriptures while taking an oath demonstrated that one had no fear of the retribution of God, who is present in his Word.

At church councils the divine presence was made manifest by the gospel codex placed on a throne, a custom first attested for the Council of Ephesus in 431, which convened "with the holy gospels lying on the throne in the middle and showing Christ himself present among us."[12] The enthroned gospel is also a frequent motif in church decorations from late antiquity and beyond as a way of representing the deity.[13] According to Isidore of Pelusium, this concept is ritually reenacted in the celebration of the liturgy at the moment of the opening of the Gospels, when the bishop removes the stole *(omophorion)* that signals his role as the representative of Christ in order to show that "the Lord himself is present."[14]

In a private context, the gospel codex could function in a slightly more indirect sense, as a reminder of the message it contained. As Epiphanius of Salamis observed, "The acquisition of Christian books is necessary for those who can use them. For the mere sight of these books renders us less inclined to sin, and incites us to believe more firmly in righteousness."[15] The use of the partially open gospel book, not for the reading of a specific text but as a reminder of the entire message it contains, is illustrated in an autobiographical story relat-

---

10. *Cod. Iust.* 3.1.13.4 (530), ed. Krueger, 2:121.

11. An early attestation of this practice is John Chrysostom, *Hom. 15.5 ad populum Antiochenum* (*PG* 49:160). It is taken for granted in the imperial legislation of the sixth century, as for example in *Cod. Iust.* 3.1.14.4 (530), ed. Krueger, 2:122; *Cod. Iust.* 4.1.12.5 (529), ed. Krueger, 2:150; and *Cod. Iust.* 5.70.7.5 (530), ed. Krueger, 2:234. For concrete examples of the application of oaths in judicial proceedings, see Erwin Seidl, *Der Eid im römisch-ägyptischen Provinzialrecht,* 2 vols. (Munich, 1933, 1935), 2:48–52.

12. Council of Ephesus (431), Mansi 4:1237C. In a famous scene, Nestorius showed his disrespect for the Gospels that were placed on a seat in the middle of the assembly at the Council of Ephesus in 431 by putting them on the floor and claiming the seat for himself. David N. Bell, trans., *Besa, The Life of Shenoute* (Kalamazoo, Mich., 1983), 78.

13. On this and related issues regarding the symbolic importance of scripture codices in late antiquity and Byzantium, see Herbert Hunger, *Schreiben und Lesen in Byzanz: Die byzantinische Buchkultur* (Munich, 1989), 12–15.

14. Isidore of Pelusium, *Ep.* 1.136 (*PG* 87:272D).

15. *Apophthegmata,* Epiphanius 8 (*PG* 65:165A), in Benedicta Ward, trans., *The Sayings of the Desert Fathers: The Alphabetical Collection,* rev. ed. (London, 1981), 58.

ed by John of Ephesus in the second half of the sixth century about one of his monastic teachers. Apa Abbi counted as his only possessions "one tunic and one cape made of pieces of rag fastened together, and a small text of the Gospel [*euaggelion*]; and he would not consent to read in any other book except that Gospel [*euaggelion*]." He spent his private time apart from the brothers, in the common chapel, his head covered and his book on his knees, "while even the book also was covered, and except a small surface only for the purpose of admitting light no part whatever of it was exposed. And thereupon he would open the book and gaze at it, and at once his tears would burst forth." The Apa remained in this position for several hours, "and he would not turn over a leaf," but he left the book open at a number of select passages, either parables or "any place where the subject was that of threats and judgement." When John himself, still an adolescent, sought Apa Abbi's guidance, "he would each time take me apart, and open that book" before dispensing his advice.[16] Only in the presence of the Word of God, signaled through a single open page of the gospel book, did the good Apa feel authorized to utter his own words.

The function of the gospel codex as a doorway to contemplation was affirmed at the Second Council of Nicaea in 787, which specified that it was to receive veneration analogous to icons and the holy cross, with incense and lights.[17] What additional forms this veneration could take we do not know, but we can gain a glimpse of a monk's intense devotion to the gospel codex from the following passage by the fifth-century Syriac author Philoxenus of Mabbug:

Salute the cross, and take the Gospel in your hands. Place it on your eyes and on your heart. Stand on your feet in front of the cross, without sitting down, and after every chapter you have read, place the Gospel on the cushion and prostrate yourself before it up to ten times. . . . Thanks to this external adoration which you give to God, you will conceive in your heart the internal adoration and the effect of divine grace which a human tongue cannot describe.[18]

16. Ernest W. Brooks, ed., *John of Ephesus, Lives of the Eastern Saints, Patrologia Orientalis* 17 (Paris, 1923), 1:214–17.

17. Mansi 13:377E. The combination of icons and gospel books has a much longer history. During the devastating Nika Riot of 532, the clergy of Constantinople carried the holy Gospels and icons of Christ into the crowds, in a vain attempt to calm down the rioters. Zonaras, *Epitome historiarum* 14.6.14, ed. Theodor Büttner-Wobst, *Ioannis Zonarae Annales*, vol. 3, Corpus Scriptorum Historiae Byzantinae 45 (Bonn, 1897), 153, lines 14–19. Zonaras, writing in the twelfth century, uses a (lost) hostile source for the reign of Justinian and should thus be considered trustworthy in his account of details.

18. Pierre Graffin, "La lettre de Philoxène de Mabboug à un supérieur de monastère sur la vie monastique," *L'Orient syrien* 6 (1961): 463–64. "Salue la croix, et prend l'Evangile dans tes mains. Place-le sur

Much more than a sign or a symbol, in certain circumstances the Bible codex embodied the actual presence of the incarnate Christ as the Word of God to dramatic effect. This and much else discussed in this chapter evokes associations of popular belief with magical practices, but it is important to bear in mind that these practices were never officially condoned by the church.[19] In fact, most of our evidence for the private use of Christian books for purposes other than reading comes from authors or church councils that point out the dubious validity of such practices and often explicitly condemn them. It was a common belief that the Bible codex could act as a miracle-working object with apotropaic and protective powers. According to John Chrysostom, the presence of the Gospels in a house would keep the devil out.[20] Hagiographical stories illustrate this; the "small book [of the Gospels]" produced by a traveling monk from his bag was able to exorcise a demon and restore the health of a young girl.[21] In this instance, the power of the gospel codex was effective regardless of the worthiness of its owner, as the guilt-ridden monk admitted that he had just stolen it. Bible codices also had the power to quell fires. Gregory of Tours reports that his relative Gallus, a rich senator and bishop of Clermont, stopped a fire in the city by first praying in front of the altar, then taking the gospel book from it, opening it, and carrying it toward the flames.[22]

Demonstrations of the tangible embodiment of the power of God in the actual object of the gospel book were an important tool in the conversion of pagans. The sorcerer Cyprian, for example, did not dare to touch the Gospels until he was baptized.[23] Similarly, in fifth-century Ireland, St. Patrick challenged a pagan wizard to subject their respective holy books to a trial by fire

---

tes yeux et sur ton coeur. Mets-toi debout devant la croix, sur tes pieds, sans t'asseoir par terre, et, après chaque chapitre que tu y auras lu, place l'Evangile sur le coussin et prosterne-toi devant lui jusqu'à dix fois. . . . Grâce à cette adoration extérieure que tu fais devant lui, prendra naissance dans ton coeur cette adoration intérieure, et l'action de grâces qu'une langue de chair ne peut exprimer telle qu'elle est."

19. See, for example, the rich material assembled in Roelof van den Broek, "Popular Religious Practices and Ecclesiastical Policies in the Early Church," in *Official and Popular Religion: Analysis of a Theme for Religious Studies,* ed. Pieter H. Vrijhof and Jacques Waardenburg (The Hague, 1979), esp. 33–35.

20. John Chrysostom, *Hom. 32 (31) in Joh.* (*PG* 59:187). Also *Concio III de Laz.,* chap. 2 (*PG* 48:994). In another context, John Chrysostom remarks that the custom of keeping a gospel codex near the bed is useless if it is not accompanied by deeds of charity. John Chrysostom, *Hom. 43 in 1 Cor.* (*PG* 61:373).

21. John Moschus, *Pratum spirituale* 8, in Elpidio Mioni, ed., "Il Pratum spirituale di Giovanni Mosco: Gli episodi inediti del Cod. Marciano greco II, 21," *Orientalia Christiana Periodica* 17 (1951): 90–91.

22. Gregory of Tours, *Life of the Fathers* 6.6, ed. Bruno Krusch, *MGH, SRM* 1.2:234, lines 8–12, in Edward James, trans., *Gregory of Tours: Life of the Fathers,* 2d ed. (Liverpool, 1991), 39.

23. Friedrich Bilabel and Adolf Grohmann, "Studien zu Kyprian dem Magier," in *Griechische,*

and water. The wizard's refusal to expose his books to this danger proved the greater power of Patrick's God and eventually resulted in the conversion of the king.[24] A much later story, preserved in the chronicle of Theophanes Continuatus, tells of an archbishop missionary to the Rus during the reign of Basil I (867–86) who demonstrated the power of Christianity by throwing a gospel book into the fire and retrieving it unharmed.[25]

The holiness of the divine Logos is not only encapsulated in the scriptural codex in its entirety, it is also present in the actual script, the letters that convey the Word of God. This is the sentiment behind canon 68 of the Quinisext Council of 692. It threatens excommunication for up to one year for anyone who destroys the books of the Old and New Testaments, or those of the church fathers, or who knowingly colludes in their destruction, either by cutting them up or by giving them to booksellers or perfume makers—the latter were well known as manufacturers of magical charms.[26] Similar concerns for the preservation of the holy word in its physical, written form may also have inspired the reuse as palimpsests of folia carrying a gospel text, as is the case in one of the manuscripts studied by Kim Haines-Eitzen in this volume. In order to avoid profanation of the written name of God, some late antique Christians continued the Jewish practice of burying religious books.[27]

Connection with Relics

Such concerns about the preservation of the holiness that resides in the concrete object in its entirety as well as in its constitutive parts suggest a connection to the use and interpretation of relics. This connection has been put forward in a seminal study by Armando Petrucci, who identifies a significant

---

koptische und arabische Texte zur Religion und religiösen Literatur in Ägyptens Spätzeit, ed. Friedrich Bilabel and Adolf Grohmann (Heidelberg, 1934), 179.

24. This story is told in the eleventh-century *Tripartite Life of Patrick* (Bethu Phatraic), in Whitley Stokes, ed., *The Tripartite Life of Patrick,* 2 vols. (London, 1887; reprint 1965), 1:57–59, cf. also 2:461. The same story is also found in a Middle Irish homily preserved in a fifteenth-century manuscript (Lebar Brecc): *On the Life of St. Patrick,* in Whitley Stokes, ed., *Three Middle-Irish Homilies of the Lives of Saints Patrick, Brigit and Columba* (Calcutta, 1877), 27.

25. Theophanes Continuatus 97, in ed. Immanuel Bekker, *Theophanes Continuatus,* Corpus Scriptorum Historiae Byzantinae 33 (Bonn, 1838), 343–44.

26. Council in Trullo, can. 68 (*PG* 137:748D–749A). Commentary by Zonaras and Balsamon in G. Rhalles and M. Potles, *Syntagma tōn theiōn kai hierōn kanonōn,* 6 vols. (Athens, 1852–59), 2:463–65.

27. Colin H. Roberts, *Buried Books in Antiquity: Habent sua fata libelli* ([London], 1963).

shift in artistic representations in the Latin West after the sixth century from a predominance of the open book to a preference for the closed, while in the Byzantine East representations of the closed and of the open book remain equally common. In Western art, the closed book thus acquires, in Petrucci's words, "the image of the closed reliquary, glowing with gems, rigidly presented for the veneration but not the comprehension of the faithful."[28]

Was the Word of God in its written form subject to the same kind of fragmentation and multiplication of holiness as the bodies of martyrs or saints, which—even when dissected into smaller particles—carried the protective and miraculous power of the whole? Alcuin of York draws this comparison in the last decades of the eighth century. He warns against the deceptive sense of accomplished piety that can result from the possession of relics or of fragments of scripture: "They carry amulets, believing them to be something holy. But it is better to imitate the examples of the saints in one's heart than to carry their bones in little bags. And it is better to hold the written teachings of the Gospels in one's mind, than to carry them, written on strips of parchment, around one's neck."[29]

The examples of Epiphanius and Apa Abbi cited above have illustrated how the closed or partially open gospel book could serve as a reminder of the entire Christian message. We have also seen how full-size gospel books could serve as protective and apotropaic devices. Both the mnemonic and the miraculous aspects are especially invoked in the use of small books that contain only selections of text, or in the use of individual written verses of scripture. Small codices with religious content were often carried around the neck by laypeople in late antiquity. Church fathers like Jerome and John Chrysostom decried this use of codices not as depositories of text but merely as reservoirs of divine power. They frequently warned their audiences against the use of phylacteries, as this entailed the danger of mistaking the object of the codex for the message it contained.[30] Jerome compares such Christian phylacteries to the Jewish

---

28. Armando Petrucci, "The Christian Conception of the Book in the Sixth and Seventh Centuries," in *Writers and Readers in Medieval Italy: Studies in the History of Written Culture,* trans. Charles M. Radding (New Haven, 1995), 30.

29. Alcuin, *Ep.* 290, ed. Ernst Dümmler, *Monumenta Germaniae Historica, Epistolae* 4:448, lines 17–21. Cf. Caesarius of Arles, *Serm.* 50.2 (*CCSL* 103:226): "Melius est in corde verba Dei retinere, quam scripta in collo suspendere."

30. See the article by Henri Leclercq, "Amulettes," *Dictionnaire d'archéologie Chrétienne et de liturgie* 1.2 (1924), cols. 1784–1860; Felix Eckstein and Jan Hendrik Waszink, "Amulett," *Reallexikon für*

tefillin, which contain only a few verses from the Torah.[31] It therefore seems reasonable to assume that references in our sources to the miraculous use of "the gospel" do not always refer to the entire combination of the four Gospels, but also to individual Gospels, or even parts thereof. Especially valuable in providing concrete physical benefits was the Gospel of John.[32] Augustine acknowledged its power to reduce a fever when placed under the head of a sick person.[33] In other instances, pieces of writing containing only the first few verses of John proved beneficial. We see the use of extracts from scripture, *pars pro toto,* to evoke the power of the *entire* Word of God in the recommendation to write psalm verses on storage jars to prevent wine from turning sour,[34] and in the Bible verses written on the walls of monks' cells in Egypt in order to preserve the holiness of the space and its inhabitant.[35]

The holiness of the Bible codex could be underscored through its combination with appropriate relics placed on its cover. An early example of this practice is the codex of the Gospel of John owned by Peter the Iberian, the fifth-century Monophysite bishop of Maiouma in Palestine, whose cover included a relic of the True Cross that miraculously oozed oil.[36] This combination of wood from the True Cross and a gospel codex seems to have been rather common, if we are to believe Jerome's complaint that it was a custom among "superstitious womenfolk" to carry both these items on their bodies.[37] Despite such criticisms of composite phylacteries, they remained popular even among the clergy. In the sixth century Gregory the Great congratulated the Lombard Queen Theode-

---

Antike und Christentum 1 (1950), cols. 397–411. Especially relevant are John Chrysostom, *Hom. 72 (73).* 2 *in Mt. 23. 1–3* (*PG* 58:669) (miniature Gospels worn around the neck by women); John Chrysostom, *Hom 19.4 ad populum Antiochenum* (*PG* 49:196) (it is better to inscribe the Gospels and the Laws in one's conscience than to wear miniature Gospels around the neck); Isidore of Pelusium, *Ep.* 2.150 (*PG* 78:604C) (women wear miniature Gospels).

31. Jerome, *Comm. in Mt. 23.5,* ed. David Hurst and Marcus Adriaen (*CCSL* 77:212). On the Jewish *tefillin,* see Emil Schürer, *The History of the Jewish People in the Age of Jesus Christ (175 B.C.–A.D. 135),* ed. Géza Vermès, Fergus Millar, and Martin Goodman, 3 vols. (Edinburgh, 1973–87), 2:479–81.

32. Edmond Le Blant, "Le premier chapitre de Saint Jean et la croyance à ses vertus secrètes," *Revue archéologique,* 3d ser., 25 (1894): 8–13.

33. Augustine, *Tract. in Ioh.* 7.12, ed. Radbod Willems (*CCSL* 36:73), lines 5–6.

34. Franz-Joseph Dölger, "Ein christlicher Brotstempel aus Karthago?" *Antike und Christentum* 1 (1929): 20–21.

35. See Ewa Wipszycka, "Le degré d'alphabétisation en Égypte byzantine," *REAug* 30 (1980): 279–96, esp. 294.

36. Richard Raabe, *Petrus der Iberer: Ein Charakterbild zur Kirchen- und Sittengeschichte des fünften Jahrhunderts* (Leipzig, 1895), 29–30.

37. Jerome, *Comm. in Mt. 23.5,* ed. D. Hurst and M. Adriaen (*CCSL* 77:212).

linda on the birth of her son by sending her a gift consisting of "a cross with holy wood from the cross of the Lord, and a reading from the holy Gospel, in a Persian box."[38] It is possible, but not entirely clear from his description, that the wood and the extract from scripture were combined into one object.

Holy Men and Holy Books

In late antiquity it was especially the hermits, monks, and holy men— themselves the embodiment of the Christian ideal—who had an intimate connection with the physical objects that contained the Word of God. From the earliest days of organized coenobitism, the existence of monastic libraries is well established, beginning with the central book depository mentioned in the *Rule of Pachomius*. In addition, there is abundant evidence that individual monks possessed gospel books of their own.[39] Seen not as worldly possessions that would bring their owners into conflict with the principle of monastic poverty, gospel codices were considered the essential equipment, or even status marker, of monks, along with their distinctive dress, the tunic. Gospel books are frequently mentioned in the context of prescriptions and regulations for the monastic life, where they are part of the furnishings of a monk's cell.[40] According to the great theoretician of monastic spirituality, Evagrius Ponticus, the monk's ultimate goal should be the continuous memory of God and the freedom from passions, "so that you possess nothing except the cell, the cloak, the tunic, and the Gospel."[41] In passages where monks are said to be owners of just one book of unspecified content, as for example in the case of a jealous monk who hides

38. Gregory the Great, *Ep.* 14.12 (*PL* 77:1316A): "Excellentissimo autem filio nostro Adulouvaldo regi transmittere phylacteria curavimus, id est crucem cum ligno sanctae crucis Domini, et lectionem sancti Evangelii theca Persica inclusam."

39. The possession of books by individual monks has to be distinguished from the communal monastic libraries, on which see Clemens Scholten, "Die Nag-Hammadi-Texte als Buchbesitz der Pachomianer," *Jahrbuch für Antike und Christentum* 30 (1988): 144–72. For the whole complex of monastic occupation with scripture, see also Gerhard J. M. Bartelink, "Die Rolle der Bibel in den asketischen Kreisen des vierten und fünften Jahrhunderts," in *The Impact of Scripture in Early Christianity*, ed. J. den Boeft and M. L. van Poll-van de Lisdonk (Leiden, 1999), 27–38.

40. Private monastic possession of more than one book is rare. One instance is Dorotheos in sixth-century Palestine, who expresses his desire to give his books to the community around Barsanuphius and John long after he had joined it. Lucien Regnault and Philippe Lemaire, trans., *Letters of Barsanuphius and John* (Solesmes, 1971), *Ep.* 326.

41. Joseph Muyldermans, ed., *Evagriana Syriaca: Textes inédits du British Museum et de la Vaticane* (Louvain, 1952), 8.3, 158, and a shorter duplicate of this passage at 3.A.7, 151.

"his own book" in the cell of Paphnutius in order to incriminate him as a thief, it is safe to assume that this was a codex of the holy scriptures.[42]

Small codices containing the Gospels or Psalms are frequently mentioned as the essential kit of traveling monks or clergy, and sometimes also of pious laymen. The *Regula Magistri* requests that monks who have to travel a long way from the monastery carry "a modest-sized little codex with some readings."[43] Maximus, a disciple of Martin of Tours, carried around his neck a gospel codex along with a small paten and a chalice—all of them miraculously preserved when his boat capsized during a crossing of the Saône River.[44] Abbot Equitius in rural Italy was so poor that he had to ride on a donkey without a proper saddle, yet he always carried *sacri codices* in a leather bag on his missionary journeys to the countryside.[45] A traveling monk in Egypt converted a prostitute by reading to her from the gospel codex he carried in a little wallet.[46] And the future hermit Amoun spent his wedding night reading to his bride from the Bible codex that he carried around his neck, in order to persuade her to agree to a chaste marriage.[47]

A number of small-size codices survive from the realms of Egyptian and Irish Christianity. The folia of the twelve Coptic and Greek fragments from Egypt, mostly on parchment, that are now preserved in the Freer Collection measure between 5.6 × 8.4 cm and 9.0 × 10.0 cm. The folia of Irish origin are slightly larger, varying in size from 12.5 × 11.2 cm to 17.5 × 14.2 cm.[48] The folia

42. John Cassian, *Conferences* 18.15.3, lines 6–7, ed. Michael Petschenig (*CSEL* 13:526).

43. *Regula Magistri* 57.4, in Adalbert de Vogüé, ed., *La règle du maître*, vol. 2 (*SC* 106:268, lines 10–12): "Si uero in uiam longiorem dirigatur, codicillum modicum cum aliquibus lectionibus de monasterio secum portet." An interesting secular parallel is the small codex of Thucydides, noted by the Antiochene rhetor Libanius in the late fourth century as his prize possession: "Its writing was fine and small, and the whole work was so easy to carry that I used to do so myself, while my slave followed behind: the burden was my pleasure." Libanius, *Autobiography* (*Or.* 1) 148, in ed. and trans. Albert F. Norman, *Libanius: Autobiography and Selected Letters* (Cambridge, Mass., 1992), 1:217.

44. Gregory of Tours, *Glory of the Confessors* 22, ed. Bruno Krusch, *MGH, SRM* 1.2, 311, lines 21–22, in Raymond van Dam, trans., *Gregory of Tours, Glory of the Confessors* (Liverpool, 1988), 37. This Maximus is not attested in the contemporary sources for St. Martin.

45. Gregory, *Dialogues* 1.4 (*PL* 77:172 A–B). Note that his monastery is said to have copyists.

46. John Moschus, *Pratum spirituale* 31 (*PG* 87.3:2880 A–C), in John Wortley, trans., *John Moschos: The Spiritual Meadow* (Kalamazoo, Mich., 1992).

47. Palladius, *Historia Lausiaca* 8.1–3, in Gerhard J. M. Bartelink, ed., *Palladio: La storia lausiaca* ([Milan], 1985), 40, line 1–42, line 29.

48. William H. Worrell, *The Coptic Manuscripts in the Freer Collection* (New York, 1923), xii–xiii; and Patrick McGurk, "The Irish Pocket Gospel Book," *Sacris Erudiri* 8 (1956): 249–70, esp. 252. Compare the large-size codices in the study by Eric G. Turner, *The Typology of the Early Codex* (Philadelphia,

are arranged into quires, but none of the specimens from either region shows any traces of binding, perhaps because the quires were intended to be carried in small wooden boxes or leather satchels.

Unfortunately, we are not often told the origin of these portable codices, nor are we informed who copied them. But there is some evidence that literate monks made it their task to copy their own codex with texts from scripture. Jerome's *Life of Hilarion* tells just such a story. In order to pay for his passage on a ship to Sicily, Hilarion intended "to pay the fare by selling a codex of the Gospels which he had written in his youth with his own hand."[49] This codex, and his monastic garb, were all he possessed. It is striking that Hilarion copied this codex "in his youth." I have previously suggested the possibility that as part of their monastic education, literate monks produced for themselves a codex of the Gospels that would remain in their private possession for the rest of their lives, just as Hilarion had done.[50] It is now possible to adduce further evidence for this. Gregory of Tours reports that his friend Leobardus, when a young boy, escaped his wealthy family and his bride, took up residence in a cell, and there began to prepare parchment with his own hands. He then wrote out for himself certain books of the scriptures, including the Psalms, in order to retain them in his memory. Once this work was completed, he devoted himself to a daily routine that included fasting, praying, chanting, reading, and on occasion also writing, in order to keep away harmful thoughts.[51] Just like Hilarion, Leobardus engaged in the preparation of a codex of the holy scriptures for his own private use as one of the first significant steps in his monastic life.

The copying of scripture was not just a mechanical activity but carried enormous spiritual significance for the copyist. According to ancient custom,

---

1977), 14, 26. The largest papyrus codex from late antiquity measures 28 × 37 cm, and the largest parchment codex 40 × 35 cm.

49. Jerome, *Life of Hilarion* 25.2, in Anton A. R. Bastiaensen, ed., *Vita di Martino, Vita di Ilarione, In memoria di Paola* ([Milan], 1975), 126, lines 2–4; English translation in Carolinne White, trans., *Early Christian Lives* (London, 1998), 109.

50. Claudia Rapp, "Christians and Their Manuscripts in the Greek East during the Fourth Century," in *Scritture, libri e testi nelle aree provinciali di Bisanzio,* ed. Guglielmo Cavallo et al. (Spoleto, 1991), 1:127–48.

51. Gregory of Tours, *Life of the Fathers* 20.2, ed. Krusch, 292, lines 16–23, in James, *Gregory of Tours,* 127–28. The crucial passage in the Latin reads: "Ibique se, propriis manibus membrana faciens, ad scribendum aptavit; ibi se, ut Scripturas Sanctas intellegeret ac Davitici carminis psalmos, qui dudum excesserant memoriae, reteneret, exercuit." The last phrase in James's translation misses the point: "There he began to make parchment with his own hands, and prepared it for writing; there he learnt to understand the Holy Scriptures and to memorise the Psalms of David, which had long passed from his mind."

the reading or writing of any text was accompanied by speaking or murmuring the words as the eye or the hand moved over the page. The physical act of writing out a text also aids in its memorization. As recent work by Raffaela Cribiore shows, the Bible provided the textbook, as it were, for the school exercises in writing that survive from late antique Egypt—presumably with the aim of imparting scriptural literacy to the pupils along with scribal skills.[52] In the monastic context, the act of copying simultaneously served the purpose of learning the scriptures by heart and engaging in *lectio divina,* having the word of God constantly on one's lips. This kind of exercise may well be the origin of six coarse scraps of papyrus—some of them reused—containing the Psalms written in a skilled but not professional hand that were found in the dwelling of a sixth-century hermit at Deir el-Naqlun in Egypt.[53]

The practice of acquiring the books of one's trade by gradually copying them out in the course of one's studies was common in the law schools of late antiquity. This was also the practice of young Manichaean devotees, as we know from Augustine. A bishop who was consulted by Augustine's mother, Monica, in her distress over her son's Manichaean leanings reminisced that when he was a child, his mother had "handed him over to the Manichees. He had not only read all their books, but had also made copies of them."[54] It is likely that Christian monks did the same. This is certainly suggested by the admonition of Abba Isaias of Scetis to novice monks: "If *you make yourself* a book, do not take care about its decoration, for this will be for you a passion."[55] It is conceivable that organized monastic communities institutionalized this practice for their literate novices. So for example in the community headed by Martin near Tours, the younger monks practiced the art of copying, while the older ones were engaged in constant prayer.[56] About a century later, at the other end of the *oikoumene,* the statutes of the monastic school of Nisi-

52. Raffaela Cribiore, *Writing, Teachers, and Students in Greco-Roman Egypt* (Atlanta, 1996).

53. Tomasz Derda, *Deir el-Naqlun: The Greek Papyri (P. Naqlun I)* (Warsaw, 1995), 41–96.

54. Augustine, *Confessions* 3.12.21, ed. Luc Verheijen (*CCSL* 27:39), in R. S. Pine-Coffin, trans., *Saint Augustine: Confessions* (London, 1961), 69.

55. Isaias of Scetis, *Logos* 3, 22–23, in Lucien Regnault and Hervé de Broc, eds., *Abbé Isaïe: Recueil ascétique,* 3d ed. (Abbaye de Bellefontaine, Maine et Loire, 1985), 51.

56. Sulpicius Severus, *Life of St. Martin* 10.6, in Jacques Fontaine, ed., *Sulpice Sévère: Vie de saint Martin,* vol. 1 (*SC* 133:274). English translation in White, *Early Christian Lives,* 144. Note that the context of this passage seems to indicate that the products of the young monks' labor were intended for sale. But this does not preclude the suggestion that these were manuscripts of the scriptures, and that the act of copying was tantamount to *lectio divina* and hence particularly suitable for the novice monk.

bis in northern Syria stipulated a three-year curriculum for novice monks, during which they had to copy parts of the Old and then of the New Testament in a particular order.[57] Similar regulations were made in the *Rules of the Monastery of Gabriel,* whose founder lived in the early seventh century. This Syrian monastery, also known as the Upper Monastery, was famous for its library and for its role in the formation of future clergy. The short *Rules* prescribe that instruction in writing should be given every Friday. The curriculum progressed from the New Testament to the Old Testament, and then to the Psalms and Prophets. It seems plausible that the young monks acquired the tools of their future trade as clerics not only through learning these texts but also by producing their own copies under the guidance of the writing instructor.[58]

This kind of appropriation of the foundational text of Christianity through a combination of memorization and scribal activity was also employed in the training of aspiring clergy. Many of the Coptic ostraca edited by Crum show prospective deacons making a firm promise to learn by heart the Gospel of John or the Gospel of Matthew, and it is conceivable that at least some deacons did so by copying these texts. Especially interesting is a Coptic ostracon containing a letter to a bishop that mentions a prospective clergyman who "writes the Gospel of John for himself and studies it"—a clear indication of the interrelationship between copying and memorization.[59]

The autograph copy of a holy man, sometimes together with his tunic, was often passed on to a favorite disciple to designate him as successor. Thus Hilarion bequeathed his precious gospel book and his monastic outfit to Hesychius, who later transported the saint's body from his last abode in Cyprus to his original monastery in Palestine.[60] Similarly, when the tomb of the apostle Barnabas in Cyprus was discovered and opened in 488, he was found to have

57. Arthur Vööbus, ed. and trans., *The Statutes of the School of Nisibis* (Stockholm, 1961), 107–9, cf. also 79.

58. Arthur Vööbus, ed. and trans., *Syriac and Arabic Documents Regarding Legislation Relative to Syrian Asceticism* (Stockholm, 1961), 187–88.

59. This rendering ("dass er das Evangelium nach Johannes für sich schreibt und studiert") is given by Derda, *Deir el-Naqlun,* 47n29, citing Martin Krause, *Apa Abraham von Hermonthis: Ein oberägyptischer Bischof um 600* (Ph.D. diss., Berlin, 1956), no. 12. But see Walter E. Crum, *Coptic Ostraca from the Collection of the Egypt Exploration Fund, the Cairo Museum and Others* (London, 1902), no. 37, p. 10: "Hemai appears to request bishop Abraham to ordain some one for him and offers to guarantee that this person (?) shall write out S. John's gospel. But little is certainly legible."

60. Jerome, *Life of Hilarion* 32.1, in Bastiaensen, *Vita di Martino,* 140, lines 4–5. English translation in White, *Early Christian Lives,* 114.

been buried with the Gospel of St. Mark on his chest, written in the evangelist's own hand, and presumably given to Barnabas as a token of deep affection.[61] A later, Western example is the manuscript now known as the Stonyhurst Gospel, which can be dated on palaeographical grounds to the late seventh or early eighth century. It was found lying next to the body of St. Cuthbert during his *translatio* to Durham Cathedral in 1104. Cuthbert either copied this codex himself or received it from his teacher, Boisil, who had carried it around his neck throughout his life.[62] The most intimate connection between the act of copying and the appointment of a successor is established in the *Life of Columba*. Columba felt his death approaching while copying Psalm 34 (Vulg. 33) and wrote, "Here, at the end of the page, I must stop. Let Baithene write what follows."[63] The scribal activity of the holy man here serves the dual functions of underscoring his enduring strength and piety to the last moments of his life and of forging a link to the generation that follows, after the page has been turned, but without any visible disruption of established pattern.

The Pious Hand

In its proximity to prayer, the copying of Christian texts as *lectio divina* was regarded as a particularly pious pursuit, whether it was practiced by monks or laypeople. Christian writers often mentioned the copying of scripture and other edifying texts to illustrate the piety of certain individuals.[64] Ambrose is thus praised by his hagiographer, Paulinus: "His constancy in prayer also was great, day and night; he did not shun the work of writing books with his own hand, unless when his body was hindered by some infirmity."[65] The holy virgin

61. Alexander the Monk, *Laudatio Barnabae* 750–66, in Peter van Deun, ed., *Hagiographica Cypria* (Turnhout, 1993), 116. Cf. also the later elaboration in the *Menologium Imperiale* 210–12, ibid., 134. A similar story of a hermit who was found dead but uncorrupted after seven years, holding a gospel book adorned with a silver cross, is told in the early seventh century: *Pratum spirituale* 87 (*PG* 87.3:2945A),in Wortley, *John Moschos*, 70.

62. T. Julian Brown, *The Stonyhurst Gospel of Saint John* (Oxford, 1969).

63. Alan Orr Anderson and Marjorie Ogilvie Anderson, eds. and trans., *Adomnan's Life of Columba* 3.23, rev. ed. (Oxford, 1991), 223. His successor, Baithene, also was active as a copyist. Ibid., 1.23, p. 51.

64. The connection between reading and copying stories of the holy men of Egypt and the desire for pilgrimage is explored by Georgia Frank, *The Memory of the Eyes: Pilgrims to Living Saints in Christian Late Antiquity* (Berkeley and Los Angeles, 2000), 6–13.

65. Paulinus, *Life of Ambrose,* chap. 9 (38), in Mary Simplicia Kaniecka, ed. and trans., *Vita sancti Ambrosii* (Washington, D.C., 1928), 80, lines 19–21: "orandi enim assiduitas magna, die ac nocte; nec operam declinabat scribendi propria manu libros, nisi cum aliqua infirmitate corpus eius attineretur."

Lidia left her native Thessalonike to visit Abba Macarius in Egypt in order to receive spiritual comfort from him. We are told that she was "a scribe writing books and living in great asceticism in the manner of men."[66] To illustrate the well-known piety of the emperor Theodosius II, later authors assume that he engaged not only in memorizing but also in copying the scriptures.[67] In Byzantium pious copying seems to have been favored especially during Lent. It is reported that the patriarch Methodius (d. 847), who in his childhood had received instruction in grammar, history, orthography, and stenography, copied one complete Psalter during each of the seven weeks of Lent, while observing a strict fast.[68] The Lenten practice of Euthymius, the future patriarch of Constantinople (d. 912), also consisted of a period of complete seclusion and fasting, during which he occupied himself not only with the composition of encomia and hymns on saints, but also with the practice of calligraphy.[69] Copying was equally treasured in the West as a pious pursuit. St. Columba's death while copying a psalm has already been mentioned.[70] And Gregory of Tours relates the story of the hermit Johannis in Chinon, who spent his time in the shade of the laurel trees he had planted, where he "either read or wrote something."[71]

The act of pious copying augmented the spiritual state of the copyist. The

66. *Life of Macarius of Alexandria,* in E. Amélineau, trans., *Monuments pour servir à l'histoire de l'Égypte chrétienne au IVe et Ve siècles,* vol. 3, *Histoire des monastères de la Basse-Égypte: Vies des saints Paul, Antoine, Macaire, Maxime et Domèce, Jean Le Nain, etc.* (Paris, 1894), 240. I am grateful to Maged Mikhail for his help with this text. English translation in Cuthbert Butler, *The Lausiac History of Palladius,* vol. 1 (Cambridge, 1898; reprint, Hildesheim, 1967), 150.

67. Socrates, *Hist. eccl.* 7.22.5, ed. Günther Christian Hansen, GCS, n. F. 1 (Berlin, 1995), 369, lines 2–5, mentions that he learned the scriptures by heart. The fourteenth-century Nicephorus Callistus, *Historia ecclesiastica* 16.3 (*PG* 146:1061D–64A), whose narration is largely dependent on earlier sources, mentions that Theodosius produced beautiful calligraphic copies of the Gospels. The ninth-century Georgios Monachos, *Chronicon,* ed. Carolus de Boor, rev. ed. Peter Wirth (Stuttgart, 1978), 604, line 9, calls him a "calligrapher." See also Jill Harries, "'Pius princeps': Theodosius II and Fifth-Century Constantinople," in *New Constantines: The Rhythm of Imperial Renewal in Byzantium, 4th–13th Centuries,* ed. Paul Magdalino (Aldershot, 1994), 35–44.

68. *Vita of Methodius, Patriarch of Constantinople,* chaps. 2, 11 (*Acta Sanctorum,* June 2, cols. 962E, 965 BC).

69. He presented a copy of his Lenten sermons "calligraphically written in his own hand" to the monks of his monastery. *Vita Euthymii Patriarchae CP* 9, ed. Patricia Karlin-Hayter (Brussels, 1970), 59, lines 4–5 (my translation). Clearly, the identity of the scribe adds a special significance to the codex when it is presented as a gift. Earlier in the same vita, the Emperor Leo VI marks his reconciliation with Euthymius by giving him "a delightful book ... and told him it was written with his own hand, and described his troubles," *Vita Euthymii* 8, 51, lines 17–19.

70. Anderson and Anderson, *Adomnan's Life of Columba* 3.23, p. 223; see also 2.16 at p. 117.

71. Gregory of Tours, *Glory of the Confessors* 23, ed. Krusch, 313; line 3, trans. van Dam, 39.

Doctrina Addai, composed in Edessa at the beginning of the fifth century, employs the act of writing as an evocative metaphor that calls all Christians to follow the divine script throughout their lives, and thereby to inscribe it into their resurrection bodies.

For the whole of that for which our Lord came into the world was that he might teach and show us that at the consummation of created things there will be a resurrection for all people. At that time their manner of life will be represented in their own persons and their bodies will become parchment skins for the books of justice. There will be no one there who cannot read, because in that day everyone will read the writings of his own book.[72]

A similar thought is expressed in an anonymous *Homily on Virginity,* which contains the promise that male and female virgins in heaven will be "holding in their hands the Psalter that is engraved in their hearts."[73] Here the body transformed through ascetic living becomes a mirror of the holy scriptures, which are inscribed on it. The equation of life and book has its roots in classical antiquity. According to the dream interpretation put forth by Artemidorus in the second century, "a book signifies the life of the person who sees it . . . and the remembrance of old deeds, for old deeds are written down in the books."[74] Scribal activity, whether real or metaphorical, thus shapes and defines the self.

Many pious men who were engaged in the production of books for a larger clientele, and even in commercial production, therefore took great care in selecting the text they were copying. Especially interesting is the case of Promotus in fifth-century Ephesus, the teacher of Markellos the Akoimetos and an accomplished calligrapher. Promotus's devotion was such that he refused to copy anything but the holy scriptures, and he did so, we are told, "not as an empty activity, but by paying attention to what he writes." It is also noted that the products of his labor enjoyed great popularity,[75] obviously because the piety of the scribe was considered to contribute to the value of his work.

A papyrus from the fifth or sixth century (*P.Köln* inv. 1473) shows the great esteem in which a venerable monastic scribe is held by his customer. Its reverential tone makes it worth quoting in full:

72. George Howard, trans., *The Teaching of Addai* (Chico, Calif., 1981), 47.

73. Anonymous, *Homily on Virginity* 57, trans. Teresa Shaw, in Vincent Wimbush, ed., *Ascetic Behavior in Greco-Roman Antiquity: A Sourcebook* (Minneapolis, 1990), 35.

74. Artemidorus, *Onirocriticon* 2.45, lines 22–25, ed. Roger A. Pack (Leipzig, 1963), 179.

75. Gilbert Dagron, "La vie ancienne de Marcel l'Acémète," *Analecta Bollandiana* 86 (1968): 271–321, esp. 289–90.

To the beloved Abba Honorius from Dionysius. I have heard that Your Piety has bought parchments. Deem us worthy, I beg, if it is possible, to trouble yourself to visit us, so that I may speak with you, so that you—when you have the time—may begin to copy for us a book on parchment, without disadvantage to yourself. For this [purpose], deem us worthy of a response or of a visit, so that I may be without worries and so that I may learn when you will begin to write for me, since I have the original [to be copied]. If you have need for anything, give the order. We will gladly be of service. Pray for us. I pray that you may be well.[76]

These examples show a further aspect of pious scribal activity that goes beyond the spiritual benefit acquired for one's own soul through the practice of *lectio divina* with the pen. Since Promotus and Honorius are not copying for their own use but for that of others, their piety adds a special quality to their work that is valued by the owners and readers of their codices.

Reflections on the effect of one's pious scribal activity on others are not frequent, but they are significant, especially as they allow us to draw a connection to hagiographic writing. The earliest relevant text is the *Vita of Melania the Younger,* who died in 439. It includes a whole paragraph that describes her engagement with scripture.[77] After praising her repeated reading and intense study of the Old and New Testaments, her memorization of the Psalms and her proficiency in Greek and Latin, the hagiographer mentions her copying activity in a rather opaque passage. It seems to mean that she practiced calligraphy on her own rather than in collaboration with others, and thus produced for "the saints" (presumably for men and women engaged in the monastic life) "examples from her own hands."[78] In other words, copying the scriptures is tan-

---

76. Ludwig Koenen, "Ein Mönch als Berufsschreiber: Zur Buchproduktion im 5./6. Jahrhundert," in *Festschrift zum 150 jährigen Bestehen des Berliner Ägyptischen Museums* (Berlin, 1974), 347–54 (Greek text and German translation at p. 352); my English translation. For a photograph, see http://www.uni-koeln.de/phil-fak/ifa/NRWakademie/papyrologie/Verstreutepub/bilder/PK1473r.jpg.

77. *Life of Melania the Younger* 26, in Denys Gorce, ed., *Vie de sainte Mélanie* (*SC* 90:178–80); see also *Life* 21 (*SC* 90:170–72) (she constantly carried a book with the scriptures in her hands); *Life* 23 (*SC* 90:174) (she divided her time between scribal activity [here the hagiographer draws attention to her skill as a calligrapher] and reading of scripture, homilies, and—as a special treat—the lives of the fathers); *Life* 33 (*SC* 90:188) (she spent her time in her cell reading and writing).

78. *Life* 26: καλλιγραφοῦσα τὸ αὔταρκες παρεῖχεν τοῖς ἁγίοις ἐκ τῶν ἰδίων χειρῶν ὑποδείγματα (*SC* 90:178). The translation by Elizabeth A. Clark, *The Life of Melania the Younger* (New York, 1984), 46, takes the word *hypodeigma* in the strictly technical sense of an original to be copied: "She copied them [the Old and the New Testaments] herself and furnished copies to the saints by her own hand." For a discussion of this passage in the context of the larger phenomenon of female scribes in early Christianity, see Kim Haines-Eitzen, *Guardians of Letters: Literacy, Power, and the Transmitters of Early Christian Literature* (Oxford, 2000), 48–49, 130–31.

tamount to providing an *exemplum* of Christian living for others. In the hand of the pious scribe, the pen acts as a substitute for lifelong exemplary conduct.

This special appreciation of pious scribal activity is reiterated by Cassiodorus in the sixth century. He declared to the monks in his southern Italian monastery of Vivarium that the act of copying allows the scribe not only to immerse himself in the scriptures but also to disseminate them to a larger public through the work of his hands.

[B]y reading the Divine Scriptures he [the scribe] wholesomely instructs his own mind and by copying the precepts of the Lord he spreads them far and wide. Happy his design, praiseworthy his zeal, to preach to men with the hand alone, to unleash tongues with the fingers, to give salvation silently to mortals, and to fight against the illicit temptations of the devil with pen and ink. Every word of the Lord written by the scribe is a wound inflicted on Satan.[79]

The authorship of a hagiographic work is often conceptualized in a similar way. The hagiographer compensates for his inability to be a living imitator of the saint in his own life by composing his work, thereby presenting an example for *imitatio* to others through his writing. Sulpicius Severus expresses this sentiment in the preface to his *Life of St. Martin:* "For even if we ourselves have not lived in such a way as to be an example to others, we have at least made an effort to prevent a man who deserves to be imitated from remaining unknown."[80]

The Miraculous Hand

Pious scribal activity thus had a twofold spiritual benefit for the scribe, as *lectio divina* and as evidence of his or her dissemination of the Christian mes-

---

79. Cassiodorus, *Institutiones* 1.30.1, lines 8–14, in R. A. B. Mynors, ed., *Cassiodori Senatoris Institutiones* (Oxford, 1937), 75: "quod et mentem suam relegendo Scripturas divinas salutariter instruunt et Domini praecepta scribendo longe lateque disseminant. felix intentio, laudanda sedulitas, manu hominibus praedicare, digitis linguas aperire, salutem mortalibus tacitum dare, et contra diaboli subreptiones illicitas calamo atramentoque pugnare. tot enim vulnera Satanas accipit, quot antiquarius Domini verba describit." Leslie Webber Jones, trans., *An Introduction to Divine and Human Readings by Cassiodorus Senator* (New York, 1946), XXX:1.

80. Sulpicius Severus, *Life of St. Martin* 1.6, in Fontaine, *Sulpice Sévère (SC* 133:252); English translation in White, *Early Christian Lives,* 136. For the efforts of Greek hagiographers of the fourth to tenth century to render present the saint through their writing, see Claudia Rapp, "Byzantine Hagiographers as Antiquarians, Seventh to Tenth Centuries," in *Bosphorus: Essays in Honour of Cyril Mango,* ed. Stephanos Efthymiadis et al., *Byzantinische Forschungen* 21 (1995): 31–44.

sage. The pious scribe can also impart a special quality to the concrete product of his or her labor, similar to the handicraft of monks or nuns offered for purchase in monastic gift shops today. In the production of copies of scripture or other texts of spiritual value, that special quality might also be rooted in the nature of the text. To understand the relationship between the holiness of the text and the holiness of the scribe, let us set biblical texts aside and look at the value attributed to the handwriting of holy men in general. This will prepare the ground for a discussion of the holiness of hagiography and its potential character as sacred text.

It was especially the letters written by a holy man in his own hand that carried miraculous powers similar to those of a contact relic. That a letter renders an absent person present is a topos in ancient epistolography and doubtless contributed to this concept. The followers of holy men often asked them for letters, since their receipt would assure a blessing and signal a special relationship of spiritual familiarity.[81]

In the case of a miracle-working letter, it is important to identify the actual medium that produced the miracle, whether the message itself, the hand in which it was written, or both. There is a long tradition in Greco-Roman antiquity of letters containing the command of a holy man that brought immediate miraculous results. Pagan holy men often addressed demonic powers in written words, which were thus close in form and function to magic spells. Pausanias and Aristides, for example, knew of letters by the god Asclepius that brought healing.[82] Apollonius of Tyana, the most famous pagan wonderworker, composed a threatening letter to a ghost in order to prevent it from harming a boy.[83]

Christians endeavored to demonstrate their power over the demons of

81. Callinicus, *Life of Hypatius* 36.7–8, ed. Gerhard J. M. Bartelink, *Callinicos: Vie d'Hypatios* (*SC* 177:226). For further examples, see Claudia Rapp, "'For Next to God, You Are My Salvation': Reflections on the Rise of the Holy Man in Late Antiquity," in *The Cult of Saints in Late Antiquity and the Early Middle Ages: Essays on the Contribution of Peter Brown,* ed. James Howard-Johnston and Paul A. Hayward (Oxford, 1999), 63–81.

82. Pausanias, *Graeciae descriptio* 10.38.13, ed. Maria Helena Rocha Pereira (Leipzig, 1981), 188; Aristides, *Logos* 23, 290, ed Wilhelm Dindorf, vol. 1 (Hildesheim, 1964), 464.

83. Philostratus, *Life of Apollonius* 3.38, ed. and trans. Frederick C. Conybeare (Cambridge, Mass., 1912), 1:316–17. For more examples of written magic, culled from hagiographical tales, see John Wortley, "Some Light on Magic and Magicians in Late Antiquity," *Greek, Roman and Byzantine Studies* 42 (2001 [2002]): 289–307.

the old world order in a similar way. Gregory the Wonder-worker, bishop of Neocaesarea in the Pontus region in the third century, stunned a pagan temple keeper by commanding the demons, who had vacated the premises while Gregory was spending the night there, to reenter their original dwelling place in the altar. He did so by simply writing on a scrap of "paper": "Gregory to Satan: Enter!"[84] Ascetic holy men in Egypt were held in high repute for issuing letters with healing commands, as Postumianus reported to Sulpicius Severus and other friends in Gaul.[85] In the sixth century, St. Eugendus in the Jura region near Basel applied this method in the exorcism of a young woman.[86] The demon—not without a sense of humor—had announced that no quantity of written papyrus from Alexandria turned into magical charms would move him, but only the express command *(iussio)* of Eugendus. The saint wrote down his command to the demon in a letter *(per scripturam istam)*, prayed, and handed it over to the messengers. His order was so effective that the demon departed from the woman before the letter had traveled even halfway to its destination. In this instance, the miraculous force resided largely in the holy man's command made manifest through the act of writing itself, not in the sufferer's physical contact with the letter containing the holy man's handwriting.

An interesting question in this context is whether the association of holy men, monks, and clergy with the holy scriptures and with writing in general gave them a special ability to write out miracle-working commands in their own hand. Indeed, recent work by David Frankfurter suggests that monks and clergy in late antique Egypt were considered "public ritual experts" and thus were often asked to copy out magic spells.[87] The relatively high degree of literacy among Egyptian clergy, monks, and ascetics would have been a further contributing factor.[88] In other regions of the empire, too, clerics were known to produce phylacteries, protective devices invoking the power of Christianity.

84. Gregory of Nyssa, *Life of Gregory the Wonderworker,* chap. 38, in Günter Heil, ed., *Gregorii Nysseni Sermones: Pars II* (Leiden, 1990), 22, line 3ff.; Michael Slusser, trans., *St. Gregory Thaumaturgus: Life and Works* (Washington, D.C., 1998), 57.

85. Sulpicius Severus, *Dialogus* 1.20.2, ed. Carolus Halm (*CSEL* 1:172, lines 9–14), trans. Alexander Roberts, *Nicene and Post-Nicene Fathers,* 2d ser. (New York, 1894), 11:33.

86. *Vita S. Eugendi,* chaps. 141–44, ed. François Martine, *Vie des pères du Jura* (*SC* 142:389–95).

87. David Frankfurter, "Ritual Expertise in Roman Egypt and the Problem of the Category 'Magician,'" in *Envisioning Magic: A Princeton Seminar and Symposium,* ed. Peter Schäfer and Hans G. Kippenberg (Leiden, 1997), esp. 125–30, and David Frankfurter, "The Perils of Love: Magic and Countermagic in Coptic Egypt," *Journal for the History of Sexuality* 10 (2001): 480–500, esp. 497–500.

88. Wipszycka, "Le degré d'alphabétisation," 279–96, esp. 288–95.

The council that convened at Laodiceia sometime in the late fourth century attempted to prohibit monks and clerics from producing such objects.[89] And in seventh-century Gaul, Eligius of Noyon criticized the custom of hanging amulets from the neck of men and cattle alike, "even if they are made by clerics, and even if it is said that this is a holy thing and that it contains passages from scripture."[90]

Distinct from letters where the message itself was intended to generate a miracle are letters in which miraculous powers reside exclusively in the handwriting and the content is of secondary importance.[91] In his *Letter to Melania,* Evagrius Ponticus describes beautiful handwriting as a metaphor for God's creation of the world; both generate in the beholder an immediate sense of the presence and intention of the creator scribe.

It is clear then, that he who is far apart from his friend can sense that one's intention through hand, finger, pen, ink, paper and all the other instruments which are at our disposition. . . . Just as someone who reads letters, by their beauty senses the power and ability of the hand and the finger which wrote them together with the intention of the writer, thus he who looks upon creation with understanding, perceives the hand and the finger of its Creator as well as his intention, that is, his love.[92]

In the early fifth century, a faithful follower of Daniel the Stylite, who lived atop a column on the outskirts of Constantinople, requested by letter a written prayer from Daniel every time a member of his household was sick, then placed the response on the sufferer and thus obtained healing. By way of explanation, the hagiographer refers to the proven efficacy of Jesus' *Letter to King Abgar* (on which more below), adding that Daniel's follower regarded this "as if the miracle had been from the hand of Christ itself."[93] Clearly, it was the combination of the holy man's prayer and his handwriting that wrought the healing.

89. Council of Laodiceia, can. 36, Mansi 2:570.

90. *Vita of Eligius of Noviomagus* 2.15 (*PL* 87:528C [= 2.16 *MGH, SRM* 4:706]): "nullus ad colla vel hominis, vel cujuslibet animalis ligamina dependere praesumat, etiamsi a clericis fiant, et si dicatur quod res sancta sit, et lectiones divinas contineat." For references to the continued involvement of clerics in the production of such protective devices, and their condemnation in the Middle Ages, see Poulin, "Entre magie et religion," 139–40.

91. Guglielmo Cavallo, "Testo e immagine: Una frontiera ambigua," in *Testo e immagine nell'alto medioevo,* Settimane di studio del Centro italiano di studi sull'alto Medioevo 41.1 (Spoleto, 1994), 31–62, esp. 59–61, draws attention to such phenomena where the text works almost like a relic or a contact relic.

92. Martin Parmentier, "Evagrius of Pontus' 'Letter to Melania,'" *Bijdragen tijdschrift voor filosofie en theologie* 46 (1985): 8, lines 27–29 and 43–47.

93. *Vita S. Danielis Stylitae* 88, ed. H. Delehaye, *Analecta Bollandiana* 32 (1913): 203.

A holy man's signature could also work miracles even if the content of his missive was unrelated and the beneficiary of the miracle was not the recipient of the letter. Venantius Fortunatus tells a story about Germanus of Auxerre in which a monk who had suffered from a fever for two years was able to "lick himself to health from the signature of the saint" on a letter Germanus had sent to the abbot Flameris. The abbot was initially reluctant to produce the document because the letter had been addressed to him and not to the monk.[94] The miraculous element here extends beyond the healing itself, to the fact that the healing powers of Germanus's signature could spill over even to people who were unknown to him.

We see the same extension of miraculous powers in a letter from Martin of Tours to Arborius, a former prefect of Rome and relative of the poet Ausonius, which cured Arborius's young daughter of a fever. "This event had such an effect on Arborius that he immediately offered his daughter to God and dedicated her to perpetual virginity. He went to find Martin and presented his daughter to him as a living witness to his special powers, in that she had been cured by him even though he was not present."[95]

A story related by Gregory of Tours about bishop Nicetius of Lyon affirms that a holy man's signature alone could be efficacious. A poor man "had obtained from him [Nicetius] letters bearing his signature," with which he went to beg for alms. He continued to do so even after Nicetius's death, for the sake of his memory—a rather lucrative business, apparently, as he was carrying six gold coins when a Burgundian thief accosted him. The pauper managed to retain the letter and took the case before the authorities, where the guilt of the thief was established because he was paralyzed as soon as his hand touched the letter.[96] This touching of a holy object whose power is invoked to certify one's testimony is reminiscent of the use of a gospel codex in the swearing of oaths. But in this instance the holiness of the scribe, not of the text, was the operative force.[97]

94. Venantius Fortunatus, *Vita of Germanus of Auxerre* 153–55, lines 15–22, ed. Bruno Krusch (*Monumenta Germaniae Historica, Auctores Antiquissimi* 4.2:23); "de sancti subscriptione sibi sanitatem linxisse" (line 22).

95. *Vita Martini* 19.1–2, ed. Fontaine, *Sulpice Sévère*, vol. 1 (*SC* 133:292), with commentary on the social implications of this miracle in vol. 2 (*SC* 134:873–83); English translation in White, *Early Christian Lives*, 151.

96. Gregory of Tours, *Life of the Fathers* 8.9, ed. Krusch, 249, line 10-250, line 4, English translation in James, *Gregory of Tours*, 60–61.

97. A late example comes from ninth-century Byzantium, when a woman reports how a fire in her

Examples of the miraculous powers of the handwriting of a holy man are particularly common on the fringes of the Christian *oikoumene*—Ireland and Scotland—where scriptural literacy and Latin learning were introduced simultaneously. Adomnan's *Life of Columba,* the sixth-century Irish founder of the monastery of Iona, dwells frequently on the holy man's constant occupation with prayer, reading, and writing. When he absentmindedly used his pen to make the sign of the cross over a dagger, brought to him while he was engaged in copying, he rendered its edge useless for killing bulls or cows. Columba was confident that it "will never wound men or cattle," and the monks exploited this miraculous effect by melting down the dagger and applying a coating of the metal to all the iron tools of the monastery, in order to render them incapable of causing accidental harm.[98] The books Columba copied were impervious to water damage, even if by some accident they had been immersed for a long time.[99] Columba's autograph books, together with his garments, produced posthumous miracles as well. During a drought, a solemn procession produced a great rainfall when the tunic he had worn at the time of his death was shaken out and books in his handwriting were read aloud.[100] The monks also obtained favorable winds by placing the saints' garments and books on the altar during their prayers.[101] This combination of miraculous objects reminds us of Hilarion's bequest of his autograph gospel and his tunic to Hesychius, and indicates that the handwriting of a holy man could be considered a contact relic in the same way that his garments were.

If the holiness of the scribe imbues his handwriting of a specific text with miraculous powers, is it possible that this special quality also extends to cop-

house was miraculously extinguished by a letter sent to her by the famous monastic reformer Theodore the Studite and bearing his handwriting: *Vita Theodori Studitae* 112 (*PG* 99:213D–16A).

98. *Adomnan's Life of Saint Columba* 2.29, ed. Anderson and Anderson, 135–75. Other episodes in the *Life* attest to the importance of monastic copying among Columba's circle: 1.23 (p. 51) mentions the copying and emendation of a Psalter by Columba's disciple and successor Baithene; 1.24 (p. 51) refers to the private reading of a book that then falls into a ewer of water; 1.25 (p. 53) tells of a clumsy visitor who knocks over Columba's ink horn. See also the Middle Irish homily *On the Life of Columba,* preserved in a fifteenth-century manuscript, in Stokes, *Three Middle-Irish Homilies,* 113, which reports that Columba copied three hundred manuscripts, all of which shared the miraculous quality of being impervious to damage by immersion in water, no matter for how long. His copying activity was linked to his missionary work. He placed a gospel "which his own hand wrote" in a church he had founded, and also applied himself to the production of "satchels and wallets for books and all church gear" (115).

99. *Adomnan's Life of Columba* 2.8–9, ed. Anderson and Anderson, 105–7.

100. Ibid., 2.44, 173–75.

101. Ibid., 2.45, 175.

ies of the original text that are made by others? This was definitely the case in Carolingian times for writing attributed to Jesus himself, such as the *Himmelsbriefe* that were still carried by soldiers during World War I, and the related phenomenon of the "Sunday Letter," a direct message from heaven encouraging the strict implementation of Sunday observance.[102] Another prominent case is Jesus' *Letter to King Abgar*.[103] According to a legend first reported in Greek by Eusebius of Caesarea, King Abgar of Edessa invited Jesus by letter to visit his city. Jesus responded by sending his regrets, along with a blessing that would render Edessa impregnable to all future enemies.[104] By the fourth century, this letter (it is unclear whether the supposed autograph or a copy of it) was affixed to the city walls of Edessa. The protective and apotropaic power of King Abgar's *Letter to Jesus* and Jesus' *Letter to King Abgar* were believed to be transferable to other circumstances. Both texts were repeated in the fifth and sixth centuries in inscriptions around doorframes and lintels in Euchaita and Ephesus.[105] Their importance was also recognized in Egypt, where Jesus' *Letter to King Abgar* was written on the walls of the cell of the hermit Theophilus, in a Coptic translation, as late as 736.[106] Both letters are found together in two Egyptian papyri of the sixth to seventh century, while a further papyrus of the same period contains only Jesus' letter. The assurance of Jesus' protection and aid is thus sought by the replication of his letter, often in conjunction with Abgar's original request. But Abgar's letter, historically proven to elicit a divine response, was also used on its own to provide a remedy for illness. A fifth-century Coptic papyrus contains the text with the addition of magical signs,

102. Lawrence Nees, "The Irish Manuscripts at St. Gall and Their Continental Affiliations," in *Sangallensia in Washington: The Arts and Letters in Medieval and Baroque St. Gall Viewed from the Late Twentieth Century,* ed. James C. King (New York, 1993), 116–19. Nees draws attention here and elsewhere to the only extant pictorial representations of Christ writing a book with his own hand in cod. Sangall. 1395 and the Utrecht Psalter.

103. The most detailed treatment of the Abgar legend remains Ernst von Dobschütz, *Christusbilder: Untersuchungen zur christlichen Legende* (Leipzig, 1899), chap. 5. For a shorter discussion, see Judah B. Segal, *Edessa: "The Blessed City"* (Oxford, 1970), 62–82.

104. Eusebius, *H.E.* 1.13, ed. Eduard Schwartz and Theodor Mommsen, rev. ed.; Friedhelm Winkelmann, *Eusebius Werke* 2.1, GCS, n. F. 6 (Berlin, 1999), 82.21–96.8, trans. Geoffrey A. Williamson, *Eusebius: The History of the Church from Christ to Constantine* (Harmondsworth, 1965), 65–69.

105. Henri Grégoire, *Recueil des inscriptions grecques-chrétiennes d'Asie Mineure,* vol. 1 (Paris, 1922; reprint Amsterdam, 1968), 37–39, no. 106.

106. F. Ll. Griffith, "Oxford Excavations in Nubia," *Annals of Archaeology and Anthropology* 14 (1927): 88–89, and plate 71.

prayers, and the name of the sufferer, Epimachus.[107] In this instance, it was not the replication of a divine autograph that was intended to perform a miracle, but a text of secondary nature.

Hagiography as Miraculous Text

This leads to our final question: could miraculous powers inhere in non-scriptural writing, and especially in hagiography? There is scattered evidence for the combination of the relics of a saint with a relevant hagiographical text, reminiscent of Peter the Iberian's gospel codex adorned by a piece from the wood of the holy cross. The hagiographer of St. Felix of Noyon explains that after the saint's burial he took away some relics, along with the martyrdom account, in order that he might benefit already in this life from the saint's assistance.[108] A similar case is reported for Northumbria in the early twelfth century, where a priest carried around his neck a book containing the *Life of Saint Cuthbert,* accompanied by contact relics from the tomb of the saint.[109] These accounts raise the possibility that, while the text authenticated and authorized the relic, text and relic could jointly hold miraculous powers.

Many hagiographical tales affirm that the saint was, in fact, present at the recital of his vita in the same way as he was present in his relics.[110] Saints' *Lives* frequently begin with an invocation by the hagiographer, asking for the saint's assistance in the composition of the text, and conclude with prayers to the saint on behalf of author and audience. Whenever the hagiographical story is recited, these passages invoke the presence of the saint. It is thus not surprising that one of the posthumous miracles of Martin of Tours involved the healing of two blind men, a miracle that occurred during the public recital of his

---

107. *P.Oxy.* 4469, ed. F. Maltomini, *The Oxyrhynchus Papyri,* vol. 65 (London, 1998), 122–29, with further references.

108. *Acta S. Felicis Martyris* (*Acta Sanctorum,* August 1, col. 28EF).

109. Reginald of Durham, *Libellus de admirandis beati Cuthberti virtutibus* 54, ed. James Raine (London, 1835), 111.

110. Els Rose, "Celebrating Saint Martin in Early Medieval Gaul," in *Christian Feast and Festival: The Dynamics of Western Liturgy and Culture,* ed. Paul Post et al. (Leuven, 2001), 267–86, explores the connection between liturgical and hagiographical texts that were recited in the commemoration of Martin of Tours. Both were closely interwoven and both could activate miraculous powers. See also the interesting remarks on the force inherent in the reading of epigrams by Joseph W. Day, "Epigram and Reader: Generic Force as (Re-)Activation of Ritual," in *Matrices of Genre: Authors, Canons and Society,* ed. Mary Depew and Dirk Obbink (Cambridge, Mass., 2000), 37–57.

vita on his feast day at Tours.[111] On a similar occasion, St. Martin was also credited with the healing of a paralytic lector, just at the moment when the lector
touched the codex to begin reading the vita of the saint.[112]

While the topos of the desired or intended presence of the saint through
the composition and ritual recital of his vita occurs frequently in Greek and
Latin hagiography, the evidence for miracle-working hagiographical texts
enshrined in written form—without reading or recital—is limited, to the
best of my knowledge, to late antique Gaul. Paulinus of Périgueux recalls in
a poem the miraculous healing of his grandson and the grandson's wife after
they touched the written account of the miracles of St. Martin. This account
had been sent to him for versification by Perpetuus, the bishop of Tours and
great propagator of Martin's powers, who not only had composed it but also
signed the document in his own hand. In the dedicatory preface to the poem
he wrote to commemorate this miraculous healing, Paulinus seems to insist
that the miracle was the result of the combination of the text on St. Martin
and the signature of Bishop Perpetuus.[113] Gregory of Tours later related this
miracle in his *Four Books on the Virtues of Saint Martin,* but with some differences: he omitted the healing of the wife and the detail about Perpetuus's signature, and added that the miracle was the result of literary blackmail, since
Perpetuus demanded it as a sign of the saint's approval for his planned versification of the text.[114] In Gregory's rendition, the resulting miracle thus operated
on two levels, in the physical healing of the poet's grandson and in the saintly
endorsement of the poet's work.

In a second story, reported by Gregory of Tours about the vita of St. Martin, a monk from Marmoutier went traveling on an errand: "For the sake of
the salvation of his soul and for the correction of his life he took with him a
book containing the *Vita* of the blessed bishop." The book accidentally ended up in a fire but was miraculously preserved without a blemish. Gregory of

111. Gregory of Tours, *De virtutibus sancti Martini episcopi* 2.29, ed. Bruno Krusch, *MGH, SRM* 1.2,
169, line 28-170, line 4, trans. Raymond van Dam, *Saints and their Miracles in Late Antique Gaul* (Princeton, 1993), 243–44.

112. Gregory of Tours, *De virtutibus sancti Martini episcopi* 2.49, ed. Krusch, 176, lines 13–19; trans.
van Dam, 253.

113. Paulinus of Périgueux, *De visitatione nepotuli sui,* ed. Michael Petschenig (*CSEL* 16:160–64);
"quem charta inscripta uirtutibus et manu beatitudinis uestrae subscripta sanauerat," 161, lines 6–7.

114. Gregory of Tours, *De virtutibus sancti Martini episcopi* 1.2, ed. Krusch, 139, lines 13–17, trans.
van Dam, 205.

Tours adds, by way of confirmation, that the book is now in his possession.[115] The characteristics of this hagiographic codex mirror those of the Bible codices discussed above: it is taken on a journey as private reading material and it is able to withstand the destructive force of fire.

A third story reported by Gregory of Tours, this time in his *Life of the Fathers,* relates how the *Miracula* of Bishop Nicetius of Lyon, his older relative and teacher, were able to cure a deacon from Autun of an eye disease.[116] The deacon was convinced that he could be healed only by visiting Nicetius's tomb, where he would take some "relic of his"—probably not bones but some of the dust or herbs that were so abundantly produced around the tombs of the saints in Gaul—or even touch the cloth that was spread out on the tomb. As he was carrying on at great length about this wish for physical contact, a clergyman approached him and said, "You are right to believe that, but to confirm your opinion of these miracles, here is a papyrus volume relating to them which will make you believe more easily what your ears have heard." The deacon eagerly seized the volume, placed it on his eyes, and immediately was able to see again "with so much clarity that he could read the tales of miracles with his own eyes." Gregory adds by way of comment, "Divine power flowed from this book, and far from leaving Nicetius without glory, it showed to many people just how glorious he was, in proving the efficacy of the miracles told in it."[117]

Implicit in this story is a hierarchical classification of miraculous agents. For those who are able to visit the tomb that encloses the saint's body, touching the cloth that covers it is more efficacious than merely collecting the dust or herbs that grow around it. But equally efficacious, even at long distance, is the physical contact with the codex that enshrines the miracles in written form. Setting one's eye on the writing on the page would, according to the cleric who brought the book, strengthen the belief that until then had been based only on oral reports, on "what your ears have heard." But before this full conversion to the power of the saint through the act of reading—through the movement of the eyes scanning the words on the open page—could occur, the

---

115. Ibid., 3.42, ed. Krusch, 192, line 27-193, line 2, trans. van Dam, 275–76.

116. Gregory of Tours, *Life of the Fathers* 8.12, ed. Krusch, 251, line 25-252, line 6, trans. James, 63–64.

117. On this episode, see also Conrad Leyser, "'Divine Power Flowed from this Book': Ascetic Language and Episcopal Authority in Gregory of Tours' *Life of the Fathers,*" in *The World of Gregory of Tours,* ed. Kathleen Mitchell and Ian Wood (Leiden, 2002), 281–94.

miracle has already taken place through the codex that is still closed. Note, however, that the final proof of the healing consists in the deacon's ability to "read the tales of the miracles with his own eyes."

Reading a hagiographic text is represented here as a physical process equal to a pilgrimage in intention and effect. In the right circumstances, the hagiographical text contains a transformative power not only as a story—as in the incident reported by Augustine at the beginning of this chapter—but also in its physical manifestation in book form. Contact with the saints in the stories written about them and the books that contain these stories could produce miracles. In this sense, hagiography may well be seen as scripture writ small.[118]

The holy book and the holy man are the most powerful icons for our interpretation of the culture and mentality of late antiquity. As the material discussed here suggests, a double movement connects the two: the pious scribe acquires holiness from copying a sacred text, but at the same time the holy man—whether as a scribe or as the subject of a hagiographical work—is also able to impart holiness to the written text.

---

118. By medieval times, the miraculous healing effect of hagiographical texts read aloud over a patient was well established. A ninth-century miscellany of medical texts, Paris, Bibliothèque Nationale, MS lat. 11218, which at a later date is recorded to have belonged to the Benedictine monastery of Saint-Bénigne, begins on fols. 2–5v with the *Passio* of Cosmas and Damian, the famous healing saints who refused payment for their services and were martyred under Diocletian. The purpose of their story in a medical compendium is explained right away: "Here begins the *passio* of the physicians Cosmas and Damian. Whoever is sick and has this *passio* read over him, the Lord will be merciful to him." In the later Middle Ages, the *Life of Saint Margaret,* another martyr of the Great Persecution, was read out in a similar way to help women in childbirth. See E. Wickersheimer, "Une Vie des saints Côme et Damien dans un manuscrit médical du IXe siècle, suivie d'une recette de collyre attribuée à la mère des deux saints," *Centaurus* 1 (1950), 38–42. I am grateful to Patrick Geary for bringing this reference to my attention.

PART VI   𝕽   THEORY AND THE BOOK

Catherine Conybeare

SANCTUM, LECTOR, PERCENSE VOLUMEN

Snakes, Readers, and the Whole Text in
Prudentius's Hamartigenia

Sanctum, lector, percense volumen: "Reader, peruse the holy book."

This paper is concerned not with books as material objects, the set of tangibles that is the province of the codicologist, but with reading. It addresses the way in which the reader constructs the book—both in the sense, now commonplace, of "constructing" the meaning of the book; and in the more literal sense of constructing the contents of the book, designating of what parts it shall consist.[1] In this sense, books truly cannot exist without readers, for who is to determine their boundaries if not the readers themselves?[2] This is especially true in a literary culture that depends on the dissemination of books in manuscript form, where the link between producer and consumer of text is so much less heavily mediated than in a print culture.

Here I examine a particularly loaded example of the way in which a read-

---

1. This chapter is, fittingly enough, a product of the sort of participatory hermeneutic that constitutes my subject. My warm thanks to the interlocutors at the Early Christian Book Conference who transformed it, to Marianne Hansen for assistance with the early printed materials, and to my student, Reverend Tony Dykes, for prompting me to read the *Hamartigenia* in the first place.

2. For an interesting discussion of these issues, see the review article by Leah Price, "The Tangible Page," *London Review of Books*, October 31, 2002, 36–39.

er may "construct" a book. In this instance, the book is a *sanctum volumen,* a holy book—the scriptures of the Christian Bible. I propose an interpretation of Prudentius's antiheretical poem, the *Hamartigenia,* which shows that the work is simultaneously an argument for the necessity of reading the Old and New Testaments as an integrated whole and a demonstration of how to produce such a reading. Further, I show that a startling extended metaphor within the poem, in which a snake is literally eviscerated by the birth of her young, encapsulates the cost of reading the Bible in the wrong way. Setting different readings—and types of reading—over against the materiality of "the book" is crucial to my discussion. The juxtaposition of reading with the material book is particularly significant when the book in question is a *sanctum volumen.* Situating the boundaries of that *volumen* incorrectly, reading it wrongly, may take the *lector* abruptly out of a mere mirage of interdependent meanings and actually imperil her immortal soul. In other words, the issue is no longer simply the *delectatio libri,* the enjoyment of reading and of textual culture per se; what is at stake is the spiritual health of the reader.

Prudentius's *Hamartigenia*[3] is an extended hexameter poem with a preface in iambics, composed in the early fifth century A.D.[4] The preface casts Marcion, a dualist heretic of the second century, as a second Cain, and the poem goes on to inveigh against dualism and account for the origin of sin in a typically Prudentian style, leavening passages of dense theological exposition with biblical *exempla* and vivid metaphors. Although there is a colorful invocation of the devil's power to lead humans astray, Prudentius ultimately lays the blame for sin upon humankind and its flawed will—"our sins are gener-

---

3. This seems to mean "the origin of sin," though *genia* is etymologically dubious. How Prudentius himself saw the work may be expressed in his *Praefatio,* v. 39: *pugnet contra haereses.*

4. The text of *Hamartigenia* used here is that of Maurice P. Cunningham, *CCSL* 126 (Turnhout, 1966). In the context of a study of readers and reading, it seemed particularly important to review a wide range of commentaries. I have accordingly consulted Victor Giselin, *In Aurelii Prudentii Clementis V. Cl. Opera Commentarius.* Part II of *Aurelius Prudentius Clemens, Theodori Pulmanni Cranenburgii, et Victoris Giselini opera: Ex fide decem librorum manuscriptorum emendatus* (Antwerp, 1564; reprinted in much fuller form in Weitz); Johann Weitz, *Aurelii Prudentii Clementis v.c. opera, noviter ad msc. fidem recensita ... a M. Iohanne Weitzio* (Hanover, 1613); Nicolaus Heinsius, *Aurelii Prudentii Clementis v.c. opera cum notis Nicolai Heinsii ... et variorum doctorum virorum maxime necessariis* (Cologne, 1701); Faustino Arévalo, ed., *M. Aureli Clementis Prudenti Carmina.* 2 vols. (Rome, 1788, 1789); Jan Stam, ed., *Prudentius: Hamartigenia* (Amsterdam, 1940); and Roberto Palla, ed., *Prudenzio: Hamartigenia* (Pisa, 1981). The doctoral dissertation of Rosemarie M. Taddei, "A Stylistic and Structural Study of Prudentius' *Hamartigenia*" (Ph.D. diss., Bryn Mawr College, 1981), is effectively a running commentary; see also Martha Malamud, "Writing Original Sin," *JECS* 10 (2002): 329–60.

ated from our own minds" (*Ham.* 554–55)—that is, the free will given to humans by God the creator. A retelling of the fatal willfulness of Lot's wife lends special poignancy to this account. The work concludes with the poet's prayer that his inevitable torments in hell be mitigated by the (appropriately orthodox) triune God.

The poem's metrical content alone signals its participation in a medium of studied pseudo-orality, the dissimulation of literary culture that is a peculiar characteristic of classical verse. Such verse may engage in complicated modes of intertextuality, but the existence of books, or of other authors, tends not to be explicitly acknowledged; the idea of textual engagement is anathema to a genre that purports to be sung. The text of the *Hamartigenia* is typical in that it is dotted with feigned markers of orality, most notably the magnificent prayer with which it closes, but also its references to *fabulae,* its repeated first-person interventions, and its direct address to interlocutors outside the text.[5] A specific appeal to biblical authority is reported as "the sacred pronouncement from the mouth of an apostolic witness."[6] So we should not, perhaps, be surprised that the text contains very few references to books. And yet it is surprising, because this poem is explicitly a counter-Marcionite work, and one of the cardinal points of Marcionism is its obliteration of swaths of scripture from the biblical canon. All the Jewish scriptures go; the Gospels are reduced to a single digest; Revelation is out; in fact, only the letters of Paul survive largely unmolested.

The obvious counter-Marcionite approach would be the one taken by the more or less contemporaneous *Carmen adversus Marcionitas.*[7] This plodding and angular work proceeds systematically through the scriptures, explaining how Christ rights the wrong perpetrated by Adam (so to have one without the other is meaningless) and how Mary rights the misplaced suasion of Eve. It lists the Old Testament prophets in order, with their achievements; it justifies the continuity of the Old Testament God with that of the New (Marcionism argues for two gods), and so on. The author of the *Carmen* sets up his argument, early in book 2, as follows:

5. The prayer: *Ham.* 931ff. *Fabula:* praef. 25. First-person interventions: e.g., *testamur,* 27, *quid loquar,* 230, *rogo,* 308, *sentio,* 637. Direct address: *haec tua vox est* (i.e., Marcion's), 124; *credite, captivi mortales,* 445; a particularly striking instance occurs at 650–55: *damna aures.*

6. *Ham.* 521–22: *sacra . . . / oris apostolici testis sententia.*

7. Edition and commentary by Karla Pollmann, *Das Carmen adversus Marcionitas: Einleitung, Text, Übersetzung und Kommentar* (Göttingen, 1991), who dates the work to between 420 and 450 (33).

suppressit nefas in tantum dementia mersos
abruptos homines numen sine fine tremendum
dividere in partes, Christi sublimia facta
falsa laude sequi culpareque gesta priora,
innumerata dei miracula, visa nec umquam
ante nec audita contemptaque corde nec ullo,
tam temere scelus illicitum componere verbis,
adversum sese duo testamenta sonare,
dissimili longe sententia velle probare,
contra prophetarum domini committere verba,
omnem legis ut infamem deducere causam
sanctorumque patrum vitam reprobare priorem,
quos in amicitiam adlexit deus ad sua dona.

C. adv. Mar. 2.13–25

Madness coerced men, submerged and cut off, into a great religious crime: to divide into parts the awe-inspiring, eternal godhead, to pursue the excellent deeds of Christ with false praise and denigrate things accomplished earlier, the numberless miracles of God, never before seen or heard, and not disdained by any heart; and rashly to concoct in words an unlawful crime: to make the two testaments sound against each other, to wish to prove them far different in teaching, to pit the words of God against those of the prophets, to conclude that every instance of the Law was unspeakable and to condemn the earlier lives of the holy fathers—whom God drew into friendship toward his own gifts.

The author explains: by Marcion the testaments are divided, pitted against each other. An "unlawful crime" is "concocted in words." The verbal, dogmatic character of the testaments is emphasized: in the course of four lines we have *verbis, testamenta sonare, sententia, verba;* and the phrase *deducere causam* seems to pun on the sense of bringing a case to judgment in the law courts.[8] Marcion treats the Jewish scriptures as despicable, but in fact God has drawn everyone together "toward his own gifts." How? Not through the mere words of the Bible (though the *Carmen* spends a great deal of space reiterating them) but through *Christus evangelium,* Christ the God-sent gospel. Paul had argued to the Galatians, says the author, that they should not take part of the gospel for the whole: "and for that reason *Christ himself* was sent as gospel into

8. *Thesaurus Linguae Latinae* 5.1, col. 280, s.v. *deduco: causa in iudicium deducta sit* (Cic. *opt. gen.* 19).

the world, not the words of a book" *(atque adeo non verba libri, sed missus in orbem / ipse Christus evangelium est)*.[9]

This sort of simple, systematic exposition is alien to Prudentius; so is the explicit dogmatism, though there are certainly plenty of imprecations against Marcion. The *Hamartigenia* contains, in fact, only three references to holy scripture as a book—twice as *liber,* once as *volumen* (never as *codex*).[10] Prudentius engages explicitly with no books other than holy scripture. And he brings into play no clear metaphors of the book: for example, Christ is never represented simply as the gospel incarnate.[11] Yet the *Hamartigenia* is profoundly and constantly concerned not with doctrine as something rigidly spelled out—in the style of *Carmen adversus Marcionitas*—but with reading: with reading as an interpretative act and hence as an ethical one, with the right and wrong motivations for reading, and with the results of right reading. Prudentius counters Marcion and related heresies not with direct refutation but with illustrative subterfuge: the poem enacts in its construction the sort of figural reading which by its very nature renders the two testaments of the Bible indispensable to each other. The reader is placed firmly at the center of the text: her reading is its justification and its extension into orthodox significance. There are, then, two books to be "read": the *sanctum volumen* and Prudentius's own poem.

I allude to Marcionism "and related heresies" because Marcionism was more or less a dead letter at this time. It seems that Prudentius, like the author of the *Carmen,* is in fact addressing dualist heresies more generally. In a work that, in the course of more than a thousand lines, is very sparing of direct quotations from the Bible, two are from classic cruces of anti-Manichaean debate.

> hoc ratio sed nostra negat, cui non licet unam
> infirmare fidem sacro quae tradita libro est.
> "nil" ait "absque deo factum, sed cuncta per ipsum,
> cuncta, nec est alius quisquam nisi factus ab ipso."
>
> Pru. *Ham.* 180–83

---

9. *C. adv. Mar.* 2.56–57. Compare Humfress's chapter in this volume on Isidore of Pelusium, the reception of the Gospels as if "invoking" Christ, and the use of the Gospels more generally to represent Christ in the courtroom.

10. At lines 181, 777, and 624. All these passages will be discussed below.

11. This omission was suggested by Sylvia Huot, "The Writer's Mirror: Watriquet de Couvin and the Development of the Author-Centered Book," in *Across Boundaries: The Book in Culture and Commerce,* ed. Bill Bell et al. (Winchester, Del., 2000), 29–46; on "Christ as a book," see 32–34.

But this [the idea that the devil has any generative powers] our reason denies, which may not weaken the one faith which is handed down in the sacred book. "Nothing," it says, "was made without God, but everything through him, everything, nor is there any other [man?] except the one made by him."

This is the first mention of a *liber,* and it is clearly designed to bring the reader up short. It is in itself, as I have mentioned, a generic transgression to acknowledge the existence of a *liber* outside the text. The importance of the book is underscored by its union of reason and faith. *Fides* represents its contents: *ratio* cannot gainsay them. Reason, faith, and book are apparently conflated as the subject of *ait*[12] to introduce an almost verbatim quotation from John 1:3—a classic locus of Manichean objection to Christianity, as we learn from Augustine's *Sermon* 1:

"Moses says," the Manichaeans say, "in the beginning God made heaven and earth," and he doesn't name the Son through whom everything was made, while John says, "in the beginning was the Word, and the Word was with God, and the Word was God.... Everything was made through Him, and without Him, nothing was made." Is this contradictory? Or rather, aren't the people who don't understand these things contradicting themselves, preferring blind reproach to pious enquiry? What then will they say, when I answer that that "beginning" *is* the Son of God, in Whom Genesis says that God made heaven and earth?[13]

This places my next passage very firmly in an anti-Manichaean context:

> sed fuit id quondam nobis sanctumque bonumque
> principio rerum, Christus cum conderet orbem.
> vidit enim deus esse bonum, velut ipse Moyses
> historicus mundi nascentis testificatus,
> "vidit" ait "deus esse bonum quodcumque creavit."
>
> Pru. *Ham.* 337–41

But it was once both holy and good for us, in the beginning of things, when Christ created the world. God saw that it was good, just as Moses himself—the historian of the burgeoning world—bore witness: "God saw," he said, "that everything which he created was good" [Gen. 1:31].

12. Palla comments: "Il soggetto di questo verbo può essere ... *ratio* o *fides* o *liber*."

13. "'Moyses enim dicit' inquiunt [Manichei] 'in principio fecit deus caelum et terram, nec nominat filium per quem facta sunt omnia, cum Iohannes dicat: in principio erat verbum, et verbum erat apud deum, et deus erat verbum ... omnia per ipsum facta sunt, et sine ipso factum est nihil.' hoccine contrarium est, an potius sibimetipsi contrarii sunt, qui ea quae non intellegunt, caecitate reprehendere quam pietate quaerere maluerunt? quid enim dicturi sunt, cum ipsum 'principium' filium dei esse respondero, in quo deum fecisse caelum et terram Genesis loquitur?"

That God—the Christian God—is creator; that the *principium* of the creation accounts in both Genesis and John should be identified with Christ; and that creation is, overall, entirely good: these presuppositions were standard loci of Manichaean criticism and Christian defense.[14]

Note the way in which a totally integrated act of biblical reading lies behind these two quotations. One is from John, one from Genesis. In the second extract, note that Christ creates the world, God sees that it is good, and Moses reports the whole. Moses is cast explicitly as a historian, a startlingly unpoetic word,[15] yet a few lines further on he is described as *sanctus vaticinator,* a "holy seer." This contrast, between the *historicus* and the *vaticinator,* epitomizes the contrast between literary culture and feigned orality. Moses bridges the gap between inspired song and historical truth, between, we might say, *fides* and *ratio* (in this case manifest as *historia*): he seems to be cast as mediator between the two testaments. The account of creation is a matter of factual, historical report as well as of present significance. Remember the amalgamation of reason and faith: logic—may we even say "the letter"?—confirms the faith that is handed down *in the sacred book.* This book—*liber* or *volumen*—must, for Prudentius's argument, be something united. Yet Prudentius is clearly aware that the Jewish and Christian scriptures emerge from two very different traditions; and John Lowden's study of early Christian book covers in this volume shows how difficult it would have been to sustain the idea of reading those scriptures as a unity. If the Gospels are bound separately, for liturgical use and ostentatious display; if the Acts and Epistles, too, are bound together and hived off from the rest of the Bible, then it will be counterintuitive for those who encounter the books in this form to argue for an integrated reading of the Bible.

14. See, once again, examples of Augustine's discussion of these points, from his commentary on Genesis directed explicitly against the Manicheans: (a) Augustine, *Gn. c. Man.* 1.8.13: "*et vidit deus lucem quia bona est* ... [hoc solent reprehendere Manichaei]: ergo non noverat deus lucem aut non noverat bonum. miseri homines, quibus displicet quod deo placuerunt opera sua ... Numquid ergo quia placet ei quod fecit, ideo non noverat bonum? *vidit ergo deus lucem quia bona est:* quibus verbis non ostenditur eluxisse deo insolitum bonum, sed placuisse perfectum."

(b) Ibid., 1.21.32: "sane non est neglegenter praetereundum quod dictum est: *et vidit deus omnia quaecumque fecit esse bona valde.* cum enim de singulis ageret, dicebat tantum: *vidit deus quia bonum est;* cum autem de omnibus diceretur, parum fuit dicere *bona,* nisi adderetur et *valde.* si enim singula opera dei, cum considerantur a prudentibus, inveniuntur habere laudabiles mensuras et numeros et ordines in suo quaeque genere constituta, quanto magis omnia simul, id est ipsa universitas quae istis singulis in unum collatis impletur!"

15. Palla points out that *historicus* is a hapax legomenon in Prudentius, and "è molto raro in poesia."

In the face of dualist criticism, however, Prudentius unites the biblical text through strategies of figural reading that he claims were taught by God:

> non conferre deo velut aequiperabile quidquam
> ausim nec domino famulum conponere signum,
> ex minimis sed grande suum voluit pater ipse
> coniectare homines, quibus ardua visere non est.
>
> <div align="right">Pru. <i>Ham.</i> 79–82</div>

I would not dare to compare anything with God as if it were on the same level, or to posit that a sign was related to the Lord, but the Father himself wished people to guess his greatness from the meanest things, for they cannot see the exalted ones.

God, in fact, pours out assistance in interpretation *per prodigialia signa;* and an emphasis on *signa,* rather than *verba,* coheres both with conventions of biblical typology and with generic fictions of orality.[16]

So far, so familiar. But at the heart of the poem Prudentius, in a striking simile, turns his gaze to the question of *how* meaning is generated. The urgent exhortation quoted in the title of this chapter comes about two-thirds of the way through the poem. Prudentius has just treated us to a hair-raising extended metaphor, an *exemplum ex ethicis,* the image of a viper who kills her mate in the act of sexual intercourse and is in turn destroyed by her young, who are born by bursting through her abdominal wall. He concludes harshly, *non dispar nostrae conceptus mentis* ("the conceiving in our own mind is no different"): the mind is destroyed again and again by *mille puerperiis,* the self-destructive births of a thousand sins. He continues:

> hinc illa est domini iusta obiurgatio Christi:
> nonne pater daemon (vos increpo, peccatores)
> concubitu carnis semen sitientis iniquum
> vos genuit? sanctum, lector, percense volumen;
> quod loquor invenies dominum dixisse profanis
> vera obiectantem mortalibus: ex patre nam vos
> esse meo genitos pietas (ait) ipsa probaret
> ac pietatis opus.
>
> <div align="right">Pru. <i>Ham.</i> 621–28 (adapting Cunningham's punctuation)</div>

---

16. So too, for example, with Prudentius's narration of the tale of Lot and his wife: "accipe gestarum monumenta *insignia* rerum, / praelusit quibus historia spectabile *signum,*" *Ham.* 723–24; and the contest

Hence that just accusation of Christ the Lord: did not a devil father (I rebuke you, sinners) beget you through a union of flesh thirsting for the evil seed? Reader, peruse the holy book: you will find that the Lord said what I am saying, adducing the truth to godless mortals: for your actual piety (he says) would prove that you are born of my father and the work of piety.

But, Prudentius goes on—returning to his extravagant imagery—the *mens bona,* invited to the bed of her lord and king (in the style of the Song of Songs), prefers to commit adultery and conceive sin instead.

Immediately behind this passage lies the *obiurgatio* of John 8:44: "you belong to your father the devil, and you want to carry out your father's desire"; and the final part seems to me (though not to Cunningham) to relate, if to anything, to John 8:31–32: "if you hold to my teaching, you are really my disciples. Then you will know the truth, and the truth will set you free." But the passage is subtly manipulative. Who, for example, is the "you" at different stages? Who are the *peccatores,* and does every instance of "you" refer to them? What about the address to the reader in the middle: who is that?

I have purposely removed from this extract the quotation marks that Cunningham gives in his text. Without these, it seems as if Christ swings round to address his own reader: peruse the holy text; find out what I am saying. This is especially shocking for the reader, as previous singular imperatives in the poem have been addressed to Marcion. It is not until we get to *dominum* that we realize that it must be Prudentius, not Christ, who is "speaking"; then again, it is not till we reach *ait* that it is certain the speaker has switched again, the change of speaker here being obscured especially by the fact that this passage does not relate very closely to anything in the relevant passage of John.

This is important for several reasons. First, because Prudentius is conflating his own voice with that of Christ, blurring the boundaries between their two speaking/writing voices. And that is a very political move in a text written to counter heretical claims, especially claims that are obsessively Christocentric: to arrogate, by implication, the authority of Christ to oneself. He exploits a similar strategy a few lines later, in the buildup to his long-deferred account of the Fall: a long passage in direct speech is introduced with *ait ipse parens opifexque et conditor Adae,* a string of synonyms for God himself, which gives the impression that it will be a versified quotation from the Bible; but it is

---

between David and Absalom is one of *signis contraria signa paternis* (567), which perhaps puns on the double meaning for *signa* of "military standards" and "signs."

nothing of the sort. Prudentius is in fact manipulating the reading of the *sanctum volumen* and blurring the boundaries between his own literary production and the scriptures. Prudentius's audience is far from necessarily familiar with the Bible, beyond (presumably) a general educated interest in Christianity:[17] there is a remarkable displacement of authority going on here.

Second, the author's manipulation is important because of the biblical context of Prudentius's quasi-quotation. This part of John (8:39–44) is a classic supersessionist text: Christ is in debate with the Jews and Pharisees (contradistinguished groups here) over the nature of revelation and truth and the meaning of their descent from Abraham. He does indeed accuse them of having the devil for a father; they, in turn, insist that he is possessed by demons. But Prudentius entirely masks the biblical context. The "you" of this passage is *not* equated with either Jews or Pharisees; given the context, both before and after, the reader might rather suppose that we are still in the realm of metaphor, that it is the mind, or soul (*mens* and *anima* interchangeable here) that thirsts for union with the flesh and engenders sins, that it is they who are the *peccatores*.[18]

This is certainly some sort of thematic sleight-of-hand, but it is not, I think, a supersessionist gesture. It could be argued that the Jews are simply being written out of Prudentius's account. However, as we have seen, the position is rather more complicated—because arguing against Marcionism and related heresies entails embracing, albeit perhaps on the quiet, the Jewish heritage and Jewish scriptures. Here we have a sort of benign misdirection: the supersessionist passage is used, but its meaning relocated. This becomes in itself a demonstration against the Marcionites of how the Old Testament may be appropriately used by Christians.

It may be relevant also that the nature of biblical time is at stake in the Johannine passage: this is where Christ says, "before Abraham was, I am." This sense of the interdependent relationship of historical event ("Abraham *was*")

17. I base this claim on contemporaneous evidence for the audience of such versified works; they seem often to have been intended for those who, educated in the pre-Christian classics, were alienated by prose style and especially by the stylistic infelicities of the Bible itself. See, for example, the letter to Macedonius of Caelius Sedulius, and my comments on it, in *Paulinus Noster: Self and Symbols in the Letters of Paulinus of Nola* (Oxford, 2000), 50–51.

18. Stam says ad loc: "the poet here refers to Jews," but what is remarkable is the *suppression* of reference to the Jews.

and ongoing revealed truth is crucial to Prudentius's integrated reading of the Bible.[19] It recalls the figure of Moses used as a bridging device, both *historicus* and *vaticinator*—both historian and singer of inspired truth. There is a variant reading in the early printed texts, including those of both Weitz and Giselin: *percurre*, "run through," for *percense*. This, if correct, would form an interesting link with *animas percurrere visu* (892) in the final vision of the poem—a passage that tells us souls can see what corporeal eyes cannot. The two readings are not, perhaps, of critical importance per se; but they epitomize the tension between historical document and spiritual vision.

We see, then, that our title quotation comes from a passage that both tests and appropriates biblical boundaries. It evokes the Jewish scriptures while remaining silent about the Jews; it coerces the reader, in the voice of Christ, to peruse—or run through—the *sanctum volumen.* Those who read rightly are in a right relationship with God, they are the "work of piety"; but those who do not are the spawn of the devil. We are in treacherous realms of reading, definition, and demarcation here. But what has the immediate context of the passage to do with reading? Can we say more about the violent extended metaphor of the snakes? The female snake, in Prudentius, "thirsts [*sitit*] obscenely, with gaping mouth, for the husband who is about to die";[20] and he recalls that thirst with his "union of flesh thirsting [*sitientis*] for the evil seed"—which is a far better description of the appalling union of the snakes than of the disputed generation of the Jews in John 8:41. This too would seem to suggest that we should read these two passages as closely interrelated.

The anomalous coupling of the snakes was a commonplace in ancient writers on natural history, and the commentary tradition, from the Isonian glosses forward, has tended to focus on amassing those sources, without discussing how or why the image is treated here.[21] Editorial ambivalence about the pur-

19. I was alerted to this consideration by John David Dawson's account of Auerbach's "discovery" of "a rich tradition of Christian figural reading of the Old Testament in which the historical reality of ancient Jews had been preserved rather than superseded." Dawson, *Christian Figural Reading and the Fashioning of Identity* (Berkeley and Los Angeles, 2002), 84.

20. *Ham.* 586–87: *moriturum obscena maritum / ore sitit patulo.*

21. Principal sources: Pliny, *Naturalis Historia* 10.169–70; Aelian, *De Natura Animalium* 1.24; Isidore, *Etym.* 12.4.10. Jerome also knew and used the image. Pliny adds the interesting detail that the snake bears only one of its brood each day; the remaining young get bored with the delay and burst their way out *(ceteri tarditatis inpatientes perrumpunt latera occisa parente).* On the Isonian glosses, see José Liébana Pérez, "Las glosas de Isón: Notas sobre un comentario carolingio a la obra de Prudencio," *Estudios clásicos* 25 (1981–83): 225–56.

pose of the passage is signaled from its very beginning. Prudentius writes, "If I may appropriate something *ex ethicis*"—or is it *"ex ethnicis"*?[22] Cunningham, with most of the printed tradition, favors *ethicis,* "the ethical sources," over the pagan ones *(ethnici).* Arévalo writes dismissively, "Aldus [Manutius] erroneously has *ex ethnicis* for *ex ethicis.* This error is embedded in several of the old manuscripts . . . which have been corrected in a more recent hand."[23] But are Manutius and the majority (in fact) of the surviving manuscripts necessarily in error? The question is an important one: is the emphasis on the ethical writings or the pagan origin of the source? What, in short, is the connection between snakes and the *sanctum volumen* that the *lector* is encouraged to peruse? Is there some link between snakes and reading or, for that matter, interpretation?

When we come to think about it, it is not so illogical that snakes and interpretation should be linked in the Judeo-Christian tradition. After all, it is the serpent in Eden who exhorts Eve to eat of the tree that will bring knowledge of good and evil. Avitus, in a verse retelling of Genesis composed some three generations after Prudentius, brings out the connection. Eve appeals to the serpent for interpretation: "Please, most learned serpent, tell us what God is calling 'death', since the thing isn't known to us uneducated people."[24] The verb Eve uses for God's denomination of death, *vocito,* is a specific term for assigning a name. That is certainly how the serpent understands it: "Woman, you are afraid of an empty name"—or a "meaningless noun" *(vacuum nomen).*[25] The result of his suasion is that Eve begins to doubt and to "bend meaning" *(flectere sensum).*[26]

---

22. *Ham.* 581: *si licet ex ethicis quidquam praesumere.*

23. "Ald. mendose *ex ethnicis* pro *ex ethicis*: qui error nonnullos veteres codices insedit . . . in quibus rec. m. correctio adhibita est . . ." He also notes the correction of the initial "e" (removing potential arguments from scansion: "e" in "ethnicus" is short by nature).

24. Avitus, *De spiritalis historiae gestis* (= *SHG*) 2:181–82: "Quid vocitet mortem, tu nunc, doctissime serpens, / pande libens, quoniam rudibus non cognita res est." The work is edited by Daniel J. Nodes, *Avitus: The Fall of Man; De spiritalis historiae gestis libri I–III* (Toronto, 1985). I read *doctissime* for his *doctissimae.*

25. *SHG* 2:185: "Terroris vacuum formidas, femina, nomen." For *vocito,* see E. Forcellini, *Totius Latinitatis Lexicon* (Padua, 1940): "est appello, frequenter voco; *chiamare, nominare.*"

26. *SHG* 2:206. P. G. W. Glare, *Oxford Latin Dictionary* (Oxford, 1982), s.v. *flectere* 8.b cites *flectam . . . sensus meos,* and gives as the meaning of *flectere* here "to alter to fit special needs or circumstances, adapt, adjust." The result is that Eve "ignorans ludit de morte futura" (*SHG* 2:216); cf. *Ham.* 723–24, cited at note 16 above.

Moreover, the description of Satan's disguise as serpent reminds us that *volumen* has another meaning. "He becomes a snake with a long neck, he mottles his gleaming neck and roughens the *volumina*—coils—of his smooth back"; and again, when God curses the serpent, he is condemned to slide in *sinuosa volumina,* looping coils, which are described as "living chains."[27] Is it by chance that Prudentius exhorts his reader to peruse the sacred *volumen?* Or is he invoking other literary coils—of less desirable reading?

This possibility naturally prompts us to look for the connections between snakes and reading elsewhere in early Christian writings. In the *vita* of Caesarius of Arles the saint has a terrible vision in which a snake binds him to a book, over which he has fallen asleep, and gnaws at his arm and shoulder. The book is one of "worldly wisdom," *sapientia mundi.* Caesarius wakes and accuses himself of having wished "to join [*copulare*] the light of the rule of salvation to the foolish wisdom of the world."[28] In a still more famous saintly dream, Jerome encapsulates his tainted asceticism—he fasts and reads Cicero, repents and reads Plautus—as the mockery of the *antiquus serpens,* the serpent of old.[29] In Martianus Capella's *De Nuptiis,* Dialectica appears holding a snake in her left hand. Eriugena, who wrote a commentary on Martianus, was under no illusions as to how to interpret this apparition: *per serpentem, sophisticas subtilitates intellige* ("by the snake, understand the logic-chopping of the sophists").[30] In each case, the serpent is associated with a hermeneutical process that is somehow suspect—and that is rooted in the *sapientia mundi.*

It seems that Manutius may not have been so deluded in taking the Prudentian metaphor of the snakes as an *exemplum ex ethnicis:* not only does the example come *from* pagan writings, but it is associated *with* pagan writings, and their inappropriate use by Christians. It is, in fact, expressive of a copula-

27. *SHG* 2:123–25: "fit longa cervica draco, splendentia colla / depingit maculis, teretisque volumina dorsi / asperat . . ."; *SHG* 3:123, "sinuosa volumina," and 3:125, "viventia vincula."

28. *Vita S. Caesarii Episcopi Arelatensis* (*MGH, SRM* 3:457–501). This passage is on p. 460: "Librum itaque, quem ei legendum doctor tradiderat, casu vigilia lassatus, in lectulo sub scapula sua posuit; supra quem dum nihilominus obdormisset, mox divinitus terribili visione percellitur, et in soporem aliquantulum resolutus, videt quasi scapulam in qua iacebat brachiumque quo innixus fuerat codici dracone conligante conrodi. Excussus ergo e somno, territus ipse visu, terribilius se ex eodem facto coepit arguere, eo quod lumen regulae salutaris stultae mundi sapientiae voluerit *copulare.*" Translation by William E. Klingshirn, *Caesarius of Arles: Life, Testament, Letters* (Liverpool, 1994), 14.

29. Jerome, *Letter* 22.30: "dum ita me antiquus serpens inluderent. . ."

30. Mart. Cap. 4.328; Cora E. Lutz, ed., *Iohannis Scotti Annotationes in Marcianum* (Cambridge, Mass., 1939), 82.

tive hermeneutic—but a misbegotten one: Prudentius may be arguing for integrated readings of the Bible, but not any sort of integration will do. Sometimes the result is not the generation of sin as such but the generation of sinful meanings: the mind, "pregnant with lethal offspring, bears the conceptions of a malign disposition from the seed of the tortuous snake."[31] And such interpretations kill the mind, or soul, that generates them. The reader is entirely complicit in her choice of right interpretation. It is imperative that she concentrate on the sacred coil—book—*volumen*.

This may throw light on an odd choice of word later in the *Hamartigenia*, in the one other place where the word *liber*, for "book," occurs. Prudentius pauses after his exposition of the *spectabile signum* of Lot to observe, *talem multa sacris speciem notat orbita libris* (777). Though the *Thesaurus Linguae Latinae* glosses this use of *orbita* as "of a way well-worn by one's ancestors," its primary meaning is of a wheel, or tracks left by a wheel.[32] The sense of the passage seems to be that "many a revolution [as of a wheel] marks out such an appearance in the sacred books," for Prudentius goes on to examine how the figural narrative revolves back on itself to treat of Ruth and Orpah, descendents of Lot. The crucial image seems to be one of cyclical repetition. Is it too fanciful to see an allusion to the *volumina* of the snakes here? Perhaps not, for in the second preface to his *Apotheosis*, Prudentius tells us of the *obliqua divortia* that sow themselves in *textis orbitis*—those, it seems, that contain *viperina . . . dogmata*.[33] The involutions of the serpents are once again connected with worldly—in this case, heretical—wisdom; and these sorts of cyclical links are made possible by the typological imaginary, which in its turn depends on the imaginative construction of readers.[34]

It is, I think, no coincidence that one of the most attentive readers of the *Hamartigenia* to date is himself very attentive to readers. Victor Giselin prides himself on creating in his commentary a *res grata* for his reader *(lector)*.[35] At

31. *Ham.* 613–14: "praegnans letale genus concepta maligni / fert opera ingenii de semine conplicis hydri." Contrast the emphasis on cognates of *concipere*, "conceive," and the generative notions involved, with the simple *componere*, "place together," in *C. adv. M.*

32. *Thesaurus Linguae Latinae* 9.2, col. 921, s.v. *orbita*: "de via ab antecessoribus trita, quam aliquis sequitur."

33. *Apoth.* 2. praef. 9–10; 3.

34. On which see Conybeare, *Paulinus Noster*, chaps. 4 and 5.

35. From Giselin's preface: "quo Lectori, rerum inprimis avido, facerem rem gratam, obscuriores dictiones, et phrases declaravi, insolentes et a communi usu remotas observavi, ad historias sacras et

line 51 he observes, "although the poet has shown the foolishness of Marcion . . . he anticipates the Reader, who he thought might have been caused to doubt by the above, and teaches how God might be One in Three."[36] A similar concern to protect the reader from doubt is shown in the note to line 555, where Giselin sees a turning point—from demonstrating that God is not the author of evil to addressing the notion of free will, and hence of the moral responsibility of the individual agent. Or reader? On some level, it seems, we do insistently return to the importance of the reader. Even in the early biographical tradition, Giselin's after-hours devotion to patristic reading was explicitly linked with his adherence to orthodoxy:[37] clearly the tradition continued that not only what but *how* you read affects your *fides*.[38]

The moral reader lies at the heart of the *Hamartigenia*. Prudentius seems to be showing us, and her, how a truly generative hermeneutic may be established by reading the Jewish and Christian scriptures in integrated form. But he also warns us of how that generative hermeneutic may go badly awry, in "l'affreuse description des noces de la vipère."[39]

The *Hamartigenia* is, most significantly, a set of poetical directives on how to read the Bible. Prudentius plays with the poetic conventions of mock orality to highlight his use of figuralism yet at the same time to make his occasional invocations of "the book" more conspicuous.[40] Like any good commentary, in the process of its creation the work also constructs the book on which it purports to comment.[41] In the *Hamartigenia,* the *sanctum volumen*

---

profanas pertinentia veris fontibus indicatis, expedivi atque illustravi: Nihil denique eorum, quae in justo commentario desiderari solent, quantum in me fuit, praetermisi."

36. "Cum Marcionis inscitiam ostendisset [poeta] . . . praeoccupat Lectorem, cui scrupulum e superioribus injectum esse putabat, & quomodo Deus in Trinitate unus sit, docet . . ."

37. Jean-François Foppens, *Bibliotheca belgica* (Brussels, 1739), 2:1151–52: "Quantum itaque per horas succisivas et curas graviores licuit, lectioni veterum Scriptorum, et praecipue Christianorum Patrum, tribuit [Giselinus]: quorum pietate erudita confirmatus, stetit recto talo in turbis religionis jactatae, nec ab Orthodoxa et Catholica fide dimoveri ratione ulla aut suasione potuit . . ."

38. Remember the discussion of *Ham.* 180–83, above.

39. The phrase is Jacques Fontaine's. See "La femme dans la poésie de Prudence," *Revue des études latines* 47 bis (1970): 55–83, reprinted in his *Études sur la poésie latine tardive d'Ausone à Prudence* (Paris, 1980), 415–43; quotation from p. 68/428. Fontaine, however, sees the episode as symbolic of "la fornication de l'âme avec Satan," but mixed with "une sorte d'horreur méthodique pour la sexualité."

40. Is it, in turn, conspicuous that Prudentius avoids the term "codex"? In the light of his argument for an integrated reading of the Bible, could he be erasing the specifically Christian term for a book in favor of words less loaded with association, or, rather, loaded in a different way?

41. For some richly suggestive reflections on this topic, see Don Fowler, "Criticism as Commen-

is assumed to be "out there"; yet at the same time it is constructed within the poem, through the directives on how to read, and through the metaphors mobilized around the notion of the *volumen*. Prudentius shows through repeated episodes, of which Lot's wife is probably the most elaborately developed, that reading the *sanctum volumen* is a constant act of willed integration. The issue with the Marcionites and their successors is what the nature of that *volumen* might be, and where its boundaries should be drawn. Prudentius demonstrates its inclusiveness, perhaps overdemonstrates it, as the boundaries seem to become ever more permeable: witness his appropriation of Christ's authoritative voice. As a warning, however, the snakes enact the generation of sinful, destructive meaning.

Reading the Bible against possible threats of heresy is a risky business. The complexities of integrated reading are considerable. "Before Abraham was, I am": this mystifying phrase captures the difficulty of observing both the historicity of the original tales and their extension into spiritual permanence.[42] This spiritual permanence is not just a one-time, fixed permanence of revelation through Christ. It is constantly, significantly reenacted through the reader's response to the Bible, and if we may take seriously Prudentius's bold conflation of his own voice with that of Christ, through the reader's response to Prudentius's own text as well.

---

tary and Commentary as Criticism in the Age of Electronic Media," in *Commentaries—Kommentare,* ed. Glenn W. Most (Göttingen, 1999), 426–42.

42. This observation is inspired, once again, by Dawson, *Christian Figural Reading:* "rather than predicated on an anti-literalism, Scripture's figurativeness is not nonliteral; its figurative character is an extension rather than obliteration of the literal sense of texts" (15).

Mark Vessey

THEORY, OR THE DREAM OF THE BOOK (MALLARMÉ TO BLANCHOT)

The Early Christian Book between History and Theory

A sickly young monk is sent to convalesce in a city not far from his island monastery. His hosts hire a tutor to give him lessons in grammar and rhetoric. One night he falls asleep over his book. As he sleeps, he dreams that his arm is being devoured. The Latin is insinuating: *videt... bracchium quo innixus fuerat codici DRACONE CONLIGANTE conrodi.* "He sees the arm on which he was leaning against the book being gnawed by a serpent that was coiling itself about [him]."[1] Or by a serpent that was coiled about the book. Or (making best sense of the first *con-* prefix) by a serpent that wound itself about him and the book, joining them in a lethal embrace. The verb *ligare* in later Latin is also used of bookbindings. This book, a spine-hinged codex rather than a *volumen* or roll, was of a kind to be bound. And it appears to have found an unusually voluminous binding, as if the snake were guarding its contents against saintly intruders. The monk wakes up in a sweat, upbraids himself for trying "to join the light of the rule of salvation with the foolish wisdom of the world," and forswears all future contact with pagan literature.[2]

---

1. Uncredited translations are mine.

2. *Vita Caesarii* 1.9, in Germain Morin, ed., *Sancti Caesarii Episcopi Arelatensis Opera Omnia,* 2 vols. (Maredsous, 1937–1942), 2:299–300; William E. Klingshirn, trans., *Caesarius of Arles: Life, Testament, Letters* (Liverpool, 1994), 13–14.

The monk's name was Caesarius. The island he left behind in the early 490s was one of the little group known then as now by the name of Lérins, on the Côte d'Azur. The monastery had been founded early in the century by Honoratus, who was said to have purged the island of snakes.[3] The city to which Caesarius came for his health was Arles, where he would abide for the remaining fifty years of his life, forty of them as bishop and metropolitan. The well-informed authors of the *Life of Caesarius,* one of whom may have been related to the sponsor of the ill-fated literature lessons, go on to describe the bishop's prowess as a Christian orator and expositor of scripture. A tireless preacher, he took care to have copies made of the sermons he delivered, so that other clerics could use them in their churches.[4] The preface to one set of sermons advises its users to heed its contents and make them available to others:

> I urge this [says the preacher] because there are many people, including perhaps some dedicated to a religious lifestyle, who like to own a number of shiny and beautifully bound books [*libros... nitidos et pulchre ligatos*], yet keep them shut up in cupboards, neither reading them themselves nor lending them to others to read. They fail to observe that there is no point in our owning books if the obstacles of this world prevent us from reading them. For a nicely bound and shiny book [*liber... bene coopertus et nitidus*], so long as it remains unread, does not make a shiny soul, whereas one that is constantly read, and on account of frequent handling [*et pro eo quod saepe revolvitur*] ceases to be beautiful without, makes the soul beautiful within.[5]

In another place, Caesarius exhorts his listeners to constant conversation with God through the medium of the sacred text. Such reading or hearing is prophylactic: "Now see if the devil can creep up on someone whom he sees intently talking with God."[6] By maintaining intimate contact with God-in-scripture,

---

3. Hilary of Arles, *Vita Honorati* 15 (*SC* 235:106–110): *Fugit horror solitudinis, cedit turba serpentium*—an episode in Lerinian mythology that surely contributed to the dream of Caesarius.

4. *Vita Caesarii* 1.52, 55. See further William E. Klingshirn, *Caesarius of Arles: The Making of a Christian Community in Late Antique Gaul* (Cambridge, 1994), 73–74 (the dream), 146–51 (Caesarius as preacher), 183–84 (preaching, the Bible, and literacy in early sixth-century Gaul).

5. Caesarius, *Serm.* 2, ed. Germain Morin (*CCSL* 103:18). The theme is ancient; see Seneca, *De tranquillitate animi* 9.6 for the Roman gentleman dozing over his books, *cui voluminum suorum frontes maxime placent tituli*. Also Jerome, *Ep.* 22.32 on the purple-dyed, gold-lettered, jewel-encrusted codices of aristocrats too mean to give succor to the poor outside their gates, with parallel passages cited by Neil Adkin, *Jerome on Virginity: A Commentary on the "Libellus de virginitate servanda" (Letter 22)* (Cambridge, 2003). See too Courtney M. Booker, "The *Codex Purpureus* and Its Role as an *Imago Regis* in Late Antiquity," in *Studies in Latin Literature and Roman History,* ed. Carl Deroux (Brussels, 1997), 8:441–77.

6. Caesarius, *Serm.* 8.3 (*CCSL* 103:44).

Christians keep the world and the devil at arm's length; to be held fast by the scriptural word is the soul's best cure. Once bitten by a book, the monk-bishop of Arles takes homeopathic measures for his flock. That may be the meaning of the dream recounted or invented by his biographers.

Other ancient readers must have fallen asleep uncomfortably over books. Some of them, if they had been reading tales of snakes and dragons, may have had nightmares like the one visited on Caesarius. Is it possible—as the famous case of Jerome might suggest—that dreams of books and book-induced visions, waking as well as sleeping, became more vivid and more common during the mutually redefining encounter of late classical literary culture with Jewish and Christian scriptures?[7] The circumstances and immediate effects of that complex transaction are considered in other essays in this volume.[8] This one takes a longer view, to argue that the coils in which certain ancient Christian readers imagined themselves ensnared are the figure of an experience of *text* or *textuality* that has also been partly determinative of recent (specifically, poststructuralist) literary theory.

Before Caesarius and Jerome, exemplary for both, was the monk Antony. In a 1967 essay on Flaubert's *La tentation de saint Antoine,* Michel Foucault underlined the proximity, in and for that work, of book to dream. *The Temptation,* he suggested,

> is not simply a book that Flaubert dreamed of writing for so long; it dreams other books, all other books that dream and that men dream of writing—books that are taken up, fragmented, displaced, combined, lost, set at an unapproachable distance by dreams, but also brought closer to the imaginary and sparkling realization of desires. In writing *The Temptation,* Flaubert produced the first literary work whose exclusive domain is that of books: following Flaubert, Mallarmé is able to write *Le Livre* and modern literature is activated—Joyce, Roussel, Kafka, Pound, Borges. The library is on fire.[9]

7. The locus classicus is of course the "vision" recounted by Jerome, *Ep.* 22.30. Paul Antin, "Autour du songe de Saint Jérôme," *Revue des études latines* 41 (1963): 350–77, measures its aftereffects, including the dream attributed to Caesarius. For an unusually sensitive reading of Jerome's and other oneiric texts, see Patricia Cox Miller, *Dreams in Late Antiquity: Studies in the Imagination of a Culture* (Princeton, 1994).

8. Especially those of Catherine Chin on Jerome and Catherine Conybeare on Prudentius. Some of the same topics are addressed in Mark Vessey, "The *Epistula Rustici ad Eucherium:* From the Library of Imperial Classics to the Library of the Fathers," in *Society and Culture in Late Antique Gaul: Revisiting the Sources,* ed. Ralph W. Mathisen and Danuta Shanzer (Aldershot, 2001), 278–97.

9. Michel Foucault, "Fantasia of the Library," in *Language, Counter-Memory, Practice: Selected Essays and Interviews,* ed. and trans. Donald F. Bouchard (Ithaca, N.Y., 1977), 92.

The roll call of modern(ist) authors is personal but programmatic. Foucault's choice of Flaubert's closet drama as the inaugural instance of a purportedly new, distinctively "bookish" kind of literary artifact fits the account that he had recently given of the emergence of modern literature, in *Les mots et les choses* (1966). On that view, "literature" in the modern sense came into being when the writer's language ceased to refer to an absolute speech, becoming instead an endless murmur of itself—when the gods fell silent or, in more ethnocentric terms, when the voice of the god of Israel (or "Israel") was no longer heard in his scriptures.[10] Foucault is of course not alone in this historical conviction. The same posttheological epoch is announced in Jacques Derrida's chapter "The End of the Book and the Beginning of Writing" at the beginning of *Of Grammatology* and in Roland Barthes's famous article on "The Death of the Author" (both 1967).[11] Around the same time and in the same Parisian milieu, Julia Kristeva was improvising a science of poetic language that would mark off modern literature from other ideological (including religious) determinations of textual activity, posit a revolution in French poetry in the age of Mallarmé, and introduce a concept—*intertextuality*—that was readily assimilable to Foucault's involuting book of books, Derrida's writing without beginning or end, and Barthes's oneiric pleasures of the text.[12]

While the blaze of which Foucault spoke forty years ago may not have swept through the Library of the Fathers in modern scholarship, several hot spots have appeared in the course of the past few decades. It has even been suggested, recently, that the main engagement of patristics or late ancient Christian studies with poststructuralist literary theory may only now be beginning.[13]

10. Foucault, *The Order of Things: An Archaeology of the Human Sciences* (New York, 1970), 44: "For now we no longer have that primary, that absolutely initial, word upon which the infinite movement of discourse was founded and by which it was limited; henceforth, language was to grow with no point of departure, no end, and no promise. It is the traversal of this futile yet fundamental space that the text of literature traces from day to day"; 300. Cf. Foucault, "Fantasia of the Library," 109: "[Flaubert's] Saint Anthony was able to triumph over the Eternal Book in becoming the languageless movement of pure matter; [his] Bouvard and Pécuchet triumph over everything alien to books, all that resists the book, by transforming themselves into the continuous movement of the book. The book opened by Saint Anthony, the book that initiated the flight of all possible temptations, is indefinitely extended by these two simple men; it is prolonged without end, without illusion, without greed, without sin, without desire."

11. For references, see notes 23 and 75 below.

12. Julia Kristeva, Σημειωτική: *Recherches pour une sémanalyse* (Paris, 1969); Julia Kristeva, *La révolution du langage poétique: L'avant-garde à la fin du XIXe siècle—Lautréamont et Mallarmé* (Paris, 1974).

13. Elizabeth A. Clark, *History, Theory, Text: Historians and the Linguistic Turn* (Cambridge, Mass., 2004), chap. 8.

If that is indeed the case, we still have time to ponder the relationship of the interlocking dream-book sequences, ancient and modern, rehearsed above. What does it mean, historically and theoretically, to (re)read the dreams of Jerome or Caesarius after Foucault—or, to take another current example, Augustine's *Confessions* in the light of Derrida's "Circumfession" and a posthumously published text of Jean-François Lyotard?[14] No one will mistake these for innocent operations. But neither should we deceive ourselves about the residue of superstition—from the side of theory!—that they are liable to convey. French poststructuralist literary critique assumes an Enlightenment history of modernity. Its theorization of modern literature takes for granted the loss of a "traditional" (i.e., Christian or Judeo-Christian) theological apprehension of the Bible as word and Word of God. Thus it habitually defines the literary text by placing the latter in more or less historical opposition to a biblical text or book whose properties are by the same gesture placed beyond the scope of history and theory. In this cosmology, which for the sake of argument I am calling superstitious, scripture or the Bible becomes the infinite-degree counterpoise to the zero-degree writing that is modern literature, the one truly—if unaccountably—exorbitant text in a universe of texts, the Archimedean point of theory that theory itself can never unsettle. Not surprisingly, the founders of theory had little to say about their own or anyone else's bibles.

By contrast, there has lately been much talk of a "religious turn" in literary studies. The frequent suggestion is that such a move is needed now in order for us to recover perspectives that have been inadvertently, if not willfully, lost in the headlong progress from old philology to new criticism to French-style theory to the ideally all-embracing but untotalizing study of culture as text. So it may be. Yet no alert reader of Western academic literary criticism and theory of the past half century can fail to notice how profoundly those discourses, especially perhaps the most influential of them, have been penetrated from the outset by the spirit of older and more avowedly "sacred" philologies and bibliologies. A polemical reminder was delivered twenty years ago by Edward Said in the pages on "Religious Criticism" that appear as a coda to *The World, the Text, and the Critic,* as part of an appeal against what he saw as the textual her-

---

14. Jacques Derrida, "Circumfession," in Geoffrey Bennington and Jacques Derrida, *Jacques Derrida,* trans. G. Bennington (Chicago, 1993); Jean-François Lyotard, *The Confession of Augustine,* trans. Richard Beardsworth (Stanford, 2000). See also John D. Caputo and Michael J. Scanlon, eds., *Augustine and Postmodernism: "Confessions" and "Circumfession"* (Bloomington, Ind., 2005).

meticism or "Alexandrianism" of the poststructuralist ascendancy in North American literature departments of the time.[15] In a different mood but no less trenchantly, George Steiner has emphasized how

[o]ur grammars, our explications, our criticisms of texts, our endeavours to pass from letter to spirit, are the immediate heirs to the textualities of western Judaeo-Christian theology and patristic exegetics. What we have done since the masked scepticism of Spinoza, since the critiques of the rationalist Enlightenment and since the positivism of the nineteenth century, is to borrow vital currency, vital investments and contracts of trust from the bank or treasure-house of theology. . . . It is loans of terminology and reference from the reserves of theology which provide the master readers in our time . . . with their licence to practise.[16]

For Steiner, a proper "return" to religion from literary studies would mean the acknowledgment, if not the (impossible) repayment, of these huge accumulated debts.

What is purposed here is no restitution but merely the beginning of a more accurate casting up of accounts. Rather than ask again what Foucault, Barthes, Derrida, or any of the other master readers of recent times can bring to our reading or deciphering of early Christian texts and books, this essay aims to elucidate the phantasmal presence of an ancient Christian "theory" of the book within the founding works of theory itself. In doing so, it acts on a suggestion made before theory in this sense was even dreamed of.

The Book as Symbol: E. R. Curtius

Half a century ago, Ernst Robert Curtius sketched the outline of a history of "The Book as Symbol" in Western literary culture from Pindar to Goethe.[17] His cue was Goethe's proposal for a study of the "life relations" encoded in literary tropes. Coming to late antiquity, Curtius pointed to verses from the *Greek Anthology* as signs of a life relation to the book that spent all its vigor, as he alleged, "in the realms of philology and the library, of calligraphy, bibliophil-

15. Edward W. Said, *The World, the Text, and the Critic* (Cambridge, Mass., 1983), 290–92.

16. George Steiner, "Real Presences," in his *No Passion Spent: Essays 1978–1995* (New Haven, 1996), 36 (from a lecture given in 1985).

17. Ernst Robert Curtius, *European Literature and the Latin Middle Ages,* trans. Willard R. Trask (Princeton, 1953), chap. 16. Page numbers are cited parenthetically in the text. Curtius's treatment of book metaphors in Christian late antiquity and the early Middle Ages has been richly supplemented by Eric Jager, *The Book of the Heart* (Chicago, 2000), chaps. 1–3.

ia, and bibliomania" (307). In one of the epigrams, "life itself is compared to a book which is unrolled until the curved stroke or flourish with the pen—the koronis—is put under the text." In another the koronis as "faithful guardian of the written pages" takes on a life and voice of its own: "And I, curved round like a snake's back, am placed at the end of this pleasant work." Curtius goes on to mention the "divine" volumes of the later Platonists, the Alexandrian book conceits of Latin poets from Catullus to Claudian, metaphors of writing and books from the Old and New Testaments, and the martyrial book language of Prudentius. That poet's *Peristephanon liber* is said to represent "the close of [an] epoch in literary terms. . . . The antique Church of the Martyrs is succeeded by the Church of the Monks. Monasticism, taking root in the West from 350, and after 500 given a form and a norm for millenniums by St. Benedict, signifies the turn from Christian Antiquity to the Christian Middle Ages" (312). Hereafter, monks would be the faithful guardians of the written word in the West, inscribing their phylacteries where snakes once lay coiled.

Curtius's narrative moves swiftly on to Cassiodorus, Isidore of Seville, and the clerkly Carolingian poets, products of "the strict, monastic school years of the Western mind" (315). Then a corner is turned and light floods a scene that opens to embrace the twelfth-century humanists, Dante, Shakespeare, and finally Goethe again. "To be sure," he concludes, "many examples of writing imagery could be found in the succeeding centuries. But it no longer possesses a unique, a felt, a conscious 'life-relationship,' could no longer possess it *after the Enlightenment shattered the authority of the book and the Technological Age changed all the relations of life*" (emphasis added). As a kind of scribal colophon to his chapter, expressive of a "timeless truth," he repeats an apophthegm of the nineteenth-century German poet Gottfried Keller: "Time is a parchment white / And thereon each doth write / With his red blood, until the day / The stream sweeps him away" (347).

Curtius is prodigal with epochs. At ease with the idea of "late antiquity" as employed by German ancient and medieval historians of his time, he makes only modest use of it as a period concept or interpretative category. Henri-Irénée Marrou's influential recasting of *die Spätantike* in terms of religious mentality ("the age of the Theopolis") appeared too late for him to notice it.[18] Unlike his fellow Romance philologist Erich Auerbach, he does not

---

18. Henri-Irénée Marrou, *Saint Augustin et la fin de la culture antique,* 2d ed. with a "Retractatio"

assign Christianity any major role in the shaping of post-Roman literary culture.[19] The customary periodizations of church history and patristics are things largely indifferent to him, useful for plotting a march down the centuries but unlikely to affect his presentation of subject matter. So it is with the reputed "turn from Christian Antiquity to the Christian Middle Ages," construed in the chapter on "The Book as Symbol" as a transition from Church of the Martyrs to Church of the Monks. Tempting as it would be for us on this occasion to make Prudentius the last Latin poet of the "early Christian book," there is nothing in *European Literature and the Latin Middle Ages* to authorize the move. The idea of an "early Christian book" is as alien to Curtius's sense of European literary history as that of an "early Christian literature," current and controversial though the latter formula had become in patristic scholarship by the 1940s.[20] Nor, writing before C. H. Roberts's British Academy paper, does he have any idea that the shift from roll to codex could have specifically Christian motivation.[21]

In one of the excursuses or supplementary chapters to *European Literature and the Latin Middle Ages,* Curtius seems to leave the door open to a partial revision of his main narrative. "The vast realm of patristics," he writes, "has not yet been explored in respect to the problems posed by *European literary history and literary theory*" (emphasis added). He continues: "We must ask: How did preoccupation with the Bible and the rise of Christian writing influence literary theory?" (446). These questions are raised at the start of a section headed "Jerome," the slender contents of which are summed up in the assertion that "for the beginning Middle Ages and later times, Jerome was the

---

(Paris, 1949), 699; Mark Vessey, "The Demise of the Christian Writer and the Remaking of 'Late Antiquity': From H.-I. Marrou's Saint Augustine (1938) to Peter Brown's Holy Man (1983)," *JECS* 6, no. 3 (1998): 383–91.

19. Erich Auerbach, *Literary Language and Its Public in Late Latin Antiquity and in the Middle Ages,* trans. Ralph Mannheim (Princeton, 1965).

20. Martin Tetz, "Altchristliche Literaturgeschichte—Patrologie," *Theologische Rundschau* 17 (1961): 1–42; Mark Vessey, "Patristics and Literary History," *Journal of Literature and Theology* 5 (1991): 342–53.

21. Colin H. Roberts, "The Codex," *Proceedings of the British Academy* 40 (1954): 169–204; Colin H. Roberts and T. C. Skeat, *The Birth of the Codex* (London, 1983). Cf. Curtius, *European Literature and the Latin Middle Ages,* 393: "The crisis of the Empire in the third century not only means a crippling of production but also produces an indifference to the older literature which was fatal to its preservation. What was no longer read was no longer copied—or rather, rewritten, for from the fourth century the papyrus scroll was replaced by the parchment codex. A technical innovation and a change of taste combined to result in a diminution of Latin literature."

great representative of the Humanism of the Church." Jerome the exemplary humanist: how Rufinus would have roared! Curtius needs this pussycat Jerome for his thesis of the grand continuity of European literature from Homer to Goethe. But we know that the "beginning Middle Ages," to say nothing yet of later times, were familiar with another Jerome as well: the protomartyr of (Christian) Latin letters, the prophet of the Vulgate, the compulsive theorist of writing and books. We have heard something of that Jerome already, and there is more to be said.[22] Until this excursus is complete, the sense of literary epoch that Curtius associated with a turn from the Church of the Martyrs to the Church of the Monks must remain an intuition. We can agree that monasticism was "one of the chief supports . . . of writing and the book" in the medieval West, but the name of Benedict by itself will not conjure the whole history.

Curtius's chapter "The Book as Symbol" has inspired a number of detailed studies in recent years, none of which can be read as a straightforward complement to his text.[23] Curtius was of the generation of European scholars that founded the science of comparative literature. In the light of later twentieth-century critiques of "Eurocentric" cultural analysis, the sense of comparison implied by this disciplinary name has become problematic. At the same time, the capital term of Curtius's carefully worded title, "literature," has been thoroughly destabilized.[24] When Curtius spoke of the need to explore "the vast realm of patristics . . . in respect to the problems posed by European literary history and literary theory," his reader might be expected to realize that he meant "European literary history" in a novel sense. No one in 1948, however, could have predicted the looming fortune of "literary theory" or the percussive effect in the next half century of the question posed the year before by another giant of the *après-Guerre*—What is literature?

In retrospect, Curtius's confidence that "writing imagery" could no lon-

22. Further indications in Mark Vessey, "From *Cursus* to *Ductus:* Figures of Writing in Western Late Antiquity (Augustine, Jerome, Cassiodorus, Bede)," in *European Literary Careers: The Author from Antiquity to the Renaissance,* ed. Patrick Cheney and Frederick A. de Armas (Toronto, 2002), 47–103, esp. 53–59.

23. Besides the work of Jager (note 17 above), Jesse M. Gellrich, *The Idea of the Book in the Middle Ages: Language Theory, Mythology, and Fiction* (Ithaca, N.Y., 1985), is largely relevant. Both authors are influenced by the use made of Curtius's chapter by Jacques Derrida, *Of Grammatology,* trans. Gayatri Spivak (Baltimore, 1976), 15.

24. For an easy way into a complex topic, see Peter Widdowson, *Literature* (London, 1999).

ger sustain a "conscious 'life-relationship'" after "the Enlightenment shattered the authority of the book and the Technological Age changed all the relations of life" seems wildly premature. The awareness of entering a new age of *communications* technology, far from annulling all prior relationships, gave rise in the immediate postwar decades to an intense interest in media and media histories, including a history of the book whose more imaginative expressions have breached the confines of the academy and show no signs of abating yet.[25] Meanwhile, a conviction that certain kinds of "authority of the book" and associated forms of knowledge were open to more penetrating question was encouraged by midcentury trends in Continental philosophy such as existentialism, phenomenology, and the revived interest in Nietzsche. It is this movement of thought, which leads to what came to be known in the Anglophone academy by the late '70s as "theory,"[26] that we shall now pursue, especially where it can be seen to summon, if only by implication or association, a longer history of (Christian) writing and the book.

The Book as Work: Stéphane Mallarmé

In the third chapter of *Qu'est-ce que la littérature?* Jean-Paul Sartre offers a short history of relations between writers and their public from the Middle Ages to the twentieth century. Partly in reaction to Julien Benda, whose *La trahison des clercs* (1927)[27] had fueled French debate on the political stance of

25. It will be enough to mention the names of Lucien Febvre, Henri-Jean Martin, Marshall McLuhan, Raymond Williams, Elizabeth Eisenstein, Robert Darnton, Roger Chartier, D. F. McKenzie, and Jerome J. McGann; for orientation, see David Finkelstein and Alistair McCleery, eds., *The Book History Reader* (London, 2002). Inferences for and from the study of late antique and early Christian textual culture in James J. O'Donnell, *Avatars of the Word: From Papyrus to Cyberspace* (Cambridge, Mass., 1998). After Jorge-Luis Borges, it was Umberto Eco in *The Name of the Rose* (1980) who made the monastic library a place of common resort. And after Luciano Canfora, *The Vanished Library,* trans. Martin Ryle (Berkeley and Los Angeles, 1987), we can now visit a modern wonder of the world at http://www.bibalex.org.

26. My own understanding of these developments owes much to Tzvetan Todorov, "La réflexion sur la littérature dans la France contemporaine," *Poétique* 38 (1979): 131–48, largely resumed in his *Literature and Its Theorists: A Personal View of Twentieth-Century Criticism,* trans. Catherine Porter (Ithaca, N.Y., 1987), 44–69; Timothy Clark, *Derrida, Heidegger, Blanchot: Sources of Derrida's Notion and Practice of Literature* (Cambridge, 1992); Patrick Ffrench, *The Time of Theory: A History of Tel Quel (1960–1983)* (Oxford, 1995).

27. "The word 'Clercs,' which occurs throughout the book, is defined by M. Benda as 'all those who speak to the world in a transcendental manner.' I do not know the English for 'all those who speak to the world in a transcendental manner.'" Translator's note (by R. Aldington) to Benda, *The Treason of the In-*

intellectuals a generation earlier, Sartre chose for his prototype of the modern writer the figure of the medieval Christian scholar, the *clericus* or *clerc*. "Literature" for Sartre defines a work of the spirit, more exactly of spiritualization, understood in the particular, de-theologizing sense of a *reprise* or taking hold again of the world and the "invincible Evil which gnaws at it without ever being able to destroy it."[28] Christianity provided a template for such world handling. It is at the origin of literature in Sartre's quasi-Hegelian narrative. "The Christian Revolution," he writes, "brought in the spiritual, that is the spirit itself, as a negation, a challenge, and a transcendence, a perpetual construction, beyond the realm of Nature, of the *antinatural* city of freedoms" (63). For this human power of transcendence to be manifest, it had first to be objectified, set apart from the ordinary existence of human beings. That was the project of Christian ideology, otherwise called theology and entrusted to a specialist corps of professional readers and writers, the *clercs*. It had nothing to do with what would later be called the humanities. To be "literate" in this context meant to be able to read the sacred texts and the commentaries upon them, and to write further commentaries that would be read by other clerics. *Literature* was alienated from society along with *spirituality,* as a condition of the future possibility of both. There was no relation yet between writer and public. Those outside the clerical class, lay aristocrats and ordinary members of society, obtained their ideas of Christianity through nonwritten media, aurally, or in the language of images. At this point Sartre pauses to recall "the sculpture of the cloisters and cathedrals, the stained glass windows, the paintings and

---

tellectuals (1928), cited by Helen Small as the epigraph to her editorial introduction to *The Public Intellectual* (Oxford, 2002). The fine essay in this volume by Rita Copeland on "Pre-modern Intellectual Biography" (40–61) leaps from Philostratus's third-century *Lives of the Sophists* to the university culture of western Europe in the twelfth and thirteenth centuries, despatching the intervening period with the observation "that what might potentially have been forms of intellectual biography [in later late antiquity and the early to central Middle Ages] were absorbed into hagiography and similar genres related to *acta sanctorum* . . . or more broadly, into the genres of ecclesiastical and dynastic chronicles" (46). The undervaluation of the "early Christian" contribution to Western ideals of the "public intellectual" is already announced in Jacques Le Goff's *Intellectuals in the Middle Ages* (1955, 1957, 1985), trans. Teresa Lavender Fagan (Oxford, 1993), and repeated, for the history of reading or textuality, by Ivan Illich, *In the Vineyard of the Text: A Commentary to Hugh's Didascalicon* (Chicago, 1993). For a narrative that would restore the late antique *clerc* to the history once evoked by Benda, see Brian Stock, *After Augustine: The Meditative Reader and the Text* (Philadelphia, 2001). I address this issue in my introduction to *Cassiodorus: "Institutions of Divine and Secular Learning" and "On the Soul,"* trans. James W. Halporn (Liverpool, 2004).

28. Jean-Paul Sartre, *What Is Literature?* trans. Bernard Frechtman (London, 2001), 121. The essays that made up *Qu'est-ce que la littérature?* (Paris, 1948) first appeared in the journal *Les temps modernes* in 1947.

the mosaics," all of which "speak of God and the Holy Story" (64). The medieval-clerical "work of the spirit" was later contested and negated in its turn, giving way to the Renaissance.

Sartre's conception of literature as "the subjectivity of a society in permanent revolution" (122) and of the history of "writing" as a serial overturning of oppressive orders—the clergy, the aristocracy, most recently the bourgeoisie—has deep roots in French and German Enlightenment thought and its Romantic sequels. The idea of the literary artist as counterpart of the cleric was formulated in the 1790s by Hegel's Jena associate Friedrich Schlegel, who adapted it from Schleiermacher.[29] Schlegel's *Geistlicher* is already Sartre's *homme d'esprit,* an individual living after the collapse of the transcendent realm once guaranteed by theology and later by its political avatar, the *ancien régime.* In crediting the "Christian Revolution" with the creation of the "spiritual" in the first place, Sartre underlines a sense of epoch made possible by the events of 1789. In the same stroke, he implicitly refers to the "crisis" of late antiquity, our concept of which was born in France with Chateaubriand's *Essais sur les révolutions anciennes et modernes* (1796) and *Le génie du Christianisme* (1802). The original vision of late antiquity as a time between two states of human consciousness was a fearful projection of the aftermath of the French Terror.[30] Chateaubriand's *Les martyrs* (1809) inaugurates a line of "romanesque" depictions of early Christian ascetics, with its sentimental portraits of a youthful Jerome and Augustine together at the tomb of the younger Scipio Africanus, sighing for a transcendent vision like that of Scipio's dream, and later of Jerome alone in his Bethlehem grotto where all that meets a visitor's eye is "the Bible, a death's head, and a few scattered leaves of the translation of the Holy Books."[31] Such verbal tableaux were inherently evocative. "Everyone," wrote Chateaubriand, "knows about Jerome's retirement in the cave at Bethlehem; everyone has seen the paintings. . . . [E]veryone knows that in his letters [he] laments being plagued in the midst of his solitude by memories of Rome."[32]

---

29. Philippe Lacoue-Labarthe and Jean-Luc Nancy, *The Literary Absolute: The Theory of Literature in German Romanticism,* trans. Philip Barnard and Cheryl Lester (Albany, N.Y., 1988), 67–70 and 139n35.

30. Reinhart Herzog, *"Wir leben in der Spätantike": Eine Zeiterfahrung und ihre Impulse für die Forschung* (Bamberg, 1987), 8–12; Reinhart Herzog, "Epochenerlebnis 'Revolution' und Epochenbewußtsein 'Spätantike': Zur Genese einer historischen Epoche bei Chateaubriand," in *Epochenschwelle und Epochenbewußtsein,* ed. Reinhart Herzog and Reinhart Koselleck (Munich, 1987), 195–219.

31. Maurice Regard, ed., *Chateaubriand: Oeuvres romanesques et voyages* (Paris, 1969), 2:180, 407.

32. Ibid., 657.

In a country where religious orders had been suppressed at the Revolution, the type of the monastic scholar—romanticized, laicized, travestied to suit changing times and tastes—enjoyed a hectic afterlife. As the abbé Migne in the 1840s and '50s set about reprinting texts of the Greek and Latin fathers in entrepreneurial succession to the great Benedictine editors of St-Maur,[33] the *poètes maudits* found other ways of playing monk without a cowl.[34] "The ancient cloisters on their great walls / Displayed in paintings the holy Truth," Baudelaire begins a sonnet on "Le mauvais moine" in *Les fleurs du mal* of 1857.[35] Piety and martyrdom were now alike out of fashion. "My soul's a tomb," the poet intones, "in which, unvirtuous cenobite, / From eternity I turn about and dwell; / Nothing decorates the walls of this hateful cloister. // O feckless monk! When shall I then have the wit to make / Of the living spectacle of my sad state / The work of my hands and passion of my eyes?"[36] As an exile from the imagined city of freedoms that had been the absolute sense of an earlier clerical culture, the writer makes an art of desolation. From the furniture of the monk's cell, he keeps only the death's head. In the absence of any Bible for him to illustrate, comment upon, or translate, the sole work of his hands and passion of his eyes are his own scattered and visionary leaves, texts in which he grapples with the nocturnal twin of an ancient noontide devil, *l'Ennui*. "You are acquainted, reader, with this subtle monster, / Hypocrite reader,— *mon semblable,—mon frère!*"[37] The hallucinogenic garden of *Les fleurs du mal* is full of creatures that bite. Remorse is the negative life force of Baudelairean aesthetics, one half of a dialectic of allegory and symbol that seeks to restore an ideal unity to human experience in the midst of disenchantment.[38]

33. R. Howard Bloch, *God's Plagiarist: Being an Account of the Fabulous Industry and Irregular Commerce of the Abbé Migne* (Chicago, 1994).

34. The role had been scripted for them in large part by their elders. Paul Bénichou, *The Consecration of the Writer, 1750–1830,* trans. Mark K. Jensen (Lincoln, Neb., 1999).

35. "Les cloîtres anciens sur leurs grandes murailles / Etalaient en tableaux la sainte Vérité" ("Le mauvais moine," lines 1–2).

36. "—Mon âme est un tombeau que, mauvais cénobite, / Depuis l'éternité je parcours et j'habite; / Rien n'embellit les murs de ce cloître odieux. // O moine fainéant! Quand saurai-je donc faire / Du spectacle vivant de ma triste misère / Le travail de mes mains et l'amour de mes yeux?" (ibid., lines 9–14).

37. "Tu le connais, lecteur, ce monstre délicat, / —Hypocrite lecteur,—mon semblable,—mon frère!" ("Au lecteur," lines 39–40).

38. Patrick Labarthe, *Baudelaire et la tradition de l'allégorie* (Geneva, 1999). Labarthe writes: "Privé de la caution de l'Absolu, l'univers devient le théâtre d'une prolifération de signes à la dérive; les assauts de la contingence vouent pour ainsi dire à une déroute du sens" (27). This generalization follows a comparison of Baudelaire's "Le Crépuscule du matin" with Prudentius, *Cathemerinon* 2 ("Ad Galli cantum").

In March 1866 Baudelaire's admirers across France learned to their dismay that the Prince of Dream had been silenced by a stroke. The mourners included a young teacher of English at the lycée of Tournon named Stéphane Mallarmé, who was then putting the last touches to a suite of poems in the style of the master, to be printed in the Parisian *Parnasse contemporain*. A voice in one of them declares: "The flesh is sad, alas! and I have read all the books." Each night Ennui tempts him with a prospect of sea voyages that he is nearly powerless to resist, despite the influence of a "young woman breast-feeding her child" and "the desert clarity of [his] lamp / On the empty paper whose whiteness protects it" ("Brise marine," lines 1, 6–8). The luminous blank of that page would be the sea room of Mallarmé's night voyage. "Before the paper," he wrote, "the artist *makes himself*."[39] Such making was self-annihilation. His *nuits blanches* had lately been given to a poem on Herodias, ideal beauty, the sight of which must cost the visionary his life. "Last night," he wrote to a friend, "I was fortunate enough to see my Poem once more in its nakedness, this evening I want to attempt the work."[40] Work, dream, poem: the words as this writer uses them are almost interchangeable. They would soon undergo an important inflection of meaning.

At Easter that year Mallarmé left his wife and infant daughter behind in Tournon and spent a week in Cannes with his friend and fellow poet Eugène Lefébure, who had just returned from an aborted trip to Egypt. Together they visited Monaco, Nice, Marseilles, and Avignon, and on April 5, a Thursday, took a boat to the island of St-Honorat (Lérins). The famous monastery founded in the early fifth century was now ruinous, the island more truly desert than it had been for centuries.[41] After the Revolution a retired actress of the Théâtre Français had converted some of the buildings and lived there for a

39. *Stéphane Mallarmé: Correspondance 1862–1871* (vol. 1 of Henri Mondor and Lloyd James Austin, eds., *Stéphane Mallarmé: Correspondance*, 11 vols. [Paris, 1959–85], hereafter *Correspondance*), 154: "Devant le papier, l'artiste *se fait*" (letter of February 1865 to Eugène Lefébure).

40. Ibid., 195 (letter of January 3, 1866, to Théodore Aubanel).

41. Lefébure held out the prospect of such a trip in a letter to Mallarmé of March 16: "Nous irions aisément jusqu'à Nice, qui n'est qu'à une heure d'ici, et nous visiterions ensemble les belles îles de Lérins, dont la plus grande est une forêt de pins immémoriaux, et dont la plus petite [St-Honorat] jadis habitée par la célèbre communauté de moines de Lérins, garde quelques ruines de vieux cloîtres, entre autres une sorte de couvent gothique fortifié avec une plateforme d'où l'on guettait l'arrivée des voiles sarrazines. Cette plate-forme, ouverte sur l'infini de l'eau, vous isole en plein rêve . . . . *Songez que vous lirez la mer de Nice dans le texte*." Henri Mondor, *Eugène Lefébure: Sa vie, ses lettres à Mallarmé* (Paris, 1951), 208–9 (emphasis added).

while; the painter Fragonard, an old lover of hers, is said to have decorated her boudoir with scenes of *galanterie*.[42] We can only guess what caught Mallarmé's eye while he was on the island, apart from the sea and the azure sky above it, which he would recall in ecstatic terms.[43] We do know, however, that during this stay in Provence he suffered some kind of crisis, one full of consequence for his idea of literary oeuvre and for a certain theory of the book.[44]

In a letter written a few weeks later Mallarmé gave an account of progress on his *Hérodiade*.

Unfortunately, in so hollowing out the verse, I have come upon two abysses, which make me despair. One is Nothingness [*le Néant*], to which I have come without knowing Buddhism, and I am still too distressed to be able to believe even in my poetry and return to the work that this crushing thought has made me abandon.

Yes, *I know*, we are only empty forms of matter, but quite sublime for having invented God and our soul. So sublime, my friend! that I want to present to myself this spectacle of a matter that is conscious of its own being and yet launches itself impetuously into the Dream that it knows not to be, singing of the Soul and all the other divine impressions of a similar kind that have piled up in us since the earliest times and that proclaim, in the face of the Nothing that is the truth, these glorious lies![45]

The other abyss was fear of an early death, as day-and-night toil threatened to undermine the poet's health. Still, the work went on. From contemplation of nothingness, Mallarmé veered to contemplation of the beautiful. His letters convey a mounting excitement, then a new sense of purpose:

I have worked harder this summer than in all my life, and I can say that I have worked for my whole life. I have laid the foundations of a magnificent work. Every man has a Secret in him, many die without having found it, and will never find it because, once they are dead, it will no longer exist, nor they. I have died, and come back to life with the bejeweled key of my last spiritual casket. It is up to me now to open it in the absence of all borrowed impressions, and its mystery will emanate in a sky[46] of great beauty. I shall need twenty years, during which

42. Jean-Jacques Antier, *Lérins: L'île sainte de la Côte d'Azur* (Paris, 1988), 281.

43. *Correspondance* 1:210, to be compared with the passage in note 41 above: "Lefébure m'a levé le rideau qui me voilait à jamais le décor de Nice et je me suis follement enivré de la Méditerranée. Ah! mon ami, que ce ciel terrestre est divin!" (letter of late April 1866 to Henri Cazalis).

44. The event has been much discussed by Mallarméans. For an account that emphasizes the religious contexts of Mallarmé's life and thought, see Bertrand Marchal, *La religion de Mallarmé* (Paris, 1988), 55–67.

45. *Correspondance* 1:207 (letter to Cazalis, quoted in note 43 above).

46. For *un fort beau ciel* Mallarmé first wrote *une fort belle oeuvre*. The analogy of work (or text) and sky is one of the constants of his poetic.

time I shall cloister myself within myself, renouncing all publicity apart from the reading of my friends.[47]

Twenty years was too modest an estimate. Mallarmé's poetic claustration lasted until his actual death more than three decades later, in 1898. As the years went by, his descriptions of the artistic work in progress gave it different names and proportions. Certain features remained more or less fixed. It was the matter of a dream. Its like had never been attempted before. It was all-encompassing. It might never be finished. It was almost impossible to begin.[48]

In 1885 Mallarmé wrote an autobiographical sketch in response to a set of questions from Paul Verlaine, who was preparing a booklet about him for a series entitled *Hommes d'aujourd'hui*. Verlaine asked about the great work. Apart from his various lesser publications over the years, wrote Mallarmé,

I have always dreamed and attempted something else, with the patience of an alchemist, ready to sacrifice all vanity and all satisfaction for it, as formerly one would set fire to one's furniture and the beams of one's roof to feed the furnace of the *Grand Oeuvre*. What is it? It is difficult to say: a book, quite simply, in several tomes, a book that would really be a book, architectural and premeditated, and not just a collection of chance inspirations, however marvelous. ... I will go further, I will say: the Book, persuaded as I am that there is only one, unwittingly attempted by anyone who writes, even by Geniuses. The Orphic explanation of the earth [*L'explication Orphique de la terre*] which is the sole duty of the poet and the literary game par excellence: for the very rhythm of the book, as impersonal in this case as it is living, even down to its pagination, juxtaposes itself to the equations of this dream, or Ode.

There you have the confession of my vice laid bare, dear friend, which a thousand times I have rejected, when my spirit was mortified or weary, but this is what possesses me and I shall perhaps succeed at it; not indeed to accomplish this work in its entirety (one would have to be I know not whom for that!) but to show a fragment of it complete, to make its glorious authenticity shine out in one place, while indicating the whole of the remainder for which one life does not suffice. To prove by the completed portions that this book exists, and that I have known what I shall not have been able to accomplish.[49]

Few passages in French literature have attracted more commentary than this one. There are two obvious points to be made here. First, Mallarmé has a

---

47. *Correspondance* 1:222 (letter of July 16, 1866, to Théodore Aubanel).

48. Lloyd James Austin, "Mallarmé et le rêve du 'Livre,'" in his *Essais sur Mallarmé*, ed. Malcolm Bowie (Manchester, 1995), 66–91. See also the works cited in note 71 below.

49. Henri Mondor and G. Jean-Aubry, eds., *Stéphane Mallarmé: Oeuvres complètes* (Paris, 1945), 662–63. A new Pléiade edition in two volumes, by Bertrand Marchal, has now appeared, but it seemed easier to retain the familiar references.

feeling for books as physical objects, volumes (in the modern sense) in which folded sheets are *bound*.[50] Second, the vision that he has of his own ultimate book has a strongly religious or quasi-religious color.[51] These features of his imagination are apparent in all his writings but perhaps most explicit in a collection of prose pieces first published together shortly before his death under the title of *Divagations*. A few brief quotations may give its flavor, even through the gauze of translation:[52]

L'écrivain, de ses maux, dragons[53] qu'il a choyés, ou d'une allegresse, doit s'instituer, au texte, le spirituel histrion.

The writer must make himself, in the text, the spiritual actor either of his sufferings, those dragons he has nurtured, or of some happiness.

"Quant au livre: L'action restreinte"

50. Daniel Moutote, *Maîtres livres de notre temps: Posterité du "Livre" de Mallarmé* (Paris, 1988), claims him as the modern master of the codex form, architect of a text made up of elements that can be juxtaposed in an infinite number of combinations, like so many (loose) leaves in a book without preordained sequence. He contrasts this model with that of the "global and durative" *volumen,* represented preeminently by the Bible, which "unfurls the total history of the Covenant and [which] the priest unfurls in the presence of the people of God" (8). For alternative reflections on the hermeneutic implications of the codex, see Guglielmo Cavallo, "Between *Volumen* and Codex: Reading in the Roman World," in *A History of Reading in the West,* ed. Guglielmo Cavallo and Roger Chartier, trans. Lydia G. Cochrane (Cambridge, 1999), 64–89, esp. 86–89: "The codex provided readers with other spaces to write on. . . . [I]t imposed a simultaneous and co-ordinated reading that moved back and forth between the principal texts and its accessories." Note that Cavallo associates such practices of "intensive" reading—as opposed to "extensive" or volumen-based reading—primarily with codices of the Bible and Roman Law!

51. Marchal, *Religion de Mallarmé,* 497ff. ("Livre et religion").

52. *Oeuvres complètes,* 370, 378–80; trans. Mary Ann Caws and Bradford Cook, *Stéphane Mallarmé: Selected Poetry and Prose* (New York, 1982), 78, 80–82.

53. The dragon or chimaera occurs repeatedly in Mallarmé's writing as a figure of impossible transcendence. Jean-Pierre Richard, *L'univers imaginaire de Mallarmé* (Paris, 1961), 157: "Cet animal cracheur de feu dont le corps s'enroule si fréquemment à cette époque autour des pieds de tables ou de consoles, c'est lui aussi qui dit allégoriquement le voeu de transcendance. *Chimériques,* à la fois le voeu d'au-delà, et 'le monstre' qui souffre et meurt un peu partout chez Mallarmé d'une agonie spectaculaire." An important train of thought associates this monster with the Christian myth of the Fall. Marchal, *Religion de Mallarmé,* 74: "Quelque chose en tout cas a commencé avec le christianisme, dans l'histoire de l'humanité, quelque chose que Mallarmé appelle la Chimère [*Correspondance* 1:246, a letter of May 17, 1867, to Eugène Lefébure] et qui se lie à la conscience tragique de la mort. Comme le serpent de la Genèse, la chimère religieuse a mordu le coeur de l'homme et lui a fait perdre définitivement l'innocence quasi édénique de l'antiquité païenne." Finally, the chimaera is the "book" itself as dreamt by Mallarmé over the years. After evoking this perfect "spiritual space" in *Crise de vers* (also included in *Divagations*), the poets exclaims: "Chimère, y avoir pensé atteste, au reflet de ses squames, combien le cycle présent, ou quart dernier de siècle, subit quelque éclair absolu . . . que, plus ou moins, tous les livres, contiennent la fusion de quelques redites comptées: *même il n'en serait qu'un—au monde, sa loi—bible comme la simulent des nations.*" Mondor and Jean-Aubry, *Oeuvres complètes,* 367 (emphasis added).

Une proposition qui émane de moi—si, diversement, citée à mon éloge ou par blâme—je la revendique avec celles qui se presseront ici—sommaire veut, que tout, au monde, existe pour aboutir à un livre.

I am the author of a statement to which there have been varying reactions, including praise and blame, and which I shall make again in the present article. Briefly, it is this: all earthly existence must ultimately be contained in a book.

Sur un banc de jardin, où telle publication neuve, je me rejouis si l'air, en passant, entr'ouvre et, au hasard, anime, d'aspects, l'extérieur du livre: plusieurs—à quoi, tant l'aperçu jaillit, personne depuis qu'on lut, peut-être n'a pensé.

Seated on a garden bench where a recent book is lying, I like to watch a passing gust half open it and breathe life into many of its outer aspects, which are so obvious that no one perhaps in the history of literature has ever thought about them.

Le pliage est, vis-à-vis de la feuille imprimée grande, un indice, quasi religieux; qui ne frappe pas autant que son tassement, en épaisseur, offrant le minuscule tombeau, certes, de l'âme.

The foldings of a book, in comparison with the large-sized open newspaper, have an almost religious significance. But an even greater significance lies in their thickness when they are piled together; for then they form a tomb in miniature for our souls.

Le livre, expansion totale de la lettre, doit d'elle tirer, directement, une mobilité et spacieux, par correspondances, instituer un jeu, on ne sait, qui confirme la fiction.

The book, which is a total expansion of the letter, must find its mobility in the letter; and in its spaciousness must establish some nameless system of relationships which will embrace and strengthen fiction.

"Quant au livre: Le livre, instrument spirituel"

One longer quotation from the same series returns us to the drama of *Hérodiade,* which is also the drama of Mallarmé and his reader:

> Lire—
> Cette pratique—
> Appuyer, selon la page, au blanc, qui l'inaugure son ingénuité, à soi, oublieuse même du titre qui parlerait trop haut: et, quand s'aligna, dans une brisure, la moindre, disséminée, le hasard vaincu mot par mot, indéfectiblement le blanc revient, tout à l'heure gratuit, certain maintenant, pour conclure que rien au delà et authentiquer le silence—
> Virginité qui solitairement, devant une transparence du regard adéquat, elle-même s'est comme divisée en ses fragments de candeur, l'un et l'autre, preuves nuptiales de l'Idée.
> L'air ou chant sous le texte, conduisant la divination d'ici là, y applique son motif et fleuron et cul-de-lampe invisibles.

Reading—

Is an exercise—

We must bend our independent minds, page by page, to the blank space which begins each one; we must forget the title, for it is too resounding. Then, in the tiniest and most scattered stopping-points upon the page, when the lines of chance have been vanquished word by word, the blanks unfailingly return; before, they were gratuitous; now they are essential; and now at last it is clear that nothing lies beyond; now silence is genuine and just.

It is a virgin space, face to face with the lucidity of our matching vision, divided of itself, in solitude, into halves of whiteness; and each of these is the lawful bride to the other at the wedding of the Idea.

Thus the invisible air, or song, beneath the words leads our divining eye from word to music; and thus, like a motif, invisibly it inscribes its fleuron and pendant there.

"Quant au livre: Le mystère dans les letters"[54]

"Death unexpectedly choked the poet ... as he was setting about the work that would be the most generous and doubtless the most enigmatic of all," wrote the editors of Mallarmé's *Oeuvres complètes* (1945).[55] Rarely can that title have been so precisely and ironically applied. The death that Mallarmé so often rehearsed, when it came, sealed the mystery of a writing life.[56] Soon to be the subject of numerous reminiscences by those who had known him, Mallarmé had himself been very sparing of personal memoir. The disappearance of the writer in the presence of the (impossible) work was the first article of his credo. His penciled reply to Verlaine was not printed until 1924. The collected correspondence did not begin to appear until 1959. In 1941, almost a century after his birth, Henri Mondor published a *Vie de Mallarmé* in two volumes with the combined dimensions of a miniature tomb.[57] Mondor drew on a large collection of little-known or unpublished documents, including letters that he was preparing to edit. His book came out in the darkest hour of France's history, a few months into the German occupation. With

54. Mondor and Jean-Aubry, *Oeuvres complètes*, 386–87, translated by Bradford Cook as *Mallarmé: Selected Prose Poems, Essays, and Letters* (Baltimore, 1956), 33–34.

55. Mondor and Jean-Aubry, *Oeuvres complètes*, xi.

56. Recent critics have been eloquent on this theme, e.g., Edward W. Said, *Beginnings: Intention and Method* (New York, 1975), 234ff.; Lawrence Lipking, *The Life of the Poet: Beginning and Ending Poetic Careers* (Chicago, 1981), 160–78 ("The Tombs of Mallarmé"); Leo Bersani, *The Death of Stéphane Mallarmé* (Cambridge, 1982). One of the sharpest formulations is Bersani's: "We might ... define Mallarmé's major enterprise ... as an effort to do away with literature. He comes to be engaged ... in the somewhat eerie strategy of celebrating writers and literature as a way of burying them" (45).

57. Paris, 1941, subsequently reissued as a single volume.

hindsight, it can be seen to inaugurate one of the dialogues that would characterize French intellectual life in the coming decades: a dialogue on European literary history, the changing role of the writer, the nature of the literary work, the ontology of "literature" itself—in short, the dialogue of "literary theory" from Sartre and Barthes to *Tel Quel*, Foucault, Derrida, and beyond; a dialogue in which ancient tropes of book and "text" would take on new and surprising forms of life. For all that it is ostensibly the least theoretical of works, Mondor's *Life of Mallarmé* marks the epoch.

The Work as Text: Maurice Blanchot

Such a chronology depends in the first instance on Blanchot (d. 2003).

According to the notice prefixed to one of his books, "Maurice Blanchot, novelist and critic, was born in 1907. His life is entirely devoted to literature and the silence that is proper to it."[58] In 1942 Blanchot wrote a review of Mondor's biography entitled "The Silence of Mallarmé." Referring to passages in the poet's letters from the years 1866–68 that had just been made public, he compared Mallarmé's experience to a mystic's dark night of the soul:

One could say that Mallarmé, through an extraordinary effort of asceticism, opened an abyss in himself where his awareness, instead of losing itself, survives and grasps its solitude in a desperate clarity. Having detached himself utterly and unceasingly from all that appears, he is like the hero of emptiness, and the night that he touches reduces him to an indefinite refusal to be no matter what—which is the very designation of the mind *(de l'esprit)*.[59]

In this darkness was born the dream of the work or book, "supreme text, plenary substitute for the universe" (105), a text of which there were only fragments and whose determinate structure and principles, it was now finally clear, would forever remain unknown, because Mallarmé had kept silent upon them. The paradoxical greatness of Mondor's biography, according to Blanchot, was to have revealed this lack. "Alas! the book is complete, and its essence is missing" (103). The book in question may be Mondor's or it may be Mallarmé's. It

58. Maurice Blanchot, *L'espace littéraire* (Paris, 1955), translated by Ann Smock as *The Space of Literature* (Lincoln, Neb., 1982). Page citations appear parenthetically in the text. On the biographical problems posed by Blanchot's oeuvre, see Leslie Hill, *Blanchot: Extreme Contemporary* (London, 1997), with a valuable bibliography of this author's texts.

59. Maurice Blanchot, *Faux pas* (Paris, 1943), English version with the same title, translated by Charlotte Mandell (Stanford, 2001), 101; Leslie Hill, "Blanchot and Mallarmé," *Modern Language Notes* 105 (1990): 889–913; Clark, *Derrida, Heidegger, Blanchot,* 73–74.

must in fact be both, since Blanchot takes the plenitudes of the poet's silence, as revealed by his biographer, and of his ultimate text, as concealed by himself, to be each other's guarantee. "This fact of having remained silent in the midst of so many words," he proposes, "may seem like the very secret whose existence should not be revealed to us" (106).

This Mallarméan, marmoreal silence was no small achievement. It had been won and sustained by an exceptional practice of *language*. A few weeks earlier, Blanchot had published a sharp response to a book called *Mallarmé l'obscur*, the author of which had tried to explain the poems by paraphrasing them. Invoking Mallarmé's own distinction between everyday and poetic language, Blanchot insisted that poetry could not be treated that way:

> What the poem signifies coincides exactly with what it is; the mind [*l'esprit*] that wants to understand it [*le comprendre*] must take it as a whole [*le prendre entier*], experience its complete reality, assimilate it materially and discern its power, when, having sought in vain to transform it the better to grasp it better, it succeeds in attaining it by the docility with which it accepts and marries it. . . . Here one must understand without dissimulation or circumlocution *(sans feinte ni détour)*, exchanging nothing but the poem for the poem. (108–9)

The near confusion in this passage between "it" pronouns standing respectively for *the reader* and *the poem* mimics an encounter in which the former, to comprehend the latter, lets him or herself be encompassed by it. In the resulting embrace, language displays its essential power, which is "to found a world, to make possible the authentic dialogue that we ourselves are and, as Hölderlin says, to name the gods" (109). Echoing an essay of Heidegger on Hölderlin, Blanchot also echoes Mallarmé's correspondence of 1866–67, as cited above. To grasp the power of language "to found a world," as Mallarmé did then, was at the same time to experience the nothingness that, in a posttheological age, is the bottomless bottom of being. "One could say," writes Blanchot, "that poetic meaning has to do with existence itself, that it is the understanding of the situation of man, that it calls what he is into question" (110). The writer or reader who submits to this interrogation is carried beyond the noise of ordinary language to a realm of silence, the realm of the perfect poem that "is recognized, in [its own] absence as the image—ultimate image—of plenitude and of the absolute." This last statement appears in a third essay of Blanchot's from 1942–43, in which he claims the ambition of the Mallarméan oeuvre for the contemporary novel.[60]

---

60. "Mallarmé and the Novel," reprinted in *Faux pas,* p. 168 in the English version.

The emphasis falls again on the literary work as locus of existential crisis; the reader will be confounded and "ravished by this book that does not depend on him but on which he depends in the most sovereign way, in a relation that puts his mind [*son esprit*] and his being in danger" (170).

In 1941 Blanchot published his own first novel, *Thomas l'obscur,* only to withdraw it from circulation shortly afterward. A decade later a revised and shorter version appeared with the same title. The book contains a vivid depiction of the engagement of reader and literary text as theorized by Blanchot. Early on, Thomas appears in the act of reading. He reads so intently that certain (unnamed, unknown) onlookers, seeing him with his book still open at the same page, suppose that he is only pretending to read. They are mistaken. This is to be a dialogue without feint or detour.

Il lisait. Il lisait avec une minutie et une attention insurpassables. Il était, auprès de chaque signe, dans la situation où se trouve le mâle quand la mante religieuse va le dévorer. L'un et l'autre se regardaient.[61]

He read. He read with a care and attention that could not be surpassed. He was, with respect to each written sign, in the situation of the male as the praying mantis is about to devour him. They stared at one another.

Initially pleasurable, the encounter becomes violent as soon as Thomas attempts to master the written signs that hold him in their gaze, each of which seems to contain within itself an endless series of signs, "like a procession of angels opening into the infinite to the very eye of the absolute" (25). In striving to grasp those signs, he is caught by them, molded by invisible hands, "bitten by a vital tooth" (26), in a word, *read.* The presence that is in the book invades the night too. He wrestles with it, becomes part of it as he contends with it, writhing on the floor, "hardly different from the serpent he would have wished to become in order to believe in the venom he felt in his mouth" (28). At every turn he finds himself "thrust back into the depths of his being by the very words which had haunted him and which he was pursuing as his nightmare and the explanation of his nightmare" (29). At last it seems to others that he is asleep, even though he is still awake. *Nuit blanchotienne.*

Mallarmé was to remain a central reference for Blanchot's reflections on literature and the literary work. From the late '40s, increasingly under the in-

---

61. Blanchot, *Thomas l'obscur,* nouvelle version (Paris, 1950), 27; Robert Lamberton, trans., *Thomas the Obscure* (Barrytown, N.Y., 1988), 25. Citations hereafter refer to Lamberton's translation.

fluence of Hegel, whose work was enjoying a new vogue in France, those reflections take a historical slant, offering a polemical alternative to the schematic literary history proposed by Sartre in *What Is Literature?*[62] According to Hegel, once the pursuit of the absolute had been reconceived in terms of historical progress, art became a thing of the past. Not so, according to Blanchot. He argued instead that at a moment not long after 1850 in France, conveniently marked in literature by Mallarmé and in painting by Cézanne, the work of art assumed a new and challenging autonomy. Whereas at successive periods in the past it had spoken for the gods, for the absence of the gods, for human beings as objects of representation (Classicism) and as creating subjects (Romanticism), it now at length became a presence to itself by becoming elusive to others, something to be forever desired and sought but never brought to light, Eurydice to the artist's Orpheus. It was at this time too, not incidentally, that the word *literature* entered general use as the common denominator for works of literary art in all genres, implying that there was a definable essence of literature, when in fact "the essence of literature is to evade every essential determination." All that mattered from now on was the *literary work* itself, even though "in the end the work is only there to lead to the search for the work; the work is the movement that carries us towards the pure point of inspiration from which it comes and which it seems able to reach only by disappearing."[63]

The movement inspired by the work defines what Blanchot calls the literary space *(l'espace littéraire)*. This topological idiom, not to be confused with the language of "structuralist" criticism emergent at the same date, is one of his distinctive contributions to literary-theoretical discourse. All signs point to Mallarmé as its strongest warrant, if not its actual source.[64] To translate

---

62. Hill, *Blanchot: Extreme Contemporary*, 104–5, citing Alexandre Kojève's *Introduction à la lecture de Hegel* (1947); Clark, *Derrida, Heidegger, Blanchot*, 70–71. A key text in this connection is Blanchot's "La littérature et le droit à la mort" (1948), reprinted in *La part du feu* (Paris, 1949), 305–45; English version in Lydia Davis, trans., *The Gaze of Orpheus and Other Literary Essays by Maurice Blanchot* (Barrytown, N.Y., 1981), 21–62, helpfully expounded by Rodolph Gasché, "The Felicities of Paradox: Blanchot on the Null-Space of Literature," in *Maurice Blanchot: The Demand of Writing*, ed. Carolyn Bailey Gill (London, 1996), 34–69. See also "Le mythe de Mallarmé" (1946) in *La part du feu*, 35–48.

63. Blanchot, "La disparition de la littérature" (1953), in *Le livre à venir* (Paris, 1959), 293; same theses in "La littérature et l'expérience originelle" (1952), in *L'espace littéraire*, 279–333 (*The Space of Literature*, 211–47). See also "L'expérience de Mallarmé" (1952), in *L'espace littéraire*, 37–52 (*The Space of Literature*, 38–48).

64. Clark, *Derrida, Heidegger, Blanchot*, 74: "Mallarmé, for Blanchot and Derrida, serves as a name to mark all that is most challenging in the literary."

l'espace littéraire as "the space of literature" is to risk a misunderstanding, since the nongeometrical space in question is strictly that of the *question of literature,* a vacancy wherein the very being of literature, with that of the author and (or as) reader, is put radically in doubt. Roland Barthes, close on Blanchot's heels in *Writing Degree Zero,* speaks of Mallarmé as the writer in whom literature as a codified set of linguistic practices first became fully visible as an object, at the price of its own destruction. In the same place, Barthes compares the bourgeois literary code to a "ritual language of priests" and names Mallarmé as one who took extreme measures to "exorcize this sacred writing" by arranging for its suicide.[65] The metaphor of ritual and exorcism is developed by Blanchot: "If to write means to enter into a *templum* which imposes upon us a certain number of usages, an implicit religion . . . then to write means first of all to want to destroy the temple before building it up—even, before crossing the threshold, to question oneself about the habits of slavery associated with the place and about the original fault that will be constituted by one's decision to confine oneself there *(s'y clôturer)."*[66] (Though less overtly iconoclastic, Derrida's early statements about the institution of literature will strike the same note.)

Up to this point, Blanchot appears principally as a theorist of literary language and the literary work. Although from time to time displaying a Mallarméan concern for the ideal or (more rarely) material volume, he could hardly on such evidence be counted a theorist of "the book." If he merits that description now, it is first of all for the collection of essays published in 1959 as *Le livre à venir* (The Book to Come). This is the instant at which the figure of the book as quasi-theological object appears on the horizon of literary theory, and at which literary theory as we know it appears as a horizon of thought. Fortuitously or not, it is also the instant of the coming of the book as history and of

65. Roland Barthes, *Le degré zéro de l'écriture* (Paris, 1953), translated as *Writing Degree Zero* by Annette Lavers and Colin Smith (New York, 1968), 74–75, continuing: "(We know all that this hypothesis of Mallarmé as a murderer of language owes to Maurice Blanchot.) This language of Mallarmé's is like Orpheus [Blanchot's figure of choice] who can save what he loves only by renouncing it, and who, just the same, cannot resist glancing round a little; it is Literature brought to the gates of the Promised Land: a world without Literature, but one to which writers would nevertheless have to bear witness" (76). Already in the opening pages of his essay Barthes takes Blanchot's Mallarmé as read. As Susan Sontag points out in her preface to the English version, *Le degré zéro de l'écriture* was partly a reaction to Sartre's *Qu'estce que la littérature?*

66. Blanchot, "La recherche du point zéro" (1953), in response to Barthes's book, reprinted in *Livre à venir,* 302–3.

the coming of the "history of the book," announced by the publication in 1958 of Lucien Febvre and Henri-Jean Martin's *L'apparition du livre*.[67] The respective fortunes of "the book" in history and theory would remain largely separate in French writing of the early 1960s, before becoming entwined in later and wider academic discourse.[68] Looking back, we should pause long enough to register the initial dissonance between a history of the book that begins with Gutenberg (Febvre and Martin) and a theory of "the book that is still to come" a century after Mallarmé (Blanchot). As students of (early) Christianity, we may also observe that a major part of Gutenberg's commerce was Bibles and that Mallarmé's dream of the absolute book came upon him in a space of imagination formerly occupied by Christian monks, if not in fact in the physical space of an island cleared once and for all of snakes by the blessed Honoratus.

The title of Blanchot's 1959 collection is shared by the only essay corresponding directly to it, the first of whose two sections bears the mock-Nietzschean title *Ecce liber* and begins: "The Book: what did Mallarmé understand by this word?"[69] Blanchot assembles some of the poet's more explicit statements concerning his great work from the time of its first projection in 1866 onward, to offer a summary account of a "Multiple book . . . not subject to randomness . . . without a personal author."[70] If these specifications seem to contradict his earlier claim (in the review of Mondor's biography) that we can finally know nothing of the Mallarméan book, the contradiction is only apparent. For what we finally know, Blanchot concludes again, is that the book is always beyond us: "the Book must never be seen as actually there. We cannot hold it" (233). *Ecce liber* means: behold the book that can never be held or be beheld, except in its absence.

Blanchot's strategy in this essay is in fact a near replica of the one he had used a decade and a half earlier in responding to *La vie de Mallarmé*. This time his pretext is a book called *Le "Livre" de Mallarmé*, in which Jacques Scherer

---

67. Lucien Febvre and Henri Jean Martin, *L'apparition du livre* (Paris, 1958), translated by David Gerard as *The Coming of the Book* (London, 1990).

68. See D. C. Greetham, *Theories of the Text* (Oxford, 1999), for an attempt at synthesis.

69. Blanchot, "Le livre à venir" (1957), in *Livre à venir*, 326–58; English version ("The Book to Come") in *The Sirens' Song: Selected Essays by Maurice Blanchot*, ed. Gabriel Josipovici and trans. Sacha Rabinovitch (Bloomington, Ind., 1982), 227–48. Citations refer to the translation.

70. *Livre nombreux . . . sans hasard . . . impersonnifié.* These sectional headings are omitted in the English version.

(at Mondor's prompting) presented a collection of the poet's notes apparently having something to do with his great enterprise.[71] Coming after Mondor's
biography, after the so-called *Oeuvres complètes* and excerpts from the letters
published as *Propos sur la poésie* (1953), on a rising tide of historical, exegetical,
and critical studies of Mallarmé, this edition of an unsuspected archive of the
poet's missing masterpiece had the air of a revelation. Blanchot remains skep-
tical. "Does this manuscript cast any light on [Mallarmé's] main project?" he
asks. "Perhaps," he answers, but only "on condition that we never lose sight of
the fact that this is not the manuscript of the Book" (246, n. 4). These random
notes, so ambiguously tied to the deceased person of their author, could not
constitute the essential (i.e., antiessentializing) work of poetry. Believe that
this was the book and we might as well believe the tales of travelers returning
with pieces of the ark of the covenant or fragments of the tablets of the Mosaic
law. Rhetorically facetious, the biblical parallels are no more carelessly chosen
than the phrase *Ecce liber.* Blanchot took Mallarmé's poetico-ontological crisis
as inaugural of a new age, prophetic of "an art to come and the future as art"
(235). The work proclaiming this new dispensation could not be any volume
issued by Gallimard. It would always be the book of the future.

The rubric for the second section of the essay echoes the opening question of the first. Having considered what Mallarmé understood by the book,
Blanchot once more expounds "A New Understanding of the Literary Space."

71. Jacques Scherer, *Le "Livre" de Mallarmé* (Paris, 1957). The edition of the notes is prefaced by
an ample essay outlining Mallarmé's ideas, under such rubrics as "Métaphysique du livre" and "Phy-
sique du livre." The first subsection is headed "Qu'est ce que la littérature?" and begins with a reference to Sartre's essay of that title. For further discussion and important revisions, see Eric Benoit,
Mallarmé et le mystère du "Livre" (Paris, 1998), especially the section on "Schèmes métaphysiques et
théologiques" (301–56), situating Mallarmé's project at the crisis of Hegelian and Romantic idealism,
between affirmation and denial of literature's potential for transcendence. Benoit concludes: "Christianisme et Littérature apparaissent simultanément dans le Livre [de Mallarmé] comme deux registres
signifiants dont aucun ne peut être ni évacué ni formulé unilatéralement. ... En effet, la Littérature
étant métaphysiquement désespérée, étant un Drame inachevable, est sentie comme un échec essentiel
dont le seul échappatoire serait le Christianisme (remède antinévrotique du fantasme métaphysique);
reciproquement, l'impossibilité pour le poète d'accepter le Christianisme comme spiritualité qui l'oblige
à faire le sacrifice de son fantasme, s'ouvre en élargissement du Christianisme et de la Passion, pascale,
dans le Drame plus large de la Littérature. Il s'agit toujours d'accouder le Songe à l'autel contre le tombeau retrouvé' [a reference to the section "Offices: Plaisir sacré" in *Divagations,* in Mondor and Jean-
Aubry, *Oeuvres complètes,* 395]: le Tombeau, vide, est le lieu *commun* de la Littérature et du Christianisme" (356).

Mallarmé [he writes] had always been aware of the fact—unrecognized before and perhaps after him—that language is a system of highly complex spatial relations whose singularity neither ordinary geometrical space nor the space of everyday life allows us to appreciate. Nothing is created and no discourse can be creative except through the preliminary exploration of the totally vacant region where language, before it is a set of given words, is a silent process of correspondences or (as he calls it) a "rhythmic scansion of the being." . . . Poetic space, the source and "outcome" of language, never exists like an object but always "spaces itself out and scatters itself." Hence Mallarmé's interest in anything that has to do with the singular essence of place—such as theatre or dance. . . . Thus poetic emotion is not an inner emotion, a subjective impression, but is a foreign "outside" [*un étrange dehors*] into which we are hurled inside ourselves out of ourselves. (345, translation modified)

These generalizations recall the scene of readerly *agon* in *Thomas the Obscure,* which already enacts the Mallarméan formula of a "rhythmic scansion of the being." Thomas falls prey to ceaselessly unfolding series of significations, experienced first as an infinite file of angels and then as a serpent's embrace.[72] His night wrestling takes place in the space of letters or poetic language specified in Blanchot's reading of Mallarmé, repeated now in "The Book to Come."[73] This literary space, for Blanchot, is the wakeful night in which humans experience the limits of their (human) being. And so once again to the project of the book outlined in Mallarmé's letter to Verlaine:

When Mallarmé says that the "Orphic explanation of the earth," the "explanation of the human being," is the mission of the poet and the purpose of the Book, what [asks Blanchot] does he mean by the repeated word explanation [*explication*]? Exactly what it stands for: the unfurling [*déploiement*] of the world and of the human being in the space of the song. Not the knowledge of what one and the other naturally are, but the development of them out of their given reality into what is mysterious and unmanifest about them, by means of the dispersing power of space and the uniting power of rhythmic becoming. Because poetry

72. Above at n. 61. For a serpent among the loose leaves of "Le Livre," see fols. 25–26 in Scherer's edition; commentary by Benoit, *Mallarmé et le mystère du "Livre,"* who detects in folios 16–26 "une réecriture à la fois de la Genèse (la Chute, le Serpent) et de l'Apocalypse (eschatologie de l'Esprit)" (188). Folios 27–33 present the scenario of an old priest who starves and is shut in a tomb ("sorte de claustration"), interpreted by Benoit as a figure of the Orphic self-sacrifice of the poet; cf. Marchal, *Religion de Mallarmé,* 508–10. For the "cloître" as one of the four main loci of the "opération" or literary-theatrical performance envisaged in Mallarmé's notes, see also fols. 102–6.

73. "A sentence is not simply projected linearly. It opens out. In this opening other sentence and word rhythms emerge, space themselves out and regroup at varying depths—words and sentences which are interrelated by definite structural affinities though not according to common logic (the logic of subordination) which destroys the space and standardises the movement" (238). For a reading of the reading-scene in *Thomas the Obscure* that aims to reveal the uncommon logic of Blanchot's prose, see Thomas Schestag, "Mantis, Relics," *Yale French Studies* 93 (1998): 221–51.

exists, not only is something changed in the universe but the universe is somehow subject to an essential change, whose significance is merely revealed or established by the bringing into being of the Book. Poetry always inaugurates *something different*. (240, translation modified)

The Book to Come: Christian Late Antiquity as a Time of Theory

With Blanchot's texts of the late 1950s we are on the threshold of the "time of theory" in France.[74] If space allowed, we might now show how themes and images from Blanchot's readings of Mallarmé (among other favorite authors of his) were adapted and developed over the next decade by writers like Barthes, Derrida, Foucault, and Kristeva, and how some of their insights were in turn assimilated by Blanchot in his later critical writings, culminating in the collection titled *L'entretien infini* (1969). Such an account would naturally include Foucault's essay on Flaubert's *Temptation of Saint Antony* (already quoted above), with its careful antedating of the postbiblical, posttheological dream of the ultimate book, and Derrida's astounding *explication* of Mallarmé in "The Double Session," as well as more immediately accessible texts like Barthes's "Death of the Author" and "From Work to Text."[75]

These further instances would help demonstrate not only the vitality of relations to the book and to writing entertained in our post-Enlightenment technological age but also, and more particularly, the intimacy of modern and putatively postmodern theories of the text to the kinds of "literary space" already projected in dreams and waking visions by Christian clerics and ascetics of late antiquity. Enough has perhaps been said already to let that intimacy begin to appear. The point is not that texts and books of early Christianity are *sources,* in any ordinary philological sense, for the pioneers of classic poststructuralist literary theory. It is rather that the theorists, in attempting to specify the conditions of their own activity as thinkers and writers of the crisis of Western modernity, were forced to reckon with the symbols that had long

74. See the study by Ffrench (cited above, note 26), esp. 28–30 and 77–78 on the ambiguous relationship to Blanchot's work of Philippe Sollers and other contributors to the journal *Tel Quel.*

75. Jacques Derrida, "The Double Session," in *Dissemination,* trans. Barbara Johnson (Chicago, 1981), 173–286; Roland Barthes, "The Death of the Author" and "From Work to Text," in Barthes, *Image, Music, Text,* trans. Stephen Heath (New York, 1977), 142–48, 155–64.

been integral to what Goethe would have called "the relations of life" in Western (Christian) culture, among which stood that of the book, and most conspicuously the Bible-as-book. One of the ways they did this, we have seen, was by revalorizing texts of relatively recent date—in France, typically, later Romantic poetry and fiction—in which the same symbolic relations were already visibly in play, if not already openly in question. Constructing his own genealogy, Foucault made Flaubert's vision of Antony, itself famously inspired by a Renaissance painting of the saint beset by demons, the beginning of a chain reaction. But the books that flanked the saint in the painting seen by Flaubert owed as much to the iconography of Jerome as they did to any *Life of Antony*. As Chateaubriand says, everyone has seen paintings of Jerome; it can hardly be coincidental that the name of Antony's malevolent disciple in Flaubert's *Temptation,* Hilarion, is shared by the hero of a much earlier romantic biography (by Jerome). Source hunting aside, the successive choices of painters, literary artists, and literary theorists cumulatively turn Jerome's fantasies of books into the kind of phantasmagoric library dreamed by Foucault and others.[76] And so it comes about that the patristic scholar, confronted by the finest exhibitions of the book in theory, is likely to be impressed most of all by their seeming contingency upon, not to say actual continuity with, experiences encoded in his or her texts of first resort.[77]

"Continuity! We have met it in a hundred forms." Casting his eye back on the road traveled in *European Literature and the Latin Middle Ages,* lamenting again the inability of the *scientia infima* of literary history to track the twisting ways of literary tradition, Curtius quotes some final instances of the "conscious reaching back for remote reserves, by which centuries are bridged." He mentions Baudelaire's taste for medieval Latin hymnody, the *précieux* medie-

---

76. For discussion of Flaubert's sources, which included Tillemont's *Mémoires pour servir à l'histoire ecclésiastique des six premiers siècles,* consult Jean Seznec, *Nouvelles études sur "La tentation de saint Antoine"* (London, 1949), and Kitty Mrosovsky's introduction to her annotated translation, *Gustave Flaubert: The Temptation of St. Antony.* (Ithaca, N.Y., 1981). The genesis and redaction of the work have been superbly studied by scholars of French literature in the wake of Foucault and poststructuralist literary and psychoanalytic theory, notably Jeanne Bem, *Désir et savoir dans l'oeuvre de Flaubert: Étude de la "Tentation de Saint Antoine"* (Neuchâtel, 1979), and Gisèle Séginger, *Naissance et métamorphoses d'un écrivain: Flaubert et "Les Tentations de saint Antoine"* (Paris, 1997). See also Jacques Chessex, *Flaubert, ou, le désert en abîme* (Paris, 1991), esp. 265–73 ("Le voeu du Livre").

77. See Geoffrey Galt Harpham, *The Ascetic Imperative in Culture and Criticism* (Chicago, 1987), esp. 1–134, for a brilliant demonstration of the kinds of short circuit that can occur between ancient and modern "theory."

valism of a J. K. Huysmans (the library of des Esseintes, so richly stocked with late Latin authors) or a Remy de Gourmont *(Le latin mystique),* and Stefan George's predilection for Nonnus: "'We still remember,' wrote [George] in his eulogy of Mallarmé, 'what a strong impression was left in us by the writings of the Byzantines and the late Latin authors, as by those of the Fathers, who could not refrain from portraying their repented sins in iridescent colors; how, in the their tormented and subjugated style we pleasurably felt the beat and throb of our own souls.'" (392). If this reminiscence speaks more directly for the literary tastes of the 1890s than it does for any known readings by Mallarmé himself, it may nonetheless attest a significant affinity; after all, one can be moved by the ancient monastic sites of Provence without ever reading a line of Jerome or Cassian. Curtius goes on to quote the first line of Verlaine's famous sonnet: *Je suis l'Empire à la fin de la décadence.* The affinity here is not just one of authors already dead. The "reaching back for remote reserves" that Curtius ascribes to the *décadents* of the last century is part of his own, highly contemporary reflection on the losses, returns, and transformations concealed by the "continuity" of a literary culture. In the next paragraph he mentions the third-century crisis of the Roman Empire, the replacement of papyrus scrolls by parchment codices in late antiquity, and the large-scale destruction of books during World War II.

Curtius was writing in the aftermath of this last event, which was also the hour of Sartre's troubling question of literature, and of H.-I. Marrou's decisive "Retractatio" (1949) of his prewar thesis on *Saint Augustin et la fin de la culture antique.*[78] Verlaine's sonnet is a reference for Marrou, too, adduced to explain his earlier readiness to cast his subject as *un lettré de la décadence.* A decade's further thought and experience had led him to revise this implicitly negative judgment. Among the sections of his book most in need of correction were those on the interpretation of obscure passages in scripture, in a chapter on "La Bible et les lettrés de la décadence" ("Retractatio," 646–51). Augustine evidently believed that God as the author of scripture sometimes veiled his meanings, just as human poets did. The Bible was a difficult book, but its difficulty was an aspect of its divine artistry. To contextualize this opinion, which must then have seemed bizarre to many readers, Marrou in 1938 looked forward to Dante, Aquinas, and medieval theories of poetic symbol-

---

78. Cited above, note 18.

ism, and backward to allegorical commentary on Homer and Christian exegesis of the Alexandrian school. (The ancient tradition of spiritual-allegorical exegesis only came into clear focus again in the 1940s and '50s, through the work of such scholars as Jean Daniélou, Henri de Lubac, and Jean Leclercq.) Almost in the same breath, he asserted the novelty of Augustine's position: "Here Augustine seems to me the first [*tout le premier*] to be sensitive to this poetry of mystery, this game of discovery. . . . [His] theory of the special value of the search for hidden meaning . . . manifests an intrinsic feature of his intellect" (492). Finally, Marrou took care to distinguish the Christian medieval understanding of symbolism from that of French symbolist poets of the 1890s and their heirs in modern criticism. For Augustine's successors, unlike Rimbaud's, the poetic symbol "does not express a kind of *sui generis* revelation that eludes discursive reason; it simply veils a truth that is perfectly defined and can easily be formulated in clear language" (490). God's obscurity, in Augustine's book, is never more than a supplementary and delightful confirmation of his clarity.

Thus Marrou in his original thesis. But such a view of the matter, he conceded in 1949, was too restrictive:

It was to forget that we are dealing here with a doctrine that is, so to speak, eternal—one of the fundamental options open to the human spirit. I was wrong to reduce the "modern" notion of poetry to that which has developed in the wake of Rimbaud (the obscure apprehension of an ineffable mystery). In the light of recent critical studies, like those of Dr. H. Mondor, I would now say that Augustine invites us to rediscover in Scripture a Mallarméan conception of poetry. (649)

Augustine a disciple of Mallarmé *avant l'homme?* Mallarmé Augustinian *à son insu?* Both of them spokesmen for an eternal doctrine of the human spirit or an eternal spirit of the book?

Marrou's "Retractatio" frames the problem of the continuity of a *literary* and *spiritual* tradition in terms exactly convergent with those of Curtius's contemporary "Epilogue," and all the more challenging when read in that connection—not least because Curtius, as we have seen, made scant allowance for the impact of Christianity on the traditions of European literature and only in an excursus stopped to ask how "preoccupation with the Bible and the rise of Christian writing" could have affected literary theory—and then Augustine is not among the authors he canvasses.

But if Mallarmé prophesies and Mondor announces the "time of theory," in what time are we to place the author of the *De doctrina christiana*?

Read closely, those pages of Marrou's self-revision give us further reason to forgo easy distinctions of times. As presented there, Augustine's propensity for "deep" spiritual readings is a concomitant of his willingness to see scripture as a literal and readily intelligible unfolding of the whole divine history of humankind. If there is any novelty about his position, it may (to use a Mallarméan phrase beloved of Derrida) be no more than that of a particular *espacement de la lecture,* as it were the spiritual redimensioning of a text that is otherwise and always read strictly *ad litteram.* As Marrou goes on to remark, Augustine's poetical hermeneutic extends to the world of signs constituted by God's creation at large and by the unfolding of history.[79] At first glance, there could seem little to choose between it and the *explication Orphique de la terre* that is the avowed aim of Mallarmé's impossible book.[80]

For modern literary theory from Blanchot to Derrida, the Bible is the book always already there, whose absence is to come, against which "literature" continually redefines itself. To speak now with Curtius, we may say that theory has a *pre*occupation with the Bible. But what if the Bible, in the sense taken for granted by theory, were in fact absent and *yet* to come? We know that Augustine "never saw a Bible."[81] Nor did he have any word for such a thing. Suppose that scripture, instead of being there "in the beginning" like the tablets of

79. Marrou, "Retractatio," 650: "Le symbole, on l'a souvent souligné, ne réside pas seulement dans les mots, les images verbales dont use l'Écriture; il s'insère dans les réalités même dont elle évoque l'existence, soit qu'elle en décrive la création, soit qu'elle en raconte l'histoire." This aspect of early Christian hermeneutics was studied under a particular angle—that of so-called figural or typological exegesis—by Curtius's fellow Romance philologist Erich Auerbach, notably in "Figura" (1944) in *Scenes from the Drama of European Literature: Six Essays,* trans. Ralph Manheim (New York, 1959), 11–76, esp. 37–43, and *Mimesis: The Representation of Reality in Western Literature* (1946), trans. Willard R. Trask (Princeton, 1953), 73–76. For a recent reassessment of Auerbach's work, without any particular reference to Augustine, see John David Dawson, *Christian Figural Reading and the Fashioning of Identity* (Berkeley and Los Angeles, 2002). On Augustine, see R. A. Markus, *Signs and Meanings: World and Text in Ancient Christianity* (Liverpool, 1996), and Karla Pollmann, "Augustine's Hermeneutics as a Universal Discipline!?" in *Augustine and the Disciplines: From Cassiciacum to "Confessions,"* ed. Karla Pollmann and Mark Vessey (Oxford, 2005), 202–31.

80. There is of course more to be seen and said than this. Begin with Hans Blumenberg, *Die Lesbarkeit der Welt* (Frankfurt am Main, 1981), 48–50 (Augustine), 310–24 (Mallarmé). Cf. note 50 above for complementary but also partly incompatible distinctions between hermeneutics of the (biblical?) volumen and of the (biblical? legal?) codex.

81. James J. O'Donnell, "Bible," in *Augustine through the Ages: An Encyclopaedia,* ed. Allan D. Fitzgerald (Grand Rapids, Mich., 1999), 99.

the law or the books of Moses, began like the literature theorized by Derrida, "with a certain relation to its own institutionality, i.e., its fragility, its absence of specificity, *its absence of object.*"[82] Should we not then try to write a *history* of the spirit of the book?[83]

82. Jacques Derrida, "'This Strange Institution Called Literature': An Interview with Jacques Derrida," in *Jacques Derrida: Acts of Literature,* ed. Derek Attridge (London, 1992), 42 (emphasis added). Derrida has just spoken of his attraction to "texts which are very sensitive to [the] crisis of the literary institution (which is more than, and other than, a crisis), to what is called 'the end of literature,' from Mallarmé to Blanchot." The interview, conducted in April 1989, is contemporary with Derrida's periphrases on Augustine's *Confessions,* composed between January 1989 and April 1990, published as "Circumfession" in Bennington and Derrida, *Jacques Derrida;* see also Mark Vessey, "Reading Like Angels: Derrida and Augustine on the Book (for a History of Literature)," in Caputo and Scanlon, *Augustine and Postmodernism,* 173–211.

83. Cf. Blanchot, "L'absence du livre," in *L'entretien infini* (Paris, 1969), translated by Susan Hanson as *The Infinite Conversation* (Minneapolis, 1993), 427: "The book begins with the Bible in which the logos is inscribed as law. Here the book attains its unsurpassable meaning, including what exceeds its bounds on all sides and cannot be overstepped. The Bible refers language to its origin: whether it be written or spoken, this language forms the basis for the theological era that opens and endures for as long as biblical space and time endure. The Bible not only offers us the preeminent model of the book, a forever unparalleled example, it also encompasses all books, no matter how alien they are to biblical revelation, knowledge, prophecy, and proverbs, because it holds in it *the spirit of the book*" (emphasis mine, translation slightly modified). This essay is the last in a volume attributed preposthumously by Blanchot (435) to "all those to whom falls the task of maintaining and prolonging the exigency to which I believe these texts . . . ceaselessly seek to respond, even unto *the absence of the book* they designate in vain." For a brief for the kind of history-in-theory that I am attempting here, see Michel Beaujour, "Genus Universum," *Glyph* 7 (1980): 15–31. My essay has been encouraged by—though alas cannot be attributed to—all those colleagues and conversation partners who keep the church fathers and the founders of theory on the same shelf, especially Elizabeth Clark and Eugene Vance.

BIBLIOGRAPHY

Adamson, Peter, Han Baltussen, and M. W. F. Stone, eds. *Philosophy, Science, and Exegesis in Greek, Arabic, and Latin Commentaries.* London, 2004.

Adkin, Neil. *Jerome on Virginity: A Commentary on the "Libellus de virginitate servanda" (Letter 22).* Cambridge, 2003.

Alexander, Loveday. "The Living Voice: Scepticism towards the Written Word in Early Christian and in Graeco-Roman Texts." In *The Bible in Three Dimensions: Essays in Celebration of Forty Years of Biblical Studies in the University of Sheffield,* ed. David J. A. Clines, Stephen E. Fowl, and Stanley E. Porter, 221–47. Sheffield, 1990.

Amélineau, E., trans. *Monuments pour servir à l'histoire de l'Égypte chrétienne au IVe et Ve siècles.* Vol. 3, *Histoire des monastères de la Basse-Égypte: Vies des saints Paul, Antoine, Macaire, Maxime et Domèce, Jean Le Nain, etc.* Annales du Musée Guimet 25. Paris, 1894.

Anderson, Alan Orr, and Marjorie Ogilvie Anderson, eds. and trans. *Adomnan's Life of Columba.* Rev. ed. Oxford, 1991.

Ando, Clifford. "The Palladium and the Pentateuch: Towards a Sacred Topography of the Later Roman Empire." *Phoenix* 55 (2001): 369–85.

Anson, John. "The Female Transvestite in Early Monasticism: Origin and Development of a Motif." *Viator: Medieval and Renaissance Studies* 5 (1974): 1–32.

Antier, Jean-Jacques. *Lérins: L'île sainte de la Côte d'Azur.* Paris, 1988.

Antin, Paul. "Autour du songe de Saint Jérôme." *Revue des études latines* 41 (1963): 350–77.

Arce, Javier. "Imperial Funerals of the Later Roman Empire: Change and Continuity." In *Rituals of Power: From Late Antiquity to the Middle Ages,* ed. Frans Theuws and Janet L. Nelson, 115–29. Leiden, 2000.

Arévalo, Faustino, ed. *M. Aureli Clementis Prudenti Carmina.* 2 vols. Rome: 1788, 1789.

Armstrong, A. H. "The Way and the Ways: Religious Tolerance and Intolerance in the Fourth Century A.D." *VC* 38 (1984): 1–17.

L'art copte en Égypte: 2000 ans de Christianisme; Exposition présentée à l'Institut du monde arabe, Paris, du 15 mai au 3 septembre 2000 et au Musée de l'Ephèbe au Cap d'Agde, du 30 septembre 2000 au 7 janvier 2001. Exh. cat. Paris, 2000.

Athanassiadi, Polymnia. "The Creation of Orthodoxy in Neoplatonism." In *Philosophy and*

Power in the Graeco-Roman World: Essays in Honour of Miriam Griffin, ed. Gillian Clark and Tessa Rajak, 271–91. Oxford, 2002.

Atiya, Aziz S., ed. *The Coptic Encyclopedia.* 8 vols. New York, 1991.

Atkins, E. M., and R. Dodaro, eds. *Augustine: Political Writings.* Cambridge, 2001.

Atkinson, John E. "Turning Crises into Drama: The Management of Epidemics in Classical Antiquity." *Acta Classica* 44 (2001): 35–52.

Aubin, Melissa. "Reversing Romance? The *Acts of Thecla* and the Ancient Novel." In *Ancient Fiction and Early Christian Narrative,* ed. Ronald F. Hock, J. Bradley Chance, and Judith Perkins, 257–72. Atlanta, 1998.

Auerbach, Erich. *Mimesis: The Representation of Reality in Western Literature.* Trans. Willard R. Trask. Princeton, 1953.

———. "Figura." In Erich Auerbach, *Scenes from the Drama of European Literature: Six Essays,* trans. Ralph Manheim, 11–76. New York, 1959.

———. *Literary Language and Its Public in Late Latin Antiquity and in the Middle Ages.* Trans. Ralph Mannheim. Princeton, 1965.

Austin, Lloyd James. "Mallarmé et le rêve du 'Livre.'" In Lloyd James Austin, *Essais sur Mallarmé,* ed. Malcolm Bowie, 66–91. Manchester, 1995.

Bagnall, Roger S. *Currency and Inflation in Fourth-Century Egypt.* Chico. Calif., 1985.

———. *Egypt in Late Antiquity.* Princeton, 1993.

Baker-Brian, N. "… *quaedam disputationes Adimanti:* Reading the Manichaean Biblical Discordance in Augustine's *contra Adimantum.*" *Augustinian Studies* 34, no. 2 (2003): 175–96.

Baldini Lippolis, Isabella. *L'oreficeria nell'impero di Costantinopoli tra IV e VII secolo.* Bari, 1999.

Baldovin, John F. *The Urban Character of Christian Worship: The Origins, Development, and Meaning of Stational Liturgy.* Rome, 1987.

Barnes, Michel René. "The Fourth Century as Trinitarian Canon." In *Christian Origins: Theology, Rhetoric, and Community,* ed. Lewis Ayres and Gareth Jones, 47–67. London, 1998.

Barnes, Timothy D. "Sossianus Hierocles and the Antecedents of the Great Persecution." *Harvard Studies in Classical Philology* 80 (1976): 239–52.

———. *Athanasius and Constantius: Theology and Politics in the Constantinian Empire.* Cambridge, Mass., 1993.

Barone Adesi, Giorgio. *L'età della "Lex Dei."* Naples, 1992.

Bartelink, Gerhard J. M. "Die Rolle der Bibel in den asketischen Kreisen des vierten und fünften Jahrhunderts." In *The Impact of Scripture in Early Christianity,* ed. J. den Boeft and M. L. van Poll-van de Lisdonk, 27–38. Leiden, 1999.

———, ed. *Palladio: La storia lausiaca.* [Milan], 1985.

Barthes, Roland. *Le degré zéro de l'écriture.* Paris, 1953. Translated by Annette Lavers and Colin Smith as *Writing Degree Zero* (New York, 1968).

———. *Image, Music, Text.* Trans. Stephen Heath. New York, 1977.

Barton, Carlin A. *The Sorrows of the Ancient Romans: The Gladiator and the Monster.* Princeton, 1993.

Bastiaensen, Anton A. R., ed. *Vita di Martino, Vita di Ilarione, In memoria di Paola.* [Milan], 1975.

Beaujour, Michel. "Genus Universum." *Glyph* 7 (1980): 15–31.

Bell, David N., trans. *Besa: The Life of Shenoute.* Kalamazoo, Mich., 1983.

Bem, Jeanne. *Désir et savoir dans l'oeuvre de Flaubert: Étude de la "Tentation de Saint Antoine."* Neuchâtel, 1979.

Bénazeth, Dominique. "Les Coutumes Funéraires." In *L'Art copte en Égypte: 2000 ans de Christianisme; Exposition présentée à l'Institut du monde arabe, Paris, du 15 mai au 3 septembre 2000 et au Musée de l'Ephèbe au Cap d'Agde, du 30 septembre 2000 au 7 janvier 2001,* 110–11. Exh. cat. Paris, 2000.

Bénichou, Paul. *The Consecration of the Writer, 1750–1830.* Trans. Mark K. Jensen. Lincoln, Neb., 1999.

Benoit, Eric. *Mallarmé et le mystère du "Livre."* Paris, 1998.

Bensly, Robert L., J. Rendel Harris, and F. Crawford Birkitt. *The Four Gospels in Syriac Transcribed from the Sinaitic Palimpsest.* Cambridge, 1894.

Bersani, Leo. *The Death of Stéphane Mallarmé.* Cambridge, 1982.

Bilabel, Friedrich, and Adolf Grohmann. "Studien zu Kyprian dem Magier." In *Griechische, koptische und arabische Texte zur Religion und religiösen Literatur in Ägyptens Spätzeit,* ed. Friedrich Bilabel and Adolf Grohmann, 32–325. Heidelberg, 1934.

Biondi, Biondo. *Il diritto Romano Cristiano.* 3 vols. Milan, 1952–54.

Blanchard, Alain. "Sur le Milieu d'Origine du papyrus Bodmer de Ménandre." *Chronique d'Égypte* 66 (1991): 211–20.

Blanchot, Maurice. *Faux pas.* Paris, 1943. English translation under the same title by Charlotte Mandell (Stanford, 2001).

———. *La part du feu.* Paris, 1949.

———. *Thomas l'obscur.* Nouvelle version. Paris, 1950. Translated by Robert Lamberton as *Thomas the Obscure* (Barrytown, N.Y., 1988).

———. *L'espace littéraire.* Paris, 1955. Translated by Ann Smock as *The Space of Literature* (Lincoln, Neb., 1982).

———. *Le livre à venir.* Paris, 1959.

———. "L'absence de livre." In *L'entretien infini,* 422–34. Paris, 1969. Translated by Susan Hanson as *The Infinite Conversation* (Minneapolis, 1993).

Blöbaum, Anke-Ilona. "Bemerkungen zu einem koptischen Brief: Das Ostrakon Louvre N 686." In *Ägypten und Nubien in Spätantiker und christlicher Zeit: Akten des 6. Internationalen Koptologenkongresses, Münster, 20.–26. Juli 1996,* ed. Stephen Emmel, Martin Krause, Siegfried G. Richter, and Sofia Schaten, 2:249–56. Wiesbaden, 1999.

Bloch, R. Howard. *God's Plagiarist: Being an Account of the Fabulous Industry and Irregular Commerce of the Abbé Migne.* Chicago, 1994.

Blumenberg, Hans. *Die Lesbarkeit der Welt.* Frankfurt am Main, 1981.

Bober, Harry. "On the Illumination of the Glazier Codex: A Contribution to Early Coptic Art, and Its Relation to Hiberno-Saxon Interlace." In *Homage to a Bookman: Essays on Manuscripts, Books and Printing Written for Hans P. Kraus on His 60th Birthday,* ed. Hellmut Lehmann-Haupt, 31–49. Berlin, 1967.

Boeft, J. den, and M. L. van Poll-van de Lisdonk, eds. *The Impact of Scripture in Early Christianity.* Leiden, 1999.

Booker, Courtney M. "The *Codex Purpureus* and Its Role as an *Imago Regis* in Late Antiquity." In *Studies in Latin Literature and Roman History,* ed. Carl Deroux, 8:441–77. Brussels, 1997.

Boter, Gerard. *The Encheiridion of Epictetus and Its Three Christian Adaptations: Transmission and Critical Editions.* Leiden, 1999.

Boud'hors, Anne. "L'Écriture, la langue et les livres." In *L'Art copte en Égypte: 2000 ans de christianisme; Exposition présentée à l'Institut du monde arabe, Paris, du 15 mai au 3 septembre 2000 et au Musée de l'Ephèbe au Cap d'Agde, du 30 septembre 2000 au 7 janvier 2001,* 64–65. Exh. cat. Paris, 2000.

Boud'hors, Anne, and Chantal Heurtel. "The Coptic Ostraca from the Tomb of Amenemope." *Egyptian Archaeology* 20 (2002): 7–9.

Bousset, Wilhelm. "Manichäisches in der Thomasakten." *Zeitschrift für die neutestamentliche Wissenschaft und die Kunde der älteren Kirche* 18 (1917–18): 1–39.

Boyarin, Daniel. *Carnal Israel: Reading Sex in Talmudic Culture.* Berkeley and Los Angeles, 1993.

——. "A Tale of Two Synods: Nicaea, Yavneh, and the Making of Orthodox Judaism." *Exemplaria* 12 (2000): 21–62.

——. "The Diadoche of the Rabbis; or, Judah the Patriarch at Yavneh." In *Jewish Culture and Society under the Christian Roman Empire,* ed. Richard Kalmin and Seth Schwartz, 285–318. Leuven, 2003.

——. "The Yavneh-Cycle of the Stammaim and the Invention of the Rabbis." In *Creation and Composition: The Contribution of the Bavli Redactors (Stammaim) to the Aggada,* ed. Jeffrey L. Rubenstein, 256–309. Tübingen, 2005.

——. "Hellenism in Rabbinic Babylonia." In *The Cambridge Companion to Rabbinic Literature,* ed. Charlotte Fonrobert and Martin Jaffee. Cambridge, forthcoming.

Boyd, Susan A. "A 'Metropolitan' Treasure from a Church in the Provinces: An Introduction to the Study of the Sion Treasure." In *Ecclesiastical Silver Plate in Sixth-Century Byzantium,* ed. Susan A. Boyd and Marlia Mundell Mango, 5–37. Washington, D.C., 1992.

——. "Art in the Service of the Liturgy: Byzantine Silver Plate." In *Heaven on Earth: Art and the Church in Byzantium,* ed. Linda Safran, 152–85. University Park, Pa., 1998.

Boyd, Susan A., and Marlia Mundell Mango, eds. *Ecclesiastical Silver Plate in Sixth-Century Byzantium.* Washington, D.C., 1992.

Bozóky, Edina. "Saints, Legends, and Charms." In *Telling Tales: Medieval Narratives and the Folk Tradition,* ed. Francesca Canadé Sauterman, Diana Chonchado, and Giuseppe C. Di Scipio, 173–88. New York, 1998.

Brakke, David. *Athanasius and Asceticism*. Baltimore, 1995.

Brock, Sebastian P., and Susan Ashbrook Harvey, trans. *Holy Women of the Syrian Orient*. Berkeley and Los Angeles, 1987.

Broek, Roelof van den. "Popular Religious Practices and Ecclesiastical Policies in the Early Church." In *Official and Popular Religion: Analysis of a Theme for Religious Studies*, ed. Pieter H. Vrijhof and Jacques Waardenburg, 11–54. The Hague, 1979.

Brooks, Ernest W., ed. *John of Ephesus: Lives of the Eastern Saints. Patrologia Orientalis* 17.1, 18.4, and 19.2. 3 vols. Paris, 1923.

Brown, Michelle P. *The Lindisfarne Gospels: Society, Spirituality, and the Scribe*. London, 2003.

Brown, Peter. *Augustine of Hippo: A Biography*. London, 1967. Rev. ed. 2000.

———. "The Diffusion of Manichaeism in the Roman Empire." *Journal of Roman Studies* 59 (1969): 92–103.

———. *The Body and Society: Men, Women, and Sexual Renunciation in Early Christianity*. New York, 1988.

———. "Images as a Substitute for Writing." In *East and West: Modes of Communication*, ed. Evangelos Chrysos and Ian Wood, 15–46. Leiden, 1999.

Brown, T. Julian, ed. *The Stonyhurst Gospel of Saint John*. Oxford, 1969.

Bruce, Lorne D. "Diocletian, the Proconsul Iulianus, and the Manichaeans." In *Studies in Latin Literature and Roman History*, ed. Carl Deroux, 3:336–47. Brussels, 1983.

Bruyn, Theodore de. "Ambivalence within a Totalizing Discourse: Augustine's Sermons on the Sack of Rome." *JECS* 1 (1993): 405–21.

Buchthal, Hugo, and Otto Kurz. *A Hand List of Illuminated Oriental Christian Manuscripts*. London, 1942.

Buckton, David, ed. *Byzantium: Treasures of Byzantine Art and Culture from British Collections*. London, 1994.

Burnaby, John. "The 'Retractations' of St Augustine: Self-criticism or Apologia?" In *Augustinus Magister*, 1:85–92. Congrès international augustinien. Paris, 1954.

Burris, Catherine. "Imagining Thecla: Rhetorical Strategies in Severus of Antioch's 97th Cathedral Homily." In *Papers Presented at the Fourteenth International Conference on Patristic Studies Held in Oxford, 2003*. Leuven, forthcoming.

Burris, Catherine, and Lucas Van Rompay. "Thecla in Syriac Christianity: Preliminary Observations." *Hugoye* 5, no. 2 (July 2002). http://syrcom.cua.edu/Hugoye/Vol5No2/HV5N2BurrisVanRompay.html.

Burrus, Virginia. *Chastity as Autonomy: Women in the Stories of the Apocryphal Acts*. Lewiston, Maine, 1987.

———. *The Making of a Heretic: Gender, Authority, and the Priscillianist Controversy*. Berkeley and Los Angeles, 1995.

———. *"Begotten Not Made": Conceiving Manhood in Late Antiquity*. Stanford, 2000.

Burton, Philip, trans. *Augustine: The Confessions*. London, 2001.

Burton-Christie, Douglas. *The Word in the Desert: Scripture and the Quest for Holiness in Early Christian Monasticism*. Oxford, 1993.

————. "Oral Culture and Biblical Interpretation in Early Egyptian Monasticism." In *Papers Presented at the Twelfth International Conference on Patristic Studies Held in Oxford, 1995,* ed. Elizabeth A. Livingstone, 2:144–150. Studia Patristica 30. Leuven, 1997.

Buschhausen, Helmut. *Die spätrömischen Metallscrinia und frühchristlichen Reliquiare.* Vienna, 1971.

Butler, Cuthbert. *The Lausiac History of Palladius.* 2 vols. Texts and Studies 6. Cambridge, 1898, 1904.

Byzance: L'art byzantin dans les collections publiques françaises: Musée du Louvre, 3 novembre 1992–1er février 1993. Exh. cat. Paris, 1992.

Calinescu, Matei. *Rereading.* New Haven, 1993.

Cameron, Alan. "The Date of Macrobius' *Saturnalia.*" *Journal of Roman Studies* 56 (1966): 25–38.

Cameron, Averil. *Christianity and the Rhetoric of Empire: The Development of a Christian Discourse.* Berkeley and Los Angeles, 1991.

Campbell, James M., and Martin R. P. McGuire, eds. *The Confessions of St Augustine, Books I–IX (Selections).* Englewood Cliffs, N.J., 1931. Reprint, Chicago, 1984.

Canfora, Luciano. *The Vanished Library.* Trans. Martin Ryle. Berkeley and Los Angeles, 1987.

Caputo, John D., and Michael J. Scanlon, eds. *Augustine and Postmodernism: "Confessions" and "Circumfession."* Bloomington, Ind., 2005.

Castelli, Elizabeth. "'I Will Make Mary Male': Pieties of the Body and Gender Transformation of Christian Women in Late Antiquity." In *BodyGuards: The Cultural Politics of Gender Ambiguity,* ed. Julia Epstein and Kristina Straub, 29–49. New York, 1991.

Cavallo, Guglielmo. "Testo e immagine: Una frontiera ambigua." In *Testo e immagine nell'alto medioevo,* 1:31–62. Settimane di studio del centro Italiano di studi sull'alto Medioevo 41.1. Spoleto, 1994.

————. "Between *Volumen* and Codex: Reading in the Roman World." In *A History of Reading in the West,* ed. Guglielmo Cavallo and Roger Chartier, trans. Lydia G. Cochrane, 64–89. Cambridge, 1999.

Caws, Mary Ann, ed. *Stéphane Mallarmé: Selected Poetry and Prose.* New York, 1982.

Certeau, Michel de. *The Writing of History.* Trans. Tom Conley. New York, 1988. Originally published as *L'écriture de l'histoire* (Paris, 1975).

Chadwick, Henry. *The Church in Ancient Society: From Galilee to Gregory the Great.* Oxford, 2001.

————, trans. *Origen: Contra Celsum.* Cambridge, 1953.

————, trans. *Saint Augustine: Confessions.* Oxford, 1992.]

Chessex, Jacques. *Flaubert, ou, le désert en abime.* Paris, 1991.

Christie, Neil. "Lost Glories? Rome at the End of Empire." In *Ancient Rome: The Archaeology of the Eternal City,* ed. Jon Coulston and Hazel Dodge, 306–31. Oxford, 2000.

Clark, Elizabeth A. *Jerome, Chrysostom, and Friends.* Lewiston, Maine, 1979.

————. *The Origenist Controversy: The Cultural Construction of an Early Christian Debate.* Princeton, 1992.

———. *Reading Renunciation: Asceticism and Scripture in Early Christianity.* Princeton, 1999.

———. *History, Theory, Text: Historians and the Linguistic Turn.* Cambridge, Mass., 2004.

———, trans. *The Life of Melania the Younger.* New York, 1984.

Clark, Elizabeth A., and Diane F. Hatch, eds. *The Golden Bough, the Oaken Cross: The Virgilian Cento of Faltonia Betitia Proba.* Chico, Calif., 1981.

Clark, Gillian. "Adam's Womb and the Salty Sea." *Proceedings of the Cambridge Philological Society* 42 (1996): 89–105.

———. "Translate into Greek: Porphyry of Tyre and the New Barbarians." In *Constructing Identities in Late Antiquity,* ed. Richard Miles, 112–32. London, 1999.

———. "Philosophic *Lives* and the Philosophic Life." In *Greek Biography and Panegyric in Late Antiquity,* ed. Tomas Hägg and Philip Rousseau, with the assistance of Christian Høgel, 29–51. Berkeley and Los Angeles, 2000.

———. "Pastoral Care: Town and Country in Late-Antique Preaching." In *Urban Centers and Rural Contexts in Late Antiquity,* ed. Thomas S. Burns and John W. Eadie, 265–84. East Lansing, Mich., 2001.

———. "City of God(s): Augustine's Virgil." *Proceedings of the Virgil Society* 25 (2004): 83–94.

———. "Pilgrims and Foreigners: Augustine on Travelling Home." In *Travel, Communication, and Geography in Late Antiquity: Sacred and Profane,* ed. Linda Ellis and Frank Kidner, 149–158. Aldershot, 2004.

———, trans. *Porphyry: On Abstinence from Killing Animals.* London, 2000.

Clark, Timothy. *Derrida, Heidegger, Blanchot: Sources of Derrida's Notion and Practice of Literature.* Cambridge, 1992.

Claussen, M. A. "*Peregrinatio* and *peregrini* in Augustine's *City of God.*" *Traditio* 46 (1991): 33–75.

Cohen, Adam S. *The Uta Codex: Art, Philosophy, and Reform in Eleventh-Century Germany.* University Park, Pa., 2000.

Cohen, Aryeh. *Rereading Talmud: Gender, Law, and the Poetics of Sugyot.* Atlanta, 1998.

Conti, Roberto. *Il Tesoro: Guida alla conoscenza del Tesoro del Duomo di Modena.* 2d ed. Monza, 1983.

Conti, Roberto, and Carlo Bertelli. *Monza: Il duomo e i suoi tesori.* Milan, 1988.

Conybeare, Catherine. *Paulinus Noster: Self and Symbols in the Letters of Paulinus of Nola.* Oxford, 2000.

Conybeare, Frederick C., ed. *The Apology and Acts of Apollonius and Other Monuments of Early Christianity.* London, 1894.

———, trans. *Philostratus: Life of Apollonius of Tyana.* 2 vols. Cambridge, Mass., 1912.

Cook, Bradford, trans. *Mallarmé: Selected Prose Poems, Essays, and Letters.* Baltimore, 1956.

Cooper, Kate. *The Virgin and the Bride: Idealized Womanhood in Late Antiquity.* Cambridge, Mass., 1996.

Copeland, Rita. "Pre-modern Intellectual Biography." In *The Public Intellectual,* ed. Helen Small, 40–61. Oxford, 2002.

Coquin, René-Georges. "Le catalogue de la bibiothèque de couvent de Saint Élie «Du Rocher» (Ostracon IFAO 13315)." *Bulletin de l'Institut Français d'Archéologie Orientale du Caire* 75 (1975): 207–39.

Corcoran, Simon. *The Empire of the Tetrarchs: Imperial Pronouncements and Government AD 284–324.* Oxford, 1996.

Cotsonis, John A. *Byzantine Figural Processional Crosses.* Washington, D.C., 1994. Exh. cat., Dumbarton Oaks, September 23, 1994–January 29, 1995.

Cramer, Frederick H. "The Expulsion of Astrologers from Ancient Rome." *Classica et Mediaevalia* 12 (1951): 21–28.

——. *Astrology in Roman Law and Politics.* Philadelphia, 1954.

Cribiore, Raffaella. *Writing, Teachers, and Students in Graeco-Roman Egypt.* Atlanta, 1996.

——. "Greek and Coptic Education in Late Antique Egypt." In *Ägypten und Nubien in Spätantiker und christlicher Zeit: Akten des 6. Internationalen Koptologenkongresses, Münster, 20.–26. Juli 1996,* ed. Stephen Emmel, Martin Krause, Siegfried G. Richter, and Sofia Schaten, 2:279–86. Wiesbaden, 1999.

Crum, Walter E. *Coptic Ostraca from the Collection of the Egypt Exploration Fund, the Cairo Museum and Others.* London, 1902.

——. "Inscriptions from Shenoute's Monastery." *Journal of Theological Studies* 5 (1904): 564–69.

——. *A Coptic Dictionary.* Oxford, 1939.

Curtius, Ernst Robert. *European Literature and the Latin Middle Ages.* Trans. Willard R. Trask. Princeton, 1953.

Cutler, Anthony. "Prolegomena to the Craft of Ivory Carving in Late Antiquity and the Early Middle Ages." In *Artistes, artisans et production artistique au Moyen Age,* ed. Xavier Barral I Altet, 2:431–71. Paris, 1987.

——. "Barberiniana: Notes on the Making, Content, and Provenance of Louvre, OA. 9603." In *Tesserae: Festschrift für Josef Engemann, Jahrbuch für Antike und Christentum, Ergänzungsband* 18 (1991): 329–39. Reprinted in his *Late Antique and Byzantine Ivory Carving* (Aldershot, 1998).

Dagron, Gilbert. "La vie ancienne de Marcel l'Acémète." *Analecta Bollandiana* 86 (1968): 271–321.

——. *Vie et miracles de sainte Thècle: Texte grec, traduction et commentaire.* Brussels, 1978.

——. *Emperor and Priest: The Imperial Office in Byzantium.* Trans. Jean Birrell. Cambridge, 2003.

Dalton, O. M. *Catalogue of the Ivory Carvings of the Christian Era.* London, 1909.

Davies, Stevan L. *The Revolt of the Widows: The Social World of the Apocryphal Acts.* Carbondale, Ill. 1980.

Davis, Stephen J. *The Cult of St. Thecla: A Tradition of Women's Piety in Late Antiquity.* Oxford, 2001.

——. "Crossed Texts, Crossed Sex: Intertextuality and Gender in Early Christian Legends of Holy Women Disguised as Men." *JECS* 10 (2002): 1–36.

Dawson, David. *Christian Figural Reading and the Fashioning of Identity.* Berkeley and Los Angeles, 2002.

Dawson, Doyne. *Cities of the Gods: Communist Utopias in Greek Thought.* New York, 1992.

Day, Joseph W. "Epigram and Reader: Generic Force as (Re-)Activation of Ritual." In *Matrices of Genre: Authors, Canons and Society,* ed. Mary Depew and Dirk Obbink, 37–57. Cambridge, Mass., 2000.

Derda, Tomasz. *Deir el-Naqlun: The Greek Papyri (P. Naqlun I).* Warsaw, 1995.

Derrida, Jacques. *Of Grammatology.* Trans. Gayatri Spivak. Baltimore, 1974.

———. "The Double Session." In *Dissemination,* trans. Barbara Johnson, 173–286. Chicago, 1981.

———. "'This Strange Institution Called Literature': An Interview with Jacques Derrida." In *Jacques Derrida: Acts of Literature,* ed. Derek Attridge, 33–75. London, 1992.

———. "Circumfession." In *Jacques Derrida,* ed. Geoffrey Bennington and Jacques Derrida, trans. G. Bennington. Chicago, 1993.

Deun, Peter van, ed. *Hagiographica Cypria.* Turnhout, 1993.

Dickie, Matthew W. *Magic and Magicians in the Greco-Roman World.* New York, 2001.

Digeser, Elizabeth DePalma. *The Making of a Christian Empire: Lactantius and Rome.* Ithaca, N.Y., 2000.

Dinkler, Erich, and Erika Dinkler von Schubert. "Kreuz." In *Lexikon der christlichen Ikonographie,* 8 vols., ed. Engelbert Kirschbaum. Vol. 2, cols. 562–90. Rome, 1970.

Dobschütz, Ernst von. *Christusbilder: Untersuchungen zur christlichen Legende.* Leipzig, 1899.

Dolbeau, François. "Les titres des sermons d'Augustin." In *Titres et articulations du texte dans les oeuvres antiques: Actes du Colloque international de Chantilly, 13–15 décembre 1994,* ed. J.-C. Fredouille, 447–68. Paris, 1977.

Dölger, Franz-Joseph. "Ein christlicher Brotstempel aus Karthago?" *Antike und Christentum* 1 (1929): 20–21.

Dombart, Bernardus, and Alfonsus Kalb, eds. *Sancti Aurelii Augustini De civitate Dei.* 2 vols. *CCSL* 47–48. Turnhout, 1955.

Doresse, Jean. "Les reliures des manuscrits gnostiques coptes découverts à Khénoboskion." *Revue d'Égyptologie* 13 (1961): 27–49.

Dostálová, Ruzena. "Der 'Bücherkatalog' Pap.Wess.Gr.Prag.I.13 im Rahmen der Nachricthen über Bücher aus Frühchristlicher Zeit." *Byzantina* 13 (1985): 537–47.

Drake, H. A. "Lambs into Lions: Explaining Early Christian Intolerance." *Past and Present* 153 (November 1996): 3–36.

Dumbarton Oaks. *Handbook of the Byzantine Collection.* Washington, D.C., 1967.

Duval, Y.-M. "Les premiers rapports de Paulin de Nole avec Jérôme." *Studi Tardoantichi* 7 (1989): 177–216.

Dyson, R. W., trans. *Augustine: The City of God against the Pagans.* Cambridge, 1998.

Eco, Umberto. *Il nome della rosa.* Milan, 1980.

Edelstein, Emma J., and Ludwig Edelstein. *Asclepius: A Collection and Interpretation of the Testimonies.* Baltimore, 1945. Reprint New York, 1975.

Edwards, Mark. "The Flowering of Latin Apologetic: Lactantius and Arnobius." In *Apologetics in the Roman Empire,* ed. Mark Edwards, Martin Goodman, and Simon Price, 197–221. Oxford, 1999.

———, trans. *Neoplatonic Saints: The Lives of Plotinus and Proclus by Their Students.* Liverpool, 2000.

Edwards, Mark, Martin Goodman, and Simon Price, eds. *Apologetics in the Roman Empire.* Oxford, 1999.

Ehrman, Bart D. *The Orthodox Corruption of Scripture: The Effect of Early Christological Controversies on the Text of the New Testament.* New York and Oxford, 1993.

———. "The Text as Window: New Testament Manuscripts and the Social History of Early Christianity." In *The Text of the New Testament in Contemporary Research: Essays on the Status Quaestionis,* ed. Bart D. Ehrman and Michael W. Holmes, 361–79. Grand Rapids, Mich., 1995.

———. "The Text of the Gospels at the End of the Second Century." In *Codex Bezae: Studies from the Lunel Colloquium, June 1994,* ed. D. C. Parker and C.-B. Amphoux, 95–122. Leiden, 1996.

Ehrman, Bart D., and Mark A. Plunkett. "The Angel and the Agony: The Textual Problem of Luke 22:43–44." *Catholic Biblical Quarterly* 45 (1983): 401–16.

Elliott, J. K. *The Apocryphal New Testament: A Collection of Apocryphal Christian Literature in an English Translation.* Oxford, 1993.

Elm, Susanna. "An Alleged Book-Theft in Fourth-Century Egypt: P.Lips. 43." *Papers of the Ninth International Conference on Patristic Studies, Oxford, 1983,* ed. Elizabeth A. Livingstone, 209–15. Studia Patristica 18.2. Kalamazoo, Mich., 1989.

———. *Virgins of God: The Making of Asceticism in Late Antiquity.* Oxford, 1994.

Elsner, Jaś. *Imperial Rome and Christian Triumph.* Oxford, 1998.

Emmel, Stephen, Martin Krause, Siegfried G. Richter, and Sofia Schaten, eds. *Ägypten und Nubien in Spätantiker und christlicher Zeit: Akten des 6. Internationalen Koptologenkongresses, Münster, 20.–26. Juli 1996.* Wiesbaden, 1999.

Epp, Eldon J. *The Theological Tendency of Codex Bezae Cantabrigiensis in Acts.* Cambridge, 1966.

Eustratiades, Sophronios. *Hagiologion tēs Orthodoxou Ekklēsias.* Athens, 1995.

Evans, Helen C., Melanie Holcomb, and Robert Hallmann. *The Arts of Byzantium.* New York, 2001.

Everett, Nicholas. *Literacy in Lombard Italy c. 568–774.* Cambridge, 2003.

Fears, J. Rufus. "The Cult of Jupiter and Roman Imperial Ideology." *ANRW* 2, no. 17.1 (1981): 3–141.

Febvre, Lucien, and Henri Jean Martin. *L'apparition du livre.* Paris, 1958. Translated by David Gerard as *The Coming of the Book* (London, 1990).

Fee, Gordon D. *The First Epistle to the Corinthians.* Grand Rapids, Mich., 1987.

Ffrench, Patrick. *The Time of Theory: A History of Tel Quel (1960–1983).* Oxford, 1995.

Fillitz, Hermann. "Habens tabulas eburneas: Der Elfenbeinschmuck des Lorscher Evangeliars." In *Das Lorscher Evangeliar: Eine Zimelie der Buchkunst des abendländischen Frühmittelalters,* ed. Hermann Schefers, 103–10. Darmstadt, 2000.

Finkelstein, David, and Alistair McCleery, eds. *The Book History Reader.* London, 2002.

Firatli, Nezih. "Un trésor du VIe s. trouvé à Kumluca, en Lycie." Akten des VII. Internationalen Kongresses für christliche Archäologie, Trier 1965. *Studi di antichità cristiana* 27 (1969): 523–25.

———. *La sculpture byzantine figurée au Musée Archéologique d'Istanbul.* Paris, 1990.

Flint, Valerie I. J. *The Rise of Magic in Early Medieval Europe.* Princeton, 1991.

———. "The Demonisation of Magic and Sorcery in Late Antiquity: Christian Redefinitions of Pagan Religions." In *Witchcraft and Magic in Europe,* vol. 2, *Ancient Greece and Rome,* ed. Bengt Ankarloo and Stuart Clark, 277–348. Philadelphia, 1999.

Fontaine, Jacques. "La femme dans la poésie de Prudence." *Revue des études latines* 47 (1970): 55–83. Reprinted in his *Études sur la poésie latine tardive d'Ausone à Prudence* (Paris, 1980), 415–43.

Foppens, Jean-François. *Bibliotheca belgica.* 2 vols. Brussels, 1739.

Foucault, Michel. *Les mots et les choses: Une archéologie des sciences humaines.* Paris, 1966. Translated as *The Order of Things: An Archaeology of the Human Sciences* (New York, 1970).

———. "Fantasia of the Library." In *Language, Counter-Memory, Practice: Selected Essays and Interviews,* ed. and trans. Donald F. Bouchard, 87–109. Ithaca, N.Y., 1977.

———. *The History of Sexuality.* Trans. Robert Hurley. 3 vols. New York, 1980.

———. "Of Other Spaces." Trans. Jay Miskowiec. *Diacritics* 16, no. 1 (1986): 22–27.

Fournet, Jean-Luc. "Une éthopée de Caïn dans le Codex des Visions de la Fondation Bodmer." *ZPE* 92 (1992): 252–66.

———. *Hellénisme dans l'Égypte du VIe siècle: La Bibliothèque et l'oeuvre de Dioscore d'Aphrodité.* Cairo, 1999.

Fowler, Don. "The Virgil Commentary of Servius." In *The Cambridge Companion to Virgil,* ed. Charles A. Martindale, 73–78. Cambridge, 1997.

———. "Criticism as Commentary and Commentary as Criticism in the Age of Electronic Media." In *Commentaries-Kommentare,* ed. Glenn W. Most, 426–42. Göttingen, 1999.

Frank, Georgia. *The Memory of the Eyes: Pilgrims to Living Saints in Christian Late Antiquity.* Berkeley and Los Angeles, 2000.

Frankfurter, David. "Ritual Expertise in Roman Egypt and the Problem of the Category 'Magician.'" In *Envisioning Magic: A Princeton Seminar and Symposium,* ed. Peter Schäfer and Hans G. Kippenberg, 115–35. Leiden, 1997.

———. *Religion in Roman Egypt: Assimilation and Resistance.* Princeton, 1998.

———. "'Things Unbefitting Christians': Violence and Christianization in Fifth-Century Panopolis." *JECS* 8 (2000): 273–95.

———. "The Perils of Love: Magic and Countermagic in Coptic Egypt." *Journal for the History of Sexuality* 10 (2001): 480–500.

Frazer, Margaret E. "Early Byzantine Silver Book Covers." In *Ecclesiastical Silver Plate in*

Sixth-Century Byzantium, ed. Susan A. Boyd and Marlia Mundell Mango, 71–76. Washington, D.C., 1992.

Fredouille, Jean-Claude, ed. *Titres et articulations du texte dans les oeuvres antiques: Actes du Colloque international de Chantilly, 13–15 décembre 1994.* Paris, 1977.

———. *Augustin d'Hippone: Sermons sur la chute de Rome.* Turnhout, 2004.

Frend, W. H. C. *Martyrdom and Persecution in the Early Church: A Study of a Conflict from the Maccabees to Donatus.* Oxford, 1965.

Gaborit-Chopin, Danielle. *Ivoires du Moyen Age.* Fribourg, 1978.

———. "Les trois fragments d'ivoire de Berlin, Paris et Nevers." In *Byzantine East, Latin West: Art-Historical Studies in Honor of Kurt Weitzmann,* ed. Doula Mouriki, Christopher F. Moss, and Katharine Kiefer, 49–63. Princeton, 1995.

Gabra, Gawdat. *Cairo, the Coptic Museum and Old Churches.* Cairo, 1999.

Gaddis, Michael. "'There Is No Crime for Those Who Have Christ': Religious Violence in the Christian Roman Empire." Ph.D. diss., Princeton University, 1999.

Gafni, Isaiah. "Nestorian Literature as a Source for the History of the Babylonian *Yeshivot*" [in Hebrew]. *Tarbiz* 51 (1982): 567–76.

Gamble, Harry Y. *Books and Readers in the Early Church: A History of Early Christian Texts.* New Haven, 1995.

Gardner, Iain, and Samuel N. C. Lieu. *Manichaean Texts from the Roman Empire.* Cambridge, 2003.

Garnsey, Peter. "Lactantius and Augustine." In *Representations of Empire: Rome and the Mediterranean World,* ed. Alan K. Bowman, Hannah M. Cotton, Martin Goodman, and Simon Price, 153–79. Oxford, 2002.

Gasché, Rodolph. "The Felicities of Paradox: Blanchot on the Null-Space of Literature." In *Maurice Blanchot: The Demand of Writing,* ed. Carolyn Bailey Gill, 34–69. London, 1996.

Gebhardt, Oskar von. *Passio S. Theclae Virginis: Die lateinischen Übersetzungen der Acta Pauli et Theclae.* Leipzig, 1902.

Geerard, M. *Clavis Apocryphorum Novi Testamenti.* Turnhout, 1992.

Gellrich, Jesse M. *The Idea of the Book in the Middle Ages: Language Theory, Mythology, and Fiction.* Ithaca, N.Y., 1985.

Gerstinger, Hans. "Ein Bücherverzeichnis aus dem VII–VIII. Jh. n. Chr. im Pap. Graec. Vindob. 26015." *Wiener Studien: Zeitschrift für klassische Philologie* 32 (1933): 185–92.

Giselin, Victor. "In Aurelii Prudentii Clementis V. Cl. Opera Commentarius." Part II of *Aurelius Prudentius Clemens, Theodori Pulmanni Cranenburgii, et Victoris Giselini opera: Ex fide decem librorum manuscriptorum emendatus.* Antwerp, 1564.

Goehring, James. "The Encroaching Desert: Literary Production and Ascetic Space in Early Christian Egypt." *JECS* 1 (1993): 218–96.

Goodblatt, David M. *Rabbinic Instruction in Sasanian Babylonia.* Leiden, 1975.

Gordon, Pamela. *Epicurus in Lycia: The Second-Century World of Diogenes of Oenoanda.* Ann Arbor, 1996.

Graffin, Pierre. "La lettre de Philoxène de Mabboug à un supérieur de monastère sur la vie monastique." *L'Orient syrien* 6 (1961): 317–52, 455–86.

Grant, Robert M. *Greek Apologists of the Second Century.* Philadelphia, 1988.

Gray, Patrick T. R. "'The Select Fathers': Canonizing the Patristic Past." *Papers Presented to the Tenth International Conference on Patristic Studies Held in Oxford, 1987,* ed. Elizabeth A. Livingstone, 5:21–36. Studia Patristica 23. Leuven, 1989.

Greetham, D. C. *Theories of the Text.* Oxford, 1999.

Gregg, Robert C., trans. *Athanasius: The Life of Antony and the Letter to Marcellinus.* New York, 1980.

Grégoire, Henri. *Recueil des inscriptions grecques-chrétiennes d'Asie Mineure.* Vol. 1. Paris, 1922. Reprint, Amsterdam, 1968.

Grégoire, Henri, and M.-A. Kugener, eds. *Marc le diacre: Vie de Porphyre, évêque de Gaza.* Paris, 1930.

Griffith, F. Ll. "Oxford Excavations in Nubia." *Annals of Archaeology and Anthropology* 14 (1927): 57–116.

Griggs, C. Wilfred. *Early Egyptian Chistianity from Its Origin to 451* CE. Leiden, 1991.

Guglielmo, Pietro, Cardinal Pandolfo, Pietro Bohier, and Ulderico Přerovský, eds. *Liber Pontificalis.* 3 vols. Studia Gratiana 21–23. Rome, 1978.

Gulácsi, Zsuzsanna. *Manichaean Art in Berlin Collections.* Turnhout, 2001.

Hagendahl, Harald. *The Latin Fathers and the Classics: A Study on the Apologists, Jerome, and Other Christian Writers.* Gothenburg, 1958.

Haines-Eitzen, Kim. "Girls Trained in Beautiful Writing: Female Scribes in Roman Antiquity and Early Christianity." *JECS* 6 (1998): 629–46.

———. *Guardians of Letters: Literacy, Power, and the Transmitters of Early Christian Literature.* Oxford, 2000.

Halivni, David. *Midrash, Mishnah, and Gemara: The Jewish Predilection for Justified Law.* Cambridge, Mass., 1986.

Halkin, François, ed. *Le Corpus Athénien de Saint Pachôme.* Geneva, 1982.

Hallett, Judith P., and Marilyn B. Skinner, eds. *Roman Sexualities.* Princeton, 1997.

Halperin, David M., John J. Winkler, and Froma I. Zeitlin, eds. *Before Sexuality: The Construction of Erotic Experience in the Ancient Greek World.* Princeton, 1990.

Halporn, James W., trans. *Cassiodorus: Institutions of Divine and Secular Learning and On the Soul.* Liverpool, 2004.

Halsberghe, G. H. "Le culte de Dea Caelestis." *ANRW* 2, no. 17.4 (1984): 2203–23.

Hamilton, Louis I. "Possidius' Augustine and Post-Augustinian Africa." *JECS* 12 (2004): 85–105.

Harpham, Geoffrey Galt. *The Ascetic Imperative in Culture and Criticism.* Chicago, 1987.

Harrauer, Hermann. "Bücher in Papyri." In *Flores litterarum Ioanni Marte sexagenario oblati: Wissenschaft in der Bibliothek,* ed. Helmut W. Lang, 59–77. Vienna, 1995.

Harries, Jill. "'Pius princeps': Theodosius II and Fifth-Century Constantinople." In *New Constantines: The Rhythm of Imperial Renewal in Byzantium, 4th–13th Centuries,* ed. Paul Magdalino, 35–44. Aldershot, 1994.

————. *Law and Empire in Late Antiquity.* Cambridge, 1999.

Harvey, Susan Ashbrook. "Women in Early Byzantine Hagiography: Reversing the Story." In *That Gentle Strength: Historical Perspectives on Women in Christianity,* ed. Lynda L. Coon, Katherine J. Haldane, and Elisabeth W. Sommer, 36–59. Richmond, Va., 1990.

Hayes, Christine. *Between the Babylonian and Palestinian Talmuds.* Oxford, 1997.

Hayne, Léonie. "Thecla and the Church Fathers." *VC* 48 (1994): 209–18.

Heil, Günter, ed. *Gregorii Nysseni Sermones: Pars II.* Gregorii Nysseni Opera 10.1. Leiden, 1990.

Heine, Ronald E. *The Commentaries of Origen and Jerome on St Paul's Epistle to the Ephesians.* Oxford, 2002.

Heinsius, Nicolaus. *Aurelii Prudentii Clementis v.c. opera cum notis Nicolai Heinsii . . . et variorum doctorum virorum maxime necessariis.* Cologne, 1701.

Hennecke, Edgar, Wilhelm Schneemelcher, and R. McL. Wilson, eds. *New Testament Apocrypha.* 2 vols. Philadelphia, 1963, 1966.

Herford, R. Travers. *Christianity in Talmud and Midrash.* London, 1903. Reprint, New York, 1978.

Herrin, Judith. "L'enseignement maternel à Byzance." In *Femmes et pouvoirs des femmes à Byzance et en Occident (VIe–XIe siècles),* ed. Stéphane Lebecq, Alain Dierkens, Régine Le Jan, and Jean-Marie Sansterre, 91–102. Lille, 1996.

Herzog, Reinhart. "Epochenerlebnis 'Revolution' und Epochenbewußtsein 'Spätantike': Zur Genese einer historischen Epoche bei Chateaubriand." In *Epochenschwelle und Epochenbewußtsein,* ed. Reinhart Herzog and Reinhart Koselleck, 195–219. Munich, 1987.

————. *"Wir leben in der Spätantike": Eine Zeiterfahrung und ihre Impulse für die Forschung.* Bamberg, 1987.

Hill, Leslie. "Blanchot and Mallarmé." *Modern Language Notes* 105 (1990): 889–913.

————. *Blanchot: Extreme Contemporary.* London, 1997.

The History of Bookbinding, 525–1950 A.D., an Exhibition Held at the Baltimore Museum of Art, November 12, 1957, to January 12, 1958. Exh. cat. Baltimore, 1957.

Holmes, Catherine, and Judith Waring, eds. *Literacy, Education and Manuscript Transmission in Byzantium and Beyond.* Leiden, 2002.

Hopkins, Keith. "Christian Number and Its Implications." *JECS* 6 (1998): 185–226.

Howard, George, trans. *The Teaching of Addai.* Chico, Calif., 1981.

Humfress, Caroline. "Law and Legal Practice in the Age of Justinian." In *Cambridge Companion to the Age of Justinian,* ed. Michael Maas, 161–84. Cambridge, 2005.

Hunger, Herbert. *Schreiben und Lesen in Byzanz: Die byzantinische Buchkultur.* Munich, 1989.

Hunt, E. D. *Holy Land Pilgrimage in the Later Roman Empire, A.D. 312–460.* Oxford, 1982.

Huot, Sylvia. "The Writer's Mirror: Watriquet de Couvin and the Development of the Author-Centered Book." In *Across Boundaries: The Book in Culture and Commerce,* ed. Bill Bell, Philip Bennet, and Jonquil Bevan, 29–46. Winchester, Del., 2000.

Ibscher, Hugo. "Koptische Einbände aus Ägypten." *Berliner Museen: Berichte aus den preussischen Kunstsammlungen* 49 (1928): 86–90.

Illich, Ivan. *In the Vineyard of the Text: A Commentary to Hugh's Didascalicon.* Chicago, 1993.

Irvine, Martin. *The Making of Textual Culture: "Grammatica" and Literary Theory 350–1100.* Cambridge, 1994.

Iser, Wolfgang. "Interaction between Text and Reader." In *The Reader in the Text: Essays on Audience and Interpretation,* ed. Susan R. Suleiman and Inge Crosman, 106–19. Princeton, 1980.

———. *The Range of Interpretation.* New York, 2000.

Jacobs, Andrew S. "The Imperial Construction of the Jew in the Early Christian Holy Land." Ph.D. diss., Duke University, 2001.

Jager, Eric. *The Book of the Heart.* Chicago, 2000.

James, Edward, trans. *Gregory of Tours: Life of the Fathers.* 2d ed. Liverpool, 1991.

Johnson, Scott F. *The Life and Miracles of Thekla: A Literary Study.* Washington, D.C., 2006.

Jones, Leslie Webber, trans. *An Introduction to Divine and Human Readings by Cassiodorus Senator.* New York, 1966.

Jordan, Robert, trans. "The *Typikon* of Gregory Pakourianos for the Monastery of the Mother of God *Petritzonitissa* in Bačkovo." In *Byzantine Monastic Foundation Documents: A Complete Translation of the Surviving Founders'* Typika *and Testaments,* ed. John Thomas and Angela Constantinides Hero, 2:507–63. Washington, D.C., 2000.

Kamesar, Adam. *Jerome, Greek Scholarship, and the Hebrew Bible.* Oxford, 1993.

Kamil, Murad. "Catalogue of the Syrian Manuscripts Newly Found in the Monastery of St. Mary Deipara in the Nitrian Desert." Unpublished English translation (ca. 1960) of an earlier Arabic catalogue.

Kaniecka, Mary Simplicia, ed. and trans. *Vita sancti Ambrosii.* Washington, D.C., 1928.

Karlin-Hayter, Patricia, ed. *Vita Euthymii Patriarchae CP.* Brussels, 1970.

Kaster, Robert. *Guardians of Language: The Grammarian and Society in Late Antiquity.* Berkeley and Los Angeles, 1988.

Keenan, James G. "A Papyrus Letter about Epicurean Philosophy Books." *J. Paul Getty Museum Journal* 5 (1977): 91–94.

Kelly, Eamonn P. "The Lough Kinale Book-Shrine." In *The Age of Migrating Ideas: Early Medieval Art in Northern Britain and Ireland,* ed. R. Michael Spearman and John Higgitt, 168–74. Edinburgh, 1993.

Kelly, J. N. D. *Jerome: His Life, Writings, and Controversies.* London, 1975.

Kenyon, Frederic. "The Library of a Greek of Oxyrhynchus." *Journal of Egyptian Archaeology* 8 (1922): 129–38.

Kessler, Herbert L. "Two Carved Plaques with St. Anne." In *Age of Spirituality,* ed. Kurt Weitzmann, 510–12.

Kirschbaum, Engelbert, Günter Bandmann, and Wolfgang Braunfels, eds. *Lexikon der christlichen Ikonographie.* 8 vols. Rome, 1968–76.

Kitzinger, Ernst. "A Pair of Silver Book Covers in the Sion Treasure." In *Gatherings in Honor of Dorothy E. Miner,* ed. Ursula E. McCracken, Lilian M. C. Randall, and Richard H. Randall Jr., 3–17. Baltimore, 1974.

Klijn, A. F. J. *The Acts of Thomas: Introduction, Text, Commentary.* Leiden, 1962.

Klingshirn, William E., trans. *Caesarius of Arles: Life, Testament, Letters.* Liverpool, 1994.

———. *Caesarius of Arles: The Making of a Christian Community in Late Antique Gaul.* Cambridge, 1994.

———. "Defining the *Sortes Sanctorum:* Gibbon, DuCange, and Early Christian Lot Divination." *JECS* 10 (2002): 77–130.

Klingshirn, William E., and Mark Vessey, eds. *The Limits of Ancient Christianity: Essays on Late Antique Thought and Culture in Honor of R. A. Markus.* Ann Arbor, 1999.

Koenen, Ludwig. "Ein Mönch als Berufsschreiber: Zur Buchproduktion im 5./6. Jahrhundert." In *Festschrift zum 150 jährigen Bestehen des Berliner Ägyptischen Museums,* 347–54. Berlin, 1974.

Koenen, Ludwig, and Wolfgang Müller-Wiener. "Zu den Papyri aus dem Arsenioskloster bei Tura." *ZPE* 2 (1968): 41–63.

Kraemer, David Charles. *The Mind of the Talmud: An Intellectual History of the Bavli.* New York, 1990.

Krause, Martin. "Apa Abraham von Hermonthis: Ein oberägyptischer Bischof um 600." Ph.D. diss., Berlin, 1956.

———. "Libraries." In *The Coptic Encyclopedia,* ed. Aziz S. Atiya, 5:1447–50. New York, 1991.

Krawiec, Rebecca. *Shenoute and the Women of the White Monastery.* Oxford, 2002.

Kristeva, Julia. *La révolution du langage poétique: L'avant-garde à la fin du XIXe siècle—Lautréamont et Mallarmé.* Paris, 1974.

———. *Σημειωτικὴ: Recherches pour une sémanalyse.* Paris, 1969.

Krueger, Derek. "Writing as Devotion: Hagiographical Composition and the Cult of the Saints in Theodoret of Cyrrhus and Cyril of Scythopolis." *Church History* 66 (1997): 707–19.

———. "Hagiography as an Ascetic Practice in the Early Christian East." *Journal of Religion* 79 (1999): 216–32.

Krueger, Paul, Theodor Mommsen, Rudolf Schoell, and Wilhelm Kroll, eds. *Corpus Iuris Civilis.* 3 vols. Berlin, 1877–95.

Kugener, M.-A., ed. *Zacharie le Scholastique: Vie de Sévère d'Antioch. Patrologia Orientalis* 2, no. 1 (1907): 68-71.

Kupiszewski, Henryk. "Dal codice-libro al codice-raccolta di precetti giuridici." *Journal of Juristic Papyrology* 20 (1990): 83–92.

Kurek, Dominka. "Some Textual Problems with Prisca and Aquila." Paper delivered to the Society of Biblical Literature, Toronto, November 25, 2002.

Labarthe, Patrick. *Baudelaire et la tradition de l'allégorie.* Geneva, 1999.

Labourt, Jérôme, ed. *Saint Jérôme: Lettres.* 8 vols. Paris, 1949–63.

Lacocque, André. *The Feminine Unconventional: Four Subversive Figures in Israel's Tradition.* Minneapolis, 1990.

Lacoue-Labarthe, Philippe, and Jean-Luc Nancy. *The Literary Absolute: The Theory of Literature in German Romanticism.* Trans. Philip Barnard and Cheryl Lester. Albany, N.Y., 1988.

Lamberton, Robert. "The Neoplatonists and Their Books." In *Homer, the Bible, and Beyond:*

Literary and Religious Canons in the Ancient World, ed. Margalit Finkelberg and Guy Stroumsa, 195–211. Leiden, 2003.

————, trans. *Thomas the Obscure.* Barrytown, N.Y., 1988.

Lampe, G. W. H., ed. *A Patristic Greek Lexicon.* Oxford, 2000.

Lange, Nicholas de. "Jews in the Age of Justinian." In *Cambridge Companion to the Age of Justinian,* ed. Michael Maas, 401–26. Cambridge, 2005

Larmour, David H. J., Paul Allen Miller, and Charles Platter, eds. *Rethinking Sexuality: Foucault and Classical Antiquity.* Princeton, 1998.

Lasko, Peter. *Ars Sacra 800–1200.* 2d ed. New Haven, 1994.

Laurence, P. "Rome et Jérome: Des amours contrariés." *Revue Bénédictine* 107 (1997): 227–49.

Laurence, Ray. "Emperors, Nature, and the City: Rome's Ritual Landscape." *The Accordia Research Papers: The Journal of the Accordia Research Centre* 4 (1994): 79–88.

————. "Ritual, Landscape, and the Destruction of Place in the Roman Imagination." In *Approaches to the Study of Ritual: Italy and the Ancient Mediterranean; Being a series of Seminars Given at the Institute of Classical Studies School of Advanced Study, University of London,* ed. John B. Wilkins, 111–21. London, 1996.

Le Blant, Edmond. "Le premier chapitre de Saint Jean et la croyance à ses vertus secrètes." *Revue archéologique,* 3d ser., 25 (1894): 8–13.

Leclercq, Henri. "Amulettes." In *Dictionnaire d'archéologie Chrétienne et de liturgie* (1924), 1.2, cols. 1784–1860.

Le Goff, Jacques. *Intellectuals in the Middle Ages.* Trans. Teresa Lavender Fagan. Oxford, 1993. Originally published as *Les intellectuels au Moyen Age* (Paris, 1955).

Leroy, Jules. *Les manuscrits coptes et coptes-arabes illustrés.* Paris, 1974.

Lewis, Agnes Smith. *Some Pages of the Four Gospels Re-transcribed from the Sinaitic Palimpsest.* London, 1896.

————. *In the Shadow of Sinai: A Story of Travel and Research from 1895 to 1897.* Cambridge, 1898.

————. *The Old Syriac Gospels, or, Evangelion da-Mepharreshê.* London, 1910.

————, ed. *Select Narratives of Holy Women from the Syro-Antiochene or Sinai Palimpsest.* Studia Sinaitica 9. London, 1900.

Lewis, Naphtali. *Life in Egypt under Roman Rule.* Atlanta, 1999.

Leyerle, Blake. "Landscape as Cartography in Early Christian Pilgrimage Narratives." *Journal of the American Academy of Religion* 64 (1996): 119–43.

Leyser, Conrad. "'Divine Power Flowed from this Book': Ascetic Language and Episcopal Authority in Gregory of Tours' *Life of the Fathers.*" In *The World of Gregory of Tours,* ed. Kathleen Mitchell and Ian Wood, 281–94. Leiden, 2002.

Liébana Pérez, José. "Las glosas de Isón: Notas sobre un comentario carolingio a la obra de Prudencio." *Estudios clásicos* 25 (1981–83): 225–56.

Liebeschuetz, J.H.W.G. *Continuity and Change in Roman Religion.* Oxford, 1979.

Lienhard, Joseph. "The Christian Reception of the Pentateuch: Patristic Commentaries on the Books of Moses." *JECS* 10 (2002): 373–88.

Lieu, Samuel N. C. *Manichaeism in the Later Roman Empire and Medieval China.* Manchester, 1985.

Lim, Richard. *Public Disputation, Power, and Social Order in Late Antiquity.* Berkeley and Los Angeles, 1994.

Lindsay, Jen. "The Edfu Collection of Coptic Books." *New Bookbinder* 21 (2001): 31–51.

Lipinsky, A. "Der Theodelinden-Schatz im Dom zu Monza." *Das Münster* 13 (1960): 146–73.

Lipking, Lawrence. *The Life of the Poet: Beginning and Ending Poetic Careers.* Chicago, 1981.

Lipsius, Richard A., and Maximilian Bonnet, eds. *Acta Apostolorum Apocrypha.* 2 vols. Leipzig, 1891, 1903.

Long, A. A. *Epictetus: A Stoic and Socratic Guide to Life.* Oxford, 2002.

Longhurst, Margaret H., and Charles Rufus Morey. "The Covers of the Lorsch Gospels." *Speculum* 3 (1928): 64–74.

Lowden, John. *Early Christian and Byzantine Art.* London, 1997.

———. "The Beginnings of Biblical Illustration." In *Imaging the Early Medieval Bible,* ed. John Williams, 9–59. University Park, Pa., 1999.

———. "Byzantium Perceived through Illuminated Manuscripts: Now and Then." In *Through the Looking Glass: Byzantium through British Eyes,* ed. Robin Cormack and Elizabeth Jeffreys, 85–106. Aldershot, 2000.

———. "The Transmission of 'Visual Knowledge' in Byzantium through Illuminated Manuscripts: Approaches and Conjectures." In *Literacy, Education and Manuscript Transmission in Byzantium and Beyond,* ed. Catherine Holmes and Judith Waring, 59–80. Leiden, 2002.

———. "Illuminated Books and the Liturgy." In *Objects, Images, and the Word: Art in the Service of the Liturgy,* ed. Colum Hourihane, 17–53. Princeton, 2003.

———. "'Reading' the *Bibles moralisées:* Images as Exegesis and the Exegesis of Images." In *Reading Images and Texts: Medieval Images and Texts as Forms of Communication,* ed. Marco Mostert and Mariëlle Hageman, 495–525. Turnhout, 2005.

———. "Les rois et les reines de France en tant que 'public' des Bibles moralisées: Une approche tangentielle à la question des liens entre les Bibles moralisées et les vitraux de la Sainte-Chapelle." In *La Sainte-Chapelle. Royaume de France et Jérusalem céleste,* ed. Yves Christe and Peter Kurmann. Forthcoming.

———. "Under the Influence of the *Bibles moralisées.*" In *Under the Influence: The Concept of Influence and the Study of Illuminated Manuscripts,* ed. John Lowden and Alixe Bovey. Forthcoming.

Lucot, A., ed. *Histoire Lausiaque.* Paris, 1912.

Lutz, Cora E., ed. *Iohannis Scotti Annotationes in Marcianum.* Cambridge, Mass., 1939.

Lyotard, Jean-François. *The Confession of Augustine.* Trans. Richard Beardsworth. Stanford, 2000.

Maas, Michael, ed. *Cambridge Companion to the Age of Justinian.* Cambridge, 2005.

MacCormack, Sabine. *The Shadows of Poetry: Vergil in the Mind of Augustine.* Berkeley and Los Angeles, 1998.

MacCoull, Leslie S. B. *Coptic Documentary Papyri from the Beinecke Library (Yale University)*. Cairo, 1986.

———. "Patronage and the Social Order in Coptic Egypt." In *Egitto e storia antica dall'ellenismo all'età araba: Bilancio di un confronto: Atti del colloquio internazionale, Bologna, 31 agosto–2 settembre 1987,* ed. Lucia Criscuolo and Giovanni Geraci, 497–502. Bologna, 1989. Reprinted in her *Coptic Perspectives on Late Antiquity* (Aldershot, 1993).

———. "The Apa Apollos Monastery of Pharoou (Aphrodito) and Its Papyrus Archive." *Le Muséon* 106 (1993): 21–63.

MacDonald, Dennis Ronald. *The Legend and the Apostle: The Battle for Paul in Story and Canon.* Philadelphia, 1983.

MacMullen, Ramsay. "Judicial Savagery in the Later Roman Empire." *Chiron* 16 (1986): 43–62.

Madec, Goulven. "Possidius de Calama et les listes des oeuvres d'Augustin." In *Titres et articulations du texte dans les oeuvres antiques: Actes du Colloque international de Chantilly, 13–15 décembre 1994,* ed. Jean-Claude Fredouille, 427–45. Paris, 1977.

Maehler, Herwig. "Byzantine Egypt: Urban Élites and Book Production." *Dialogos: Hellenic Studies Review* 4 (1997): 118–36.

Malamud, Martha. "Writing Original Sin." *JECS* 10 (2002): 329–60.

Mango, Marlia Mundell. *Silver from Early Byzantium: The Kaper Koraon and Related Treasures.* Baltimore, 1986. Published in conjunction with the exhibition "Silver Treasure from Early Byzantium," Walters Art Gallery, April 18–August 17, 1986.

———. "The Monetary Value of Silver Revetments and Objects Belonging to Churches, A.D. 300–700." In *Ecclesiastical Silver Plate in Sixth-Century Byzantium,* ed. Susan A. Boyd and Marlia Mundell Mango, 123–36. Washington, D.C., 1992.

Marchal, Bertrand. *La religion de Mallarmé.* Paris, 1988.

Marin, Louis. "The Frontiers of Utopia." In *Utopias and the Millennium,* ed. Krishan Kumar and Stephen Bann, 7–16. London, 1993.

Markus, R. A. *Signs and Meanings: World and Text in Ancient Christianity.* Liverpool, 1996.

Marrou, Henri-Irénée. Μουσικὸς ἀνήρ: *Étude sur les scènes de la vie intellectuelle sur les monuments funéraires romains.* Grenoble, 1937.

———. *Saint Augustin et la fin de la culture antique.* 2d ed. with a "Retractatio." Paris, 1949.

Martin, Annick. "L'Église et la Khôra Égyptienne au IVe Siècle." *REAug* 25 (1979): 3–26.

Martin, Dale B. *The Corinthian Body.* New Haven, 1995.

Martini, Luciana, and Clementina Rizzardi. *Avori bizantini e medievali nel Museo Nazionale di Ravenna.* Ravenna, 1990.

Mathews, Thomas F. *The Early Churches of Constantinople: Architecture and Liturgy.* University Park, Pa., 1971.

———. *The Clash of Gods: A Reinterpretation of Early Christian Art.* 2d ed. Princeton, 1999.

McDonald, Mary Francis, trans. *Lactantius: The Divine Institutes, Books I–VII.* Washington, D.C., 1964.

McGill, Scott. *Virgil Recomposed: The Mythological and Secular Centos in Antiquity.* New York, 2005.

McGurk, Patrick. "The Irish Pocket Gospel Book." *Sacris Erudiri* 8 (1956): 249–70.

McLynn, Neil B. *Ambrose of Milan: Church and Court in a Christian Capital.* Berkeley and Los Angeles, 1994.

———. "Augustine's Roman Empire." In *History, Apocalypse, and the Secular Imagination: New Essays on Augustine's City of God,* ed. Mark Vessey, Karla Pollmann, and Allan D. Fitzgerald, 29–44. Bowling Green, Ohio, 1999.

Meredith, Anthony. "Orthodoxy, Heresy, and Philosophy in the Latter Half of the Fourth Century." *Heythrop Journal* 16, no. 1 (1975): 5–21.

———. "Porphyry and Julian against the Christians." *ANRW* 2, no. 23.2 (1980): 1119–49.

Metzger, Bruce M. *The Early Versions of the New Testament: Their Origin, Transmission, and Limitations.* Oxford, 1977.

———. *Manuscripts of the Greek Bible: An Introduction to Greek Palaeography.* New York and Oxford, 1981.

———. *The Text of the New Testament: Its Transmission, Corruption, and Restoration.* 3d ed. New York, 1992.

Meyer, Robert T., trans. *Palladius: The Lausiac History.* New York, 1965.

Millar, Fergus. *The Roman Near East 31 B.C.–A.D. 337.* Cambridge, Mass., 1993.

Miller, Patricia Cox. *Dreams in Late Antiquity: Studies in the Imagination of a Culture.* Princeton, 1994.

———. "Jerome's Centaur: A Hyper-Icon of the Desert." *JECS* 4 (1996): 209–33.

Miner, Dorothy Eugenia, ed. *Early Christian and Byzantine Art: An Exhibition Held at the Baltimore Museum of Art, April 25–June 22 [1947].* Exh. cat. Baltimore, 1947.

Mioni, Elpidio. "Il Pratum Spirituale di Giovanni Mosco: Gli episodi inediti del Cod. Marciano greco II, 21." *Orientalia Christiana Periodica* 17 (1951): 61–94.

Mommsen, Theodor, and Paul M. Meyer, eds. *Theodosiani Libri XVI cum Constitutionibus Sirmondianis.* 2d ed. 2 vols. Berlin, 1954.

Mondor, Henri. *Vie de Mallarmé.* 2 vols. Paris, 1941.

———. *Eugène Lefébure: Sa vie, ses lettres à Mallarmé.* Paris, 1951.

Mondor, Henri, and G. Jean-Aubry, eds. *Stéphane Mallarmé: Oeuvres complètes.* Paris, 1945.

Mondor, Henri, and Lloyd James Austin, eds. *Stéphane Mallarmé: Correspondance.* 11 vols. Paris, 1959–85.

Monteserrat-Torrents, Josep. "The Social and Cultural Setting of the Coptic Gnostic Library." In *Papers Presented at the Twelfth International Conference on Patristic Studies Held in Oxford, 1995,* ed. Elizabeth A. Livingstone, 3:464–81. Studia Patristica 31. Leuven, 1997.

Morey, Charles Rufus. "The Painted Covers of the Washington Manuscript of the Gospels." In *East Christian Paintings in the Freer Collection,* ed. Charles Rufus Morey, 63–81. New York, 1914.

Morin, Germain, ed. *Sancti Caesarii Episcopi Arelatensis Opera Omnia.* 2 vols. Maredsous, 1937–42.

Morin, Germain, and Antonio Casamassa, eds. *Miscellanea Agostiniana: Testi e studi, pubblicati a cura dell'ordine eremitano di s. Agostino nel XV centenario dalla morte del santo dottore.* 2 vols. Rome, 1930, 1931.

Moutote, Daniel. *Maîtres livres de notre temps: Posterité du "Livre" de Mallarmé.* Paris, 1988.

Mratschek, Sigrid. *Der Briefwechsel des Paulinus von Nola.* Göttingen, 2001.

Mrosovsky, Kitty, trans. *Gustave Flaubert: The Temptation of St. Antony.* Ithaca, N.Y., 1981.

Musurillo, Herbert, trans. "The Acts of the Scillitan Martyrs." In *The Acts of the Christian Martyrs,* 86–89. Oxford, 1972.

Muyldermans, Joseph, ed. *Evagriana Syriaca: Textes inédits du British Museum et de la Vaticane.* Louvain, 1952.

Mynors, R. A. B., ed. *Cassiodori Senatoris Institutiones.* Oxford, 1937.

Nathan, Geoffrey. "The Rogation Ceremonies of Late Antique Gaul: Creation, Transmission, and the Role of the Bishop." *Classica et Mediaevalia* 49 (1998): 275–303.

Nautin, Pierre. "Études de chronologie hiéronymienne (393–397): III. Les premières relations entre Jérome et Paulin de Nole." *REAug* 19 (1973): 213–39.

Needham, Paul. *Twelve Centuries of Bookbindings 400–1600.* New York, 1979.

Nees, Lawrence. "The Irish Manuscripts at St. Gall and Their Continental Affiliations." In *Sangallensia in Washington: The Arts and Letters in Medieval and Baroque St. Gall Viewed from the Late Twentieth Century,* ed. James C. King, 95–132. New York, 1993.

Neuschäfer, Bernhard. *Origenes als Philologe.* 2 vols. Basel, 1987.

Neusner, Jacob. *Judaism in Society: The Evidence of the Yerushalmi; Toward the Natural History of a Religion.* Atlanta, 1991.

Newman, Hillel I. "Between Jerusalem and Bethlehem: Jerome and the Holy Places of Palestine." In *Sanctity of Time and Space in Tradition and Modernity,* ed. Alberdina Houtman, Marcel J. H. M. Poorthuis, and Joshua Schwartz, 215–27. Leiden, 1998.

Niccum, Curt. "The Voice of the Manuscripts on the Silence of Women: The External Evidence for 1 Cor. 14:34–35." *New Testament Studies* 43 (1997): 242–55.

Niccum, Curt, and Jeffrey Childers. "'Anti-Feminist' Tendency in the 'Western' Text of Acts?" In *Essays on Women in Earliest Christianity,* ed. Carroll D. Osburn, 1:469–92. Joplin, Miss., 1993.

Nicholson, Oliver. "*Civitas quae adhuc sustentat omnia:* Lactantius and the City of Rome." In *The Limits of Ancient Christianity: Essays on Late Antique Thought and Culture in Honor of R. A. Markus,* ed. William E. Klingshirn and Mark Vessey, 7–25. Ann Arbor, 1999.

Nodes, Daniel J., ed. *Avitus: The Fall of Man; De spiritalis historiae gestis libri I–III.* Toronto, 1985.

Norman, Albert F., trans. *Libanius: Autobiography and Selected Letters.* 2 vols. Cambridge, 1992.

O'Daly, Gerard. *Augustine's City of God: A Reader's Guide.* Oxford, 1999.

O'Donnell, James J. *Augustine.* Boston, 1985.

———. *Avatars of the Word: From Papyrus to Cyberspace.* Cambridge, 1998.

———. "Bible." In *Augustine through the Ages: An Encyclopaedia,* ed. Allan D. Fitzgerald, 99–103. Grand Rapids, Mich., 1999.

———. "The Next Life of Augustine." In *The Limits of Ancient Christianity: Essays on Late Antique Thought and Culture in Honor of R. A. Markus,* ed. William E. Klingshirn and Mark Vessey, 215–31. Ann Arbor, 1999.

———, ed. *Augustine: Confessions.* 3 vols. Oxford, 1992.

O'Meara, Dominic J. *Pythagoras Revived: Mathematics and Philosophy in Late Antiquity.* Oxford, 1989.

Orlandi, Tito. "The Library of the Monastery of Saint Shenute at Atripe." In *Perspectives on Panopolis: An Egyptian Town from Alexander the Great to the Arab Conquest,* ed. A. Egberts, B. P. Muhs, and J. van der Vliet, 211–19. Leiden, 2002.

Otranto, Rosa. *Antiche liste di libri su papiro.* Rome, 2000.

Palla, Roberto, ed. *Prudenzio: Hamartigenia.* Pisa, 1981.

Parássoglou, George M. "A Book Illuminator in Byzantine Egypt." *Byzantion* 44 (1974): 362–68.

Parmentier, Martin. "Evagrius of Pontus' 'Letter to Melania.'" *Bijdragen tijdschrift voor filosofie en theologie* 46 (1985): 2–38.

Paschoud, François. *Roma aeterna: Études sur le patriotisme romain dans l'Occident latin à l'époque des grandes invasions.* Paris, 1968.

Patlagean, Evelyne. "L'histoire de la femme déguisée en moine et l'évolution de la sainteté féminine à Byzance." *Studi Medievali,* 3d ser., 17 (1976): 597–623.

Payne, Philip B. "Fuldensis, Sigla for Variants in Vaticanus, and 1 Cor. 14:34–35." *New Testament Studies* 41 (1995): 240–62.

———. "Ms. 88 as Evidence for a Text without 1 Cor. 14:34–35." *New Testament Studies* 44 (1998): 152–58.

Pazaris, Theocharis. *The Rotunda of Saint George in Thessaloniki.* Thessalonike, 1985.

Peshitta Institute. *List of Old Testament Peshitta Manuscripts (Preliminary Issue).* Leiden, 1961.

———. "Peshitta Institute Communications VII." *Vetus Testamentum* 18 (1968): 128–43.

Pesthy, Monika. "Thecla in the Fathers of the Church." In *The Apocryphal Acts of Paul and Thecla,* ed. Jan N. Bremmer, 168–71. Kampen, 1996.

Petrucci, Armando. "The Christian Conception of the Book in the Sixth and Seventh Centuries." In *Writers and Readers in Medieval Italy: Studies in the History of Written Culture,* trans. Charles M. Radding. New Haven, 1995.

Pharr, Clyde. "The Interdiction of Magic in Roman Law." *Transactions and Proceeding of the American Philological Association* 63 (1932): 269–95.

———, trans. *The Theodosian Code and Novels and the Sirmondian Constitutions.* Princeton, 1952.

Pine-Coffin, R. S., trans. *Saint Augustine: Confessions.* London, 1961.

Pines, Shlomo. "Notes on the Parallelism between Syriac Terminology and Mishnaic Hebrew" [in Hebrew]. In *Sefer zikaron le-Ya'akov Fridman: Kovets mehkarim [Ya'akov Fridman Memorial Volume],* ed. Shlomo Pines, 205–13. Jerusalem, 1974.

Plumer, Eric. *Augustine's Commentary on Galatians.* Oxford, 2003.

Pollmann, Karla. *Das Carmen adversus Marcionitas: Einleitung, Text, Übersetzung und Kommentar.* Göttingen, 1991.

———. *St. Augustine the Algerian.* Göttingen, 2003.

———. "Sex and Salvation in the Vergilian Cento of the Fourth Century." In *Romane Memento: Vergil in the Fourth Century,* ed. Roger Rees, 79–96. London, 2004.

———. "Augustine's Hermeneutics as a Universal Discipline!?" In *Augustine and the Disciplines: From Cassiciacum to Confessions,* ed. Karla Pollmann and Mark Vessey, 202–31. Oxford, 2005.

Poque, Suzanne. *Le Langage symbolique dans la prédication d'Augustin d'Hippone: Images héroïques.* 2 vols. Paris, 1984.

Potter, David S. "Martyrdom as Spectacle." In *Theater and Society in the Classical World,* ed. Ruth Scodel, 53–88. Ann Arbor, 1993.

Poulin, Joseph-Claude. "Entre magie et religion: Recherches sur les utilisations marginales de l'écrit dans la culture populaire du haut Moyen Age." In *La culture populaire au moyen âge: Études présentées au Quatrième colloque de l'Institut d'études médiévales de l'Université de Montréal, 2–3 avril 1977,* ed. Pierre Boglioni, 123–43. Montreal, 1979.

Price, A. Whigham. *The Ladies of Castlebrae: A Story of Nineteenth-Century Travel and Research.* Gloucester, 1985.

Price, Leah. "The Tangible Page." *London Review of Books,* October 31, 2002, 36–39.

Price, Simon. "Latin Christian Apologetics: Minucius Felix, Tertullian, and Cyprian." In *Apologetics in the Roman Empire,* ed. Mark Edwards, Martin Goodman, and Simon Price, 105–29. Oxford, 1999.

Provoost, A. "Le caractère et l'évolution des images bibliques dans l'art chrétien primitif." In J. den Boeft and M. L. van Poll-van de Lisdonk, *The Impact of Scripture in Early Christianity,* 79–101. Leiden, 1999.

Pugliese, Giovanni. "A Suggestion on the Collatio." *Israel Law Review* 29 (1995): 161–75.

Raabe, Richard. *Petrus der Iberer: Ein Charakterbild zur Kirchen- und Sittengeschichte des fünften Jahrhunderts.* Leipzig, 1895.

Rapp, Claudia. "Christians and Their Manuscripts in the Greek East in the Fourth Century." In *Scritture, libri e testi nelle aree provinciali di Bizanzio,* ed. Guglielmo Cavallo, Giuseppe de Gregorio, and Marilena Maniaci, 1:127–48. Spoleto, 1991.

———. "Byzantine Hagiographers as Antiquarians, Seventh to Tenth Centuries." In *Bosphorus: Essays in Honour of Cyril Mango,* ed. Stephanos Efthymiadis, Claudia Rapp, and Dimitris Tsougarakis. *Byzantinische Forschungen* 21 (1995): 31–44.

———. "'For Next to God, You Are My Salvation': Reflections on the Rise of the Holy Man in Late Antiquity." In *The Cult of Saints in Late Antiquity and the Early Middle Ages: Essays on the Contribution of Peter Brown,* ed. James Howard-Johnston and Paul A. Hayward, 63–81. Oxford, 1999.

Rebenich, Stefan. *Hieronymus und sein Kreis.* Stuttgart, 1992.

Rebillard, Éric. "A New Style of Argument in Christian Polemic: Augustine and the Use of Patristic Citations." *JECS* 8 (2000): 559–78.

Regard, Maurice, ed. *Chateaubriand: Oeuvres romanesques et voyages.* 2 vols. Paris, 1969.

Regnault, Lucien, and Hervé de Broc, eds. *Abbé Isaïe: Recueil ascétique.* 3d ed. Abbaye de Bellefontaine, Maine et Loire, 1985.

Regnault, Lucien, and Philippe Lemaire, trans. *Letters of Barsanuphius and John.* Solesmes, 1971.

Revillout, Eugène. "Textes coptes extraits de la correspondance de St. Pésunthius, évêque de Coptos et de plusieurs documents analogues (juristique ou économique)." *Revúe Égyptologique* 12 (1914): 2–33.

Rhalles, G., and M. Potles. *Syntagma tōn theiōn kai hierōn kanonōn tōn te hagiōn kai paneuphemōn Apostolōn.* 6 vols. Athens, 1852–59.

Richard, Jean-Pierre. *L'univers imaginaire de Mallarmé.* Paris, 1961.

Richard, Marcel. "Les florilèges diphysites du Ve et VIe siècle." In *Das Konzil von Chalkedon: Geschichte und Gegenwart,* ed. Alois Grillmeier and Heinrich Bacht, 1:721–48. Würzburg, 1951.

Rist, John. *Augustine: Ancient Thought Baptized.* Cambridge, 1994.

Robbins, Geoffrey A. "'Fifty Copies of the Sacred Writings' (*VC* 4.36): Entire Bibles or Gospel Books?" In *Papers Presented to the Tenth International Conference on Patristic Studies Held in Oxford, 1987,* ed. Elizabeth A. Livingstone, 1:91–98. Studia Patristica 19. Louvain, 1989.

Roberts, Colin H. "The Codex." *Proceedings of the British Academy* 40 (1954): 169–204.

———. *Buried Books in Antiquity: Habent sua fata libelli.* [London], 1963.

———. *Manuscript, Society, and Belief in Early Christian Egypt.* London, 1979.

Roberts, Colin H., and T. C. Skeat. *The Birth of the Codex.* London, 1983.

Robinson, James M. *The Facsimile Edition of the Nag Hammadi Codices: Introduction.* Leiden, 1972.

———. "The Construction of the Nag Hammadi Codices." In *Essays on the Nag Hammadi Texts: In Honour of Pahor Labib,* ed. Martin Krause, 170–90. Leiden, 1975.

———. *The Pachomian Monastic Library at the Chester Beatty Library and the Bibliothèque Bodmer.* Occasional Papers 19. Claremont, 1990.

Rose, Els. "Celebrating Saint Martin in Early Medieval Gaul." In *Christian Feast and Festival: The Dynamics of Western Liturgy and Culture,* ed. Paul Post, G. Rouwhorst, A. Scheer, and L. van Tongeren, 267–86. Leuven, 2001.

Rotelle, John E., ed. *The Works of Saint Augustine for the Twenty-First Century.* Part 3, vol. 4, *Sermons on the New Testament, 94A–147A.* Trans. Edmund Hill. Brooklyn, N.Y., 1992.

Rousseau, Philip. *Pachomius: The Making of a Community in Fourth-Century Egypt.* Berkeley and Los Angeles, 1985.

Rousselle, Aline. *Porneia: On Desire and the Body in Antiquity.* Trans. Felicia Pheasant. Oxford, 1988.

Rubenstein, Jeffrey L. *Talmudic Stories: Narrative Art, Composition, and Culture.* Baltimore, 1999.

———. "The Thematization of Dialectics in Bavli Aggada." *Journal of Jewish Studies* 53, no. 2 (2002): 1–14.

———. *The Culture of the Babylonian Talmud*. Baltimore, 2003.

Rutschowscaya, Marie-Hélène. *Catalogue des bois de l'Egypte copte*. Paris, 1986.

Ruether, Rosemary Radford. "Judaism and Christianity: Two Fourth-Century Religions." *Sciences Religieuses/Studies in Religion* 2 (1972): 1–10.

Safran, Linda, ed. *Heaven on Earth: Art and the Church in Byzantium*. University Park, Pa., 1998.

Said, Edward W. *Beginnings: Intention and Method*. New York, 1975.

———. *The World, the Text, and the Critic*. Cambridge, Mass., 1983.

Sanders, Henry A., ed. "New Manuscripts of the Bible from Egypt." *American Journal of Archaeology* 12 (1908): 49–55.

———. *Facsimile of the Washington Manuscript of the Four Gospels in the Freer Collection*. Ann Arbor, 1913.

Sarefield, Daniel. "'Burning Knowledge': Studies of Bookburning in Ancient Rome." Ph.D. diss., Ohio State University, 2004.

Sartre, Jean-Paul. *Qu'est-ce que la littérature?* Paris, 1948. Translated by Bernard Frechtman as *What Is Literature?* (London, 2001).

Schäublin, Christoph. *Untersuchungen zu Methode und Herkunft der antiochenischen Exegese*. Cologne, 1974.

Scherer, Jacques. *Le "Livre" de Mallarmé*. Paris, 1957.

Schestag, Thomas. "Mantis, Relics." *Yale French Studies* 93 (1998): 221–51.

Schmidt, Carl, ed. *Acta Pauli aus der Heidelberger koptischen Papyrushandschrift Nr. 1*. Leipzig, 1904. Reprint, Hildesheim, 1965.

Scholten, Clemens. "Die Nag-Hammadi-Texte als Buchbesitz der Pachomianer." *Jahrbuch für Antike und Christentum* 30 (1988): 144–72.

Schürer, Emil. *The History of the Jewish People in the Age of Jesus Christ (175 B.C.–A.D. 135)*. Ed. Géza Vermès, Fergus Millar, and Martin Goodman. 3 vols. Edinburgh, 1973–87.

Schüssler-Fiorenza, Elizabeth. *In Memory of Her: A Feminist Theological Reconstruction of Christian Origins*. New York, 1983.

Scullard, H. H. *Festivals and Ceremonies of the Roman Republic*. Ithaca, N.Y., 1981.

Sedley, David. "Philosophical Allegiance in the Greco-Roman World." In *Philosophia Togata: Essays on Philosophy and Roman Society,* ed. Miriam Griffin and Jonathan Barnes, 97–119. Oxford, 1989.

Segal, Judah B. *Edessa: "The Blessed City."* Oxford, 1970.

Séginger, Gisèle. *Naissance et métamorphoses d'un écrivain: Flaubert et "Les Tentations de saint Antoine."* Paris, 1997.

Seidl, Erwin. *Der Eid im römisch-ägyptischen Provinzialrecht*. 2 vols. Munich, 1933, 1935.

Seznec, Jean. *Nouvelles études sur "La tentation de saint Antoine."* London, 1949.

Shanzer, Danuta. "The Anonymous Carmen contra paganos and the Date and Identity of the Centonist Proba." *REAug* 32 (1986): 232–48.

———. "The Date and Identity of the Centonist Proba." *Recherches Augustiniennes* 27 (1994): 75–96.

Sharpe, Richard. "Dispute Settlement in Medieval Ireland: A Preliminary Inquiry." In *The*

Settlement of Disputes in Early Medieval Europe, ed. Wendy Davies and Paul Fouracre, 169–89. Cambridge, 1992.

Simmons, Michael Bland. *Arnobius of Sicca: Religious Conflict and Competition in the Age of Diocletian.* Oxford, 1995.

Singer, P. N., trans. *Galen: Selected Works.* Oxford, 1997.

Skeat, T. C. "The Length of the Standard Papyrus Roll and the Cost-Advantage of the Codex." *ZPE* 45 (1982): 169–74.

———. "Was Papyrus Regarded as 'Cheap' or 'Expensive' in the Ancient World?" *Aegyptus* 75 (1995): 74–93.

Slusser, Michael, trans. *St. Gregory Thaumaturgus: Life and Works.* Washington, D.C., 1998.

Small, Helen, ed. *The Public Intellectual.* Oxford, 2002.

Smalley, Beryl. *English Friars and Antiquity in the Early Fourteenth Century.* Oxford, 1960.

Smith, Andrew. "Porphyrian Studies since 1913." *ANRW* 2, no. 39.2 (1987): 717–73.

Smith, Martin Ferguson. *Diogenes of Oinoanda: The Epicurean Inscription.* Naples, 1993.

———. "Excavations at Oinoanda 1997: The New Epicurean Texts." *Anatolian Studies* 48 (1998): 125–70.

Snyder, H. Gregory. *Teachers and Texts in the Ancient World: Philosophers, Jews, and Christians.* London, 2000.

Sodini, Jean-Pierre. "Les ambons médiévaux à Byzance: Vestiges et problèmes." In *Thymiama stē mnēmē tēs Laskarinas Boura,* 1:303–7. Athens, 1994.

Sotinel, Claire. "Emperors and Popes in the Sixth Century: The Western View." In *Cambridge Companion to the Age of Justinian,* ed. Michael Maas, 267–90. Cambridge, 2005.

Spatharakis, Ioannis. "Early Christian Illustrated Gospel Books from the East." In J. den Boeft and M. L. van Poll-van de Lisdonk, *The Impact of Scripture in Early Christianity,* 102–21. Leiden, 1999.

Speyer, Wolfgang. *Büchervernichtung und Zensur des Geistes bei Heiden, Juden und Christen.* Bibliothek des Buchwesens 7. Stuttgart, 1981.

Splendori di Bisanzio: Testimonianze e riflessi d'arte e cultura bizantina nelle chiese d'Italia. Exh. cat. Milan, 1990.

Springer, Carl P. E. "Jerome and the *Cento* of Proba." In *Papers Presented at the Eleventh International Conference on Patristic Studies Held in Oxford, 1991,* ed. Elizabeth A. Livingstone, 5:96–105. Studia Patristica 28. Louvain, 1993.

Stam, Jan, ed. *Prudentius: Hamartigenia.* Amsterdam, 1940.

Steenbock, Frauke. *Der kirchliche Prachteinband im frühen Mittelalter, von den Anfängen bis zum Beginn der Gotik.* Berlin, 1965.

Steiner, George. "Real Presences." In George Steiner, *No Passion Spent: Essays 1978–1995,* 20–39. New Haven, 1996.

Stephens, Anthony. "The Sun State and Its Shadow: On the Condition of Utopian Writing." In *Utopias: Papers from the Annual Symposium of the Australian Academy of the Humanities,* ed. Eugene Kamenka, 1–19. Melbourne, 1987.

Stock, Brian. *Augustine the Reader.* Cambridge, Mass., 1996.

——. *After Augustine: The Meditative Reader and the Text*. Philadelphia, 2001.

Stokes, Whitley, ed. *Three Middle-Irish Homilies of the Lives of Saints Patrick, Brigit, and Columba*. Calcutta, 1877.

——. *The Tripartite Life of Patrick*. 2 vols. London, 1887. Reprint, Wiesbaden, 1965.

Stramara, Daniel F. "ΑΔΕΛΦΟΤΗΣ: Two Frequently Overlooked Meanings." *VC* 51 (1997): 316–20.

Strzygowski, Josef. *Koptische Kunst: Catalogue général des antiquités égyptiennes du Musée du Caire, nos. 7001–7394 et 8742–9200*. Vienna, 1904.

Swanson, R. N., ed. *The Church and the Book: Papers Read at the 2000 Summer Meeting and the 2001 Winter Meeting of the Ecclesiastical History Society*. Studies in Church History 38. Woodbridge, 2004.

Szirmai, J. A. *The Archaeology of Medieval Bookbinding*. Aldershot, 1999.

Taddei, Rosemarie M. "A Stylistic and Structural Study of Prudentius' *Hamartigenia*." Ph.D. diss., Bryn Mawr College, 1981.

Tait, John. "Some Notes on Demotic Scribal Training in the Roman Period." In *Proceedings of the 20th International Congress of Papyrologists, Copenhagen 23–29 August 1992,* ed. Adam Bülow-Jacobsen, 188–92. Copenhagen, 1994.

——. "How to Read Hieroglyphs?" In *Studies on Ancient Egypt in Honour of H. S. Smith,* ed. Anthony Leahy and John Tait, 317–19. London, 1999.

Tefnin, Ronald. "A Coptic Workshop in a Pharaonic Tomb." *Egyptian Archaeology* 20 (2002): 6.

Tetz, Martin. "Altchristliche Literaturgeschichte—Patrologie." *Theologische Rundschau* 17 (1961): 1–42.

Tkacz, Catherine Brown. *The Key to the Brescia Casket: Typology and the Early Christian Imagination*. South Bend, Ind., 2002.

Todorov, Tzvetan. "La réflexion sur la littérature dans la France contemporaine." *Poétique* 38 (1979): 131–48.

——. *Literature and Its Theorists: A Personal View of Twentieth-Century Criticism*. Trans. Catherine Porter. Ithaca, N.Y., 1987.

——. "The Journey and Its Narratives." Trans. Alyson Waters. In *Transports: Travel, Pleasure, and Imaginative Geography, 1600–1830,* ed. Chloe Chard and Helen Langdon, 287–96. New Haven, 1996.

Treu, Kurt. "Antike Literatur im Byzantinischen Ägypten im Lichte der Papyri." *Byzantinoslavica* 47 (1986): 1–7.

Trout, Dennis E. "The Dates of the Ordination of Paulinus of Bordeaux and of His Departure for Nola." *REAug* 37 (1991): 237–60.

——. *Paulinus of Nola: Life, Letters, and Poems*. Berkeley and Los Angeles, 1999.

Turaev, Boris. *Koptskiia zametki* [*Coptic Observations*]. St. Petersburg, 1907.

Turner, Eric G. *The Typology of the Early Codex*. Philadelphia, 1977.

Vaggione, Richard Paul. *Eunomius of Cyzicus and the Nicene Revolution*. New York, 2000.

Van Dael, P. C. J. "Biblical Cycles on Church Walls: Pro Lectione Pictura." In J. den Boeft and M. L. van Poll-van de Lisdonk, *The Impact of Scripture in Early Christianity*, 122–32. Leiden, 1999.

Van Dam, Raymond. *Leadership and Community in Late Antique Gaul*. Berkeley and Los Angeles, 1985.

———. *Saints and Their Miracles in Late Antique Gaul*. Princeton, 1993.

———, trans. *Gregory of Tours: Glory of the Confessors*. Liverpool, 1988.

Van Lantschoot, Arnold. *Recueil des colophons des manuscrits chrétiens d'Égypte*. Louvain, 1929.

Van Rompay, Lucas, and Andrea Schmidt. "Takritans in the Egyptian Desert: The Monastery of the Syrians in the Ninth Century." *Journal of the Canadian Society of Syriac Studies* 1 (2001): 41–60.

Vasilake, Maria, ed. *The Mother of God: Representations of the Virgin in Byzantine Art*. Milan, 2000. Published in connection with an exhibition held at the Benaki Museum, Athens, Greece, October 20, 2000–January 20, 2001.

Veilleux, Armand, ed. *Pachomian Koinonia*. 3 vols. Cistercian Studies Series 45–47. Kalamazoo, Mich., 1980–82.

Vessey, Mark. "Ideas of Christian Writing in Late Roman Gaul." D.Phil. diss., Oxford University, 1988.

———. "Patristics and Literary History." *Journal of Literature and Theology* 5 (1991): 342–53. Reprinted in his *Latin Christian Writers in Late Antiquity and Their Texts* (Aldershot, 2005).

———. "Conference and Confession: Literary Pragmatics in Augustine's *Apologia contra Hieronymum*." *JECS* 1 (1993): 175–213. Reprinted in his *Latin Christian Writers in Late Antiquity and Their Texts* (Aldershot, 2005).

———. "Jerome's Origen: The Making of a Christian Literary *Persona*." In *Papers Presented at the Eleventh International Conference on Patristic Studies Held in Oxford, 1991*, ed. Elizabeth A. Livingstone, 5:135–45. Studia Patristica 28. Louvain, 1993. Reprinted in his *Latin Christian Writers in Late Antiquity and Their Texts* (Aldershot, 2005).

———. "The Forging of Orthodoxy in Latin Christian Literature: A Case Study." *JECS* 4 (1996): 495–513. Reprinted in his *Latin Christian Writers in Late Antiquity and Their Texts* (Aldershot, 2005).

———. "The Demise of the Christian Writer and the Remaking of 'Late Antiquity': From H.-I. Marrou's Saint Augustine (1938) to Peter Brown's Holy Man (1983)." *JECS* 6, no. 3 (1998): 377–411. Reprinted in his *Latin Christian Writers in Late Antiquity and Their Texts* (Aldershot, 2005).

———. "*Opus Imperfectum*: Augustine and His Readers, 426–435 A.D." *VC* 52 (1998): 264–85. Reprinted in his *Latin Christian Writers in Late Antiquity and Their Texts* (Aldershot, 2005).

———. "The *Epistula Rustici ad Eucherium*: From the Library of Imperial Classics to the Library of the Fathers." In *Society and Culture in Late Antique Gaul: Revisiting the Sources*, ed. Ralph W. Mathisen and Danuta Shanzer, 278–97. Aldershot, 2001. Reprinted in his *Latin Christian Writers in Late Antiquity and Their Texts* (Aldershot, 2005).

————. "From *Cursus* to *Ductus:* Figures of Writing in Western Late Antiquity (Augustine, Jerome, Cassiodorus, Bede)." In *European Literary Careers: The Author from Antiquity to the Renaissance,* ed. Patrick Cheney and Frederick A. de Armas, 47–103. Toronto, 2002.

————. *Latin Christian Writers in Late Antiquity and Their Texts.* Aldershot, 2005.

————. "Reading Like Angels: Derrida and Augustine on the Book (for a History of Literature)." In *Augustine and Postmodernism: "Confessions" and "Circumfession,"* ed. John D. Caputo and Michael J. Scanlon, 173–211. Bloomington, Ind., 2005.

Vezin, Jean. "Les livres utilisés comme amulettes et comme reliques." In *Das Buch als magisches und als Repräsentationsobjekt,* ed. Peter Ganz, 101–116. Wiesbaden, 1992.

Vikan, Gary. "Byzantine Art as a Mirror of Its Public." *Apollo* 118 (1983): 164–67.

Visotzky, Burton L. *Fathers of the World: Essays in Rabbinic and Patristic Literatures.* Tübingen, 1995.

Vleeming, Sven P. "Some Notes on Demotic Scribal Training in the Ptolemaic Period." In *Proceedings of the 20th International Congress of Papyrologists, Copenhagen 23–29 August 1992,* ed. Adam Bülow-Jacobsen, 185–87. Copenhagen, 1994.

Volbach, Wolfgang Fritz. *Elfenbeinarbeiten der Spätantike und des frühen Mittelalters.* 3d ed. Mainz, 1976.

Vööbus, Arthur, ed. and trans. *The Statutes of the School of Nisibis.* Stockholm, 1961.

————. *Syriac and Arabic Documents Regarding Legislation Relative to Syrian Asceticism.* Stockholm, 1961.

Vorster, Johannes N. "Construction of Culture through the Construction of Person: The *Acts of Thecla* as an Example." In *The Rhetorical Analysis of Scripture: Essays from the 1995 London Conference,* ed. Stanley E. Porter and Thomas H. Olbricht, 445–75. Sheffield, 1997.

Wal, Nicolaas van der, and Bernard H. Stolte, eds. *Collectio Tripartita: Justinian on Religious and Ecclesiastical Affairs.* Groningen, 1994.

Ward, Benedicta, trans. *The Sayings of the Desert Fathers: The Alphabetical Collection.* Rev. ed. Kalamazoo, Mich., 1984.

Waring, Judith. "Literacies of Lists: Reading Byzantine Monastic Inventories." In *Literacy, Education, and Manuscript Transmission in Byzantium and Beyond,* ed. Catherine Holmes and Judith Waring, 165–86. Leiden, 2002.

Waszink, Jan Hendrik. "Amulett." *Reallexikon für Antike und Christentum* (1950), vol. 1, cols. 397–411.

Weber, Manfred. "Zur Ausschmückung koptischer Bücher." *Enchoria* 3 (1973): 53–62.

Weiss, Abraham. "On the Literary Development of the Amoraic Sugya in Its Formative Period" [in Hebrew]. In *Mehkarim ba-Talmud* [Studies in Talmud], 124–59. Jerusalem, 1975.

Weitz, Johann. *Aurelii Prudentii Clementis v.c. opera, noviter ad msc. fidem recensita . . . a M. Iohanne Weitzio.* Hanover, 1613.

Weitzmann, Kurt. "An Early Coptic/Arabic Miniature in Leningrad." *Ars Islamica* 10 (1943): 119–34.

———. *Illustrations in Roll and Codex: A Study of the Origin and the Method of Text Illustration.* Reprinted with addenda. Princeton, 1970.

———. *The Monastery of Saint Catherine at Mount Sinai: The Icons.* Vol. 1: *From the Sixth to the Tenth Century.* Princeton, 1976.

———, ed. *Age of Spirituality: Late Antique and Early Christian Art, Third to Seventh Century; Catalogue of the Exhibition at the Metropolitan Museum of Art, November 19, 1977, through February 12, 1978.* New York, 1979.

White, Carolinne, trans. *Early Christian Lives.* London, 1998.

Wickersheimer, Ernst. "Une Vie des saints Côme et Damien dans un manuscrit médical du IXe siècle, suivie d'une recette de collyre attribuée à la mère des deux saints." *Centaurus* 1 (1950): 38–42.

Widdowson, Peter. *Literature.* London, 1999.

Wieacker, Franz. *Textstufen klassischer Juristen.* Göttingen, 1960.

Wilfong, Terry J. *Women of Jeme: Lives in a Coptic Town in Late Antique Egypt.* Ann Arbor, 2002.

Williams, Stephen. *Diocletian and the Roman Recovery.* London, 1985.

Williamson, Geoffrey A., trans. *Eusebius: The History of the Church from Christ to Constantine.* Harmondsworth, 1965.

Wimbush, Vincent, ed. *Ascetic Behavior in Greco-Roman Antiquity: A Sourcebook.* Minneapolis, 1990.

Winlock, Henry E., and Walter E. Crum. *The Monastery of Epiphanius at Thebes. Part 1.* New York, 1926.

Winter, John Garrett. *Life and Letters in the Papyri.* Ann Arbor, 1933.

Wipszycka, Ewa. "Le degré d'alphabétisation en Égypte byzantine." *REAug* 30 (1980): 279–96.

———. "The Nag Hammadi Library and the Monks: A Papyrologist's Point of View." *Journal of Juristic Papyrology* 30 (2000): 183–91.

Wire, Antoinette. *The Corinthian Women Prophets: A Reconstruction through Paul's Polemic.* Minneapolis, 1990.

Witherington, Ben. "The Anti-Feminist Tendencies of the 'Western' Text in Acts." *Journal of Biblical Literature* 103 (1984): 82–84.

Worp, Klaas A. *Checklist of Editions of Greek, Latin, Demotic and Coptic Papyri, Ostraca and Tablets.* http://scriptorium.lib.duke.edu/papyrus/texts/clist.html (accessed August 2005).

Worrell, William H. *The Coptic Manuscripts in the Freer Collection.* New York, 1923.

Wortley, John. "Some Light on Magic and Magicians in Late Antiquity." *Greek, Roman and Byzantine Studies* 42 (2001 [2002]): 289–307.

———, trans. *John Moschos: The Spiritual Meadow.* Kalamazoo, Mich., 1992.

Wright, William. *Catalogue of Syriac Manuscripts in the British Museum, Acquired since the Year 1838.* 3 vols. London, 1870–72.

———. *Apocryphal Acts of the Apostles.* 2 vols. London, 1871.

Young, Frances. *Biblical Exegesis and the Formation of Christian Culture.* Cambridge, 1997.

Zanker, Paul *The Mask of Socrates: The Image of the Intellectual in Antiquity.* Trans. Alan Shapiro. Berkeley and Los Angeles, 1995.

Zimmermann, Barbara. "Die Codexillustration als neuer Kunstzweig: Spiegel einer geänderten Funktion des Buches in der Spätantike?" In *The Use of Sacred Books in the Ancient World,* ed. Leonard V. Rutgers, Peter W. van der Horst, Henriette W. Havelaar, and Lieve M. Teugels, 263–85. Leuven, 1998.

———. "Illustrierte Prachtcodices. Bücherluxus in der Spätantike." In *Epochenwandel? Kunst und Kultur zwischen Antike und Mittelalter,* ed. Norbert Zimmermann and Franz Alto Bauer, 45–56. Mainz, 2001.

———. *Die Wiener Genesis im Rahmen der antiken Buchmalerei: Ikonographie, Darstellung, Illustrationsverfahren und Aussageintention.* Wiesbaden, 2003.

CONTRIBUTORS

Daniel Boyarin is the Hermann P. and Sophia Taubman Professor of Talmudic Culture, University of California at Berkeley. His books include *Carnal Israel: Reading Sex in Talmudic Culture* (University of California Press, 1993); *A Radical Jew: Paul and the Politics of Identity* (University of California Press, 1994); *Unheroic Conduct: The Rise of Heterosexuality and the Invention of the Jewish Man* (University of California Press, 1997); *Dying for God: Martyrdom and the Making of Christianity and Judaism* (Stanford University Press, 1999); and *Border Lines: The Partition of Judaeo-Christianity* (University of Pennsylvania Press, 2004). He teaches in the departments of Near Eastern Studies and Rhetoric, and currently serves as Chair of the Department of Near Eastern Studies. His current projects are a study of dialogue and dialectic in Plato's fifth-century and the Babylonian Talmud and an investigation of the Son of Man figure and concept in Judaism (including the Gospels) from I Enoch to late antiquity.

Catherine Burris is a doctoral candidate in religious studies at the University of North Carolina. She has published two articles, with Lucas Van Rompay, on Thecla in Syriac tradition, and another on Severus of Antioch. She is currently writing a dissertation on the Syriac *Book of Women.*

Catherine M. Chin is Assistant Professor of Church History and Historical Theology at the Catholic University of America. She specializes in Latin Patristics and Early Christian Studies, with an emphasis on the development of Latin Christian literature. She has published articles in *Augustinian Studies, The Journal of Early Christian Studies, Hugoye: The Journal of Syriac Studies,* and *Studia Patristica.* Her book, on the ideologies of literary education in late antiquity, is forthcoming from the University of Pennsylvania Press.

Gillian Clark is Professor of Ancient History at the University of Bristol. She works on the interaction of Christianity and Graeco-Roman culture in the early centuries A.D., with a particular interest in gender history. Publications include *Women in Late Antiquity* (Oxford University Press, 1993); *Augustine: Confessions 1–4* (Cambridge Greek and Latin Classics, 1995), *Porphyry: On Abstinence* (Duckworth and Cornell, 2000), and *Christianity and Roman Society* (Cambridge University Press, 2004). She is currently directing a collaborative international commentary on Augustine's *City of God,* to be published by Oxford University Press. She co-edits the scholarly annotated translations *Translated Texts for Historians,* A.D. *300–900* (Liverpool University Press) and *Oxford Early Christian Studies* (Oxford University Press).

Catherine Conybeare is Associate Professor of Greek, Latin, and Classical Studies, Bryn Mawr College. Her major publications are *Paulinus Noster: Self and Symbols in the Letters of Paulinus of Nola* (Oxford University Press, 2000) and *The Irrational Augustine* (Oxford University Press, 2006). She is a senior editor of *Bryn Mawr Classical Review.*

Kim Haines-Eitzen is Associate Professor of early Christianity and early Judaism and chair of the Department of Near Eastern Studies at Cornell University. Her *Guardians of Letters: Literacy, Power, and the Transmitters of Early Christian Literature* (Oxford University Press, 2000) is a social history of the scribes who copied Christian texts in the second and third centuries. She is working on a book that deals with the intersection of gender, text transmission, and literacy in early Christianity.

Caroline Humfress is Lecturer in Late Antique and Early Medieval History, Department of History, Classics and Archaeology, Birkbeck College, University of London. Her publications include *The Evolution of Late Antiquity* (with Peter Garnsey) (Cambridge: Orchard Academic, 2001); "Law and Legal Practice," in *The Cambridge Companion to the Age of Justinian,* ed. Michael Maas (Cambridge University Press, 2005); and "Roman Law, Forensic Argument and the Formation of Christian Orthodoxy (III–VI Centuries)," in *Orthodoxie, christianisme, histoire—Orthodoxy, Christianity, History: Travaux du groupe de recherches "Definir, maintenir et remettre en cause l'orthodoxie dans l'histoire du christianisme,"* ed. Susanna Elm, Eric Rebillard, and Antonella Romano (École française de Rome, 2001), 1–26.

Chrysi Kotsifou is a Visiting Associate Curator and Fellow at the Institute for Christian Oriental Research and the Department of Semitic and Egyptian Languages and Literatures at the Catholic University of America. She completed a Ph.D. at King's College, London, in 2002 with a dissertation entitled "Travel to and within Byzantine Egypt: The Evidence from Hagiography." In 2002–3 she was an Andrew W. Mellon research fellow at the Center for the Study of Early Christianity at Catholic

University, in 2003–4 a postdoctoral fellow in Hellenic Studies at Princeton University, and in 2004–5 a postdoctoral fellow at the Classics Department at Columbia University. She has also taught at the American University in Cairo.

John Lowden is Professor of the History of Art at the Courtauld Institute of Art, University of London. His *Illuminated Prophet Books* (1988) and *The Octateuchs* (1992) studied Byzantine material with a particular concern for basic issues of method and questions of pictorial transmission. *The Making of the Bibles Moralisées* (2000), in two volumes, considered French material of the thirteenth to fifteenth centuries, with special emphasis again on the codicological foundations of art-historical arguments, and issues of novelty, narrative, and consumption. It was awarded the 2002 Otto Gründler Prize. His *Early Christian and Byzantine Art* (Phaidon, 1997) has been reprinted three times, and translated into French, Greek, Japanese, and Korean.

Claudia Rapp is Professor in the Department of History at the University of California, Los Angeles. She is the author of *Holy Bishops in Late Antiquity: The Nature of Christian Leadership in a Time of Transition* (University of California Press, 2005), the co-editor of *Elites in Late Antiquity,* special issue, *Arethusa* 33 (2000) and *Bosphorus: Essays in Honor of Cyril Mango,* special issue, *Byzantinische Forschungen* 21 (1995), and has written numerous articles on hagiography and the cult of saints.

Philip Rousseau is Andrew W. Mellon Professor of Early Christian Studies at the Catholic University of America. He is the author of numerous books on asceticism and early Christianity, most recently *The Early Christian Centuries* (2002), and is editor of Blackwell's forthcoming *Companion to Late Antiquity.*

Daniel Sarefield completed his Ph.D. in Greek and Roman History at the Ohio State University in 2004 and is now Visiting Assistant Professor in the Department of History. He has articles forthcoming on book burning in the ancient world and on religion and violence in the modern world, and is currently revising his dissertation for publication.

Mark Vessey is Professor of English and the holder of a Canada Research Chair in Literature/Christianity and Culture at the University of British Columbia. He is the editor, most recently, of *Cassiodorus: Institutions of Divine and Secular Learning and On the Soul* (with James W. Halporn), published by Liverpool University Press (2004) and of *Augustine and the Disciplines: From Cassiciacum to Confessions*(with Karla Pollmann), published by Oxford University Press (2005). A collection of his articles was published in 2005 as *Latin Christian Writers in Late Antiquity and Their Texts.*

INDEX

The Early Christian Book was designed and typeset in Garamond Premier Pro
by Kachergis Book Design of Pittsboro, North Carolina. It was printed on 60-pound
Natures Natural and bound by Thomson-Shore of Dexter, Michigan.